Investment Mathematics

Andrew T. Adams PhD, AIA
School of Management, University of Edinburgh

Philip M. Booth FIA, FSS
Sir John Cass Business School, City of London and the
Institute of Economic Affairs, London

David C. Bowie PhD, FFA
Hymans Robertson, Glasgow

Della S. Freeth PhD, FSS
Health Care Development Unit, City University, London

WILEY

Copyright © 2003 John Wiley & Sons Ltd,
    The Atrium, Southern Gate, Chichester,
    West Sussex PO19 8SQ, England

    Telephone (+44) 1243 779777
    Email (for orders and customer service enquiries): cs-books@wiley.co.uk
    Visit our Home Page on www.wileyeurope.com or www.wiley.com

This publication is designed to provide accurate and authoritative information in regard to the subject matter covered. It is sold on the understanding that the Publisher is not engaged in rendering professional services. If professional advice or other expert assistance is required, the services of a competent professional should be sought.

Other Wiley Editorial Offices

John Wiley & Sons Inc., 111 River Street,
Hoboken, NJ 07030, USA

Jossey-Bass, 989 Market Street,
San Francisco, CA 94103-1741, USA

Wiley-VCH Verlag GmbH, Boschstr. 12,
D-69469 Weinheim, Germany

John Wiley & Sons Australia Ltd, 33 Park Road, Milton,
Queensland 4064, Australia

John Wiley & Sons (Asia) Pte Ltd, 2 Clementi Loop #02-01,
Jin Xing Distripark, Singapore 129809

John Wiley & Sons Canada Ltd, 22 Worcester Road,
Etobicoke, Ontario, Canada M9W 1L1

Wiley also publishes its books in a variety of electronic formats. Some content that appears in print may not be available in electronic books.

British Library Cataloguing in Publication Data

A catalogue record for this book is available from the British Library

ISBN 0-471-99882-6

Typeset in 10/12pt Times by Mathematical Composition Setters Ltd, Salisbury, Wiltshire
Printed and bound in Great Britain by Biddles Ltd, Guildford and King's Lynn
This book is printed on acid-free paper responsibly manufactured from sustainable forestry in which at least two trees are planted for each one used for paper production.

Contents

Preface

This book is intended for practitioners in the investment world, particularly those studying for professional examinations. It is also suitable for students of finance and investment in higher education, either as a main text or as an additional reference book.

The book is divided into three parts. Part I looks at the fundamental analysis of investments from a mathematical viewpoint, relying heavily on compound interest techniques which are developed in the first chapter. There is particular emphasis on the valuation of investments and the calculation of rates of return. Mathematical developments are illustrated with practical examples. The material is presented in such a way that those without formal training in mathematics will be able to follow the text without difficulty.

Part II provides the necessary statistical background for investment specialists. Modern financial economics and developments in the actuarial field have emphasised the importance of probability distributions and have made investors more aware of the concept that expected investment returns are the expected values of random variables. The statistical topics in Part II complete the foundation which allows the reader to tackle topics in Part III. Like Part I, the approach in Part II assumes little formal mathematical training.

Part III deals with a number of specialist topics which are applications of the material covered in Parts I and II. It is expected that readers will only study those chapters of Part III which are relevant to their particular work or course. Topics covered are modern portfolio theory and asset pricing, market indices, portfolio performance measurement, bond analysis, option pricing models, and stochastic investment models.

An important feature of this international text is the way in which chapters are self-contained, and yet follow logically one from another. This will enable readers to choose a reading path appropriate to their own specific needs without a loss of continuity; it also enables the text to be used as a reference manual. *Investment Mathematics* is an accessible text which will provide readers with a sound analytical framework within which the valuation of investments and investment in a wider context may be studied.

ATA, PMB, DCB, DSF

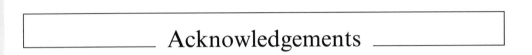

Acknowledgements

We wish to thank Dr Peter England for his generous help.

Part I
Security Analysis

The first part of this book develops the foundations of security analysis, drawing heavily upon the concept of compound interest. Consequently, the first chapter is devoted to explaining the basics of compound interest. Chapters 2 and 3 use these techniques in the analysis of fixed-interest bonds, equities and real estate. Chapter 4 deals with the mathematical problems of investment in inflationary conditions and Chapter 5 deals with the analysis of index-linked bonds. Chapter 6 makes use of the material presented in Chapters 4 and 5 to consider the mathematics associated with foreign currency investments. There has been dramatic growth in the market for derivative securities in recent times and the basics of these instruments are outlined in Chapter 7.

1
Compound Interest

1.1 INTRODUCTION

The purpose of this chapter is to provide an introduction to *compound interest* which is the foundation of investment mathematics. In particular, methods are developed for calculating the accumulated value and present value of an investment. Although we concentrate on financial investment in securities in this book, for completeness, the second half of this chapter is devoted to discussion of real investment in projects.

Readers unfamiliar with the concepts of *exponents* and *geometric series*, which occur frequently in compound interest calculations, should first read the Annex to this chapter.

1.2 ACCUMULATED VALUES

Suppose that a woman deposits £100 with a bank which pays a rate of interest of 6% per annum to its depositors and that she leaves any interest earned to accumulate within the account. At the start of the second year she would have £100 × 1.06 = £106 in the account, which would earn 6% interest during the second year. So in the second year the £106 grows at 6% to £106 × 1.06, or alternatively £100$(1.06)^2$, which equals £112.36. The important point to grasp here is that interest is itself earning interest. This is the essence of what is known as *compound interest*. If interest were spent rather than left in the account, total interest received at the end of the second year would amount to only £12 rather than £12.36.

By the end of the third year, the £112.36 will grow to £112.36 × 1.06, or alternatively £100$(1.06)^3$, which equals £119.10. Continuing the process further, the £100 grows to £100$(1.06)^4$ after four years, £100$(1.06)^5$ after 5 years and so on. In the general case, £100 grows to £100$(1.06)^n$ after n years.

We may generalise the above *compounding* process further. Suppose that an amount $A(0)$ is invested at time 0 at a compound interest rate of i per interval, where i is written as a decimal rather than a percentage. Then the accumulated amount $A(n)$ after n intervals of time is given by the formula

$$A(n) = A(0)(1 + i)^n \qquad (1.1)$$

This may be represented diagrammatically as shown in Figure 1.1. Note that the rate at which interest accrues has not been expressed as a rate *per annum* but as a rate *per interval*. A unit interval of time is not restricted to one year. It could be a half-year, a quarter of a year, an hour or any other interval of time.

Equation (1.1) is valid not only for an integral number of time intervals but also for fractions of time intervals, provided the rate of growth is constant. Consider the amount by which the investment has grown after $1/m$ of a time interval (where m is an integer). If the sum has grown by a factor $1 + y$, we can say that

$$(1 + y)^m = 1 + i$$

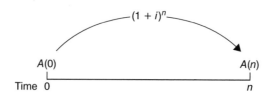

Figure 1.1

or

$$(1 + y) = (1 + i)^{1/m}$$

Thus, after n time intervals and r periods of $1/m$ time intervals (r and m integers), the sum $A(0)$ would grow to

$$A(0) \cdot (1 + i)^{n + (r/m)}$$

In other words, after any time period t, $A(0)$ would grow to $A(0) \cdot (1 + i)^t$.

Example 1.1

What is the accumulated value of £300 invested at 5% per annum for (a) 6 years? (b) $12\frac{1}{2}$ years?

Answer

(a) $A(6) = £300(1.05)^6 = £402.03$.
(b) $A(12.5) = £300(1.05)^{12.5} = £552.06$.

Example 1.2

What is the accumulated value of $200 invested for $8\frac{1}{4}$ years where the rate of interest is (a) 3% per half-year? (b) 2% per quarter?

Answer

(a) The unit interval of time is a half-year so that n is $8.25 \times 2 = 16.5$

$$A(16.5) = \$200(1.03)^{16.5} = \$325.72$$

(b) The unit interval of time is a quarter so that n is $8.25 \times 4 = 33$

$$A(33) = \$200(1.02)^{33} = \$384.45$$

Example 1.3

What is the accumulated value in 6 years' time of £200 invested now, £400 invested at the end of year 3 and £300 invested at the end of year 5, if the rate of interest is 5% per annum?

Answer

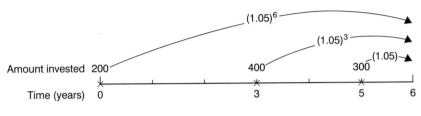

Figure 1.2

In this case there are a number of payments at different points in time. The solution is straightforward when it is realised that the accumulated values of the payments can be considered separately and then simply added together (see Figure 1.2).
    £200 is invested for 6 years, £400 for 3 years and £300 for 1 year, so

$$\text{Accumulated value} = £200(1.05)^6 + £400(1.05)^3 + £300(1.05)$$

$$= \underline{£1046.07}$$

1.3 EFFECTIVE AND NOMINAL RATES OF INTEREST

Rates of interest only have meaning when they are related to a time interval. Thus, in Examples 1.1 and 1.3 above, the rate of interest was 5% *per annum* whereas in Example 1.2(a) the rate of interest was 3% *per half-year* and in Example 1.2(b) the rate of interest was 2% *per quarter*. Rates of interest expressed in this way give the actual rate of increase over the stated interval of time. They are known as *effective* rates of interest.

Example 1.4

If the effective annual rate of interest is 7%, what is the effective monthly rate of interest?

Answer

Let the effective monthly rate of interest be j. Then

$$(1+j)^{12} = 1.07$$

$$1+j = 1.00565$$

$$j = 0.565\%$$

Where the effective rate of interest is expressed in terms of $1/p$ of a year, it is often converted to an annual rate by simply multiplying by p. Thus, 3% per half-year would be quoted as being "6% per annum, convertible half-yearly". Similarly, 2% per quarter would be quoted as being "8% per annum, convertible quarterly". Interest rates quoted in this way are known as *nominal* rates of interest. Quoted interest rates on savings products offered by banks are often nominal rates, e.g. convertible half-yearly.

Corresponding to a nominal rate of interest there always exists an effective annual rate of interest. For example, suppose £100 is invested for a year at a rate of interest of 8% per annum, convertible half-yearly (i.e. an effective rate of interest of 4% per half-year). This is not the same as an effective rate of interest of 8% per annum. The amount at the end of the year would be £100$(1 + 0.08/2)^2$. If the corresponding annual rate of interest is i per annum, the amount at the end of the year may also be written as £100$(1 + i)$. We therefore have

$$£100(1 + 0.08/2)^2 = £100(1 + i)$$

or

$$(1 + 0.08/2)^2 = 1 + i$$

$$1.0816 = 1 + i \qquad (1.2)$$

$$i = 0.0816 \quad \text{or} \quad 8.16\%$$

That is, a rate of interest expressed as 8% per annum convertible half-yearly is the same as an effective rate of interest of 8.16% per annum.

Equation (1.2) above may be generalised. Suppose we are given a rate of interest per annum, convertible p times a year (denoted by the symbol $i^{(p)}$). Then the equivalent rate of interest per annum (denoted by the symbol i) is given by

$$\left(1 + \frac{i^{(p)}}{p}\right)^p = 1 + i \qquad (1.3)$$

If p is greater than 1 so that interest is convertible more frequently than once a year, interest itself earns interest within the year, and the effective rate of interest i exceeds the nominal rate of interest, $i^{(p)}$. As p increases so that intervals between additional interest become smaller and smaller, the margin between i and $i^{(p)}$ widens at a decreasing rate, tending to a limit which corresponds to interest being *continuously compounded*. In this case (for which p is infinite), the resultant annual convertible rate of interest is referred to as the *force of interest* and is given the symbol δ. The equivalent rate of interest per annum is given by

$$e^\delta = 1 + i$$

where

$$e = \lim_{p \to \infty} \left(1 + \frac{1}{p}\right)^p = 2.718$$

If the force of interest is quoted, then we have:

$$A(t) = A(0)e^{\delta t} \qquad (1.4)$$

Example 1.5

If the effective annual rate of interest is 6%, what is (a) the annual rate of interest convertible half-yearly? (b) the force of interest?

Answer

(a) Let the annual rate of interest convertible half-yearly be $i^{(2)}$. Then

$$\left(1 + \frac{i^{(2)}}{2}\right)^2 = 1.06$$

$$1 + \frac{i^{(2)}}{2} = 1.029\ 56$$

$$\frac{i^{(2)}}{2} = 0.029\ 56$$

$$i^{(2)} = \underline{5.912\%}$$

(b) Let the force of interest be δ. Then

$$e^{\delta} = 1.06$$

$$\delta = \log_e 1.06$$

$$\delta = 0.0583$$

$$\delta = \underline{5.83\%}$$

1.4 THE ACCUMULATED VALUE OF AN ANNUITY-CERTAIN

An annuity-certain is a series of payments at fixed intervals of time for a fixed period of time. The payments may be of a constant amount or they may vary.

(1) A series of payments of one per interval payable in arrears for n intervals

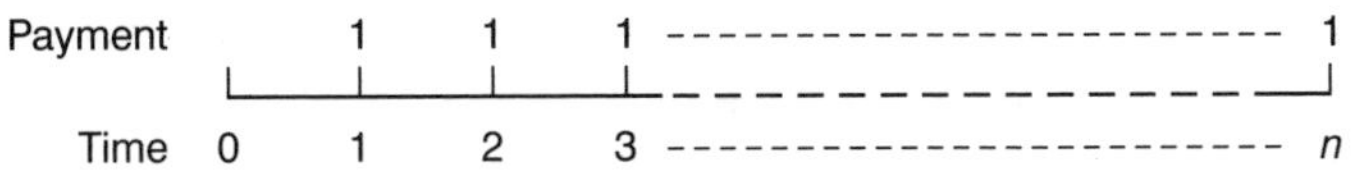

Figure 1.3

The accumulated value of this series of payments is often denoted by the symbol $s_{\overline{n}|}$. Occasionally it is necessary to make clear the ruling rate of interest by placing it to the right, e.g. $s_{\overline{n}|}10\%$.

Suppose that the rate of interest is i per interval, Then

$$s_{\overline{n}|} = (1+i)^{n-1} + (1+i)^{n-2} + \cdots + (1+i) + 1$$

or, reversing the order of the terms on the right-hand side,

$$s_{\overline{n}|} = 1 + (1+i) + \cdots + (1+i)^{n-2} + (1+i)^{n-1}$$

The right-hand side of this equation is the sum of a geometric series with first term equal to 1 and common ratio equal to $1 + i$. There are n terms in the series. The sum of this geometric series is

$$\frac{1 \cdot (1 - (1+i)^n)}{1 - (1+i)} \qquad \text{using equation (1.22)}$$

We therefore have the result:

$$s_{\overline{n}|} = \frac{(1+i)^n - 1}{i} \qquad (1.5)$$

It is not usually necessary to calculate $s_{\overline{n}|}$ as values can be obtained from compound interest tables (see back of this book).

(2) A series of payments of one per interval payable in advance for n intervals

Figure 1.4

The accumulated value of this series of payments is often denoted by the symbol $\ddot{s}_{\overline{n}|}$. Note that this is the same as the series of payments in (1) above except that each payment accumulates for one additional interval. It therefore follows that

$$\ddot{s}_{\overline{n}|} = (1+i)s_{\overline{n}|} \qquad (1.6)$$

1.5 PRESENT VALUES

We have considered how to determine the accumulated value of a payment (or a number of payments) at some point in the future. We now consider the reverse problem of determining the amount which must be invested now to provide for a payment (or a number of payments) at some point (or points) in the future. In other words, we wish to determine the present value of amounts received at specified future points in time. As with accumulated values, present values depend on the ruling rate of interest but instead of *accumulating* we are *discounting*.

Suppose that we wish to make a payment of £600 in exactly 7 years from now and that the rate of interest is 9% per annum. How much must be invested at the present time to provide this amount? If the initial amount invested is $A(0)$, then using equation (1.1) derived earlier, we obtain

$$£600 = A(0)(1.09)^7$$

so that

$$A(0) = \frac{£600}{(1.09)^7}$$

$$= £328.22$$

In general, the amount $A(0)$ which must be invested now to provide $A(t)$ after t intervals of time is given by

$$A(0) = \frac{A(t)}{(1+i)^t} \tag{1.7}$$

where i is the rate of interest per interval, and t need not be an integer. Alternatively, if δ is the force of interest,

$$A(0) = A(t)e^{-\delta t}$$

$A(0)$ is known as the *present value* of $A(t)$.

Equation (1.7) may be represented diagrammatically as in Figure 1.5.

$1/(1+i)$ is often given the symbol v and so equation (1.7) would then become

$$A(0) = A(t) \cdot v^t \tag{1.8}$$

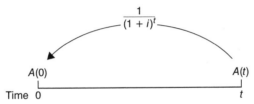

Figure 1.5

Example 1.6

What is the present value of £100 due in exactly 8 years from now if the rate of interest is 7% per annum?

Answer

Here we have

$$t = 8 \qquad A(t) = £100 \qquad i = 0.07$$

So

$$\text{Present value} = \frac{£100}{(1.07)^8}$$

$$= \underline{£58.20}$$

Note that the present value is less than the amount due in the future.

Example 1.7

Assuming a rate of interest of 4% per half-year, how much must be invested now to
provide the following payments?

$$£200 \text{ after 2 years}$$

$$\text{plus} \quad £600 \text{ after } 3\tfrac{1}{2} \text{ years}$$

$$\text{plus} \quad £500 \text{ after 5 years}$$

Answer

The unit interval of time is a half-year in this case.

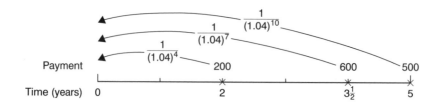

Figure 1.6

The amount which must be invested now is

$$\frac{£200}{(1.04)^4} + \frac{£600}{(1.04)^7} + \frac{£500}{(1.04)^{10}} = \underline{£964.69}$$

1.6   THE PRESENT VALUE OF AN ANNUITY-CERTAIN

The following types of annuity-certain are particularly important in investment and it is
therefore useful to know the general formulae for their present values.

(1) A series of payments of one per interval payable in arrears for n intervals

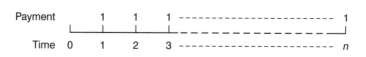

Figure 1.7

The present value of this series of payments is often denoted by the symbol $a_{\overline{n}|}$. Suppose
that the rate of interest is i per interval. Then

$$a_{\overline{n}|} = \frac{1}{(1+i)} + \frac{1}{(1+i)^2} + \cdots + \frac{1}{(1+i)^n}$$

The right-hand side of this equation is the sum of a geometric series with first term equal to $1/(1+i)$ and common ratio equal to $1/(1+i)$.

The sum of this geometric series is

$$\frac{\dfrac{1}{(1+i)}\left(1-\dfrac{1}{(1+i)^n}\right)}{1-\dfrac{1}{(1+i)}}$$

Multiplying the numerator and denominator by $1+i$, we obtain

$$\frac{1-\dfrac{1}{(1+i)^n}}{1+i-1}=\frac{1-\dfrac{1}{(1+i)^n}}{i}$$

We therefore have the result:

$$a_{\overline{n}|}=\frac{1-\dfrac{1}{(1+i)^n}}{i} \tag{1.9}$$

Values of $a_{\overline{n}|}$ are commonly found in compound interest tables (see back of book).

(2) A series of payments of one per interval payable in advance for n intervals

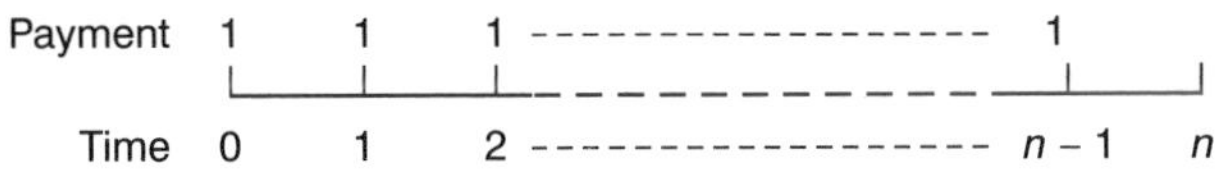

Figure 1.8

The present value of this series of payments is often denoted by the symbol $\ddot{a}_{\overline{n}|}$. This is the same as the series of payments in (1) above except that each payment is discounted for one interval fewer. It therefore follows that

$$\ddot{a}_{\overline{n}|}=(1+i)a_{\overline{n}|} \tag{1.10}$$

(3) An infinite series of payments made at the end of each interval; the first payment is d_1 and each subsequent payment is $(1+g)$ times the previous payment

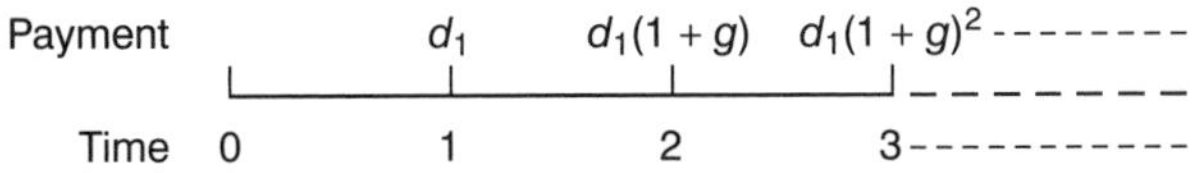

Figure 1.9

Suppose again that the rate of interest is i per interval. Then

$$\text{Present value} = \frac{d_1}{(1+i)} + \frac{d_1(1+g)}{(1+i)^2} + \frac{d_1(1+g)^2}{(1+i)^3} + \cdots$$

The right-hand side of this equation is an infinite geometric series with first term equal to $d_1/(1+i)$ and common ratio equal to $(1+g)/(1+i)$. If i is greater than g, the series is convergent and the sum of the series is

$$\frac{\dfrac{d_1}{(1+i)}}{1 - \dfrac{(1+g)}{(1+i)}}$$

Multiplying the numerator and denominator by $1+i$ we obtain

$$\frac{d_1}{(1+i) - (1+g)}$$

so that the present value equals

$$\frac{d_1}{i-g} \tag{1.11}$$

Note that when there is zero growth, i.e. $g = 0$, we have an infinite series of payments (known as a *perpetuity*) of d_1 per interval, payable in arrears with present value equal to d_1/i. The same result can be obtained by multiplying equation (1.9) by d_1 and setting $n = \infty$.

(4) An increasing annuity in which the first payment is one after one interval, the second payment is two after two intervals, and so on, with a final payment of n after n intervals

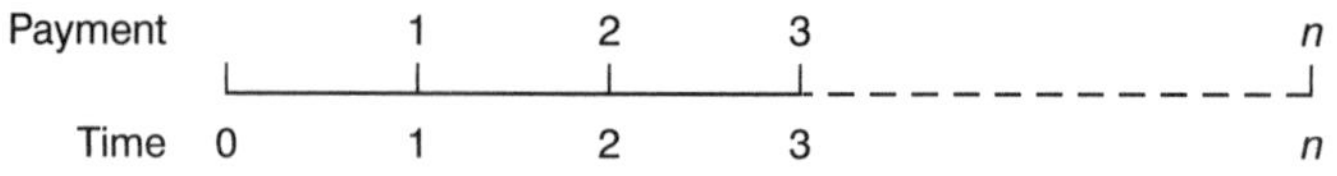

Payment		1	2	3		n
Time	0	1	2	3		n

Figure 1.10

The present value of this series of payments is often denoted by the symbol $(Ia)_{\overline{n}|}$. It is convenient to use v for $1/(1+i)$. Then

$$(Ia)_{\overline{n}|} = v + 2v^2 + \cdots + nv^n \tag{1.12}$$

$$(1+i)(Ia)_{\overline{n}|} = 1 + 2v + 3v^2 + \cdots + nv^{n-1} \tag{1.13}$$

Subtracting equation (1.12) from equation (1.13),

$$i(Ia)_{\overline{n}|} = 1 + v + v^2 + \cdots + v^{n-1} - nv^n$$

$$(Ia)_{\overline{n}|} = \frac{\ddot{a}_{\overline{n}|} - nv^n}{i} \tag{1.14}$$

(5) A series of payments of one per interval payable p times per interval in arrears for n intervals

Figure 1.11

The present value of this series of payments is often denoted by the symbol $a_{\overline{n}|}^{(p)}$. Again, it is convenient to use v for $1/(1+i)$. We then have

$$a_{\overline{n}|}^{(p)} = \frac{1}{p}\,v^{1/p} + \frac{1}{p}\,v^{2/p} + \cdots + \frac{1}{p}\,v^{np/p}$$

The right-hand side is a geometric series with first term $(1/p)v^{1/p}$ and the common ratio $v^{1/p}$. There are np terms. So

$$a_{\overline{n}|}^{(p)} = \frac{1}{p}\,v^{1/p}\left\{\frac{1-v^n}{1-v^{1/p}}\right\}$$

$$= \frac{1-v^n}{p(1+i)^{1/p}(1-v^{1/p})}$$

$$= \frac{1-v^n}{p\{(1+i)^{1/p}-1\}}$$

$$= \frac{i a_{\overline{n}|}}{p\{(1+i)^{1/p}-1\}} \qquad \text{using equation (1.9)}$$

$$= \frac{i}{i^{(p)}}\,a_{\overline{n}|} \qquad \text{using equation (1.3)}$$

We therefore have the result

$$a_{\overline{n}|}^{(p)} = \frac{i}{i^{(p)}}\,a_{\overline{n}|} \qquad\qquad (1.15)$$

(6) A series of payments of one per interval payable p times per interval in advance for n intervals

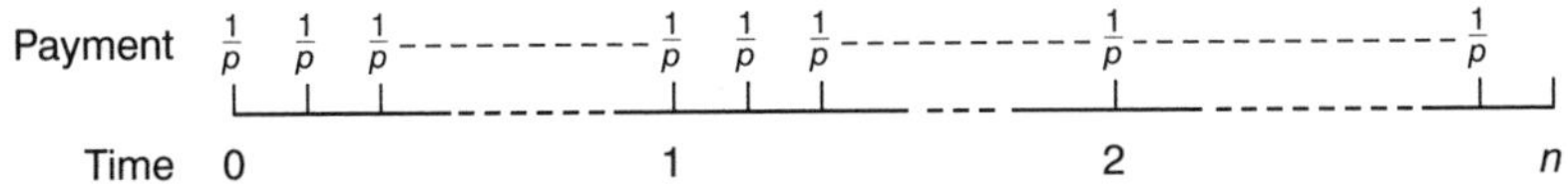

Figure 1.12

The present value of this series of payments is often denoted by the symbol $\ddot{a}_{\overline{n}|}^{(p)}$. The problem is the same as in (5) above except that each payment must be discounted by $1/p$ of an interval less. So

$$\ddot{a}_{\overline{n}|}^{(p)} = (1+i)^{1/p} a_{\overline{n}|}^{(p)}$$

$$= (1+i)^{1/p} \left(\frac{i}{i^{(p)}}\right) a_{\overline{n}|} \qquad \text{using equation (1.15)}$$

$$= \left(1+\frac{i^{(p)}}{p}\right)\left(\frac{i}{i^{(p)}}\right) a_{\overline{n}|} \qquad \text{using equation (1.3)}$$

or

$$\ddot{a}_{\overline{n}|}^{(p)} = \left(\frac{i}{i^{(p)}} + \frac{i}{p}\right) a_{\overline{n}|} \qquad (1.16)$$

Excel Application 1.1

Excel contains several functions useful for financial calculations.

The PV function, for example, can be used for calculating several present value calculations, including simple annuities.

The PV function can take 5 parameters: the rate of interest per period (rate), the number of periods (nper), the (constant) amount paid each period (pmt), any additional amount paid in the future (fv) and an indicator as to whether payments are made at the beginning or end of each period (0 for the end, 1 for the beginning).

Example 1: To calculate the present value of $100 paid in 10 years, when the rate of interest is 10% p.a., you could enter in any cell on the spreadsheet:

=PV(10%,10,0,100,0)

This returns a value of −38.55. The negative sign is a convention in Excel – if the future value is positive, then the present value is represented as a negative.

Example 2: To calculate the present value of an annuity of 10 per month (paid in arrear) for 10 years at a rate of interest of 12% p.a. (convertible monthly), you would enter (in any cell in the spreadsheet):

=PV(12%/12,120,10,0,0)

This returns −697.01 as present value for the annuity.

The function FV is very similar to PV, but produces the future value rather than the present value. For example, the accumulated value at the end of the 10 years is given by:

=FV(12%/12,120,10,0,0)

This produces a number of −2300.39.

1.7 INVESTMENT PROJECT ANALYSIS

The term "investment" has a double meaning. It can mean real investment in projects or it can mean financial investment in equities, bonds or other securities. For the rest of this chapter we will confine our attention to the former. More precisely, we will consider the appraisal of investment projects by companies using discounted cash flow (DCF) techniques. These techniques are based on compound interest theory. After this chapter, however, the emphasis will be on financial investment in securities.

The application of DCF techniques is a straightforward aspect of project appraisal. The difficult part is estimating the inputs of the model, namely the expected cash flows and the appropriate rate of interest.[1] Many investment projects have intangible or unmeasurable benefits or costs, including synergies with the rest of the business; the measurement of such costs or benefits may involve a degree of subjectivity. Furthermore, all project appraisal decisions involve a choice, accept or reject, so they should be defined in terms of *incremental* cash flow by comparing the project with the "base case", i.e. the status quo.

We will assume that all cash flows are discrete, thus ignoring the possibility of continuous payments. In other words, we assume that any continuous payments can be approximated by a set of discrete payments. The *net cash flow* is simply the cash inflow minus the cash outflow. For most projects encountered in practice, there is a *conventional* net cash flow pattern. This means that there are net cash outflows for one or more years followed by net cash inflows for all subsequent years. *Unconventional* net cash flow patterns have more than one change of sign in the sequence of net cash flows.

1.8 NET PRESENT VALUE

Let C_{t_j} be the net cash flow at time t_j ($j = 1, 2, ..., n$). The *net present value* (NPV) of an investment project at a rate of interest i is given by:

$$\text{NPV} = \sum_{j=1}^{n} C_{t_j}(1+i)^{-t_j} \tag{1.17}$$

In other words, we take all the net cash flows and discount them to the start of the project. The NPV measures the added value to the company of undertaking the project. It should be calculated using a rate of interest equal to the rate of return that the company would expect to pay to finance the project (the "cost of capital"). This could be the return shareholders expect on equity capital or the return that has to be paid on debt capital, or a weighted average of the two. However, account should be taken of the risk of the project. The higher the risk, the higher the volatility of shareholders' returns and hence the higher the rate of interest that should be employed to discount payments.

Cash outflows must not include interest payments as these are taken into account implicitly in the discounting process. For example, if cash inflows occur later than cash outflows, the former will be discounted more in the NPV calculation.

In a sense, NPV measures the overall profit of the project, expressed at the beginning of the project. This concept becomes more obvious if we first look at the *accumulated*

---

[1] In addition, there may be some optionality in that projects that are not feasible now may become so later.

profit at the end of the project. If the project ends T years from now, the accumulated profit (A) is given by:

$$A = \sum_{j=1}^{n} C_{t_j}(1+i)^{T-t_j} \tag{1.18}$$

If we then multiply equation (1.18) by $(1+i)^{-T}$, we obtain the NPV equation (1.17). This demonstrates the point that the NPV is just the present value of the accumulated profit.

1.9   INTERNAL RATE OF RETURN

The *internal rate of return* (IRR) of an investment project is the rate of interest at which the NPV (or, alternatively, the accumulated profit)[2] of the investment project is equal to zero. It is called the *internal* rate of return because it is the return earned by the project itself. No external market rate of interest is involved in the calculation.

Imagine a hypothetical bank account that represents the project. The amounts invested can be thought of as being paid out of the bank account and cash inflows received from the project can be thought of as being paid into the bank account. A fixed rate of interest is charged on negative balances ("overdrafts") and the same fixed rate is paid on positive cash balances ("deposits"). Interest is left to accumulate within the account. Then if balances in the bank account are accumulated at the IRR, the final balance of the bank account will be exactly zero.

For project appraisal purposes, the IRR must be compared with the cost of capital. In simple terms, if the internal rate of return is higher than the cost of capital, the project is worthwhile because it will provide a higher rate of return than that which the company will have to pay to finance the project.

If we are appraising a single investment project with a conventional net cash flow pattern, NPV and IRR lead to consistent decisions. Let i_0 be the IRR and i_1 be the cost of capital. If there is a conventional net cash flow pattern, the NPV of a project will be a continuously decreasing function of the rate of interest. Therefore because $\text{NPV}(i_0) = 0$, we have $\text{NPV}(i_1) > 0$ if and only if $i_0 > i_1$.

If, on the other hand, we are appraising a project with an unconventional net cash flow pattern, there may be more than one possible value for the IRR.[3] For such projects, decision-making using the IRR can be problematic.

Example 1.8

A company intends to put \$2,238,600 into an investment project which provides \$1.2m, \$1.5m and \$2m at the end of 3 years, 8 years and 12 years respectively. Show that the internal rate of return is 10% per annum.

---

[2] We can set up an *equation of value* at any time. The important point to remember is that all cash inflows and all cash outflows must be discounted (or accumulated) to the *same* point in time. It is not sensible to compare cash flows discounted to different points in time.

[3] This corresponds to negative cash balances arising in the hypothetical bank account at some stage in the life of the project.

Answer

The NPV of the project (in $m) is given by:

$$NPV = -2.2386 + \frac{1.2}{(1+i)^3} + \frac{1.5}{(1+i)^8} + \frac{2}{(1+i)^{12}} \qquad (1.19)$$

Substituting $i = 0.1$ we see that the right-hand side of equation (1.19) is equal to zero. Thus the internal rate of return is 10% per annum.

1.10   DISCOUNTED PAYBACK PERIOD

The *discounted payback period* of a project is the time it takes for the discounted incoming cash flows to recover the discounted outgoing cash flows. In other words, at the end of the discounted payback period, all incoming cash flows have repaid all outgoing cash flows together with any interest due on loans necessary to finance outgoing cash flows. It can be regarded as the time it takes for the project to become profitable.

Knowledge of discounted payback period may be useful if capital is scarce. A project which becomes profitable earlier may be considered to be better than one which becomes profitable later because it will allow capital to be repaid and investment in another project to go ahead. However, it does not tell the investor about the overall profitability of a project. A project which carries on for longer but which pays back capital more slowly might have a higher NPV. If the rate of interest used in the NPV calculation is the appropriate one, it should not matter when the project becomes profitable. Later cash flows are discounted more. However, an investor's view of risk might be such that it is appropriate to use a higher interest rate for discounting cash flows from projects that are "longer", and this would be a better way to take account of time preferences than using discounted payback period. Nevertheless, despite these drawbacks, it may still be considered useful to know the discounted payback period for the purposes of budgeting and financial planning.

The *payback period* is the same as the discounted payback period except that the cash flows are not discounted. It is the period after which the sum of incoming cash flows is first not less than the sum of outgoing cash flows. It is difficult to find a good reason to use the payback period in investment project appraisal. It is one way of ensuring that the preference for early cash flows over late cash flows is taken into account but it is better to do this using an NPV approach.

Example 1.9

A machine can be purchased for £5000, which will give rise to the cash inflows and costs shown in Table 1.1.

The machine can be sold after 6 years for £1000. All cash flows are at the end of the year. The cost of capital is 10% per annum effective. Calculate

(i) the net present value of the project;
(ii) the discounted payback period.

Table 1.1

Year	Inflows from sales (£)	Maintenance costs (£)
1	1000	50
2	1500	50
3	2000	100
4	1500	100
5	1000	150
6	500	200

Answer

(1) Time	(2) Net cash flow (£)	(3) Discount factor	(4) DCF (£)	(5) $\sum$ DCF (£)
0	−5000	1.000000	−5000	−5000
1	950	0.909091	863.6	−4136.4
2	1450	0.826446	1198.3	−2938.1
3	1900	0.751315	1427.5	−1510.6
4	1400	0.683013	956.2	−554.4
5	850	0.620921	527.8	−26.6
6	1300	0.564474	733.8	+707.2

(i) NPV $= \sum$ Column (4) $= \pm£707.2$.

(ii) From Column (5), discounted payback period is 6 years.

Excel Application 1.2

Another very useful pair of functions in Excel are XNPV and XIRR, which can be used to calculate net present values and internal rates of return, respectively.

The parameters for XNPV are, first of all, a rate of interest (rate) and then two ranges of numbers, the amounts of the payments and the dates of the payments.

For example, to calculate the net present value in example 1.9, enter in cells A1 to A7, 1 Jan 2002, 31 Dec 2002, 31 Dec 2003, 31 Dec 2004, 31 Dec 2005, 31 Dec 2006, 31 Dec 2007 (i.e. arbitrary dates representing the times "now" and then 6 dates at annual intervals) and enter in cells B1 to B7, −5000, 950, 1450, 1900, 1400, 850, 1300 (i.e. the amounts corresponding to the dates).

If you enter the formula =XNPV(10%,B1:B7,A1:A7), it returns the answer 707.84. This is slightly different from the answer in the solution to example 1.9, because the XNPV calculation is based on days and it is assumed that there are exactly 365 days in the year.

If this function is not available, run the Setup program to install the Analysis ToolPak. After you install the Analysis ToolPak, you must enable it by using the **Add-Ins** command on the **Tools** menu.

The function XIRR returns the internal rate of return for an arbitrary set of dates and cash flows. It requires the dates and amounts of the cash flows to be entered as well as an initial guess as to what the answer might be.

Example 1.8 can be replicated in Excel by entering the following dates in cells A1 to A4, 1 Jan 2002, 31 Dec 2004, 31 Dec 2009, 31 Dec 2013 and the following amounts in cells B1 to B4, −2.2386, 1.2, 1.5 and 2.0. If the formula = XIRR(B1:B4,A1:A4,5%), it returns the answer 0.09996, which is extremely close to 10%.

1.11 ANALYSIS OF DECISION CRITERIA

We have already rejected as inadequate the payback method of appraisal. Cash flows after the payback period are ignored, the time value of money is ignored and the method cannot cope with unconventional cash flow patterns. The discounted payback method can provide some useful information but suffers from the same drawbacks as the payback method apart from taking the time value of money into account.

How does the IRR criterion compare with the NPV criterion? We have established that they will normally lead to the same conclusion if they are applied to a single project. But the IRR and NPV criteria can conflict if we are comparing two projects. Consider two projects that are mutually exclusive. One gives the higher NPV and the other the higher IRR. Which project is better? The most common reason for this situation is that the projects differ in scale, that is, one project (the one with the higher NPV) is longer or requires more capital than the other. If the cost of capital is 10%, is an IRR of 100% on an initial outlay of £1 better than an IRR of 25% on an initial outlay of £1,000,000? And which is better, a return of 100% per annum for a day or a return of 25% per annum for a year, with the same initial outlay? If two projects are mutually exclusive, the one with the greater NPV should be chosen, as this will maximise shareholders' wealth.

1.12 SENSITIVITY ANALYSIS

NPV is an important concept because it is the ultimate measure of profitability of a project. However, the input variables are generally uncertain. For this reason it is often useful to conduct a sensitivity analysis. This involves varying the key parameters of the project, one at a time, to assess the sensitivity of the project NPV (or IRR) to variation in each parameter. For example, we could set upper and lower bounds for revenues, costs and the starting date for incoming cash flows. The NPV is then calculated with one of the variables at the upper or lower bound, while each of the other variables is set equal to the best estimate. The NPV calculation is repeated to test the sensitivity of the project NPV to each of the variables. This process can be carried out easily nowadays with the use of spreadsheets.

Sensitivity analysis disaggregates the problem. By identifying the factors causing most concern, it indicates what further information would be useful and how the project might be re-designed to reduce the risk.

Annex 1.1   Exponents

An *exponent* (also known as an *index* or a *power*) is a number placed at the right of and above a symbol, number or expression. If the exponent is a positive integer it indicates that the symbol is to be multiplied by itself as many times as there are units in the integer. For example,

$$3^2 = 3 \times 3 = 9$$

or

$$y^3 = y \times y \times y$$

Suppose that the exponent of y is of the form $1/q$ where q is an integer. Then $y^{1/q}$ is a number which when raised to the power q equals y. Thus

$$12^{1/5} = z \qquad \text{where} \qquad z^5 = 12$$

In practice, expressions such as $12^{1/5}$ may be calculated on a hand-held calculator using the $y^{1/x}$ button (with $y = 12$ and $x = 5$) or the y^x button (with $y = 12$ and $x = 0.2$). Both methods give an answer of 1.64375 for $12^{1/5}$.

If the exponent of y is a fraction p/q then $y^{p/q}$ is defined as $(y^{1/q})^p$. Thus $12^{4/5}$ should be interpreted as $(12^{1/5})^4$. In practice, expressions of the form $y^{p/q}$ may be calculated using the y^x button of a hand-held calculator. For the expression $12^{4/5}$, we enter $y = 12$ and $x = 4/5 = 0.8$ to obtain 7.30037.

A negative exponent indicates that, in addition to the operations indicated by the numerical value of the exponent, the quantity is to be reciprocated. It makes no difference whether the reciprocation is performed before or after the other exponential operations. For example,

$$3^{-2} = (3^2)^{-1} = (9)^{-1} = \frac{1}{9}$$

or

$$3^{-2} = (3^{-1})^2 = \left(\frac{1}{3}\right)^2 = \frac{1}{9}$$

If a and b are positive numbers, the following *laws of exponents* are valid:

(i) $a^n \cdot a^m = a^{n+m}$
(ii) $a^m / a^n = a^{m-n}$
(iii) $(a^m)^n = a^{mn}$
(iv) $(ab)^n = a^n \cdot b^n$
(v) $(a/b)^n = a^n / b^n$

where m and n are any numbers.

Annex 1.2   Geometric series

The summation of the general form of a finite geometric series is

$$a + aR + aR^2 + aR^3 + \cdots + aR^{n-1}$$

where a and R are constants. There are n terms in the series. Note that each term of the series can be obtained by multiplying the previous term by a common ratio, R. For example,

$$\text{Third term} = \text{Second term} \times R$$
$$= aR \times R$$
$$= aR^2$$

Examples of a finite geometric series are

(i) $2 + 10 + 50 + 250$

   In this case, the first term is 2, the common ratio is 5 and there are four terms in the series.

(ii) $1 + \dfrac{1}{2} + \dfrac{1}{4} + \dfrac{1}{8} + \dfrac{1}{16}$

   In this case, the first term is 1, the common ratio is $\frac{1}{2}$ and there are five terms in the series.

The above series may be evaluated by simply adding up the terms. Thus, the sum of series (i) is 312 and the sum of series (ii) is $1\frac{15}{16}$. However, adding up the terms in a geometric series is an extremely laborious process when there are a large number of terms. In such a situation we use the following formula, the proof of which is given below.

$$S_n = \frac{a(1 - R^n)}{1 - R}$$

where n = the number of terms in the series
         a = the first term of the series
         R = the common ratio
         S_n = the sum of the series.

Proof

$$S_n = a + aR + aR^2 + \cdots + aR^{n-1} \tag{1.20}$$

Multiplying equation (1.20) by R we obtain

$$RS_n = aR + aR^2 + aR^3 + \cdots + aR^n \tag{1.21}$$

Subtracting equation (1.21) from equation (1.20) gives

$$S_n - RS_n = a - aR^n$$
$$S_n(1 - R) = a(1 - R^n)$$

so that

$$S_n = \frac{a(1 - R^n)}{1 - R} \qquad (1.22)$$

Consider again the series (i) and (ii) above to confirm the validity of the formula:

(i) $2 + 10 + 50 + 250$. Thus $a = 2$, $R = 5$ and $n = 4$. So the sum of the series is

$$\frac{2(1 - 5^4)}{1 - 5} = \frac{2(-624)}{-4}$$

$$= \underline{312} \text{ as before.}$$

(ii) $1 + \frac{1}{2} + \frac{1}{4} + \frac{1}{8} + \frac{1}{16}$. Thus $a = 1$, $R = \frac{1}{2}$ and $n = 5$. So the sum of the series is

$$\frac{1(1 - (\frac{1}{2})^5)}{1 - \frac{1}{2}} = \frac{\frac{31}{32}}{\frac{1}{2}}$$

$$= \underline{1\frac{15}{16}} \text{ as before}$$

An infinite geometric series has an infinite number of terms and is therefore of the form

$$a + aR + aR^2 + aR^3 + \cdots$$

where the symbol ... indicates that the series extends indefinitely. If R is numerically greater than 1, the series does not have a finite sum and is said to be *divergent*. If R is numerically less than 1, the sum of the series moves closer to a finite limit as more terms are added. Such a series is said to be *convergent* and its sum, S, is given by the following formula:

$$S = \frac{a}{1 - R} \qquad \text{(where } -1 < R < +1) \qquad (1.23)$$

Consider the series $1 + \frac{1}{2} + \frac{1}{4} + \frac{1}{8} + \cdots$.

The sum of the first three terms is $1\frac{3}{4}$

The sum of the first four terms is $1\frac{7}{8}$

The sum of the first five terms is $1\frac{15}{16}$

Intuitively, we see that as we add more and more terms, the sum gets closer and closer to the limit 2. In this case, $a = 1$ and $R = \frac{1}{2}$, and substituting these values into equation (1.23), we see that the sum of the series is in fact

$$\frac{1}{1 - \frac{1}{2}} = 2$$

REFERENCES

Booth, P.M., Chadburn, R., Cooper, D., Haberman, S. and James, D. (1999), *Modern Actuarial Theory and Practice*, Chapman and Hall.

Donald, D.W.A. (1975), *Compound Interest and Annuities-Certain*, Heinemann.

McCutcheon, J.J. and Scott, W.F. (1991), *An Introduction to the Mathematics of Finance*, Heinemann.

2
Fixed-interest Bonds

2.1 INTRODUCTION

Bonds are securitised loans which may be bought or sold before they are repaid. The purchaser of a bond receives a certificate which stipulates the rate of interest to be paid and the amount to be repaid at the end of the loan.

In this chapter, we are concerned only with bonds which pay a fixed income, often known as the *coupon* or *interest payment*. Such bonds (sometimes described as *straight bonds*) are the most important type of bond. They are usually repayable at *nominal* or *par* value on a single date, known as the *maturity date* or *redemption date*. Current market prices, determined by supply and demand, are expressed as a percentage of the bond's nominal value.

The profile of cash returns from a straight bond with a single redemption date n years from now is illustrated in Figure 2.1. It has been assumed that the annual coupon D is payable in equal half-yearly instalments and that an interest payment has just been made.

Figure 2.1

2.2 TYPES OF BOND

Bonds may be classified into three separate categories: (a) domestic bonds, (b) foreign bonds, (c) Eurobonds.

(a) *Domestic bonds* are an important investment medium in many countries. They are issued by a domestic borrower, denominated in the local currency and sold mainly to domestic investors. The US bond market is by far the most important domestic bond market. It includes Treasury notes and bonds, government agency bonds, municipal bonds and corporate bonds. Treasury issues, which form the largest market, carry a central government guarantee and generally pay interest in equal half-yearly instalments. Treasury notes have an orignal term of from 1 to 10 years, whereas Treasury bonds have an original term of over 10 years. The Japanese domestic bond market is the second largest after the US and is dominated by Japanese government bonds (JGBs). Interest is payable in equal half-yearly instalments. The UK bond market is dominated by *British Government bonds* (*gilt-edged securities* or *gilts*), which are guaranteed by the British Government. In conventional issues, interest is generally payable in equal half-yearly instalments.

(b) *Foreign bonds* are denominated in the local currency but issued by a foreign borrower. New issues and secondary trading are under the supervision of local market authorities. The main foreign bond markets are those of the United States (Yankee), Japan (Samurai) and Switzerland.

(c) *Eurobonds* are usually issued internationally by a syndicate of banks. Free from controls of any government, many different types of Eurobonds have been developed in response to the requirements of borrowers and lenders. Bonds may be issued in a variety of currencies including the US dollar, sterling, yen, Swiss franc, deutschmark and the Euro. Thus, in this international bond market, governments or large companies may borrow dollars from German investors or yen from the Swiss.

Eurobonds normally have an original term of up to 10 years, although bonds with longer terms are sometimes issued. They are in *bearer* form, meaning that transfer is effected simply by passing the bond certificate from one person to another. Interest is paid annually without deduction of tax.

2.3   ACCRUED INTEREST

If a bond is purchased between interest payment dates, the total price paid by the investor includes *accrued interest*. Broadly speaking, accrued interest is the amount of interest that would have been paid between the last interest payment date and the settlement date, if interest were paid on a daily basis. Although accrued interest is included in the total price paid by investors, it is not generally included in the quoted market price. Prices which do not include accrued interest are known as *clean* prices whereas prices which include accrued interest are known as *dirty* prices.

The manner in which accrued interest is calculated depends on the bond market in question. In the case of US Treasury issues, accrued interest is calculated according to the exact number of days between coupons. Thus, if accrued interest is to be calculated 35 days from the last interest payment and there are 183 days between the interest payments, accrued interest would be 35/183 of the semi-annual coupon.

In the Eurobond market, accrued interest is based on a 30-day month and a 360-day year. Thus, the holder of a bond for one month receives 30/360 or one-twelfth of the annual coupon. Accrued interest to a settlement date on the thirty-first calendar day of a month is the same as that to the thirtieth calendar day of the same month; for example, accrued interest from 2 December to 31 December would equal 28/360 of the annual coupon, the same as that for the period 2 December to 30 December. On the other hand, accrued interest from 15 February to 1 March would equal 16/360 of the annual coupon compared with 13/360 of the annual coupon for the period 15 February to 28 February.

In the UK and Japan, accrued interest is calculated on the basis of a 365-day year (including leap years). Accrued interest is proportional to the number of days since the last interest payment.

Example 2.1

Interest payment dates for a 15% British Government bond are 27 April and 27 October. Calculate the accrued interest per £100 nominal of stock if the settlement date for a deal is 15 July.

Answer

Number of days from last interest payment date to settlement date

$$= 3 + 31 + 30 + 15$$

$$= 79$$

Thus,

$$\text{Accrued interest} = \frac{79}{365} \times £15$$

$$= \underline{£3.2466}$$

Table 2.1 summarises the methods for calculating accrued interest in major bond markets.

A complication can arise in calculating accrued interest for British Government bonds. When a bond is quoted *cum dividend*, a buyer is entitled to the next interest payment but when a bond is quoted *ex dividend*, a buyer is not entitled to the next interest payment. Gilts normally go ex dividend 7 working days before an interest

Table 2.1

Bond market	Day count	Usual frequency of coupon
US Treasury bonds	Actual/actual	Semi-annual
Eurobonds	30/360	Annual
Japanese Government bonds	Actual/365	Semi-annual
British Government bonds	Actual/365	Semi-annual

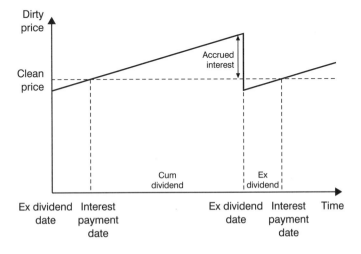

Figure 2.2

payment is due. Note that when a bond is quoted ex dividend, accrued interest will be negative, based on the time between the settlement date and the next interest payment date. Accrued interest is negative because it will be more than 6 months before a buyer receives a semi-annual coupon.

Figure 2.2 shows the way accrued interest for a British Government bond varies over time. It has been assumed that the clean price remains constant over the period.

2.4   PRESENT VALUE OF PAYMENTS

The value of a bond is equal to the present value of coupons to be received plus the present value of the redemption amount, using an appropriate rate of interest. This value may then be compared with the bond's (dirty) market price to assess whether the bond is cheap or dear. However, in practice, investors normally assess bonds using redemption yield (see Sections 2.7 and 2.8) which is essentially an internal rate of return approach.

2.5   INTEREST YIELD

Interest yield (sometimes called *current yield, running yield* or *flat yield*) is a measure of the annual interest in relation to the amount invested.

Gross interest yield is obtained by dividing the coupon by the clean price, and expressing the result as a percentage. That is,

$$\text{Gross interest yield} = \frac{\text{coupon}}{\text{clean price}} \times 100\% \qquad (2.1)$$

Net interest yield is similar to gross interest yield, but takes into account tax on income.

$$\text{Net interest yield} = (1 - t) \times \frac{\text{coupon}}{\text{clean price}} \times 100\% \qquad (2.2)$$

where t = the investor's rate of tax on income.

If interest yield after expenses is required, transaction costs should be added to the clean price in the case of a purchase, or deducted from the clean price in the case of a sale.

Example 2.2

The quoted price of a 10% bond is £102 (per £100 nominal). Calculate the interest yield to an investor who pays no tax.

Answer

$$\text{Gross interest yield} = \frac{£10}{£102} \times 100\%$$

$$= \underline{9.80\%}$$

Interest yields are of very limited use, except where a stock is undated, in which case there are no redemption proceeds to consider. Normally, interest yield is only useful in judging whether the income produced by a given stock will be sufficient for the needs of a particular investor. In order to make comparisons with other investments, allowance must be made for any capital gains or losses at redemption.

We will now take into account the gain (or loss) on redemption as well as coupon payments in calculating yields. It will be assumed that coupon payments are made in equal half-yearly instalments.

2.6   SIMPLE YIELD TO MATURITY

In Japanese bond markets, the concept of simple interest is used when calculating the yield to maturity (simple yield to maturity) rather than the usual compound interest method (redemption yield). The capital gain (or loss) is deemed to occur uniformly over the bond's life. The simple yield to maturity is therefore not a true yield, unlike redemption yield which will be discussed in Section 2.7.

$$\text{Simple yield to maturity} = \frac{D}{P} + \left\{ \frac{100 - P}{P} \times \frac{1}{n} \right\} \tag{2.3}$$

where P = current price, including accrued interest
$\quad\quad\quad D$ = coupon (payable in half-yearly instalments)
$\quad\quad\quad n$ = outstanding term to redemption (in years).

The historical rationale for this incorrect formula is the ease of calculation. It understates (or overstates) the yield if the bond stands above (or below) the nominal value.

2.7   GROSS REDEMPTION YIELD

Broadly speaking, *gross redemption yield* or *gross yield to maturity* is the annual rate of return to redemption for an investor who pays no tax. However, if interest is paid half-yearly, it is usual in the US and the UK to calculate and express the redemption yield as a yield per annum, convertible half-yearly, i.e. the half-yearly internal rate of return is calculated and then multiplied by 2.[1]

To simplify matters, assume for the moment that settlement coincides with an interest payment date. This means that accrued interest is zero so that the dirty price is simply equal to the quoted clean price. Then the gross redemption yield is defined as $2i$, where i is a solution of the following equation:

$$P = \frac{D a_{\overline{2n}|}}{2} + \frac{100}{(1 + i)^{2n}} \tag{2.4}$$

---

[1] Most Europeans calculate the true effective annual yield, giving a higher figure for bonds paying interest half-yearly or more frequently, due to the compounding effect.

Equation (2.4) is simply the equation of value at the present time using a half-yearly rate of interest i. The right-hand side of the equation is the present value of interest payments and redemption proceeds.

Example 2.3

A US Treasury bond has a term to redemption of exactly 14 years. If the coupon rate is 13% and the gross redemption yield is 9.82%, what is the current market price?

Answer

We have

$$D = 13 \qquad n = 14 \qquad i = \frac{0.0982}{2} = 0.0491$$

$$a_{\overline{2n}|} = \frac{1 - \dfrac{1}{(1+i)^{2n}}}{i} = \frac{1 - \dfrac{1}{(1.0491)^{28}}}{0.0491}$$

$$= 15.045$$

Substituting these values into equation (2.4),

$$P = 6.5 \times 15.045 + \frac{100}{(1.0491)^{28}}$$

$$= \underline{123.9}$$

Excel Application 2.1

Excel contains many functions that are useful for bond analysis. We outline just two in this application, namely the PRICE and MDURATION functions.

The PRICE function

PRICE(settlement,maturity,rate,yld,redemption,frequency,basis) returns the price of bond. Settlement is the date at which the bond was bought, maturity is the date at which redemption occurs, rate is the annual coupon rate, yld is the yield to maturity of the bond, redemption is the rate of redemption per 100 of nominal, frequency is the frequency with which coupons are paid and basis is an indicator which tells Excel which convention to use for calculating the number of days between dates (details can be found by using the help menu in Excel).

For example, to calculate the price of the bond in example 2.3, you would enter: =Price(1 Jan 2002, 31 Dec 2014, 13%, 9.82%, 100, 2, 0). This returns 123.07. Again, this is slightly different from the answer that ignores the subtleties involved with the actual conventions associated with expressing interest rates and dealing with coupons.

> The YIELD function would calculate the yield associated with a given price.
>
> The MDURATION function (see Section 2.10).
>
> MDURATION(settlement,maturity,coupon,yld,frequency,basis) calculates the modified duration of a bond. For the same bond as above, the modified duration or volatility is given by:
>   =MDURATION(1 Jan 2002, 31 Dec 2014, 13%, 9.82%, 2, 0), which returns 6.86.

In Example 2.3, we calculated the market price, given the gross redemption yield. It is more usual, however, to be confronted with the problem of calculating the gross redemption yield, as current market prices are readily available. Unfortunately, it is not usually possible to find a solution to equation (2.4) analytically and "successive approximation" methods must be employed.

Equation (2.4) may be rearranged as follows:

Substituting

$$a_{\overline{2n}|} = \frac{1 - \dfrac{1}{(1+i)^{2n}}}{i}$$

we obtain

$$P = \frac{D}{2}\left\{\frac{1 - \dfrac{1}{(1+i)^{2n}}}{i}\right\} + \frac{100}{(1+i)^{2n}}$$

Multiplying both sides by $(1+i)^{2n}$,

$$P(1+i)^{2n} = \frac{D}{2}\left\{\frac{(1+i)^{2n} - 1}{i}\right\} + 100$$

Subtracting P from both sides,

$$P\{(1+i)^{2n} - 1\} = \frac{D}{2}\left\{\frac{(1+i)^{2n} - 1}{i}\right\} + (100 - P)$$

Multiplying by $2i/\{(1+i)^{2n} - 1\}P$,

$$2i = \frac{D}{P} + \left(\frac{100 - P}{P} \times \frac{2i}{(1+i)^{2n} - 1}\right) \tag{2.5}$$

Remember that equation (2.4) is only valid on an interest payment date. Equation (2.5) is therefore correct on an interest payment date but may lead to inaccurate results at other times. The first term on the right-hand side is the gross interest yield. The second term on the right-hand side gives the capital element in the gross redemption yield.

Note the similarity between equation (2.5) and equation (2.3). In fact, equation (2.3) is a first approximation to equation (2.5), as can be seen as follows.

Using the binomial expansion,

$$(1+i)^{2n} = 1 + 2ni + \cdots$$

Hence, ignoring terms in i^2 and higher-order terms,

$$\frac{2i}{(1+i)^{2n} - 1} \simeq \frac{2i}{1 + 2ni - 1} = \frac{1}{n}$$

Substituting into equation (2.5) we obtain

$$2i = \frac{D}{P} + \left(\frac{100 - P}{P} \times \frac{1}{n} \right) \qquad \text{as in equation (2.3)}$$

Equation (2.5) may be solved for $2i$ using numerical approximation techniques. Nowadays, redemption yield calculations may be done on programmable pocket calculators, so there should be no need to do the calculations by hand.

Consider now the more general case in which there is less than half a year to the next coupon payment. This is illustrated in Figure 2.3.

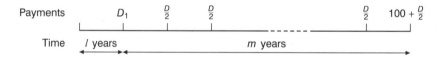

Figure 2.3

Then the equation of value at the present time is

$$P = \frac{1}{(1+i)^{2l}} \left\{ D_1 + \frac{D}{2} a_{\overline{2m}|} + \frac{100}{(1+i)^{2m}} \right\} \qquad (2.6)$$

where D_1 = next interest payment (normally $D/2$)
         l = period to next interest payment (in years)
         m = period from next interest payment to redemption date (in years)

N.B. For a British Government bond which is ex dividend, set $D_1 = 0$ because the next interest payment will not be received by a buyer.

2.8   NET REDEMPTION YIELD

Net redemption yield is calculated in a similar way to gross redemption yield but takes taxation into account. It is therefore dependent not only on the characteristics of the stock being considered, but also on the tax position of the investor. Assuming that the investor (or the bond) is free from capital gains tax, it is only necessary to allow for tax on income. Then if the present time is an interest payment date, net redemption yield is $2i$ where i is a solution of the following equation:

$$P = (1 - t)\, \frac{D}{2}\, a_{\overline{2n}|} + \frac{100}{(1 + i)^{2n}} \qquad (2.7)$$

where $t =$ the investor's rate of tax on income.

Net redemption yields may be calculated using the same numerical approximation techniques that are used to calculate gross redemption yields.

2.9 HOLDING PERIOD RETURN

Up to now we have looked at yields on the assumption that bonds are held to redemption. However, investors do not normally hold bonds to redemption, so they are concerned with the return over the period held and also with the possible change in the price of a bond caused by a change in the general level of yields (volatility — see Section 2.10).

Holding period return is simply the internal rate of return over the period that the stock is held by the investor. It may be very different from the redemption yield at the time of purchase.

Example 2.4

An investor who pays no tax purchased a US Treasury bond with coupon rate $12\frac{1}{2}\%$ at a price of \$114.25. Accrued interest on the settlement date was zero. After holding the bond for exactly 3 years, the investor sold at \$126.75. Ignoring expenses, show that the holding period return was 7% per half-year.

Answer

Equation of value at time of purchase:

$$114.25 = \frac{12.5}{2}\, a_{\overline{6}|} + \frac{126.75}{(1 + j)^6}$$

where j is the holding period return.

Substituting $j = 0.07$ we obtain a value of 114.25 for the right-hand side of the above equation, which equals the left-hand side. So the holding period return was 7% per half-year or, alternatively, 14% per annum convertible half-yearly.

2.10 VOLATILITY

The *volatility* (or *modified duration*) of an individual bond is a measure of its price sensitivity to changes in gross redemption yield. When the price rises (or falls), the yield falls (or rises), but this relationship between price changes and yield changes is not a simple one and depends on the bond's individual characteristics.

In the technical definition of volatility, the use of differentials rather than differences avoids the problem that the proportionate change in price corresponding to a rise in yields may be different from the proportionate change in price corresponding to a fall in yields. Thus,

$$\text{Volatility} = -\frac{1}{P} \times \frac{dP}{dy} \tag{2.8}$$

where P = dirty price
and y = gross redemption yield ($= 2i$)

The minus sign in equation (2.8) ensures that volatility is positive.

Nevertheless, most investors prefer to define volatility in terms of finite yield differences rather than in terms of differential calculus. Thus, in simple terms:

"Volatility is the percentage change in price for a 0.01% change in yield."

Volatility is a function of the following:

(1) *Term to redemption.* Normally, for a given coupon rate, volatility increases as term to redemption increases. It should be intuitively reasonable that for an investor who has a 20-year bond, the reduction in price necessary to provide an extra 0.01% redemption yield over 20 years must be greater than the reduction in price necessary to provide an extra 0.01% yield over 1 year. However, there are exceptions to this rule; for low-coupon bonds with a very long term, volatility can fall as term to redemption increases (see Section 15.5).

(2) *Coupon rate.* For a given term to redemption, volatility increases as coupon rate falls. This is because the lower the coupon rate, the greater the importance of redemption proceeds as a proportion of total present value. The redemption proceeds are the payments farthest away, and thus their present value is most sensitive to changes in the valuation rate of interest.

Table 2.2   Rises in price for a 1% fall in yield

Bond	Term to redemption (years)	Coupon (£)	Gross redemption yield (%)	Price (£)	Rise in price (%)
A	10	5	11	$64\frac{1}{8}$	7.4
			10	$68\frac{7}{8}$	
B	20	5	11	$51\frac{7}{8}$	10.1
			10	$57\frac{1}{8}$	
C	10	15	11	$123\frac{7}{8}$	5.9
			10	$131\frac{1}{8}$	
A	10	5	6	$92\frac{9}{16}$	8.0
			5	100	

(3) *The general level of yields.* For a given term to redemption and coupon rate, volatility increases as the general level of yields in the market falls. Again, the lower the level of yields, the greater the importance of redemption proceeds as a proportion of total present value.

Table 2.2 shows the percentage change in price of £100 nominal of a fixed-interest sterling bond with half-yearly interest payments and redeemable at par, for a 1% fall in gross redemption yield. Bond B is more volatile than Bond A, the former having a longer term to redemption. Bond A has a greater volatility than Bond C, which has a higher coupon. Note also that the rise in price of Bond A is higher when the yield starts at 6% than when it starts at 11%.

The concept of volatility will be discussed further in Chapter 15, particularly with regard to its role in bond portfolio management.

2.11   DURATION

Duration, sometimes known as *effective mean term* or *discounted mean term*, is the mean term of the present value of payments received. More precisely, it is a weighted average of the times of payments (i.e. coupons and redemption proceeds), where the weights are the present values (using a rate of interest equal to the gross redemption yield) of the payments.

Again assuming that coupon payments are made in equal half-yearly instalments and that the present time is an interest payment date,

$$\text{Duration} = \frac{1 \cdot \dfrac{Dv}{2} + 2 \cdot \dfrac{Dv^2}{2} + \cdots + 2n \cdot \dfrac{Dv^{2n}}{2} + 2n \cdot 100v^{2n}}{\dfrac{Dv}{2} + \dfrac{Dv^2}{2} + \cdots + \dfrac{Dv^{2n}}{2} + 100v^{2n}} \quad \text{half-years}$$

$$= \frac{1}{2} \times \frac{1}{P} \times \left\{ \frac{Dv}{2} + \frac{2Dv^2}{2} + \cdots + 2n \cdot \frac{2nDv^{2n}}{2} + 200nv^{2n} \right\} \quad \text{years} \quad (2.9)$$

Thus, duration is calculated by taking the time of a payment and multiplying by the present value of the payment; the sum is then taken over all the times at which the payments are made and this is divided by the price of the bond. Dividing the result by 2 gives duration in years.

The concept of duration is frequently used in a bond portfolio management technique known as *immunisation* (see Chapter 15).

2.12   THE RELATIONSHIP BETWEEN DURATION AND VOLATILITY

There is a close relationship between duration and volatility which is discussed fully in Section 15.4. It can be shown that

$$\text{Duration} = (1 + i) \times \text{volatility} \quad (2.10)$$

where $2i$ is the gross redemption yield.

Thus, an increase in duration occurs if and only if there is an increase in volatility, and the factors affecting volatility also affect duration.

2.13 CONVEXITY

Equation (2.8) can be rearranged to give:

$$dP = -P \cdot V \cdot dy \qquad (2.11)$$

where V is volatility.

We can use equation (2.11) to estimate the change in price of a bond for a small change in the (gross) redemption yield. As redemption yield changes, however, a bond's volatility also changes. Volatility is thus only an accurate predictor of price changes for infinitesimally small changes in redemption yield.

Convexity measures the sensitivity of volatility to changes in redemption yield. It arises from the fact that a straight bond's price–redemption yield curve is convex to the origin of the graph (see Figure 2.4).

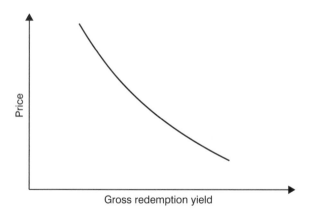

Figure 2.4 Convexity for a fixed-interest bond

Convexity may be defined (approximately) as the difference between the actual percentage change in price and the percentage change in price predicted by the bond's volatility. We will discuss convexity further in Section 15.6.

2.14 YIELD CURVES

The yield curve for a government bond market is a graph of the relationship between gross redemption yield and term to redemption[2] at a given point in time. Yield curves exist for each bond market. In practice, there are a number of factors, other than term to redemption, reflected in the gross redemption yields of individual government bonds, so that elaborate curve-fitting techniques are required to determine the shape of the curve.

---

[2] The use of duration has been advocated by many market operators as an alternative to term to redemption.

In Sections 2.15 to 2.18, we consider various theories for the shape of the yield curve. It is unlikely that the observed yield curve at any given time will be entirely consistent with only one of these theories. They may all be reflected in the shape of the yield curve to some extent.

2.15   THE EXPECTATIONS THEORY

Under the expectations theory, all market participants are indifferent to whether stocks are long-term or short-term. A long-term investment is therefore equivalent to a series of short-term investments and investors' expectations of future short-term interest rates will determine the shape of the yield curve. When short-term interest rates are expected to remain constant in the future, the yield curve will be flat. But if the majority of investors expect interest rates to rise (or fall), the yield curve will slope upwards (or downwards) as illustrated in Figure 2.5.

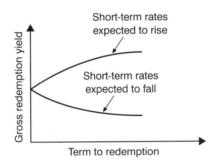

Figure 2.5

Let i_1, i_2, ..., i_{2n} per half-year be a series of *assumed* short-term interest rates which are expected by the market, where i_k is the expected half-yearly rate of interest for a half-year loan maturing k half-years from now. The analysis is simplified if we consider a bond priced at par with coupon D payable semi-annually. Then the gross redemption yield is $D\%$.

According to the expectations theory, D is given by

$$100 = \frac{D/2}{1 + i_1} + \frac{D/2}{(1 + i_1)(1 + i_2)} + \cdots + \frac{D/2 + 100}{(1 + i_1)(1 + i_2) \dots (1 + i_{2n})}$$

Multiplying by $(1 + i_1)(1 + i_2) \dots (1 + i_{2n})$ and solving,

$$\frac{D}{2}\% = \frac{(1 + i_1)(1 + i_2) \dots (1 + i_{2n}) - 1}{\{(1 + i_2)(1 + i_3) \dots (1 + i_{2n})\} + \{(1 + i_3)(1 + i_4) \dots (1 + i_{2n})\} + \cdots + (1 + i_{2n}) + 1}$$

$$(2.12)$$

Note the following:

(i) If the assumed short-term rates are equal, i.e. $i_1 = i_2 = \cdots = i_{2n} (= i)$, then

$$\frac{D}{2}\% = \frac{(1 + i)^{2n} - 1}{(1 + i)^{2n - 1} + (1 + i)^{2n - 2} + \cdots + (1 + i) + 1}$$

The denominator of the right-hand side is a geometric series, the sum of which is $[(1 + i)^{2n} - 1]/i$. Hence

$$\frac{D}{2}\% = i \qquad \text{or} \qquad D\% = 2i$$

Thus, in this case the yield curve is flat.

(ii) If short-term interest rates are expected to fall over the next year, say $i_1 = 10\%$ and $i_2 = 5\%$, then considering a 1-year bond,

$$\frac{D}{2}\% = \frac{(1.1)(1.05) - 1}{1.05 + 1}$$

$$= 0.076$$

$$= 7.6\%$$

We therefore have a pure expectation yield curve which initially slopes downwards.

Expectations theory assumes that market participants are "risk neutral", but under real-world conditions this is not the case so that the "pure expectations" yield curve must be modified.

2.16   THE LIQUIDITY PREFERENCE THEORY

Long-term stocks are generally more volatile than short-term stocks (see Section 2.10) so there is greater risk of capital loss if there is a general rise in yields. According to the liquidity preference theory, the relative riskiness of longer-dated stocks means that they must offer a higher yield to induce investors to hold them. Thus, yields will include a *risk premium* which increases with term to redemption, giving an upward bias superimposed on the pure expectations curve. For example, according to this theory, when short-term interest rates are expected to remain constant over time, there will be a tendency for the yield curve to slope upwards (see Figure 2.6).

Liquidity preference is consistent with the investment policy of investors with short-term liabilities (e.g. banks), but other investors (e.g. traditional life assurance funds) may require the certainty of income provided by long-dated stocks.

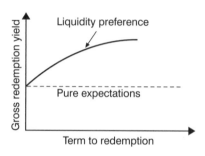

Figure 2.6

2.17   THE MARKET SEGMENTATION THEORY

This theory states that yields on each "maturity segment" are determined independently by supply and demand. The investment policy of each class of investor is regarded as being dominated by the length of their liabilities so they have "preferred habitats" in the bond market. Investors with short-term liabilities will exert an influence on the short end of the market, whereas investors with long-term liabilities will deal mainly in long-dated bonds. On the supply side, the funding requirements and preferences of the government in question will clearly have an influence on the yield curve.

As with other theories, market segmentation is an oversimplification of investor behaviour. Matching is the safest investment strategy when liabilities are fixed in money terms, but for those investors with liabilities denominated in real terms (e.g. UK final salary pension funds), simply matching by length is not appropriate.

2.18   INFLATION RISK PREMIUM

Although expected inflation is incorporated into interest rates, unexpected inflation still constitutes a risk. As long-term bonds have a greater inflation risk than short-term bonds, yields will include an *inflation risk premium*, which increases with term to redemption, suggesting an upward bias for the yield curve.

2.19   PAR YIELD CURVES

Broadly speaking, the *par yield curve* is a graph of the relationship between the coupon rate that a new issue would have to offer to be priced at par, and the term to redemption. Note that when a stock stands at par, coupon rate and gross redemption yield are equal on a coupon payment date.

The par yield curve is designed to standardise yields so as to eliminate the effect of coupon difference on the yield curve. It is not a relationship between average market yield and term to redemption.

2.20   SPOT AND FORWARD INTEREST RATES

A *spot interest rate* is the rate paid when money is borrowed now to be repaid at a single date in the future. It is an average rate of interest per annum between the current date and the payment date.

Define $_0i_n$ to be the annual spot rate between now and n years in the future. For example, $_0i_1$ is the annual rate paid on a loan between now and 1 year from now; $_0i_2$ is the annual rate paid on a loan between now and 2 years' time. Then the present value $A(0)$ of an amount $A(n)$ payable n years from now is given by

$$A(0) = \frac{A(n)}{(1 + {}_0i_n)^n}$$

A *forward interest rate* applies to contracts made for a period "forward" in time. Terms are determined now, but the actual loan occurs later. Thus, an interest rate could be agreed now for a 1-year loan to be made in 3 months time and repaid in 15 months time.

Forward interest rates can be calculated from the relevant spot rates. For example, if we define the forward rate of interest from the end of year 1 to the end of year 2 to be $_1i_2$, we have

$$(1 + {}_0i_1)(1 + {}_1i_2) = (1 + {}_0i_2)^2$$

$$_1i_2 = \frac{(1 + {}_0i_2)^2}{1 + {}_0i_1} - 1$$

2.21 SPOT RATES AND REDEMPTION YIELDS

Given the details of a particular bond, including its price, the gross redemption yield can be calculated unambiguously, and its use facilitates comparisons between bonds with different terms to redemption. However, attempting to express the return from bonds, which have intervening payments before redemption, in a single statistic is an oversimplification which can lead to problems.

Consider a 10% bond paying coupons annually with exactly 2 years to redemption. If the bond's price is equal to the present value of coupon and redemption payments,

$$P = \frac{10}{(1 + {}_0i_1)} + \frac{10 + 100}{(1 + {}_0i_2)^2}$$

Given P, we cannot estimate $_0i_1$ and $_0i_2$ from the information given. There is an infinite number of combinations of 1-year and 2-year spot rates which will give the correct value. The gross redemption yield *can* be calculated because an additional constraint is imposed, namely that 1-year and 2-year spot rates are set equal.

If, however, we are also given the details and price of either a 1-year bond or a different 2-year bond in the same bond market, it is possible to estimate the spot rates. We have two equations and two unknowns.

Example 2.5

Government bonds X and Y both pay annual coupons and are to be redeemed at par exactly 2 years from now. A coupon payment has just been made in both cases. Bond X has a coupon rate of 13% and stands at a price of 105 in the market. Bond Y has a coupon rate of 5% and stands at a price of 91.25 in the market. Calculate the 1-year and 2-year annual spot rates.

Answer

For Bond X we have

$$105 = \frac{13}{1 + {}_0i_1} + \frac{113}{(1 + {}_0i_2)^2} \tag{2.13}$$

For Bond Y we have

$$91.25 = \frac{5}{1 + {}_0i_1} + \frac{105}{(1 + {}_0i_2)^2} \tag{2.14}$$

Multiplying equation (2.13) by $\frac{5}{13}$,

$$\frac{5}{13} \times 105 = \frac{5}{1 + _0i_1} + \frac{5 \times 113}{13(1 + _0i_2)^2} \tag{2.15}$$

Subtracting equation (2.15) from equation (2.14),

$$91.25 - 40.385 = \frac{(105 - 43.462)}{(1 + _0i_2)^2}$$

$$(1 + _0i_2)^2 = \frac{61.538}{50.865}$$

$$_0i_2 = \underline{10\%}$$

Substituting this value of $_0i_2$ in equation (2.13),

$$105 = \frac{13}{1 + _0i_1} + \frac{113}{(1.1)^2}$$

$$105 - 93.388 = \frac{13}{1 + _0i_1}$$

$$1 + _0i_1 = \frac{13}{11.612}$$

$$_0i_1 = \underline{12\%}$$

If there is a sufficiently wide variety of bonds in a government bond market, it should be possible to calculate or estimate the whole range of spot rates, from short rates through to long rates. But if a common set of spot rates which make price equal to the present value of payments cannot be found, it follows that the cash flow from at least one bond can be provided more cheaply by a combination of other bonds.

The main advantage of using spot rates rather than redemption yields in analysing bonds is that payments made by different bonds at the same point in time are valued using the same rate of interest. This is not the case with redemption yields. Furthermore, two bonds with the same term to redemption but with different coupons will in general have different redemption yields, quite apart from any taxation effects. This makes drawing the yield curve difficult and leads to a scattering around it. Alternative approaches would be to draw a number of yield curves, each for a different level of coupon, or to concentrate on the spot rate curve (i.e. the zero coupon yield curve).

2.22 STRIPS

There are no US Treasury nor British Government zero-coupon bonds in issue. However, a bond is effectively a portfolio of coupon payments plus one repayment of principal. For example, a five year bond paying coupons twice a year can be considered to have 11 components–10 coupon payments plus one principal repayment. If each of these components could be traded separately in the market, they would constitute 11 zero-coupon bonds.

In 1982, a number of US investment banks created synthetic zero-coupon Treasury bonds. They bought US Treasury bonds and reissued them as separate zero-coupon bonds. The idea proved popular with investors and in 1985 the US Treasury decided to initiate an official programme whereby investors could exchange Treasury bonds for stripped bonds. These were commonly known as *strips*, an acronym for Separately Traded and Registered Interest and Principal Securities. Since 1997, all US Treasury bond issues have been strippable. The logic of the strip market stemmed from the observation that two bonds with the same coupon rate, paying coupons on the same day, but having different maturity dates, have a series of common components that should in an efficient market have the same price.

Following the success of the US Treasury strip market, the British Government launched a strip market in 1997. All main gilts are now issued as strippable with the same coupon days — 7 June and 7 December. Unfortunately, the gilt strip market has been slow to develop and there persists a lack of liquidity in the market. So gilt strips cannot be relied upon to provide true spot rates.

2.23   CORPORATE BONDS

Companies issue corporate bonds to raise long-term loan capital. Some issues are secured by means of a charge on the assets of the company. Most issues, however, are unsecured, meaning that security for the loan is the general creditworthiness of the company in question.

Some corporate bonds are not redeemable at par. In this case, 100 is simply replaced by R in the gross redemption yield equation (2.4), where £R is the redemption price per £100 nominal, provided that the other simplifying assumptions in Section 2.7 apply.

Corporate bonds generally offer a higher gross redemption yield than a corresponding government bond due to the credit risk. That is, investors require a risk premium in the yield. The greater the risk of default, the higher the premium. Corporate bonds also tend to have poorer marketability than a corresponding government bond, which increases the yield premium.

Corporate and other non-government bonds are discussed in more detail in Section 15.7.

REFERENCES

Association of International Bond Dealers (1990), *Formulae for Yield and Other Calculations*, AIBD.
Benninga, S. (2000), *Financial Modeling*, Part IV, The MIT Press.
Booth, P.M., Chadburn, R., Cooper, D., Haberman, S. and James, D. (1999), *Modern Actuarial Theory and Practice*, Chapman and Hall.
Kritzman, M. (1992), "What Practitioners Need to Know About Duration and Convexity", *Financial Analysts Journal*, 48, November–December, 17–20.
Livingston, M. (1999), *Bonds and Bond Derivatives*, Blackwell.
Phillips, F.P.S. (1987), *Inside the New Gilt-edged Market*, Woodhead-Faulkner.
Shaeffer, S. (1977), "The Problem with Redemption Yields", *Financial Analysts Journal*, July–August.
Sharpe, W.F., Alexander, G.J. and Bailey, J.V. (1999), *Investments*, 6th edition, Prentice-Hall International.
Tuckman, B. (1996), *Fixed Income Securities: Tools for Today's Markets*, John Wiley & Sons.

3
Equities and Real Estate

3.1 INTRODUCTION

We now consider two forms of investment that are backed by real assets — *equities* and *real estate*. Income is in the form of dividends for equities and rent for real estate.

Equities (also known as *ordinary shares* or *common stock*) represent ownership of a company. Thus, equity holders (also known as *shareholders* or *stockholders*) have a residual claim on the profits and assets of the company. If the business is successful, a flow of increasing dividends can be expected in line with the improving level of profits. If, on the other hand, the business goes into decline and is eventually liquidated, equity holders are the last to receive any repayment of capital. For equities which are actively traded on a stock market, there is a central market price based upon actual transactions.

Real estate consists of legal interests in land and buildings. As each unit of real estate is unique and cannot easily be subdivided, there is no central market price. Therefore, estimating the prices for which real estate can be purchased or sold is partly a matter of professional judgement.

We will concentrate on a fundamental approach to valuing these investments, based upon discounting future cash flows. In practice, however, equities and real estate are often valued using investment ratio comparisons with similar assets (see Sections 3.3 and 3.7).

International equity investment has become important owing to its risk diversification benefits and the range of opportunities which are available. Investment in foreign real estate, however, is not at present common for institutional investors. Each country has its own laws affecting real estate, and its own set of relationships between landlord and tenant. Taxation, unforeseen risks and the difficulty of managing and monitoring real estate located abroad are all serious problems.

We first discuss equities, returning to real estate in Section 3.7. To simplify the discussion, we will assume henceforth in Chapter 3 that the investor in question pays no tax. The investment mathematics aspects of foreign equity investment will be introduced in Chapter 6.

3.2 DISCOUNTED DIVIDEND MODEL

Owning a share gives the right to receive a stream of future dividends. Thus, directly estimating the present value (V_0) of a share involves estimating the present value of future dividends. We will assume that dividends are paid annually. If a dividend has just been paid, we obtain

$$V_0 + \frac{d_1}{(1+r)} + \frac{d_2}{(1+r)^2} + \frac{d_3}{(1+r)^3} + \cdots \tag{3.1}$$

where d_i = estimated gross dividend per share after i years
and r = investor's required annual rate of return (or just "required return" for short).

It might seem that equation (3.1) could give an infinite value for the share. This is mathematically possible but unrealistic. In practice, the rate of dividend growth in the long run will be lower than the required rate of return. Thus, the present values of more and more distant dividends will eventually become smaller and smaller until they can be ignored.

Estimating future dividend payments is not an easy matter. The usual approach would be to estimate the company's profits and hence earnings per share, and then multiply by an estimate of the proportion of earnings paid out in dividends. All relevant available information must be taken into account and all future dividends, until such time as their present values become negligible, must be estimated.

Although few investors would value a share directly by discounting future dividends, it is worth considering equation (3.1) further as it gives insights into the factors which influence the value of a share. For example, suppose that dividends are expected to grow at a positive constant annual rate g. Then the right-hand side of equation (3.1) becomes a geometric series, which is convergent provided g is less than r, the required return. Thus equation (3.1) simplifies to

$$V_0 = \frac{d_1}{r - g} \qquad (3.2)$$

(see equation (1.11) — in this case the rate of interest is r).

The investor's task is reduced to choosing an appropriate required return and estimating the next dividend together with the dividend growth rate thereafter.

The following observations can be made from a study of equation (3.2).

(a) The higher the estimate of the next dividend, the higher the value of the share.
(b) The higher the estimated growth rate of dividends, the higher the value of the share.
(c) The higher the required return, the lower the value of the share.
(d) The lower the denominator of the right-hand side of equation (3.2), i.e. $r - g$, the more volatile the value of the share in response to given changes in r or g.

Example 3.1

Suppose Mr Smith's required return for share XTC is 15% per annum, and he estimates that: (i) an annual dividend of 12p will be paid in exactly one year; (ii) dividends will grow at a constant rate of 10% per annum thereafter.

Calculate the value of an XTC share to Mr Smith.

Answer

Using equation (3.2),

$$V_0 = \frac{12}{0.15 - 0.10}$$

$$= \underline{240p}$$

A more refined approach is to estimate individual dividend payments for a few years and then assume a constant growth rate thereafter. For example, if $d_1, ..., d_{m+1}$ are the estimated annual dividend payments up to year $m+1$ and g' is the constant growth rate of dividends thereafter:

$$V_0 = \frac{d_1}{(1+r)} + \frac{d_2}{(1+r)^2} + \cdots + \frac{d_m}{(1+r)^m} + \frac{1}{(1+r)^m} \times \frac{d_{m+1}}{r-g'}$$

where it has been assumed that the first dividend d_1 is payable after exactly 1 year, and equation (3.2) has been applied after m years.

Example 3.2

An investor is considering the purchase of 100 ordinary shares in Adam Entertainments PLC. Dividends from the shares will be paid annually. The next dividend is due in 6 months and is expected to be 6p per share. The second, third and fourth dividends are expected to be 25% greater than their predecessors; thereafter dividends are expected to grow at a constant rate of 5% per annum in perpetuity. Calculate the present value of the dividends if the investor's required rate of return is 14% per annum.

Answer

The present value (in £s) is

$$6\left(\frac{1}{1.14^{0.5}} + \frac{1.25}{1.14^{1.5}} + \frac{1.25^2}{1.14^{2.5}} + \frac{1.25^3}{1.14^{3.5}}\right)$$

$$+ \frac{6 \times 1.25^3 \times 1.05}{1.14^{3.5}}\left(\frac{1}{1.14} + \frac{1.05}{1.14^2} + \frac{1.05^2}{1.14^3} + \cdots\right)$$

$$= 6(0.9366 + 1.0270 + 1.1261 + 1.2347) + 7.7786\left(\frac{1}{0.14 - 0.05}\right)$$

$$= 25.946 + 86.429$$

$$= \underline{£112.38}$$

In practice, a three-stage process is commonly used in estimating future dividends. Individual dividend payments are estimated for a few years, then an average dividend growth rate is applied for groups of similar companies for a further period of years and, finally, a constant dividend growth rate for all companies in the economy is applied thereafter.

Choosing the appropriate required (rate of) return is not easy as it involves consideration of the risk associated with the share. In general, investors are risk-averse, so the higher the investor's perception of the share's risk, the higher the required return (see Chapter 12). There may also be other factors to consider in assessing the required return, including marketability.

A comparison between current market price P and estimated present value V_0 of a share indicates whether or not that share is attractive to the long-term investor. If P is greater (or less) than V_0, the share is expensive (or cheap).

There may be a number of reasons for a share price being different from its estimated value:

(a) The investor's estimate of future dividends is different from the market's estimate. In this case, the important question to ask is whether the investor knows something that the market does not know. If not, then perhaps the market knows something that the investor does not know.
(b) The investor's required return is different from the market's expected return. This may be because the investor's perception of risk is different from that of the market. In the case of an investor who does not hold a diversified portfolio of shares, for example, it is likely that the required return for a share which has a high level of risk specific to that company will be greater than the market's expected return.
(c) Irrational valuation of the share by the market, e.g. a "speculative bubble" or, conversely, an "oversold" situation.

3.3 INVESTMENT RATIOS

In practice, equity analysts generally use indirect methods of share valuation rather than valuing future dividends directly. These methods often involve the use of key investment ratios such as the *dividend yield* and the *price/earnings ratio*.

Dividend yield is the gross annual dividend per share divided by the current share price in the market. It is an indication of the current level of income from a share. We define dividend yield using a forecast gross dividend per share d_1 although published dividend yields in the financial press are usually based upon the actual historic gross dividend.

$$\text{Dividend yield} = \frac{d_1}{P}$$

Price/earnings ratio is the current share price in the market expressed as a multiple of net earnings per share. Again, our definition is based upon forecast net earnings per share e_1 for the current year, whereas the financial press tends to quote price/earnings ratios based on the latest reported net earnings per share.

$$\text{Price/earnings ratio} = \frac{P}{e_1}$$

Assuming that annual dividends are expected to grow at a constant rate, we can use equation (3.2) to isolate the factors which should influence the investor's *required* dividend yield d_1/V_0 and *required* price/earnings ratio V_0/e_1.

Rearranging equation (3.2),

$$\frac{d_1}{V_0} = r - g \tag{3.3}$$

Thus, the investor's required dividend yield d_1/V_0 is simply the required return r less the expected dividend growth rate g. If the actual dividend yield d_1/P based on a dividend forecast and the current market price is greater (or less) than the required dividend yield, the share is cheap (or expensive).

Dividing equation (3.2) by prospective net earnings per share e_1 from which the next dividend d_1 is paid,

$$\frac{V_0}{e_1} = \frac{d_1/e_1}{r - g} \tag{3.4}$$

Thus, the investor's required price/earnings ratio V_0/e_1 reflects the estimated d_1/e_1 ratio, the required return and dividend growth expectations. If the actual price/earnings ratio P/e_1 based on an earnings forecast and the current market price is greater (or less) than the required price/earnings ratio, the share is expensive (or cheap).

Average price/earnings ratios across international markets vary considerably, reflecting differences in the proportion of earnings paid out in dividends, required returns and dividend growth expectations. Furthermore

(i) net earnings per share are not calculated on a consistent basis over different national markets;

(ii) equities in different national markets may not be efficiently priced, one relative to another; and

(iii) the tax treatment of dividends is not standardised internationally.

The value of a company's underlying net assets is sometimes used as a measure of fundamental value, particularly in a takeover or liquidation situation, or for companies which are investment vehicles for specific types of assets (e.g. UK investment trusts or US closed-end funds). For a continuing business, however, earnings and dividends are generally more important than net asset value.

3.4   SCRIP ISSUES AND STOCK SPLITS

A *scrip issue* (*bonus issue* or *capitalisation issue*) is an issue of further shares to existing shareholders in proportion to their holdings where no payment is required. There is no change in the company's assets and an individual shareholder's proportionate ownership of the company does not alter.

By having a scrip issue, the directors increase the number of shares in issue, thereby reducing the share price. The fall in the market price of the old shares occurs when they are first quoted *ex-scrip*. This coincides with initial dealings in the new shares. However, there may be a slight movement in the share price before the shares go ex-scrip, in response to the scrip issue announcement, for the following reasons:

(a) A scrip issue is usually regarded as an indication of confidence on the part of the board of directors. They would be unlikely to announce a scrip issue if they felt that the share price might fall substantially, subsequent to the issue.

(b) The announcement may be accompanied by new information, e.g. a dividend forecast.
(c) It might also be argued that there is the prospect of increased marketability as there is increased divisibility of share holdings.

General Formula for Theoretical Price After a Scrip Issue

Suppose that the directors of a company decide to make an m for n scrip issue. This means that a shareholder receives m new shares at no cost for every n held prior to the issue.

Consider a holding of n old shares each priced P_1 on the day the new shares are posted to shareholders. On the following business day, the holding will consist of n old shares ex-scrip together with m new shares.

Suppose the opening price of the old shares ex-scrip is P_2. Then, ignoring any difference in settlement dates between the old and new shares, the new shares should also be priced P_2 in the market. As the market value of the company and the shareholder's proportionate ownership of the company should not change as a result of the issue, we have for a holder of n shares before the issue:

Value of holding after issue = Value of holding before issue

$$(n + m)P_2 = nP_1$$

$$P_2 = \left(\frac{n}{n + m}\right)P_1 \tag{3.5}$$

Example 3.3

The directors of a company decide to make a 2 for 1 scrip issue. On the day before the old shares go ex-scrip, the old shares stand at a price of 540p in the market. What market price would you expect for the old shares ex-scrip?

Answer

Substituting $m = 2$, $n = 1$ and $P = 540$p into equation (3.5),

$$\text{Expected price for old shares ex-scrip} = \frac{1}{1 + 2} \times 540\text{p}$$

$$= \underline{180\text{p}}$$

In practice, the actual share price may be different from the theoretical value P_2 derived above, simply reflecting news which may have arisen since the previous business day.

Figure 3.1 shows how the price of a share might be expected to behave assuming that the market receives no news other than the scrip issue announcement.

A *stock split* is similar to a scrip issue but, as the name suggests, existing shares are cancelled and replaced by a larger number of new shares. For example, in a 5 for 1 stock

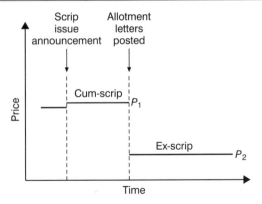

Figure 3.1

split, the company replaces each existing share by five new ones. Thus, a 5 for 1 stock split is equivalent to a 4 for 1 scrip issue. As with a scrip issue, the effect of a stock split is to reduce the share price. However, unlike a scrip issue, a stock split does not involve turning shareholders' reserves into share capital within the company's balance sheet.

3.5   RIGHTS ISSUES

A *rights issue* (or *privileged subscription*) is an offer to existing shareholders in the company, enabling them to subscribe cash for new shares in proportion to their existing holdings. The company is raising additional finance, perhaps for a new project or to repay short-term borrowings. Although rights issues are unusual in the US,[1] the rights issue is a common method for quoted companies to issue new shares in many other countries including the UK.

The issue price will be at a discount to the market price when the announcement is made. This is to try to ensure that the issue price is below the market price at the last date for acceptance and payment. Clearly, shareholders will not take up their rights if the shares can be purchased more cheaply in the market.

An example of a rights issue would be the issue of 100,000 shares on the basis of "1 for 4 at 100p". This means that a shareholder receives the right to purchase one new share at a price of 100p for every four shares already held.

There may be share price movement before a rights issue is carried out in response to the rights issue announcement, depending on the reasons for the additional finance. For example, the issue may be an indication that the company is unable to maintain its business from retained profits alone. On the other hand, the company may have the opportunity to invest in a particularly attractive project for which it requires finance. There may also be other new information in the announcement, e.g. a dividend forecast,

---

[1] In the US, the *seasoned equity offer* is the most common method by which companies already quoted on a stock market sell further shares to investors. The shares are offered to investors generally, not just to existing shareholders. The offer price is typically at or just below the market price. Rights issues were common in the US before the 1970s but are now very rare. This is somewhat surprising as the costs involved in a seasoned equity offer are significantly higher than those of a rights issue (Eckbo and Masulis, 1992).

and it is possible that the prospect of an additional supply of shares onto the market in a heavy rights issue will tend to depress the share price.

Initially, the new shares are in the form of tradable certificates issued to each shareholder indicating the number of shares for which subscription is authorised. These certificates are sometimes known as *nil paid* shares, meaning that the subscription price has not yet been paid. But after payment of the subscription price, the new shares become *fully paid*.

On receiving their certificates, shareholders have a choice of four courses of action. They can take up their subscription rights in full, sell all of the rights, take up part of the rights and sell the balance, or do nothing and let the rights lapse. If one or more shareholders take no action even though their rights have some value, it is usual for the company to sell the rights for their benefit.

General Formula for Theoretical Price After a Rights Issue

Suppose that a company decides to make an m for n rights issue at a price P. This means that a shareholder has the right to purchase m new shares at a price P per share for every n shares held prior to the issue.

Consider a holding of n old shares which carry the right to subscribe to the issue, known as *cum rights* shares or *rights-on* shares, each priced P_1 on the day before dealings in the new *nil paid* shares commence. When dealings commence on the following business day, the holding will consist of n old shares *ex-rights* and m new nil paid shares. Now that the old shares are ex-rights, they no longer carry the right to subscribe to the issue.

Suppose that the opening price of the old shares ex-rights is P_2. Then the new nil paid shares might be expected to trade at a price $P_2 - P$, assuming that P_2 is greater than P, because the nil paid shares become equivalent to an ex-rights share when the subscription price P has been paid.

No money has yet been subscribed and therefore,

$$\text{Value of old ex-rights shares} + \text{Value of new nil paid shares} = \text{Value of old cum rights shares}$$

$$nP_2 + m(P_2 - P) = nP_1$$

$$(n + m)P_2 = nP_1 + mP$$

$$P_2 = \frac{nP_1 + mP}{n + m} \tag{3.6}$$

As might be expected, the opening price of the old shares ex-rights is a weighted average of the cum rights price and the subscription price.

Example 3.4

The directors of a company decide to make a 3 for 4 rights issue at 200p. On the day before they go ex-rights, the old shares stand at a price of 230p in the market. What price would you expect for the old shares ex-rights?

Answer

Substituting $m = 3$, $n = 4$, $P = 200p$ and $P_1 = 230p$ in equation (3.6),

$$\text{Expected price for old shares ex-rights} = \frac{4 \times 230p + 3 \times 200p}{4 + 3}$$

$$= 217p$$

It should be noted that equation (3.6) is only approximate as new information may have been received by the market since the previous business day. Furthermore, holders of such shares in effect possess an option. They can discard their certificates rather than subscribe if the price of the old shares is below the subscription price at the last date for acceptance. The price of the new nil paid shares will therefore be greater than $P_2 - P$ and can never be negative. Strictly speaking, option pricing theory is required to value the nil paid shares (see Chapter 16).

Figure 3.2 shows how both the old shares and new shares in a UK rights issue might be expected to behave assuming that the issue is seen as neutral by the market and no other news which could affect the share price is received by the market over the period shown.

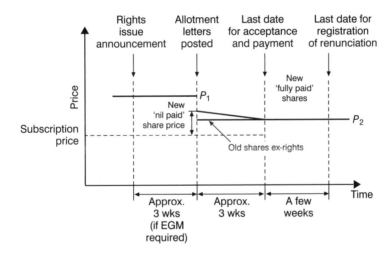

Figure 3.2

3.6 MARKET EFFICIENCY

Academic research in the 1960s and earlier seemed to suggest that share prices followed a random walk. That is, successive price changes were independent of each other. The search for an explanation of this apparent randomness led to the formation of the *Efficient Market Hypothesis* (EMH). If true in one of its stronger forms, the EMH has implications far beyond the mere independence of successive share price changes. The EMH has been the subject of much research and discussion, and has been a major source of disagreement between academics and practitioners. While academics have forcefully promoted acceptance of the hypothesis, practitioners have tended to reject it.

What exactly do we mean by informational efficiency? A stock market is said to be *efficient* if share prices fully reflect all available information. Since there are normally positive information and trading costs, however, a more practical definition is that share prices fully reflect all available information to the point where the benefits of acting on the information equal the costs of collecting it.

There is no way of formally proving informational efficiency for a given stock market but it is possible to carry out a number of tests. Tests of informational efficiency were traditionally divided into three categories — weak form, semi-strong form and strong form (Fama, 1970). Each deals with a different type of information.

A market is *weak form efficient* if share prices fully reflect information contained in past share prices. This implies that attempts to predict future share price movements from the study of share price history are a waste of time.

A market is *semi-strong form efficient* if share prices fully reflect all publicly available information. This implies that share prices adjust instantaneously to newly published information. It is therefore not possible *consistently* to achieve superior investment performance without access to non-public information.

A market is *strong form efficient* if share prices fully reflect all knowable information. It is therefore not possible consistently to achieve superior investment performance. This would imply that insiders could not profit from dealing on inside information. Even information held only by directors of a company would be fully reflected in the company's share price.

Note that as we move from weak form tests through to strong form tests we are referring to progressively more information. Thus strong form efficiency implies semi-strong form efficiency, which in turn implies weak form efficiency. Conversely, weak form inefficiency implies semi-strong form inefficiency, which in turn implies strong form inefficiency.

Research that tested the efficient market hypothesis in the 1970s was not controversial. The general view among academics was that the weak form hypothesis was true, the semi-strong form was mainly true and the strong form was probably not true. But market efficiency became a highly controversial area again in the 1980s due to the discovery of a number of apparent stock market "anomalies". These included the January effect (share prices rise in January far more than the average monthly amount) and the small firm effect (over long periods and in many countries, shares in small firms have produced significantly higher returns than shares in large firms).

The stock market crash of 1987 brought home the distinction between informational efficiency and rational fundamental valuation. While the weight of evidence might indicate that share prices react efficiently to new information, this does not necessarily mean that share prices always reflect "true" fundamental values. For example, a share price may instantly and fully incorporate news of a dividend increase and yet still be undervalued or overvalued by a significant amount. Rational valuation is a more difficult concept to define and test compared to informational efficiency but it is perhaps no less important.

Behavioural finance has been gaining momentum as a legitimate area for research since the 1990s. A basic precept of behavioural finance is that people do not make choices on a rational basis but instead act, or do not act, under the powerful influence of their emotions. As a result, share prices can depart from fundamental values for extended periods. Behavioural finance comprises a variety of theories, each suggesting a different type of irrational behaviour. According to proponents of behavioural finance, behavioural finance provides plausible explanations for the existence of various stock market anomalies. But proponents of market efficiency, such as Fama (1998), dismiss behavioural finance, believing that it is not the route to superior investment performance.

3.7   REAL ESTATE

The valuation of real estate using an explicit discounted cash flow approach is considered in this section.

Typical lease terms in the main commercial property markets around the world are given in Table 3.1. We will concentrate on freehold real estate let at open market rental level with regular rent reviews (either to open market rental level or in line with an index). It is assumed that rent is payable p times per year in advance (e.g. if rents were payable quarterly in advance, then $p = 4$).

Let

V_0 = value of real estate
R_1 = initial rental income, net of annual outgoings
g = growth in full rental value (or index) per annum (assumed constant)
n = rent review period
$\ddot{a}_{\overline{n}|}^{(p)}$ = present value of an annuity of 1 per annum payable p times per year in advance for n years, using an annual rate of interest r.

The following further simplifying assumptions are made.

(i)   A rent review has just been carried out.
(ii)   No tenant defaults and leases at expiry are immediately renewed, on similar terms.
(iii)   Refurbishment and redevelopment costs together with other non-annual outgoings are ignored.
(iv)   Constant rental growth is assumed at each rent review, so the annual rent (net of annual outgoings) increases by $(1 + g)^n$ at a rent review, with no allowance for ageing or obsolescence.

The value of freehold real estate let with regular rent reviews is then given by

$$V_0 = R_1 \ddot{a}_{\overline{n}|}^{(p)} + \frac{R_1(1+g)^n}{(1+r)^n} \ddot{a}_{\overline{n}|}^{(p)} + \frac{R_1(1+g)^{2n}}{(1+r)^{2n}} \ddot{a}_{\overline{n}|}^{(p)} + \cdots$$

$$= R_1 \ddot{a}_{\overline{n}|}^{(p)} \left[1 + \left(\frac{1+g}{1+r}\right)^n + \left(\frac{1+g}{1+r}\right)^{2n} + \cdots \right]$$

$$= \frac{R_1 \ddot{a}_{\overline{n}|}^{(p)}}{1 - \left(\dfrac{1+g}{1+r}\right)^n} \tag{3.7}$$

Table 3.1 Typical lease terms

	London	New York	Tokyo	Paris	Frankfurt
Method of paying rent	Quarterly in advance	Monthly in advance	Monthly in advance	Quarterly in advance	Monthly in advance
Initial deposit	Not usual	Three months' rent or letter of credit	12–15 months	A quarter's rent or sometimes a bank or corporate guarantee	Bank guarantee to cover a quarter's rent
Length of lease	15–25 years	5–10 years	2 years	9 years	5 with option to renew, 10 with 5 year break
Rental increases	Rent reviewed to open market levels every 5 years	Fixed step up or fair market value	By negotiation on request of landlord, on 2-yearly basis	Annual or triennial indexation to INSEE Construction Index	Indexation to Consumer Price Index
Break clauses	10, 15 or 20 years subject to negotiation	None	Tenant's option on 6 months' notice	Tenant's option at 3 and 6 years can be contracted away	See above
Renewal right	Legal right to new lease at market rent	No legal entitlement	Legal right to new lease at market rent	No legal entitlement	No legal entitlement

Source: ATIS REAL Weatheralls Ltd (2002). Reproduced with permission.

Different required rates of return should be used for different assets, the main distinguishing factor being the perceived "risk". The higher the perceived risk, the higher the required rate of return (r). Important risk factors are the probability of reletting should the current tenant fail, unforeseen physical, environmental or economic obsolescence and unforeseen changes in real estate or planning law. Risk that is "specific" to a particular asset may be given less importance by investors holding well-diversified portfolios.

Just as equity investors in shares use dividend yield as a means of comparison in assessing investments, real estate investors may consider the initial rental yield in making buy or sell decisions concerning freehold interests in let real estate, where rental yield may be defined as

$$\text{Rental yield} = \frac{\text{Rental income (net of annual outgoings)}}{\text{Market value} + \text{purchaser's costs}} \times 100\% \qquad (3.8)$$

Note that equation (3.7) may be rearranged to give

$$\frac{R_1}{V_0} = \frac{1 - \left(\dfrac{1+g}{1+r}\right)^n}{\ddot{a}_{\overline{n}|}^{(p)}}$$

Ignoring purchasers' costs, we therefore have

$$\text{Rental yield} = \frac{1 - \left(\dfrac{1+g}{1+r}\right)^n}{\ddot{a}_{\overline{n}|}^{(p)}} \qquad (3.9)$$

Note that, with $R_1/V_0 = k$,

$$g = (1+r)[1 - k\ddot{a}_{\overline{n}|}^{(p)}]^{1/n} - 1$$

which can be used as a check on the implied rental growth for a known value of r.

For further discussion of property investment appraisal, the reader is referred to Adams, Booth and MacGregor (1999).

Example 3.5

A tax-exempt institutional investor is considering buying the freehold of an office block for £1,000,000. Rents will be payable quarterly in advance, with the first payment being due at the purchase date. The rent will begin at a level of £40,000 per annum and is expected to increase on each fifth anniversary of purchase by 25%. In 20 years from purchase the institution expects to spend £150,000 refurbishing the office and, exactly 40 years after purchase, it expects to sell the freehold for £6,000,000. Calculate the net present value of the investment using a required rate of return of 9% per annum convertible half-yearly.

Answer

It is convenient to work in half-years in this example. Rent of £20,000 per half-year is paid in two equal instalments in advance. The required rate of return is $4\frac{1}{2}\%$ per half-year.

The present value of rents in the first 10 half-years is

$$20{,}000\ddot{a}^{(2)}_{\overline{10}|}$$

where the annuity function is calculated at a rate of interest of $4\frac{1}{2}\%$.

The present value of rents in the second period of 10 half-years is

$$\frac{1.25}{(1.045)^{10}} \times 20{,}000\ddot{a}^{(2)}_{\overline{10}|} \text{ and so on.}$$

The present value of rents in the eighth period of 10 half-years is

$$\frac{(1.25)^7}{(1.045)^{70}} \times 20{,}000\ddot{a}^{(2)}_{\overline{10}|}$$

The above form a geometric series with first term of $20{,}000\ddot{a}^{(2)}_{\overline{10}|}$ and common ratio $1.25/(1.045)^{10} = 0.80491$, with 8 terms. Using equation (1.16),

$$\ddot{a}^{(2)}_{\overline{10}|} = \left(\frac{0.045}{0.0445} + \frac{0.045}{2} \right) a_{\overline{10}|}$$

$$= 1.03374 \times 7.9127$$

$$= 8.17964$$

So the first term of the series is

$$20{,}000 \times 8.17964 = 163{,}593$$

Therefore the present value of rent is

$$163{,}593 \left\{ \frac{1 - (0.80491)^8}{1 - (0.80491)} \right\} = 690{,}808$$

The present value of refurbishment costs is

$$\frac{150{,}000}{(1.045)^{40}} = 25{,}789$$

The present value of the sale price is

$$\frac{6{,}000{,}000}{(1.045)^{80}} = 177{,}357$$

Hence the net present value of the investment is

$$690{,}808 - 25{,}789 + 177{,}357 - 1{,}000{,}000 = -\text{£}157{,}624$$

Clearly, the freehold should not be bought on the basis of a required rate of return of 9% per annum convertible half-yearly, as the investment has a negative net present value.

3.8   YIELD GAPS

The initial gross dividend yield on equities (normally obtained from published indices) less the gross redemption yield for an index of secure long-dated fixed-interest government bonds of the same country may be either positive or negative. Ignoring tax complications, this depends largely on the growth prospects for equity dividends and the relative risk of the two types of investment, as perceived by investors in the market. Note that equities could be perceived as less risky than government bonds in a market dominated by long-term investors with liabilities denominated in real terms. Let

$$\frac{d_1}{P_0} = \text{initial dividend yield on the equity index}$$

$$Y = \text{redemption yield for the government bond index}$$
$$g = \text{market's expected growth rate for equity dividends}$$
$$r = \text{market's expected return for equities} = Y + r^*$$

where r^* might be described as a "risk" premium but could also reflect other factors such as marketability. We know that

$$\frac{d_1}{P_0} = r - g$$

$$\Rightarrow \quad \frac{d_1}{P_0} = Y + r^* - g$$

$$\Rightarrow \quad Y - \frac{d_1}{P_0} = g - r^* \tag{3.10}$$

$Y - d_1/P_0$ is known as a *yield gap*.

Consideration of the yield gap for equities may be a useful tool for investors deciding on the balance between equities and fixed-interest bonds. Similarly, making decisions about overall investment in different types of real estate may involve studying the corresponding yield gap. However, it is important to take future price inflation into account. For example, dividend (or rental) growth of at least 5% per annum is highly likely if inflation is expected to be 7% per annum but highly unlikely if a steady inflation rate of 0% per annum is expected.

Chapter 5 introduces the concept of a *real* yield gap which may be useful in comparing the attraction of equities (or real estate) and index-linked bonds.

REFERENCES

Adams, A.T. (1989), *Investment*, Graham & Trotman.

Adams, A.T., Booth, P.M. and MacGregor, B. (1999), "Property Investment Appraisal", *British Actuarial Journal*, 5, 5, 955–82.

Armitage, S. (1998), "Seasoned Equity Offers and Rights Issues: A Review of the Evidence", *The European Journal of Finance*, 4, 29–59.

Brealey, R. and Myers, S. (2002), *Principles of Corporate Finance*, 7th edition, McGraw-Hill.

Day, J.G. and Jamieson, A.T. (1980), *Institutional Investment — Volume IV*, Institute of Actuaries.

Eckbo, B.E. and Masulis, R.W. (1992), "Adverse Selection and the Rights Offer Paradox", *Journal of Financial Economics*, 32, 293–332.

Fama, E.F. (1970), "Efficient Capital Markets: A Review of Theory and Empirical Work", *Journal of Finance*, 25, 383–417.

Fama, E.F. (1998), "Market Efficiency, Long-term Returns and Behavioral Finance", *Journal of Financial Economics*, 49, 282–306.

Lofthouse, S. (2001), *Investment Management*, 2nd edition, John Wiley & Sons.

4
Real Returns

4.1 INTRODUCTION

In general, investors invest in order that they can purchase more goods at the end of the period of investment than they could at the beginning. In times of stable prices, this is achieved by increasing the local currency value of one's investment. In times of inflation, however, it is quite possible that the value of an investment will increase in local currency terms yet fall in purchasing power or *real* terms. This is even true at times of moderate inflation. The UK government's current inflation target is 2.5%. At this rate, the value of money will halve in 28 years. A pension contribution invested at the beginning of an individual's working life may be invested for 47 years before it is used to help purchase an annuity. At a 2.5% rate of inflation, £1 invested at age 18 would be worth only 31p at retirement. Because of the desire of most investors to increase the purchasing power value of their investments, a study of real returns is an important aspect of financial mathematics.

Owing to the problems associated with investment in times of inflation, securities have been issued which link returns to the level of retail prices: these will be considered in Chapter 5. The calculation of real returns involves transforming units of one currency (e.g. sterling) into units of another (purchasing power units). Therefore, a study of real returns leads naturally to a study of investments denominated in foreign currencies: these will be considered in Chapter 6.

4.2 THE CALCULATION OF REAL RETURNS GIVEN A CONSTANT RATE OF INFLATION

The easiest calculations arise when we estimate prospective real rates of return or calculate present values under the assumption of a constant future rate of inflation. We will assume that the constant future rate of inflation is f, where f is expressed in decimal form.

If a cash flow of £X buys a certain quantity of goods at the beginning of a year, a cash flow of £$X(1 + f)$ will be required to buy the same quantity of goods at the end of the year. Alternatively, a cash flow of £X at the end of the year will purchase what £$X/(1 + f)$ purchased at the beginning of the year.

Thus, by dividing all cash flows at the end of the year by $(1 + f)$, we can re-express those cash flows in beginning-of-year purchasing power terms. Having made this adjustment to allow for the effects of inflation, we can proceed to calculate present values of, or real yields from, investments. This can be done by the usual procedures of discounting sums of money at a given yield to the present day (or accumulating them to some future date); the following example illustrates this idea.

Example 4.1

A bond, which has one year to maturity, is purchased for £97. At maturity, the investor receives £100 principal repayment and a £5 interest payment. Inflation over the year is expected to be 2%. Calculate the real return from holding the bond.

Answer

The total payment at maturity is £105. At the end of the year, this will purchase what £[105/1.02] would have purchased at the beginning of the year. Thus, in current purchasing power terms, our investment is worth £102.94 at the end of the year and the real return is j such that

$$97(1 + j) = £102.94$$

Therefore $j = \underline{6.12\%}$

The return here is described as the real return because it measures the increase in the amount of real goods the investor can buy as a result of the investment, rather than simply the increase in the number of units of local currency held.

It is worth noting that, as long as all cash flows are re-expressed in purchasing power terms at the same point in time, it does not matter what point in time we choose. In the above example, we could have expressed all cash flows in end-year sterling terms and multiplied the yield equation through by $(1 + f)$; this would have given the same answer for the yield. In such real yield calculations, we are taking various local currency cash flows and transforming them so that they are all in units of local currency which would have the same purchasing power at any given date: it does not matter which particular date we choose.

4.3   VALUATION OF A SERIES OF CASH FLOWS GIVEN A CONSTANT RATE OF INFLATION

We can now look at the valuation of a series of cash flows, in real terms, under the assumption of a constant rate of inflation. If the price level is growing at a constant rate f per annum then prices, on average, will be higher by a factor $(1 + f)$ after one year; after two years, prices will be higher, on average, by a factor $(1 + f)(1 + f)$ or $(1 + f)^2$; after n years they will be higher by a factor $(1 + f)^n$. The situation is analogous to that of a sum of money growing with interest. After half a year, the price level will be greater by a factor $(1 + f)^{1/2}$, after 1.5 years by a factor $(1 + f)^{1.5}$, etc.

Thus, if we receive a cash flow after t years have elapsed and the rate of inflation is f per annum, to re-express the cash flow in real terms (i.e. allowing for the fall in the purchasing power of money) we divide the payment by a factor $(1 + f)^t$.

If we are valuing a series of cash flows and adjusting for the fall in the purchasing power of money, we adjust the cash flows, as described above, to allow for the effect of the rise in the price level. We then discount each payment back to the valuation point, in the usual way, using the real rate of return. If we know the present value of the series, but we do not know the real rate of return, we solve the equation of value for the latter.

The most straightforward application of the calculation of the real return from a series of cash flows, or the calculation of the present value of a series of cash flows for a given real return, under the assumption of a constant rate of inflation, is the valuation of the payments from a conventional bond. This case will be illustrated below by example.

Example 4.2

A bond with 10 years to maturity, paying a coupon at a rate of 5% *per annum* payable half-yearly is purchased by an investment fund to give a real return of 3% *per annum* on the assumption of future inflation of 2% *per annum* for the next 10 years. Calculate the present value.

Answer

Each half-yearly coupon payment will be £2.50 per £100 nominal of stock held; there will also be a final payment of £100 per £100 nominal held at redemption in 10 years' time. The purchase price is the present value of the payments, after allowing for the fall in the purchasing power of money, valued at a real rate of interest of 3%.

Let the purchase price $= P$. For any value of f and j,

$$P = \frac{2.5}{(1+f)^{1/2}(1+j)^{1/2}} + \frac{2.5}{(1+f)(1+j)} + \cdots + \frac{2.5}{(1+f)^{10}(1+j)^{10}} + \frac{100}{(1+f)^{10}(1+j)^{10}}$$

The first twenty terms form a geometric progression with first term

$$\frac{2.5}{(1+f)^{1/2}(1+j)^{1/2}}$$

and common ratio

$$\frac{1}{(1+f)^{1/2}(1+j)^{1/2}}$$

where j is the real return and f is the rate of inflation. Therefore,

$$P = \frac{2.5}{(1+f)^{1/2}(1+j)^{1/2}} \times \frac{1 - [(1+f)(1+j)]^{-10}}{1 - [(1+f)(1+j)]^{-1/2}} + \frac{100}{[(1+f)(1+j)]^{10}} \qquad (4.1)$$

and, with $f = 0.02$ and $j = 0.03$

$$P = \underline{100.02}$$

In this case, a price to give an annual effective real yield has been calculated. In the UK, annual yields convertible *half-yearly* are normally quoted for gilt-edged stocks (see Chapter 2). The calculation of the price for a given half-yearly yield would pose no additional problems here: we would simply replace $(1+j)^{1/2}$, $(1+j)$, $(1+j)^{3/2}$, etc. by $(1+j^{(2)}/2)$, $(1+j^{(2)}/2)^2$, $(1+j^{(2)}/2)^3$, etc., where $j^{(2)}/2$, is the half-yearly effective yield. This would give a slightly different geometric progression. The real yield *per annum* convertible half-yearly is twice the half-yearly effective yield.

4.4   THE RELATIONSHIP BETWEEN REAL AND NOMINAL YIELDS

It is worth noting the relationship between the effective annual real yield and the effective annual nominal yield for a given constant rate of inflation. Calling the effective annual nominal yield i in Example 4.2, then

$$100.02 = \frac{2.5}{(1+i)^{1/2}} + \frac{2.5}{(1+i)} + \cdots + \frac{2.5}{(1+i)^{10}} + \frac{100}{(1+i)^{10}} \qquad (4.2)$$

Summing the first twenty terms on the right-hand side as a geometric progression, with a first term of $2.5(1+i)^{1/2}$ and common ratio $1/(1+i)^{1/2}$ and adding the final term, we find that

$$100.02 = \frac{2.5}{(1+i)^{1/2}} \times \frac{[1-(1+i)^{-10}]}{[1-(1+i)^{-1/2}]} + \frac{100}{(1+i)^{10}} \qquad (4.3)$$

The right-hand side of equation (4.3) is the same as the right-hand side of equation (4.1) which was used to calculate the price for a given real yield but with $(1+i)$ equal to $(1+f)(1+j)$. This would imply that

$$\frac{(1+i)}{(1+f)} = (1+j)$$

hence
$$j = \frac{(i-f)}{(1+f)}$$

where i is the *nominal* effective yield *per annum*, f is the constant future rate of inflation and j is the *real* effective yield *per annum*. Thus, if we are given the price of a bond, we can calculate the nominal yield and then calculate the real yield using the above relationship, for a given assumed constant future rate of inflation.

Working in terms of real and nominal yields convertible *half-yearly*, the relationship between them would be as follows

$$\frac{j^{(2)}}{2} = \frac{\dfrac{i^{(2)}}{2} - \dfrac{f^{(2)}}{2}}{1 + \dfrac{f^{(2)}}{2}} \qquad (4.4)$$

where

$j^{(2)}/2$ is the real effective yield per half-year (i.e. the real yield *per annum* convertible half-yearly is $j^{(2)}$);
$i^{(2)}/2$ is the nominal effective yield per half-year (i.e. the nominal yield *per annum* convertible half-yearly is $i^{(2)}$);
$f^{(2)}/2$ is the rate of inflation per half-year; and
$f^{(2)}/2 = (1+f)^{1/2} - 1$.

All we have done in this case is changed the time unit from one year to half a year and then derived a similar relationship to that derived above from equations (4.1) and (4.3).

4.5 ESTIMATION OF THE RATE OF INFLATION

The rate of inflation to be used, when calculating real yields or when calculating prices for given real yields, is the prospective rate over the term of the security: this is unlikely to be the current inflation rate. Various methods of estimating future inflation can be employed, including stochastic and econometric models. It is, however, very difficult to estimate the rate of inflation over long time periods with any degree of certainty. Many monetary zones (for example, the Eurozone, the UK) operate inflation targetting regimes. Markets may well accept the inflation target as an estimate of long-term average inflation. However, the monetary regime would have to be "credible", for example, managed by an independent central bank with no political interference.

4.6 REAL RETURNS FROM EQUITY INVESTMENTS

Another application of the calculation of real returns or of present values for a given real return is in the analysis of equity investments. No new concepts are involved here, so we will simply illustrate the idea by example.

Example 4.3

An analyst is estimating the rate of return from the equity of a UK company. The price of a share is currently £1.50. The gross dividend per share, paid yesterday, was 4.5p. Dividends, which are paid annually, are expected to rise by 4% *per annum* in future years and inflation is expected to be 3% *per annum*.

 (i) Calculate (a) the historic gross dividend yield; (b) the real effective annual rate of return; (c) the nominal effective annual rate of return.
 (ii) Another analyst expects that the declared dividend for this company will grow exactly in line with inflation. Calculate the real return from the shares, estimated by the analyst.

Answer

 (i) (a) The historic gross dividend yield is the amount of the dividend, divided by the share price (see Chapter 3). It is therefore 4.5/150 or 3%.
     (b) Given an expected growth rate of dividends of 4% and inflation of 3%, the present value of the dividend stream, with payments expressed in real terms, is

$$0.045 \times \left\{ \frac{1.04}{(1.03)(1+j)} + \frac{1.04^2}{(1.03)^2(1+j)^2} + \frac{1.04^3}{(1.03)^3(1+j)^3} + \cdots \right\} \quad (4.5)$$

where j is the real effective annual return and the series is summed to infinity.

We know that the present value is equal to £1.5, but do not know j, the annual effective real rate of return. Equation (4.5) is the sum of a geometric progression, with first term equal to $0.045 \times 1.04/[(1.03(1+j)]$ and a common ratio of $1.04/[(1.03)(1+j)]$. The series converges provided $(1+j) > 1.04/1.03$. Using equation (1.23):

$$1.5 = \frac{0.045 \times 1.04}{(1+j)(1.03)} \times \frac{1}{1 - \dfrac{1.04}{(1.03)(1+j)}}$$

This can be rearranged to give

$$33.013 = \frac{1}{(j - 0.009709)} \qquad \text{so } j = 0.0400 \text{ or } \underline{4.00\%}$$

(c) There are several approaches to this part. Firstly, we could note the result of Section 4.4, that is $(i - f)(1 + f) = j$, where i is the nominal return per annum, f the constant rate of future inflation and j the real return per annum. Therefore,

$$i = j(1 + f) + f = 0.04(1.03) + 0.03$$

$$\text{or} \quad \underline{7.12\%}$$

This answer could also be derived from first principles by replacing $(1 + j)(1 + f)$ with $(1 + i)$ in the geometric progression in part (b) and solving for i, the nominal return (because if the nominal return is being calculated, there is no need to adjust the cash flows, by dividing by the $(1 + f)$ factors to allow for the falling purchasing power of money).

(ii) Working from first principles, the present value of the dividends from the share is the sum of the following progression:

$$0.045[(1 + j)^{-1} + (1 + j)^{-2} + (1 + j)^{-3} + \cdots]$$

The $(1 + \textit{growth rate})$ and $(1 + \textit{rate of inflation})$ factors cancel out, whatever the common inflation and dividend growth rates are.

The sum also forms a geometric progression, with an infinite number of terms, which converges as long as the real rate of interest is positive. The first term is $0.045/(1 + j)$ and the common ratio is $1/(1 + j)$. The sum of the progression is therefore

$$\frac{0.045}{(1 + j) - 1} = \frac{0.045}{j}$$

where j is the real rate of return.

$$1.5 = \frac{0.045}{j}, \qquad \text{therefore } j = \frac{0.045}{1.5} \quad \text{or} \quad \underline{3\%}$$

This result deserves special comment: the real return is exactly equal to the historical dividend yield. This is because the analyst has assumed that future dividends will grow in line with inflation. All the future dividends are equal, in real terms, to the dividend just declared. There is no real dividend growth and thus the investment can be treated as a perpetuity with a level sum, in real terms, being paid at the end of each year; the yield therefore is equal to the initial rate of dividend per unit invested.

There are alternative ways of approaching part (i) (c) and part (ii) and it is of interest to consider further some of the issues raised, whilst deriving some further useful relationships. As in Example 4.3 above, it will be assumed in what follows that the latest dividend has just been paid and that the next dividend will be paid in exactly one year's time. In part (i) (c), we can use a relationship similar to that derived in Chapter 3, so that the nominal yield, i, is equal to

$$i = g + (1 + g) \frac{d_0}{P} \tag{4.6}$$

where d_0/P is the historical dividend yield, based on the market price (P), i is the return on the share estimated by the analyst and g is the expected growth rate (in Chapter 3 the notation V_0 was used to denote the investor's valuation and r to denote the rate of return that the investor required on the equity). This could be written more usefully as

$$i = g + \frac{d_1}{P} \tag{4.7}$$

where d_1/P is the prospective dividend yield, based on the estimate of the dividend to be paid at the end of the first year.

The real return (j) is equal to $(i - f)/(1 + f)$ where f is the rate of inflation and, using equation (4.6) for i, we can say that

$$j = \frac{g + (1 + g) \dfrac{d_0}{P} - f}{(1 + f)} \tag{4.8}$$

If $f = g$ (as in part (ii)), the above expression simplifies to give $d_0/P = j$, i.e. the real return is equal to the historical dividend yield.

This leads to an alternative way of analysing equity investments: the profits of a company arise from selling real goods and services, and income from selling those goods and services will rise, on average, in line with the rate of inflation. It may well be a more sensible starting point to estimate the rate at which dividends are expected to grow in excess of the price level, i.e. the real dividend growth rate. For techniques of appraising equity investments and estimating dividend growth, see, for example, Bodie, Kane and Marcus (2002) or Blake (2000). The real dividend growth rate is likely to be more predictable than the nominal dividend growth rate, which depends on both the rate of inflation and the real dividend growth rate.

If we define the real dividend growth rate to be g_r, given an historical dividend of d_0, then

$$g_r = \frac{\dfrac{d_0(1 + g)}{(1 + f)} - d_0}{d_0} \tag{4.9}$$

That is, the real growth rate of dividends is the prospective dividend, adjusted for the fall in the purchasing power of money, minus the beginning year dividend, divided by the beginning year dividend. Rearranging (4.9), we obtain

$$g_r = \frac{\dfrac{d_0 + gd_0 - d_0 - d_0 f}{1+f}}{d_0}$$

therefore

$$g_r = \frac{\dfrac{gd_0 - d_0 f}{1+f}}{d_0} \qquad (4.10)$$

and

$$g_r = \frac{g-f}{1+f} \qquad (4.11)$$

From equation (4.8) the real rate of return (or real yield)

$$j = \frac{g + (1+g)\dfrac{d_0}{P} - f}{(1+f)}$$

thus

$$j = \frac{(g-f)}{(1+f)} + \frac{(1+g)\dfrac{d_0}{P}}{(1+f)} \qquad (4.12)$$

and, substituting g_r for $(g-f)/(1+f)$ (equation 4.11) and $(1+g_r)$ for $(1+g)/(1+f)$, equation (4.12) can be written as

$$j = g_r + (1+g_r)\frac{d_0}{P} \qquad (4.13)$$

If the prospective real dividend yield (i.e. the prospective dividend, in real terms, divided by the current share price) is defined as d_{r_1}/P, which is equal to $(1+g_r)d_0/P$, the above expression can be written as:

$$j = g_r + \frac{d_{r_1}}{P} \qquad (4.14)$$

and equations (4.13) and (4.14) can be compared with equations (4.6) and (4.7) respectively.

Equation (4.14) has effectively been derived by replacing the expression for the real growth rate in the equation for the real return (expressed in terms of the nominal growth rate, the rate of inflation and dividend yield). The similarities between equations (4.13) and (4.6) and between equations (4.14) and (4.7) merely confirm the statement made at the beginning of the chapter that performing calculations in real terms is merely re-expressing returns in units of a different currency.

For a given assumed rate of inflation and real growth rate, the nominal growth rate and the prospective nominal return can be calculated easily. For reasons which have been explained above, it is often more logical to begin by estimating a prospective real growth rate for dividends.

4.7 ESTIMATION OF EQUITY VALUES FOR A GIVEN REAL RATE OF RETURN

If an investor's estimate of the value of a share (V_0) is required, given assumed future dividend growth rates and also required returns, this can be calculated by using formulae similar to (4.6), (4.7), (4.13) or (4.14). Thus,

$$j_r = g_r + (1 + g_r) \frac{d_0}{V_0} \qquad (4.15)$$

and

$$j_r = g_r + \frac{d_{r_1}}{V_0} \qquad (4.16)$$

These equations can then be solved for V_0. The investor's *required* real rate of return is given the symbol j_r to distinguish it from the investor's expected return (j) calculated for a given market price (P).

If we are given a nominal growth rate of dividends, the real growth rate can be calculated by first using equation (4.11). If a nominal return is required and we are given a real dividend growth rate, this can be found by using equation (4.16) and then using the relationship between real and nominal returns.

Example 4.4

An investor requires a real rate of return of 4% and anticipates that the real rate of growth of dividends from a particular equity investment will be 1%. Calculate the required dividend yield and the price the investor would be willing to pay for one share if an annual dividend of 4.5p per share has just been paid.

Answer

We will use equation (4.15) above, $j_r = g_r + (1 + g_r)d_0/V_0$ where j_r is the required real rate of return, g_r is the real rate of dividend growth and d_0/V_0 is the required historical dividend yield. Hence the required dividend yield to ensure that the required real rate of return is achieved, given the anticipated dividend growth rate, is

$$\frac{d_0}{V_0} = \frac{j_r - g_r}{1 + g_r}.$$

Therefore, in this case,

$$\frac{d_0}{V_0} = \frac{0.04 - 0.01}{1.01} = 0.0297 \text{ (or } \underline{2.97\%})$$

The dividend yield is equal to the dividend divided by the share price the investor is willing to pay, which is $4.5/V_0$ where V_0 is the share price. Therefore,

$$0.0297 = \frac{4.5}{V_0} \quad \text{and} \quad V_0 = \frac{4.5}{0.0297} = 151.52\text{p} \quad \text{or} \quad \underline{\pounds1.52}$$

4.8   CALCULATING REAL RETURNS WITH VARYING RATES OF INFLATION

If we are calculating historical rather than prospective rates of return, it is unlikely that the rate of inflation which is used to deflate local currency payments and transform them into constant purchasing power units will be constant for any significant period of time. In addition, we may wish to calculate prospective real returns from securities for a given price or price for a given return, under the assumption of a varying rate of inflation. It will be useful, therefore, to take an approach which is more general than that which has been taken hitherto.

The general level of prices and thus the rate of inflation in a country can be measured by reference to an index. The index number itself has no particular meaning but successive index numbers can be used to measure the rate of change of the price level. The use of indices in calculating the rate of inflation will be described briefly below.

The index which is generally used to measure the price level in the UK is the Retail Price Index (or RPI). More comprehensive indices can be used, but the RPI is published relatively quickly after the date to which it refers and is rarely revised after publication. The RPI measures the price level of a typical basket of consumer goods and thus excludes capital goods.[1] In most developed countries, an index with similar characteristics is published and therefore this section is readily applicable to any country where reliable price level statistics are produced.

Let the retail price index at time t be RPI_t. The ratio of the general level of prices at time t_2 to that at time t_1, can therefore be written as RPI_{t_2}/RPI_{t_1}. The rate of change of prices (or rate of inflation) over the time period t_1 to t_2 is $(RPI_{t_2} - RPI_{t_1})/RPI_{t_1}$ which we will define to be $_{t_1}f_{t_2}$. The factor by which the price level is higher will simply be the ratio of the price index at time t_2 to that at time t_1, RPI_{t_2}/RPI_{t_1}, which equals $(1 + _{t_1}f_{t_2})$.

We may need to express a cash flow which occurs at time t_2 in terms of a unit of money which has the same purchasing power as a unit of money at time t_1 thus the cash

---

[1] See www.statistics.gov.uk/themes/economy/articles/prices and inflation, from the UK Government National Statistics Office website for technical details of the RPI.

flow which occurs at time t_2 needs to be deflated according to the factor by which the price level increased between time t_1 and time t_2. In other words, to re-express a payment at time t_2 in purchasing power terms as at time t_1 we need to divide by $(1 + {}_{t_1}f_{t_2})$ or equivalently divide by RPI_{t_2}/RPI_{t_1}, which is the same as multiplying by RPI_{t_1}/RPI_{t_2}. This is exactly the same operation as we performed in the examples above except that the factors by which the price level had risen after each payment, if a number of payments were made, formed successive powers of $(1 + f)$ where f, the rate of inflation, was constant.

If prospective real returns from or present values of securities are to be calculated, it is necessary to estimate the factor by which the price level will rise between the base date and each date at which a cash flow will take place; in other words, it is necessary to calculate successive values of the retail price index, using estimates of future rates of inflation. The inflation factors, or retail price index values, can then be applied to future cash flows in order to express the cash flows in purchasing power terms, as at the base date.

The RPI is only calculated once per month and therefore, if historical real returns are to be calculated given past values of the RPI, it may be necessary to estimate its value at a date between two calculation dates. If the rate of inflation is constant between two dates, the logarithm of the RPI will be a linear function and thus it is appropriate to estimate values of the RPI by interpolation between logarithms of successive published values. Given the usually erratic nature of the Retail Price Index, however, the slightly easier process of linear interpolation between successive absolute values will normally be adequate. The techniques of estimation are discussed in Wilkie (1984), from which the next examples are adapted. While some of the examples relate to a period many years ago, during which OECD inflation was much higher than today, the techniques are illustrated very effectively by these examples.

When re-expressing local currency cash flows in purchasing power terms, the base date that is usually chosen is the beginning of the transaction. In the following examples, we will transform monetary cash flows into purchasing power terms as measured at the beginning of the transaction; but the reader should note that any other date could be chosen as the base date.

Example 4.5

Exchequer 10.5% 1988 paid interest of £5.25 per £100 nominal on 10 May and 10 November each year and was redeemed at par on 10 May 1988. If the real yield to redemption, when the stock was purchased on 10 May 1983, was 3.83% *per annum* convertible half-yearly, calculate the purchase price assuming inflation from 10 May 1983 of 9%, 8%, 7%, 6% and 5% *per annum* in successive years.

Answer

First, we need to calculate values of the Retail Price Index on all dates on which payments were made under the assumptions given. As has been stated, the particular starting value of the Retail Price Index is of no significance as we are only concerned with the ratio of the price level on one date to the price level on another date. We will therefore assume that the retail price index had a value of 100 on 10 May 1983.

Given that inflation was at a rate of 9% *per annum* in the first year, the Retail Price Index on 9 May 1984 would have been 109; the value on later dates would be as follows:

10 May 1985:   109(1.08) = 117.72 (given a rate of inflation of 8% in the following
                                         year)
10 May 1986:   109(1.08)(1.07) = 125.96
10 May 1987:   109(1.08)(1.07)(1.06) = 133.52
10 May 1988:   109(1.08)(1.07)(1.06)(1.05) = 140.19

It is sufficiently accurate, for the purposes of this problem, to assume that 10 November is exactly half a year after 10 May. To obtain values of the Retail Price Index at the November dates we can therefore take the value of the RPI on 10 May each year and multiply by a factor $(1+f)^{1/2}$ where f is the rate of inflation in the year concerned. Thus the value of the retail price index on 10 November 1983 will be $100(1.09)^{1/2} =$ 104.40 and the values on later November dates are as follows:

10 November 1984: $109(1.08)^{1/2} = 113.28$
10 November 1985: $109(1.08)(1.07)^{1/2} = 121.77$
10 November 1986: $109(1.08)(1.07)(1.06)^{1/2} = 129.68$
10 November 1987: $109(1.08)(1.07)(1.06)(1.05)^{1/2} = 136.82$

We now need to discount all the payments back to the purchase date after having multiplied each payment by the ratio of the price index at the base date (which we have defined to be 100) to the price index at the time the payment is made. It is convenient to work in half-years, as we have been given a value for the yield convertible half-yearly.

The real yield $j^{(2)}/2$, is (3.83/2)% per half-year = 1.915%. If $v = (1+j^{(2)}/2)^{-1}$, then the price (P) is calculated as follows:

$$P = 5.25 \times 100 \left\{ \frac{v}{104.4} + \frac{v^2}{109} + \frac{v^3}{113.28} + \frac{v^4}{117.72} + \frac{v^5}{121.77} + \frac{v^6}{125.96} \right.$$

$$\left. + \frac{v^7}{129.68} + \frac{v^8}{133.52} + \frac{v^9}{136.82} + \frac{v^{10}}{140.19} \right\} + 100 \times \frac{100v^{10}}{140.19}$$

hence

$$P = £98 \text{ per £100 nominal of stock}$$

The following example involves estimating the value of a price index on a date between two dates on which a value has been given.

Example 4.6

A fixed-interest stock, issued in a certain country, with a coupon rate of 9% *per annum* payable half-yearly and which was redeemable 5 years from the issue date, was issued on 11 November 1994. Interest payments were made on 11 May and 11 November each year. The retail price index for that country was known to have the following values at the times stated below:

11 November 1994	300	11 November 1997	—
11 May 1995	304	11 May 1998	360
11 November 1995	312	11 November 1998	370
11 May 1996	314	11 May 1999	382
11 November 1996	320	11 November 1999	398
11 May 1997	330		

The value on 11 November 1997 is not known, but it is known that the value of the retail price index on 16 October 1997 was 340 and the value on 18 November 1997 was 346.

(a) Calculate an appropriate estimate of the retail price index which could be used for 11 November 1997.
(b) Calculate the price an investor would have paid to purchase the fixed interest stock on 11 November 1994 to obtain a real yield of 3% *per annum* convertible half-yearly, assuming the stock was held to redemption.

Answer

(a) As has been stated above, if the retail price index is rising at a constant rate between two dates, estimates of the value of the index between the dates should be calculated by interpolating between logs of the successive values of the index. It can be seen from studying the retail price index values given that the retail price index is not rising at a constant rate or following any particular pattern. Interpolating between the actual values, rather than the logs of the values of the price index would therefore be quite acceptable. This is because the assumption implicit behind log linear interpolation (namely that the index rises at a constant *rate*) is clearly not fulfilled. In order to illustrate the technique of log linear interpolation, however, this method will be used here.

The number of days between 16 October and 18 November is 33; the number of days between 16 October and 11 November is 26. If linear interpolation were being used, the value of the retail price index on 11 November would be taken as (26/33) times the difference between the two successive values plus the value on 16 October. That is, we would assume that the price index followed a straight line from its value on 16 October to its value on 18 November. With log linear interpolation, we assume that the log of the index follows a straight line between the two dates. Thus,

$$\ln(RPI,\ 11\ November) = \ln(RPI,\ 16\ October)$$
$$+ \frac{26}{33} \times [\ln(RPI,\ 18\ November) - \ln(RPI,\ 16\ October)]$$

Therefore

$$\ln(RPI,\ 11\ November) = \ln 340 + \frac{26}{33} \times (\ln 346 - \ln 340) = 5.8427$$

Thus $(RPI,\ 11\ November) = 344.71$, or <u>345</u> to the nearest whole number.

(b) This estimated value of the retail price index can be used, together with the quoted values, to calculate the present value of the payments. The real rate of return can then be found by solving the equation of value.

We are given a rate of return *per annum* convertible half-yearly of 3%, which implies a rate of return of 1.5% per half-year. It is therefore sensible to work in half-years with

$$v = \left(1 + \frac{j^{(2)}}{2}\right)^{-1} = \frac{1}{1.015} = 0.98522$$

The present value of the payments from the security is

$$P = 4.5 \times 300 \left\{ \frac{v}{304} + \frac{v^2}{312} + \frac{v^3}{314} + \frac{v^4}{320} + \frac{v^5}{330} + \frac{v^6}{345} + \frac{v^7}{360} + \frac{v^8}{370} + \frac{v^9}{382} + \frac{v^{10}}{398} \right\}$$
$$+ \frac{100 \times v^{10} \times 300}{398}$$

By inserting successive values of v^n, a price of 101.62 is obtained.

The above techniques have merely applied the ideas of discounting and accumulating money with interest, which have been discussed in earlier chapters, to a situation where money values are not constant and investors are interested in analysing investments in real terms. Once a payment, expressed in the investor's currency, has been adjusted to allow for the fall in the value of money, the same principles of financial mathematics apply and equations of value can be solved for yields, present values and accumulated values. A grounding in these techniques now allows us to move on to the study of index-linked securities and foreign currency investments.

REFERENCES

Blake, D. (2000), *Financial Market Analysis*, 2nd edition, Wiley, UK.
Bodie, Z., Kane, A. and Marcus, A.J. (2002), *Investments*, 5th edition, McGraw-Hill, US.
Wilkie, A.D. (1984), "On the Calculation of Real Investment Returns", *Journal of the Institute of Actuaries*, 111, 11–172.
http://www.statistics.gov.uk

5
Index-linked Bonds

5.1 INTRODUCTION

Index-linked bonds are now an important asset category in many investment markets. In general, the capital value and income from equity and real estate investments tend to rise as the price level rises. However, the returns from conventional fixed-interest bonds, by definition, do not increase as the price level rises; thus an increase in inflation, above the anticipated level, leads to a reduced real return. This is a particular problem for pension funds, which are generally more concerned about achieving a particular *real* rate of return than about achieving a particular nominal rate of return.

A number of international index-linked bond markets have developed in recent years. Some derive their origin from periods of high inflation in the country concerned. For example, Argentina began issuing index-linked bonds in 1972 and Poland began issuing in 1992. However, some of the more recent markets which have developed, such as the US, where the first issue was in 1997, derive their origin from a desire by the bond issuing authorities to widen their portfolio of debt. By doing so, they reduce the risk to the government of disinflationary shocks and take advantage of the lower inflation risk premium available from indexed debt. An up-to-date list of international issuers of index-linked bonds can be found on the UK Debt Management Office's website at http://www.dmo.gov.uk/gilts/index.htm

In this chapter, we study the characteristics of index-linked bonds and techniques of valuation. A method of comparing the relative value of index-linked bonds and equities is also discussed. The discussion concentrates mainly on UK index-linked bonds but many of the principles involved apply equally to index-linked bonds issued in other countries (see Section 5.2).

5.2 CHARACTERISTICS OF INDEX-LINKED BONDS

The most important characteristics of index-linked bonds, issued by the UK government, are the following:

(1) Both coupon and capital payments are linked to the Retail Price Index (RPI) and all payments are guaranteed by the UK government.

(2) The initial running yield is low, commonly around $2\frac{1}{2}\%$. Because the capital value of the bond is protected against inflation, the initial running yield can be close to the expected long-term real return. Table 5.1 shows the real rates of return available from sample UK index-linked bonds on 25th October 2002, assuming future inflation of 5% *per annum* (column a) and 3% *per annum* (column b).

(3) The coupon and capital values are indexed to the RPI with a lag of 8 months. This means that the real return from index-linked bonds *can* vary slightly if the rate of inflation varies (as is seen in Table 5.1). In particular, if the rate of inflation in the last 8

Table 5.1 Typical real yields to maturity on UK government index-linked bonds

Index-linked bond	Real yield to maturity*	
	(a)	(b)
Treasury $2\frac{1}{2}$% 2009	2.20%	2.38%
Treasury $2\frac{1}{2}$% 2013	2.27%	2.39%
Treasury $4\frac{1}{8}$% 2030	2.18%	2.24%

*Column (a) assumes 5% p.a. future inflation; column (b) assumes 3% p.a. future inflation.

months of the bond's life is different from that in the 8 months before the bond was issued, the bond may not give full protection against inflation. For this reason, when real yields to redemption from index-linked bonds are quoted in the financial press, they are normally quoted at two different prospective rates of inflation. In general, the lower the inflation rate during the period for which the bond is held, the higher will be the real return, other things being equal; this is because full inflation protection is not given by a bond which is subject to indexation lags.

(4) The investor obtains a more or less guaranteed real return if the bond is held to maturity. However, if the bond is sold before the maturity date, there is no such guarantee, because the price of the bond will rise and fall in the market as the general level of real yields changes. As will be seen from a later example, it is quite possible for the investor to achieve a *negative* real yield over the holding period.

(5) Index-linked bonds are attractive to two particular groups of investors: high-income tax payers and investors with long-term real liabilities. High-income taxpayers find index-linked bonds attractive because of the low coupon rate. They are attractive to investors with long-term liabilities which tend to rise as the price level rises (e.g. UK final salary pension funds) because long-dated index-linked bonds can be regarded as a defensive, secure, long-term investment, with a relatively certain real yield to maturity.

The precise characteristics of index-linked bonds vary from market to market. In most index-linked markets, bonds pay indexed coupon and capital payments. There have also been zero coupon bond issues and, in the case of Poland, an issue where only the capital payment and not the coupon payment was indexed. As well as an inflation risk arising from the indexation lag (see Section 5.5), there is also an inflation risk arising from the absence of indexation of the coupon in this case (see Booth and Stroinski, 1996).

All index-linked bonds incorporate an indexation lag, as discussed in (3) above. The UK is unusual in incorporating an 8-month indexation time lag in its index-linked bond structure. In all other major index-linked markets (for example, Australia, Canada, New Zealand, the US and France) a 3-month indexation lag is used, and both coupon and capital payments are indexed. There are some other differences between international index-linked markets. French index-linked bonds pay coupons annually. Those issued by the New Zealand and Australian governments pay coupons quarterly and those issued by the US and Canadian governments pay coupons half-yearly. These differences in detail do not affect the principles of valuation which are developed in the valuation formulae for UK index-linked bonds in Sections 5.4 to 5.6. The details and conventions, however, are different.

5.3   INDEX-LINKED BONDS: SIMPLE CASE

Before considering the type of index-linked bonds which are normally issued in practice, it is of interest to consider mathematically the valuation of an index-linked bond in the case where payments are linked precisely to an index of prices.

A number of assumptions will be made. The bond is bought on the issue date. Coupons are paid twice per year, at a nominal rate of $D\%$ per annum, linked to the rise in the price index between the time when the stock was issued and the time of payment. The bond is redeemable at par value, linked also to the rise in the price index. Inflation is at a rate of f per annum. There are n years to redemption and the investor requires a real return of $j^{(2)}$ per annum convertible half-yearly over the term to redemption.

The price of £100 nominal of such a bond, to yield $j^{(2)}$ per annum, convertible half-yearly would be

$$P = \frac{D}{2} \left\{ \frac{(1+f)^{1/2}v}{(1+f)^{1/2}} + \frac{(1+f)v^2}{(1+f)} + \cdots + \frac{(1+f)^n v^{2n}}{(1+f)^n} \right\} + \frac{100(1+f)^n v^{2n}}{(1+f)^n}$$

where v is calculated at a real rate of interest of $j^{(2)}/2$. The payments are constant, in real terms, at a rate of D per annum and thus all the $(1+f)$ factors cancel out, leaving the conventional bond formula

$$P = \frac{D}{2}\, a_{\overline{2n|}} + 100v^{2n} \tag{5.1}$$

where

$$a_{\overline{2n|}} = \frac{(1-v^{2n})}{\frac{1}{2}j^{(2)}} \qquad \text{and} \qquad v = (1 + \tfrac{1}{2}j^{(2)})^{-1}$$

but where the compound interest functions are calculated at the required *real* rate of return.

For a number of reasons, explained below, the payments from an index-linked bond are likely to be linked to an index of prices with a time lag. We therefore need a more general model.

5.4   INDEX-LINKED BONDS: A MORE GENERAL APPROACH

It will be helpful to consider index-linked bonds in the more general sense and then apply this to the particular form of index-linked bonds which have been issued in the UK. In general, there is a lag between a change in the price index and the corresponding change in the payments from an index-linked bond, partly because price indices tend to be calculated and published in arrears.

It is convenient, at first, to ignore the relationship between the price index which is used to convert payments from an index-linked bond into real terms and that which is used to calculate monetary payments from the bond. The value of the new index, which is used to calculate the monetary payments from the bond, will be denoted by I_t, at time t. If t_0 is the base date (that is the date from which payments are indexed) then I_{t_0} is the value, at the base date, of the index used to calculate monetary payments from the index-linked bond. The time at which the first payment from the bond is due will be denoted by t_1, the time at which the second payment is due, by t_2, etc.

The monetary amount of a payment at time t will be determined by what is known as the *nominal* payment, increased according to the ratio of the value of the index I_t, at time t, to its value at the base date. For example, if the bond has a nominal annual coupon of 3% payable half-yearly, the nominal payment due 6 months after the bond is issued is £1.50 per £100 nominal of bond. If the index used for calculating the monetary payment from the nominal payments was 200 at the base date (when the bond was issued) and 220 at the time the payment was made (i.e. it had increased by 10%), the monetary payment after 6 months would be calculated as follows.

The ratio of the value of the index used to calculate monetary payments, at the time the payment is due, to its value at the base date is: $I_{t_1}/I_{t_0} = (220/200) = 1.1$. The amount of the monetary payment per £100 nominal is found by taking this ratio and multiplying it by the amount of the nominal payment to give £$(1.1 \times 1.5) =$ £1.65.

There is a further reason, in addition to the complication caused by the indexation lag, for using a separate index to calculate monetary payments from the specified nominal payments. When the present value of a payment is calculated in real terms, given the values of the price index at the chosen base date and at the time the payment is made, the value of the price index is needed on the precise day on which the payment was made: if the value on the actual date on which the payment was made is not available, techniques of interpolation may be used to calculate an estimate of the value (see Example 4.6). The index which is used to calculate monetary payments from an index-linked bond, however, is often designed so that it takes the same value throughout any individual month (although note comments in Section 5.6 about international markets). This situation is best illustrated by referring to the particular case of index-linked bonds in the UK.

In the UK, payments are linked to the RPI with an 8-month lag. This means that the next coupon payment is always known and accrued interest can be calculated (see Section 5.8). Assume that a bond was issued in January of a particular year and a payment is due in July of that year. The month which falls 8 months before January is May of the previous year. So the base date value of the index used to calculate monetary payments from the bond will be the value of the RPI calculated in May of the previous year. This May value will be used whatever the precise date of issue and will be denoted by I_{t_0} as before. The value of the index used to calculate the first monetary payment, in July, will be the value of the RPI calculated in November of the previous year, denoted by I_{t_1}. Again, this index value will not depend on the precise date of the payment in July. Therefore the monetary payment, due in July, would be equal to the pre-determined nominal payment multiplied by I_{t_1}/I_{t_0}. The index I_t only changes once every calendar month and is equal, at any time, to the value of the RPI calculated in the calendar month 8 months previously.

The effects of the indexation lag are best shown by deriving a general valuation formula for an index-linked bond purchased on a coupon payment date. In this case, the index to which payments are linked is considered explicitly and there is a time lag between an increase in the retail price index and the index to which payments are linked. This leads to a result somewhat different from equation (5.3), where there was no indexation lag.

Consider an index-linked bond which has a term to redemption of n half-years and an annual coupon rate of D, paid half-yearly. Interest and capital payments are indexed with reference to a retail price index, with a time lag of 8 months. The assumed future rate of inflation is f per annum and a real yield of $j^{(2)}$ per annum convertible half-yearly is required.

The base date value of the index used to calculate the monetary coupon payments from the nominal coupon rate is the value of the retail price index calculated 8 months before the bond was issued. Using the symbols' defined above, this is I_{t_0}. The value of the index used to calculate the monetary amount of the first coupon is the retail price index calculated 8 months before payment (I_{t_1} using the defined notation). The amount of the first coupon is therefore

$$\frac{D}{2} \times \frac{I_{t_1}}{I_{t_0}}$$

The value of the index used to calculate the monetary amount of the second coupon payment (12 months after the bond is issued) is the value of the retail price index 4 months after issue. This is 6 months after the retail price index value used to calculate the first monetary payment was calculated. Thus the value is $(1+f)^{1/2} \times I_{t_1}$. The second coupon payment, assuming inflation at rate f per annum, is therefore

$$\frac{D}{2} \times (1+f)^{1/2} \times \frac{I_{t_1}}{I_{t_0}}$$

Given the assumed constant rate of inflation, the index used to calculate the monetary payments from the nominal coupon rate will rise by a factor of $(1+f)^{1/2}$ between each coupon payment. The third coupon payment is therefore

$$\frac{D}{2} \times (1+f) \times \frac{I_{t_1}}{I_{t_0}}$$

The last coupon payment will be paid after n half-years and the value of the index used to calculate the monetary payment will be the value of the retail price index 8 months before the last payment, which will be

$$(1+f)^{(n-1)/2} \times \frac{I_{t_1}}{I_{t_0}}$$

This takes account of inflation from 8 months before the bond was issued until 2 months before the bond was issued, and then for the $(n-1)$ half-years until 8 months before the bond is redeemed.

The monetary payments now have to be transformed into purchasing power terms as at the base date. At the time the first coupon payment is made, the retail price index is a factor $(1+f)^{1/2}$ greater than its value at the base date (thus allowing for inflation for half a year). The real value of the first payment is therefore

$$\frac{\frac{D}{2} \times \frac{I_{t_1}}{I_{t_0}}}{(1+f)^{1/2}}$$

When the second coupon payment is made, the retail price index is higher than at the base data (purchase date) by a factor $(1+f)$. The real value of the second payment is therefore

$$\frac{\dfrac{D}{2} \times (1+f)^{1/2} \times \dfrac{I_{t_1}}{I_{t_0}}}{(1+f)} = \frac{\dfrac{D}{2} \times \dfrac{I_{t_1}}{I_{t_0}}}{(1+f)^{1/2}}$$

When the third coupon payment is made, the retail price index has risen by a factor $(1+f)^{3/2}$. The real value of this coupon payment is therefore

$$\frac{\dfrac{D}{2} \times (1+f) \times \dfrac{I_{t_1}}{I_{t_0}}}{(1+f)^{3/2}} = \frac{\dfrac{D}{2} \times \dfrac{I_{t_1}}{I_{t_0}}}{(1+f)^{1/2}}$$

This sequence continues, with the factors of $(1+f)$ cancelling out leaving I_{t_1}/I_{t_0} in the numerator of the expression for the real value of each payment and $(1+f)^{1/2}$ in the denominator. In real terms, therefore, each coupon payment is of the same amount. The capital repayment, in purchasing power terms as at the base date, is

$$100 \times \frac{I_{t_1}/I_{t_0}}{(1+f)^{1/2}}$$

It is now necessary to calculate the present value of the payments. The real rate of interest is $j^{(2)}/2$ per half-year. The real rate of return was quoted as a rate *per annum* convertible half-yearly, this being the market convention for bonds with semi-annual coupons. Let $v = (1 + \frac{1}{2}j^{(2)})^{-1}$, where $j^{(2)}$ is the real rate of return *per annum* convertible half-yearly. The coupon payments form an annuity where each payment, in real terms, is as specified above. The present value of the coupon payments and redemption payment is

$$\frac{D}{2} \times \frac{I_{t_1}/I_{t_0}}{(1+f)^{1/2}} (v + v^2 + \cdots + v^n) + 100 \times \frac{I_{t_1}/I_{t_0}}{(1+f)^{1/2}} \times v^n \qquad (5.2)$$

Noting that the successive powers of v form a geometric progression, equation (5.2) simplifies to

$$\frac{I_{t_1}/I_{t_0}}{(1+f)^{1/2}} \left\{ \frac{D}{2} \times \frac{1 - v^n}{\frac{1}{2}j^{(2)}} + 100v^n \right\} \qquad (5.3)$$

Thus

$$\text{Issue price of the bond} = \frac{I_{t_1}/I_{t_0}}{(1+f)^{1/2}} \times \left\{ \frac{D}{2} \times a_{\overline{n}|} + 100v^n \right\} \qquad (5.4)$$

where the compound interest functions are calculated at a rate of interest of $j^{(2)}/2$.

It is worth noting, at this point, the similarities and differences between equation (5.4) and equation (5.1). In the case of the bond which is priced using equation (5.4), the payments are linked to the price index with lag. The present value therefore depends on the assumed future rate of inflation. Furthermore, it should also be noted that the first payment from the bond is actually known in monetary terms. This payment could therefore be discounted at a nominal rate of interest (or, equivalently, transform the payment into real terms and then discount at the real rate of interest).

It should also be noted, in this derivation, that it has been assumed that there is exactly half a year between payments. In practice, this would not be the case (there may, for example be 181, 182, 183 or 184 days between any two consecutive payments). When considering the valuation of a bond in practice, the exact time between the date of purchase and the receipt of payments should be considered.

Example 5.1

On 17 May 2002, the government of a country issued an index-linked bond of term 15 years. Interest is payable half-yearly in arrears and the annual coupon rate is 3%. Interest and capital repayments are indexed by reference to a retail price index with a time lag of 8 months. The retail price index value calculated in September 2001 was 212.00 and that calculated in March 2002 was 218.23.

The issue price of the bond was calculated so that, if the retail price index were to increase continuously at a rate of 7% *per annum* from March 2002, a purchaser of the bond at issue would obtain a real yield of 4% *per annum* convertible half-yearly, measured in relation to the retail price index. Calculate the issue price for the bond.

Answer

Equation (5.4) can be used to calculate the price of a bond for a given assumption about the future rate of inflation. In this example, the bond is of length 15 years, so that n is 30 half-years. Therefore,

$$\frac{I_{t_1}/I_{t_0}}{(1+f)^{1/2}} = 0.99515; \qquad \frac{D}{2} \times \frac{1-v^n}{\frac{1}{2}j^{(2)}} = 33.59475 \qquad \text{and} \qquad 100v^n = 55.20709$$

Substituting these values into equation (5.4), a price of £88.37 per £100 nominal of bond is obtained.

5.5   THE EFFECT OF INDEXATION LAGS

It is of interest to study the effect of the lag between changes in the price index and changes in the payments from an index-linked bond. Our study will be confined to an examination of the effect of the lag if a bond is to be held to maturity, given a constant future rate of inflation. This was the situation assumed when deriving equation (5.4).

In the UK, the rate of inflation during the time between purchase and maturity, compared with the rate of inflation in the 8 months before the bond was purchased, is of particular significance. This is because the real return will be calculated using the rate of inflation which pertained whilst the bond was held, but the rate of inflation during the period 8 months before the bond was purchased is relevant when calculating the payments which will be provided by the bond.

A change in the rate of inflation from that which was assumed when the bond was valued will therefore lead to a change in the real yield from an index-linked bond. This is because it will cause the value of the payments, measured in real terms, to change. As can be seen from the right-hand side of equation (5.4), a rise (or fall) in the constant assumed rate of inflation will reduce (or increase) the present value of the payments, for a given real yield. Thus, to equate the present value to the price, the real yield must be reduced (or increased). Specifically, therefore, a rise in the rate of inflation during the currency of the bond will lead to a fall in the real yield, as the investor will not be fully compensated for the rise in the price level.

The effect on the real yield of a change in the uniform rate of inflation is greater if the bond has a shorter life to maturity. The major reason for this is that the 8 months for which indexation effectively does not take place form a greater proportion of the time to payment, the closer a payment is to the present day.

Section 5.6 illustrates the method of valuation of index-linked bonds if the investor is purchasing a bond between coupon payment dates. The reader who is only interested in the principles of valuation, as described above, can omit the next section without loss of continuity.

5.6   A FURTHER GENERALISATION OF THE MODEL

So far, it has been assumed that bonds have been purchased at the issue date and that it is exactly half a year before the first coupon payment date. It has also been assumed that the last known price index value was that published 2 months before the bond was issued (i.e. the price index number used to determine the first coupon payment after issue, where there is an 8-month indexation lag).

This model can be generalised. An 8-month time lag will still be assumed between calculation of a price index value and the indexing of the payments from the bond. However, we will deal with the case where a price index number after the one which is used to determine the first monetary payment is known. In addition, valuation will be carried out at a time which is not necessarily half a year before the next coupon payment date.

If the next payment from the bond is the rth coupon payment after issue, this will be of fixed amount

$$\frac{I_{t_r}}{I_{t_0}} \times \frac{D}{2} = C_r$$

where D is the nominal coupon rate *per annum*. I_{t_r} is the value of the price index which was calculated 8 months before the due date of the first coupon after purchase: it is therefore used to determine the first coupon payment after purchase, where we have an 8-month indexation lag.

Now consider the second coupon payment after purchase (or the $(r + 1)$th coupon payment after issue). If a further price index number is known, after I_{t_r}, it will be convenient to assume a constant rate of inflation from the time of this latest price index date, rather than from the time to which I_{t_r}, relates. The $(r + 1)$th coupon payment will then be of amount:

$$\frac{(\text{latest RPI value}) \times (1+f)^{y/12}}{I_{t_0}} \times \frac{D}{2} = C_{r+1}$$

where y is the number of months between the date on which the latest known retail price index figure was calculated and the date of calculation of the price index figure which determines the $(r+1)$th monetary payment.

For example, if the second coupon payment after purchase is due 9 months after the bond was purchased and the last known price index value was that calculated 1 month ago, the index number used to determine that monetary payment would be the latest price index value increased to allow for 2 months' inflation (thus providing an estimate of the price index number to be calculated in 1 months' time or 8 months before the second coupon payment after purchase).

Each successive payment will be higher by a factor of $(1+f)^{1/2}$ if the price index is assumed to rise at a rate of f *per annum* from the latest calculated value.

The next two stages in deriving the present value of the bond involve expressing the series of monetary coupon payments in real terms and discounting back to the purchase date. It will also be assumed that there are x days until the next coupon payment date; that there are exactly 182.5 days between each coupon payment; and that there are n remaining coupon payments. The present value of the series of coupon payments and final redemption payment will be

$$P = \frac{v^{x/182.5}}{(1+f)^{x/365}} \left\{ C_r + \frac{C_{r+1}v}{(1+f)^{1/2}} + \frac{C_{r+1}(1+f)^{1/2}v^2}{(1+f)} + \cdots + \frac{C_{r+1}(1+f)^{(n-2)/2}v^{n-1}}{(1+f)^{(n-2)/2}} \right.$$

$$\left. + 100 \times \frac{(\text{latest RPI})(1+f)^{y/12}(1+f)^{(n-2)/2}v^{n-1}}{I_{t_0}(1+f)^{(n-1)/2}} \right\}$$

where v is calculated at the real yield per half-year.

The first coupon payment has to be discounted back $x/182.5$ half-years; the second coupon payment $x/182.5$ half-years plus one half-year, and so on. When calculating the real value of payments, inflation for $x/365$ years has to be allowed for in the case of the first coupon payment; $x/365$ plus a half-year, in the case of the second coupon payment, etc. The above formula can be simplified to give

$$P = \frac{v^{x/182.5}}{(1+f)^{x/365}} \left\{ C_r + \frac{C_{r+1}}{(1+f)^{1/2}} \times a_{\overline{n-1|}} + 100 \times \frac{(\text{latest RPI})(1+f)^{y/12}v^{n-1}}{I_{t_0}(1+f)^{1/2}} \right\}$$

$$(5.5)$$

As mentioned in Section 5.2, the details and conventions of index-linked bond valuation formulae are different in different countries. For example, in Canada and the US, I_t would be calculated differently for each day in the month by interpolation between the consumer price index calculated three months before t and the consumer price index calculated two months before t. Details of bond issues can be found on the websites of the issuers. For example, a comprehensive guide to the 1998 French inflation-linked OAT can be found at http://www.francetresor.gouv.fr/oat/oati/us/ broch.html Further details of valuation formulae can be found in Deacon and Derry (1998).

5.7   HOLDING PERIOD RETURNS

If a holding period return is to be calculated, the monetary payments from the bond will be known. The actual price index values will also be known and interpolation can be used to estimate price index values on the days on which payments were received, so that present values of payments can be obtained in real terms. To calculate holding period returns and construct the appropriate equations of value, one simply needs to go back to first principles. This is illustrated in Example 5.2 which is based on an example from Wilkie (1984). Like Example 4.5, Example 5.2 is based on a real situation some time ago. However, it has been chosen because it illustrates the principles clearly.

Example 5.2

An investor subscribed to a quantity of 2% Index-Linked Treasury 1996 on the issue date. The following instalments per £100 nominal of bond were paid: £35 on 27 March 1981, £30 on 1 May 1981 and £35 on 26 May 1981. The investor received interest payments per £100 nominal of £0.80 on 16 September 1981, £1.10 on 16 March 1982 and £1.15 on 16 September 1982. The bond was sold for £107.50 per £100 nominal on 31 December 1982. Show that the real return over the holding period was approximately −0.3% per half-year, ignoring tax.

The RPI values which will be required in our calculations are:

15 July 1980	267.9	13 October 1981	303.7
17 March 1981	284.0	12 January 1982	310.6
14 April 1981	292.2	16 March 1982	313.4
19 May 1981	294.1	14 September 1982	322.9
16 June 1981	295.8	12 October 1982	324.5
14 July 1981	297.1	14 December 1982	325.5
15 September 1981	301.1	11 January 1983	325.9

Answer

In order to calculate the real yield, estimates of the RPI are required on those days on which a payment is made but on which the RPI was not calculated. These values are found by interpolation between the logarithms of the calculated RPI values, as shown in Example 4.6. This gives values as follows:

27 March 1981	286.90
1 May 1981	293.12
26 May 1981	294.52
16 September 1981	301.10
16 September 1982	323.01
31 December 1982	325.74

16 March 1982 was a calculation date and therefore the known value of 313.4 can be used directly in the calculation.

The coupon payments from the bond are given. However, it is a useful exercise to check one of those payments. It is not possible to calculate the amount of the first coupon easily because it is adjusted to allow for the fact that the bond was paid for in instalments. The second payment is calculated as follows.

On 16 March 1982, the coupon payment should be

$$1 \times \frac{\text{RPI July 1981}}{\text{RPI July 1980}} = \frac{297.1}{267.9} = 1.1 \text{ or } £1.10$$

The nominal amount of each coupon payment is £1 and the bond was issued 8 calendar months after July 1980, with the first full coupon payment being 8 months after July 1981.

The real return will be calculated as a half-yearly rate of return and therefore, in deriving the equation of value, it is necessary to calculate the time between each payment and the issue date in half-years. If half a year is 182.5 days, the times between the issue date and each payment date, in units of half a year, are as follows:

27 March 1981 to 1 May 1981	= 35/182.5 half-years	= 0.1918 units
27 March 1981 to 26 May 1981	= 60/182.5 half-years	= 0.3288 units
27 March 1981 to 16 September 1981	= 173/182.5 half-years	= 0.9479 units
27 March 1981 to 16 March 1982	= 354/182.5 half-years	= 1.9397 units
27 March.1981 to 16 September 1982	= 538/182.5 half-years	= 2.9479 units
27 March 1981 to 31 December 1982	= 644/182.5 half-years	= 3.5288 units

The exact timing of each payment has been used here to determine the number of time units between the outset of the transaction and each payment. Market practice may involve the use of various approximations.

The equation of value equates the present value of the outgoing payments (the instalments paid by the investor) to the present value of the incoming payments (the three coupon payments and the sale price), after adjusting for the fall in the purchasing power of money. The base date will be taken as the date on which the first instalment was paid (27 March 1981). The value of the RPI on the base date has been estimated as 286.9. For illustrative purposes, it is useful to insert this initial value into the equation of value, although it is unnecessary to do so because it cancels out. The equation of value is

$$35(286.9/286.9) + 30(286.9/293.12)v^{0.1918} + 35(286.9/294.52)v^{0.3288}$$

$$= 0.8(286.9/301.1)v^{0.9479} + 1.1(286.9/313.4)v^{1.9397} + 1.15(286.9/323.01)v^{2.9479}$$

$$+ 107.5(286.9/325.74)v^{3.5288}$$

where $v = (1+j)^{-1}$ and $j = -0.003$ or -0.3% (the real yield).

Thus, it can be seen that all the initial values of the RPI cancel out, illustrating the fact that it is merely a scaling factor. Inserting the appropriate value of $v = 1.003$ and cancelling the initial value of the RPI, the value of the left-hand side is

$$0.12199 + 0.1024 \times 1.0006 + 0.11884 \times 1.001 = 0.3434$$

and the right-hand side is

$$0.00266 \times 1.003 + 0.00351 \times 1.006 + 0.00356 \times 1.009 + 0.33002 \times 1.011 = 0.3434$$

Therefore, the real yield is -0.3% per half-year.

5.8 ACCRUED INTEREST

If the bond is purchased between interest payment dates, accrued interest must be added to the clean price in order to obtain the total purchase price. Similarly, if it is desired to calculate the clean price from a given total price, accrued interest must be deducted.

Accrued interest is calculated in the same way as for conventional fixed-interest securities, by assuming that the next interest payment (the monetary amount of which can be calculated exactly, because of the indexation lag) accrues linearly in the total price from one interest payment date to the next. The precise nature of the calculation will depend on the accrued interest method used in the country concerned (see Section 2.3).

Example 5.3

The interest payment dates for a UK-style index-linked bond, with a 2% coupon, redeemable in 2006, issued on 27th March 1991 are 16 September and 16 March. Calculate the accrued interest per £100 nominal of the bond if the settlement date for a deal was 14 May 2000. The RPI for July 1990 was 67.9 and for January 2000 was 119.5.

Answer

The number of days since the last interest payment is 59; the nominal annual coupon rate is 2% *per annum* and the index for calculating monetary payments has a value of 67.9 in March 1991 (when the bond was issued) and 119.5 in September 2000 (when the first coupon payment after the settlement date was due). Therefore, the accrued interest is calculated as follows:

$$\text{Accrued interest} = £2 \times \frac{59}{365} \times \frac{119.5}{67.9} = \underline{£0.57}$$

5.9 THE REAL YIELD GAP

The *yield gap* was defined in Section 3.8 as the gross redemption yield for an index of secure fixed-interest government bonds of a particular country less the initial gross dividend yield on equities (normally obtained from published indices) in the same country. It should reflect the relative perceived risk of equity investments and fixed-interest government bonds and the extent to which investors believe that future dividends will increase.

The analysis of the yield gap is complicated by the fact that it draws comparison between two fundamentally different types of investments. Equities are inherently real investments but fixed-interest investments are denominated in nominal currency terms. The analysis of the yield gap therefore requires an analysis of three aspects: the difference in risk between the types of investment being compared, the increase in money dividends from equities caused by the effect of inflation and the increase in real dividends from equities (which could be negative).

As was stated in Section 4.6, it is often useful to consider real rather than money dividend growth in the analysis of equities. One should perhaps extend this logic and analyse the difference between the dividend yield on equities and the real gross redemption yield on index-linked bonds. The *real* yield gap, so defined, should reflect the expectations of investors for real dividend growth and the difference between the risk from purchasing index-linked investments and that from purchasing equity type investments.

Equation (4.13) showed that

$$j = g_r + (1 + g_r) \times \frac{d_0}{P}$$

where j is the real return from equities, g_r is the real growth rate of equity dividends, which is assumed to be constant, and d_0/P the historical dividend yield.

Although the real yield to maturity of an index-linked bond is not independent of the rate of inflation, it is not significantly affected by it. This is particularly true in the case of long-dated index-linked bonds. It would be reasonable to postulate therefore that the difference between the prospective real return (j) from equities and the real yield to redemption from index-linked bonds (which will be defined as j_{il} in this context) depends only on the risk premium (r_p) which the investor demands from equities (i.e. the additional real return which compensates for the extra risk of equity investments) and an error term (e) (caused, for example, by investments being inefficiently priced). Thus it could be said that

$$j - j_{il} = r_p + e \qquad (5.6)$$

Substituting the expression for j from equation (4.13) gives

$$g_r + (1 + g_r) \times \frac{d_0}{P} - j_{il} = r_p + e \qquad (5.7)$$

Re-arranging this expression, we obtain an expression for the real yield gap, which depends only on the theory behind equation (5.6) and the discounted dividend model being correct. Thus,

$$\frac{d_0}{P} - j_{il} = r_p - g_r - g_r \times \frac{d_0}{P} + e \qquad (5.8)$$

Ignoring the third term on the right-hand side (which will be small), the real yield gap is dependent only on the risk premium demanded by investors for investing in equities, the expected real growth rate of equity dividends and an error term which may reflect the inefficient pricing of investments at any time.

An investor may study the real yield gap over a period of time and use it in determining the allocation of investment funds between asset categories. If the current real yield gap cannot be explained by the investor's perceptions of prospective real dividend growth rates and the relative risk of equities compared with index-linked bonds, the investor might decide to allocate more assets to the category which appears to be relatively cheap. However, the timing of any such investment decision may depend on other, short-term, factors.

Because the real yield gap should be independent of investors' expectations of inflation, one would expect it to be more stable than the yield gap. The real yield on index-linked securities can vary slightly as inflation varies, as has been demonstrated earlier; in addition, the real return from equities may vary as the rate of inflation varies (because of lags in the transmission mechanisms of inflation through the economic system and the costs and frictions caused by inflation itself). However, apart from these factors, if the market is efficient, the difference between the dividend yield on equities and the real yield on index-linked bonds should reflect only the prospects for real growth of equity dividends and the difference in risk between the two types of investment, as perceived by the market as a whole.

There is further discussion in Lofthouse (2001) of the real yield gap (described by Lofthouse as the "modern yield gap"). In particular, Lofthouse discusses its use in asset allocation. As is also discussed by Lofthouse, interpreting the real yield gap in international markets can be difficult because of the relative illiquidity of some index-linked markets and the different tax position of index-linked bonds.

Example 5.4

On 22 June 2001, the dividend yield on the FT Actuaries All Share Index (UK) was 2.42%; the real yield to redemption on the FTSE Actuaries All Stocks Index-linked bond index was 2.31% (assuming inflation at 5% *per annum*). Calculate the real yield gap and comment on your answer.

Answer

The real yield gap is the difference between the dividend yield on equities and the real yield on index-linked bonds and is therefore 0.11%. This means that the sum of the equity risk premium and expected real dividend growth from equities was 0.11%.

It may be of interest to note that the real yield gap in the US market was −2.18% and in France −1.38%.

These levels of the real yield gap were low historically. This reflected historically low dividend yields from equities. In the UK, but not in the other markets, yields from index-linked gilts are also relatively low by historic standards.

5.10 ESTIMATING MARKET EXPECTATIONS OF INFLATION

The existence of index-linked bonds allows us to develop methods to estimate the market's expectation of future inflation by comparing real yields to maturity from index-linked bonds with nominal yields to maturity from conventional bonds. Deacon and Derry (1994) defined the methods of doing so.

5.10.1 Index-linked and Conventional Bonds: Basic Relationships

Deacon and Derry (1994) describe three approaches to the estimation of market expectations of inflation. The first of these is the so-called "simple approach". The simple approach uses basic relationships between index-linked bond and conventional bond yields to maturity to estimate market expectations of inflation. We will assume that we are dealing with a government bond market where the credit risk from any long-term bond is negligible. We also assume, when using the simple approach, that we have an index-linked bond market where there are no indexation lags.

Let the real yield to maturity from index-linked bonds and the expected real yield to maturity from conventional bonds both equal j and let the nominal yield from conventional bonds be i (quoted as effective rates per annum). If the expected rate of inflation is f per annum and prices adjust in each asset market so that the expected real return from both conventional and index-linked gilts is the same, the following relationship from Section 4.4 would hold:

$$(1+j)(1+f) = (1+i)$$

Thus:

$$f = (i-j)/(1+j)$$

At low values of j it is reasonable to use the approximate relationship:

$$f \approx i - j \tag{5.9}$$

However, it could be argued that there should be a risk premium from conventional bonds because they carry an inflation risk so that the expected real yield to maturity from conventional bonds and the expected real yield to maturity from index-linked bonds are not equal.[1] This inflation risk premium may be difficult to estimate. Investors with different liabilities or objectives will have different risk-free instruments (see Chapter 17). Indexed-linked and conventional bond markets could therefore become segmented with expected real yields being determined by supply and demand in each market. The expected real yields would not necessarily be the same in each market but it would be difficult to estimate the magnitude of the difference. This argument can be countered by suggesting that there will be investors, at the margin, who invest to try to obtain the highest risk-adjusted return. Such investors may lead conventional and index-linked bonds to be priced so that their expected returns are equal or so that their risk-adjusted expected returns are equal, leading again to a risk premium for conventional bonds. The outcome would depend on how such marginal investors viewed inflation risk.

These arguments implying the possible existence of a risk premium, as a result of the behaviour of investors, ignore the issuing policy of the authorities. The issuer of bonds may wish to ensure the lowest possible real cost of funding government debt. If the expected real yield to maturity from index-linked bonds were less than that from conventional bonds, we might expect the issuing authorities to issue more index-linked bonds until the real yields became such that the real cost of funding using conventional and indexed instruments was equalised. The difference between conventional and index-linked bond yields would, in these circumstances, reflect the inflation expectations of the issuing authority. However, even this reasoning may not hold. The issuing authority may wish to maintain a diverse portfolio of funding instruments even if this does not lead to the lowest expected real cost of funding, in order to reduce the risk of

---

[1] There may also be a liquidity premium, most likely in the index-linked bond market.

particular types of economic shock affecting the real funding cost of government debt (see www.dmo.gov.uk for a statement of the objectives of government debt-funding policy in the UK). The issuing authority may also be willing to pay a higher expected cost of funding conventional debt because conventional debt gives the issuer the option to devalue the debt in real terms, an option which does not exist with index-linked debt.

Given all these considerations, one would not expect the expected real yield to maturity from conventional gilts to equal the real yield to maturity from index-linked gilts. There will probably be a positive risk premium from conventional gilts, the magnitude of which will be hard to estimate without independent estimates of the inflation expectations. There is little work in the financial economics literature on the likely size of this inflation risk premium.

Incorporating a risk premium in the approximation (5.9) above, we obtain:

$$f \approx i - j - r_p \tag{5.10}$$

where r_p is the risk premium from conventional gilts.

5.10.2 Problems with the Simple Approach to Estimating Inflation Expectations

There are a number of problems with the simple approach to estimation that are identified by Deacon and Derry (1994).

(1) The real yield to maturity from index-linked bonds is not independent of the expected rate of inflation because of indexation lags: this is known as the problem of internal consistency.
(2) As noted above, the risk premium required from conventional gilts is unobservable.
(3) The conventional bond and index-linked bond used (or the indices used) to estimate inflation expectations will have different durations. Even if the bonds used have the same term to redemption, the different pattern of payments from the conventional and indexed instruments means that they represent yields over different time periods. If yield curves are steeply sloping, this problem invalidates the whole analysis because the difference between conventional and index-linked bond yields would include a yield curve as well as an inflation effect.

5.10.3 Solving the Problem of Internal Consistency: Break-even Inflation Rates

We can obtain an idea of the magnitude of the problem of internal consistency by looking at index-linked bond real yields to maturity at different rates of inflation. For example, on 24 May 2002, the real yield to maturity of Treasury 2.5% 2009 was 2.3% assuming 5% future inflation and 2.47% assuming 3% future inflation. A change in the inflation assumption of 2% p.a. would change the inflation expectation estimate by 0.17%. The effect is, of course, greater for shorter-dated stocks. If, for example, we use a 5% inflation assumption to calculate the real yield to maturity from index-linked bonds and the market's expectation of inflation is less than 5%, we will under-estimate the investor's required real yield to maturity from index-linked bonds (which, we note from Section 5.5, is higher, the lower is expected inflation over the life of the bond). Using the simple method of estimating inflation expectations, we will therefore over-estimate inflation expectations.

The simple approach will give rise to reasonable results, as long as the rate of inflation used in the equation of value for the index-linked bond is reasonably close to the calculated estimate of inflation expectations. However, the break-even method of estimating inflation expectations (described below) is not difficult to apply, as long as appropriate computation facilities are available to solve the equations of value. The break-even methodology gives accurate results if the yield curves for index-linked and conventional bonds are reasonably flat.

We will show how to calculate break-even inflation rates in the UK market, where there is an 8-month indexation lag. Ignoring the risk premium we have three equations and three unknowns. The following notation will be used:

$i^{(2)}/2$ is the effective nominal yield to maturity per half-year from a conventional bond
$j^{(2)}/2$ is the effective real yield to maturity per half-year from an index-linked bond
n is the term to redemption of both bonds (in half-years)
I_{t_0} is the value of the retail price index 8 months before issue
I_{t_1} is the value of the retail price index 2 months before purchase
$f^{(2)}/2$ is the constant assumed effective future rate of inflation per half year
f is the constant assumed annual effective rate of inflation
D_c is the coupon rate per annum from the conventional bond
D_{il} is the nominal rate of coupon per annum from the index-linked bond
P_c is the price of the conventional bond and
P_{il} is the price of the index-linked bond
$f^{(2)}$, $i^{(2)}$ and $j^{(2)}$ are unknown.

The relationship between the half-yearly rate of inflation $f^{(2)}/2$ and the annual effective rate of inflation f is: $f = (1 + f^{(2)}/2)^2 - 1$.

It will be assumed that the term to redemption is an integer number of half-years (the principle of solving the equations is no different if that is not the case: see, for example, equation 5.5).

The following three equations need to be solved for $i^{(2)}$, $f^{(2)}$ and $j^{(2)}$:

$$P_c = (D_c/2)a_{\overline{n}|} + 100v^n \tag{5.11}$$

($a_{\overline{n}|}$ and v^n are to be calculated at $i^{(2)}/2\%$: compare with equation 2.4, although note the different definition of n)

$$P_{il} = \frac{I_{t_1}/I_{t_0}}{(1+f)^{1/2}} [(D_{il}/2)a_{\overline{n}|} + 100v^n] \tag{5.12}$$

($a_{\overline{n}|}$ and v^n are to be calculated at $j^{(2)}/2\%$: compare with equation 5.4).

If the expected real return from conventional and index-linked bonds were equal, the following relationship would hold:

$$(i^{(2)}/2 - f^{(2)}/2)/(1 + f^{(2)}/2) = j^{(2)}/2 \tag{5.13}$$

The left-hand side is the expression for the expected real return from the conventional bond (with variables expressed as yields per annum convertible half-yearly) and the right-hand side is the real return from the index-linked bond.

The following procedure can be used to solve equations 5.11 to 5.13. The equation of value for the conventional bond (5.11) can be solved for $i^{(2)}$. Using equation 5.12 we can express the actuarial functions ($a_{\overline{n}|}$ and v^n) for the index-linked bond, replacing the real yield to maturity $j^{(2)}$ by $(i^{(2)}/2 - f^{(2)}/2)/(1 + f^{(2)}/2)$ (see equation 5.13). Equation 5.12 can then be solved for $f^{(2)}$. The break-even rate of inflation f can then be found using the relationship between $f^{(2)}$ and f, above.

If we need to take account of the risk premium, an appropriate assumption should be made and the following equation will be used instead of equation 5.13:

$$(i^{(2)}/2 - f^{(2)}/2)/(1 + f^{(2)}/2) - r_p = j^{(2)}/2 \qquad (5.14)$$

where r_p is the assumed risk premium, now expressed as a half-yearly effective yield.

Given the existence of an unobservable risk premium, interpreting changes in the calculated break-even rate of inflation can be difficult. A change in the calculated break-even rate of inflation may imply a change in market expectations of inflation or a change in the inflation risk premium. Given that the inflation risk premium is not observable, any change in the break-even inflation rate requires further market analysis to estimate likely changes in the inflation risk premium required from conventional bonds, before firm conclusions can be drawn.

5.10.4 Solving the Problem of Differing Durations

If break-even estimates of inflation expectations are calculated using a conventional bond and an index-linked bond of the same term to maturity, the estimate of inflation expectations does not relate to that term to maturity because the indexed and conventional instruments have different payment structures. If indexed and conventional instruments of the same duration are used, it is difficult to interpret the inflation expectation as applying to any particular term. For example, if a twenty-year fixed interest bond has a duration of thirteen years and a sixteen-year index-linked bond has the same duration, to what term does an estimate of inflation expectations estimated from the two bonds apply? This problem may not be important if the yield curves of real yields to maturity from index-linked bonds and of nominal yields to maturity from conventional bonds are not flat. However, we can address the problem by using the techniques introduced in Section 5.10.5.

5.10.5 Forward and Spot Inflation Expectations

If the yield curves have significant slopes or if a very accurate decomposition of nominal yields into real yields and inflation expectations is required, we need to fit full index-linked gilt and conventional gilt yield curves. The techniques for doing this are beyond the scope of this text (see, for example, Anderson and Sleath, 2001, and the references contained therein) but the principles will be explained so that the reader can interpret published "yield curves" of inflation expectations.

In principle, it is possible to estimate a yield curve for conventional bonds and a yield curve for index-linked bonds from market data. The yield curve for index-linked bonds would show the relationship between real yields to maturity and term to maturity in a particular market. In particular, spot (or zero coupon) and forward (or implied

forward) rate yield curves can be derived (see Sections 2.14, 2.20 and 2.21). We assume
that the yield curves relate to annual effective rates of interest. The following definitions
will be used:

$_0i_t = t$ year nominal spot rate at time zero
$_{t-1}i_t = t$ year nominal forward rate at time zero
$_0j_t = t$ year real spot rate at time zero
$_{t-1}j_t = t$ year real forward rate at time zero
$_0f_t = t$ year spot rate of inflation at time zero
$_{t-1}f_t = t$ year forward rate of inflation at time zero

Ignoring the inflation risk premium, we can then derive spot and forward inflation rates
using the following relationships:

$$(1 + _0i_t)^n = (1 + _0j_t)^n(1 + _0f_t)^n \qquad (5.15)$$

and

$$(1 + _{t-1}i_t) = (1 + _{t-1}j_t)(1 + _{t-1}f_t) \qquad (5.16)$$

There is, in fact, a complication in the practical computation of these yield curves. If a
yield curve were fitted through index-linked bond yields, with the yields calculated
under a given inflation assumption, the method described here would solve the problem
of mismatching durations but the problem of internal consistency would reappear. This
is because the spot and forward yields estimated for index-linked bonds would depend
on the inflation assumption used. Thus, the real yield curve must be fitted using
iterative techniques. When the real yield curves and inflation expectation curves have
finally been derived, the real spot and forward yields from indexed-linked bonds are
calculated using assumptions for future inflation that are the same as the calculated
market expectations of inflation.

The interpretation of $_0f_t$ is that it is the average compound rate of inflation *per annum*
the market expects between the current time and time t. For example, if t is 10, it is the
compound average rate of inflation over the next ten years. This is probably the
meaning people normally ascribe to the phrase "inflation expectations over the next ten
years". This measure of inflation expectations has many applications. For example, it
can be used in equity valuation models, which build up nominal dividend expectations
from real dividend growth expectations and inflation expectations.

The interpretation of $_{t-1}f_t$ is that it is the expected one year rate of inflation at the
current time between future time $t - 1$ and future time t. The whole yield curve of such
forward rates can be used when individual expected annual inflation rates are needed.
One such application arises when valuing pensions in payment in a UK pension scheme.
Such pensions are often indexed to retail prices but with a cap on the increase in any
individual year. Forward rates of inflation expectations could be used to determine
market expectations of the increase in pension in a particular year. Hence, market
expectations of whether the cap would be effective (because inflation was expected to
exceed the cap) could be derived.

Thus the derivation of a full yield curve allows the investor to derive a market inflation
expectation for each year (or between any two times). Average market compound
expected rates of inflation over any time period could then be derived. If the real or

nominal yield curves are sloping, this can remove the inaccuracies of the break-even rate approach which does not take proper account of the periods over which real or nominal yields (and hence derived inflation expectations) pertain.

REFERENCES

Anderson, N. and Sleath, J. (2001), *New Estimate of the UK Real and Nominal Yield Curves*, Bank of England Working Paper Series, No. 126, Bank of England (www.bankofengland.co.uk).

Booth, P.M. and Stroinski, K. (1996), "The Joint Development of Insurance and Investment Markets in Poland: An Analysis of Actuarial Risk", *British Actuarial Journal*, 2, 3 (8), 741–63.

Deacon, M. and Derry, A. (1994), *Deriving Estimates of Inflation Expectations from the Prices of UK Government Bonds*, Bank of England, Working Paper Series, No. 23, Bank of England (www.bankofengland.co.uk).

Deacon, M. and Derry, A. (1998), *Inflation-indexed Securities*, Prentice-Hall.

Lofthouse, S. (2001), *Investment Management*, John Wiley & Sons.

Wilkie, A.D. (1981), "Indexing Long Term Financial Contracts", *Journal of the Institute of Actuaries*, 108, 299–341.

Wilkie, A.D. (1984), "On the Calculation of Real Investment Returns", *Journal of the Institute of Actuaries*, 111, 149–72.

http://www.dmo.gov.uk

http://www.dmo.gov.uk/gilts/index.htm

http://www.francetresor.gouv.fr/oat/oati/us/broch.html

6
Foreign Currency Investments

6.1 INTRODUCTION

The financial mathematics techniques discussed in Chapters 4 and 5 can readily be applied to the analysis of foreign currency investments. When real returns are calculated, the analyst is simply expressing payments denominated in one currency (the domestic currency) in units of another currency (purchasing power units). A variant of this valuation technique can be applied when foreign currency investments are valued. Instead of transforming all payments made at any time into purchasing power units, they can be transformed into units of the domestic currency.

After discussing the valuation of foreign currency denominated investments, arbitrage and hedging conditions will be derived. Mathematical aspects of the processes by which foreign exchange spot markets, foreign exchange forward markets and capital markets can be brought into equilibrium will then be discussed. We will then apply these ideas to the valuation of longer-term international investments.

6.2 EXCHANGE RATES

Throughout this chapter, the exchange rate will be defined as the number of units of foreign currency which can be obtained for one unit of domestic currency. This is equivalent to the price of domestic currency in foreign currency terms and is the method of quoting exchange rates in the UK.

If the exchange rate at time t is denoted by E_t, it is possible to convert a payment of E_t units of foreign currency, due at time t, into one unit of the domestic currency or vice versa. Alternatively, it is possible to convert $1/E_t$ units of domestic currency into one unit of foreign currency or vice versa. Thus, the reciprocal of the exchange rate could be regarded as the price of foreign currency. Transaction costs will be ignored in the analysis that follows.

A 5% rise (fall) in the value of the domestic currency means that one unit of the domestic currency will buy 5% more (fewer) units of the foreign currency. A rise in the domestic currency value, by 5%, would therefore imply a 5% rise in the quoted exchange rate (as defined above). The reciprocal of the exchange rate, or the price of foreign currency, however, will change by a slightly different percentage. A 5% rise in the exchange rate means that one unit of the domestic currency will buy $1.05 \times E_t$ units of foreign currency. One unit of foreign currency will therefore buy $1/(1.05 \times E_t)$ units of domestic currency, which is the new price of foreign exchange. The price of foreign exchange, or the number of units of the domestic currency per unit of foreign currency, has thus fallen by

$$\frac{[(1/E_t) - 1/(1.05 \times E_t)]}{(1/E_t)} \times 100\%$$

or

$$4.76\%$$

Thus a 5% rise in the sterling dollar exchange rate means that 5% more dollars can be purchased with every pound of sterling; that 5% more dollars are required to purchase every pound of sterling; and that 4.76% fewer pounds of sterling are purchased with every dollar. It is important to recognise this when dealing with exchange rates which may be quoted in different forms.

Example 6.1

A US investor places $500 in a sterling deposit account, at a fixed rate of interest of 6% *per annum*, for one year. The exchange rate is currently $1.40 per pound sterling and the dollar is expected to appreciate against sterling by 5% during the course of the year. Calculate the expected return in dollar terms.

Answer

At the beginning of the year, $1.4 will buy £1 and thus each $1 will buy £(1/1.4); at the end of the year, we are told that each $1 will buy 5% more sterling so each $1 will buy £[(1/1.4)1.05] or £0.75. Therefore, each £1 will buy $1.333.

At the beginning of the year, £(500/1.4) are purchased and, at the end of the year, the sterling investment purchases $[1.06 × (500/1.4) × 1.333] or $504.636 after allowing for interest and reconversion back at the new exchange rate. The yield, in dollar terms, from the transaction, is i, where

$$500(1 + i) = 504.636$$

therefore,

$$i = 0.93\%.$$

6.3   EXCHANGE RATES, INFLATION RATES AND INTEREST RATES

In the following sections, relationships between exchange rates, inflation rates and interest rates will be discussed. An understanding of these relationships is an important step in the analysis of foreign currency investments. Firstly, it is important to define some terms which will be used throughout the analysis.

E_s = *spot exchange rate (i.e. the number of units of foreign currency which can be purchased for one unit of the domestic currency)*

E_f = *forward exchange rate (i.e. the number of units of foreign currency which can be purchased for one unit of the domestic currency for a contract in which settlement and delivery takes place at some specified future date)*

E_e = *expected spot exchange rate at some specified future time*

i_d = *domestic interest rate over a specified time period*

i_a = *foreign interest rate over a specified time period*

f_d = *the expected domestic rate of inflation over a specified time period*

f_a = *the expected rate of inflation in a specified foreign country over a specified time period*

The interest rate may be obtained from Treasury bills in the country concerned, from short-dated bonds or from commercial paper. We will assume it is a risk-free rate. With regard to forward exchange rates there is no limit, in theory, to the amount of time over which a forward contract may operate but, in practice, the forward markets normally offer contracts for settlement in 30 days, 90 days or one year.

6.4   COVERED INTEREST ARBITRAGE

Covered interest arbitrage is a risk-free method of investment. Its use by investors can help ensure consistency between foreign currency spot rates, foreign currency forward rates and interest rates.

An investor can obtain a risk-free return, expressed in units of the domestic currency, in two ways. Firstly, investment could be undertaken which guaranteed a fixed domestic currency rate of interest over the term of the transaction. Secondly, a foreign currency investment could be bought and the maturity and interest proceeds sold on the forward foreign exchange market, at a price determined at the outset of the investment.

For an initial capital outlay of one unit of the domestic currency, the maturity proceeds from the first method of investment will be

$$(1 + i_d) \qquad\qquad (6.1)$$

If the second method of investment is employed, E_s units of the foreign currency are bought which accumulate to $E_s(1 + i_a)$ at the end of the period of investment. After exchanging the maturity proceeds, at the predetermined forward exchange rates, the proceeds in domestic currency will be

$$\frac{E_s(1 + i_a)}{E_f} \qquad\qquad (6.2)$$

In equilibrium, it would be expected that, ignoring dealing costs and exchange rate spreads, the maturity proceeds from the two methods of investment would be the same. The capital requirements are identical and, if the borrowers are of equal credit risk, there is no greater risk attached to one method of investment than to the other. Thus, equating expressions (6.1) and (6.2), we obtain

$$(1 + i_d) = \frac{E_s}{E_f} \times (1 + i_a) \qquad\qquad (6.3)$$

This can be written as

$$\frac{(i_d - i_a)}{(1 + i_a)} = \frac{(E_s - E_f)}{E_f} \qquad\qquad (6.4)$$

or (for small values of i_a)

$$i_d - i_a \simeq \frac{(E_s - E_f)}{E_f}$$

Given that

$$\frac{E_f}{E_s} + \frac{(1 + i_a)}{(1 + i_d)}$$

equation (6.4) can be rewritten as

$$\frac{(i_d - i_a)}{(1 + i_d)} = \frac{(E_s - E_f)}{E_s} \tag{6.5}$$

Multiplying throughout by -1 gives

$$\frac{(i_a - i_d)}{(1 + i_d)} = \frac{(E_f - E_s)}{E_s} \tag{6.6}$$

$(E_f - E_s)/E_s$ could be defined as the *forward discount on foreign currency* in the foreign exchange market. If the discount is positive, it implies that the number of units of foreign currency, per unit of domestic currency, which can be obtained in the forward market, is greater than the number which can be obtained in the spot market (so that the domestic currency is more expensive on the forward market). Such a situation may be combined with higher interest rates in the foreign country because, for example, higher inflation is expected in the foreign country.

If the left-hand side of equation (6.6) is greater than the right-hand side, investors will invest in such a way that interest rates and spot and forward exchange rates adjust sufficiently to allow equilibrium to be restored. If $(i_a - i_d)/(1 + i_d)$ is defined as the interest rate differential, the forward discount on foreign currency must be less than the interest rate differential, if investment in the foreign currency is to be profitable. If the right-hand side of equation (6.6) is greater than the left-hand side, investors will invest in the domestic market and holders of foreign currency will buy the domestic currency spot and sell it forward, until equilibrium is restored.

When the market has moved to equilibrium, the interest rate differential exactly compensates for the fact that, if the forward discount is positive (negative), one unit of the foreign currency, when sold forward, buys fewer (more) units of the domestic currency than were necessary to buy each unit of foreign currency spot.

It is the pure arbitrageur who acts to ensure that the above equilibrium condition holds. We will move on to consider other operators in the market who affect forward exchange rates, spot exchange rates and interest rates. Traders in foreign exchange markets will generally be those who make use of arbitrage opportunities. The transaction described is a relatively simple arbitrage transaction. However, more complex arbitrage transactions using derivatives markets as well as foreign exchange and investment contracts operate according to similar principles.

6.5 THE OPERATION OF SPECULATORS

A speculator in the foreign exchange market takes a foreign exchange risk with the aim of making a profit. Pure speculation can involve the speculator buying a currency in the forward market, with the intention of selling the currency on the spot market, when the forward contract matures. The currency may also be sold in the forward market, with the intention of buying the currency on the spot market to deliver the forward contract when it matures. Pure speculation requires no capital. The pure speculator is simply trying to gain from a movement in exchange rates not anticipated by the forward exchange markets.

An alternative form of speculation, sometimes known as arbitrage speculation, but here described simply as speculation, involves buying foreign currency in the spot markets to sell at a later time in the spot markets, in the hope of gaining from a change in exchange rates. The speculator does not take out forward cover.

We can consider equations which express the gains from the alternative methods of speculation. Again, assume that one unit of the domestic currency is available for speculation by either method. If pure speculation is carried out, the expected value, at the end of the period, of one unit invested at the beginning of the period, will be

$$\frac{(1 + i_d)}{E_e} E_f \tag{6.7}$$

One unit is invested at the domestic interest rate and then $(1 + i_d)E_f$ units of the foreign currency can be bought on the forward exchange market, under the contract made at the outset of the period. It is expected that the foreign currency can then be exchanged for the domestic currency at the exchange rate E_e.

If speculation is carried out, the expected accumulation of one unit will be

$$\frac{E_s(1 + i_a)}{E_e} \tag{6.8}$$

One unit of domestic currency is exchanged for the foreign currency and invested at the interest rate prevailing in the foreign country. The investor then expects to exchange the accumulation at the end of the transaction at the exchange rate E_e, which is the expected exchange rate at the end of the transaction.

As speculators consider pure speculation and speculation as alternatives, it is important to consider the conditions under which one or the other may be more profitable.

Equations (6.7) and (6.8) show the number of units of domestic currency which are expected to arise from pure speculation and speculation respectively. Speculation will therefore be pursued until the forward and spot exchange rates and the domestic and foreign interest rates move to an equilibrium level such that

$$\frac{E_s(1 + i_a)}{E_e} = \frac{(1 + i_d)}{E_e} E_f \tag{6.9}$$

It can be seen that this is equivalent to equation (6.3), the covered interest arbitrage equilibrium condition. The forms of speculation described here are relatively simple. But, again, they are similar, in principle, to speculation which may be undertaken by traders in all financial markets when forward and futures prices are out of line with expectations and with underlying asset and currency prices.

6.6 PURCHASING POWER PARITY THEORY

By proposing further relationships between interest rates and inflation, and exchange rates and inflation, a set of consistent conditions can be derived which show how spot exchange rates, expected exchange rates, forward exchange rates, interest rates and inflation can be related. This can provide a basis for the analysis of foreign currency investments.

The purchasing power parity theory suggests that exchange rate movements should reflect the relative price changes of tradable goods in different countries. It will be assumed that the rate of inflation in a country is the same as the average rate of increase in the prices of *tradable* goods.

Assume, for example, that the rate of increase of the price of cars in two countries reflects the average rate of increase in the prices of tradable goods. Consider a simple bilateral foreign exchange market for yen and sterling and assume that it is in equilibrium. If the price of cars in the UK were to rise by 10%, consumers in the UK would purchase more Japanese cars and consumers in Japan would wish to purchase more domestic vehicles. All other things being equal, this would lead to a movement in the exchange rate to offset the increase in the price of cars in the UK. Thus the yen would become 10% more expensive in sterling terms.

If the purchasing power parity theory holds, expected exchange rate movements will reflect expected rates of inflation in various countries. Algebraically, the implications of purchasing power parity theory can therefore be expressed using the relationship

$$\frac{E_e}{E_s} = \frac{(1+f_a)}{(1+f_d)} \tag{6.10}$$

Although purchasing power parity theory is not thought to hold in practice in the short term, it is a worthwhile starting point in the analysis of international investments. It may well be easier to analyse expected real changes in exchange rates (after taking into account future expected inflation in the countries under consideration) than nominal changes in exchange rates, when analysing international investments.

One of the implications of purchasing power parity theory is that real returns from a foreign currency investment would be independent of the domestic currency of the investor. If the investor's domestic currency depreciates over the term of the investment, this will simply reflect higher inflation in the domestic country than in the country in which the investment takes place. There will therefore be a higher domestic currency return, but this will be offset by the higher rate of inflation when real returns are calculated.

6.7 THE INTERNATIONAL FISHER EFFECT

The *international Fisher effect* hypothesises a relationship between expected inflation rates and interest rates in different countries. Specifically, Fisher (1930) proposed that real interest rates will tend to equality in different countries. Fisher also suggested that real interest rates tended to remain stable over time, so that fluctuations in interest rates tended to arise as a result of changes in inflationary expectations.

It is fairly clear why real, as compared with nominal, interest rates may be expected to be relatively stable over time in an individual country. If inflationary expectations increase, investors will wish to be compensated for the fall in the purchasing power of money and this will tend to put upward pressure on nominal interest rates. However, it should be said that óther factors are particularly important in determining short-term interest rates.

Furthermore, investors in international investment markets seek the highest possible real return (for a given level of risk). If capital moves freely between world investment markets and if exchange rate movements reflect inflation differentials between different countries, real interest rates will have a tendency to converge in international investment markets. If we consider two countries, higher nominal interest rates will be required, by an investor, in the country where the currency is expected to fall in value the most. If purchasing power parity theory holds, the relative depreciation of the weakest currency will only reflect additional inflation in that currency. Therefore, the higher level of nominal interest rates, necessary to compensate the investor for the additional fall in the exchange rate of the high inflation country, must also reflect relative inflation rates. If nominal interest rates are higher in a particular country only to the extent that inflation is higher, this implies that real rates are equal in the two countries.

Using the relationship between nominal interest rates, real interest rates and inflation established in Section 4.4, the international Fisher relationship leads to the following relationship between interest rates and inflation in the domestic and foreign investment markets:

$$\frac{i_d - f_d}{1 + f_d} = \frac{i_a - f_a}{1 + f_a} \qquad (6.11)$$

6.8   INTERACTIONS BETWEEN EXCHANGE RATES, INTEREST RATES AND INFLATION

We will now move on to consider covered interest arbitrage and speculation as alternative forms of investment. By considering equations (6.2) and (6.8), which show the returns from investing one unit of currency using these alternative methods, we can see that, if investors are indifferent between the two forms of investment, covered interest arbitrage will be pursued if the following relationship holds:

$$\frac{E_s(1 + i_a)}{E_f} > \frac{E_s(1 + i_a)}{E_e}$$

If investors could predict the expected exchange rate with perfect foresight or if they were risk neutral, they would invest through the method of covered interest arbitrage, until such time as the forward rate was exactly equal to the expected exchange rate. It is sometimes suggested that, because speculation is a more risky transaction than covered interest arbitrage, the expected exchange rate should be lower than the forward rate (so that more domestic currency can be bought with one unit of foreign currency at the expected exchange rate than at the forward exchange rate). However, the existence of different investors with different risk profiles and liabilities, together with the effect of investors from the foreign market (who require to be able to buy more of *their own* currency at the expected rate than at the forward rate, if they regard speculation as more risky) investing in the domestic market means that, in aggregate, the forward exchange rate should adjust to reflect future exchange rate expectations. For the purposes of the model which is being developed, it will be assumed that the forward exchange rate is a market indicator of the expected exchange rate.

If parity holds between forward and expected exchange rates, equation (6.3) can be re-written, replacing the forward exchange rate with the expected exchange rate, as follows:

$$(1 + i_d) = \frac{E_s}{E_e} (1 + i_a) \tag{6.12}$$

Equation (6.12) could have been derived from first principles, if it had been assumed that investors were risk neutral. The left-hand side of the equation shows the return from investing one unit in the domestic market. The right-hand side shows the return from investing in the foreign investment market and then exchanging the proceeds back at the expected exchange rate.

Using equation (6.10) (the purchasing power parity condition), we can replace E_s/E_e, in equation (6.12) by $(1 + f_d)/(1 + f_a)$, to give

$$(1 + i_d) = \frac{(1 + f_d)}{(1 + f_a)} \times (1 + i_a)$$

Dividing both sides by $(1 + f_d)$ and adding $(1 + f_d)/(1 + f_d)$ to the left-hand side and $(1 + f_a)/(1 + f_a)$ to the right-hand side, we obtain

$$\frac{i_d - f_d}{1 + f_d} = \frac{i_a - f_a}{1 + f_a} \tag{6.13}$$

Thus, the international Fisher effect can be shown to be an implication of purchasing power parity theory, forward and expected exchange rate parity and of the free movement of capital, so that investors are free to take advantage of the most favourable investment opportunities.

It is perhaps intuitively reasonable that, if exchange rate movements reflect differentials in inflation rates, interest rates in different countries should also reflect differentials in inflation rates. This will ensure that if an investor is adversely affected by a weakening of the foreign currency in which investment takes place, that investor will be compensated by a higher level of interest rates in the country concerned.

Example 6.2

A UK investor has a choice of investing in a particular foreign country through the method of covered interest arbitrage or investing without taking forward cover. The investor may also invest in the domestic money market. The interest rate in the foreign country, for an investment of appropriate maturity, is 6% *per annum*; the current spot exchange rate is 2 units of foreign currency per unit of sterling and the relevant forward exchange rate is 2.03 units of foreign currency per unit of sterling. The investor is risk neutral.

(a) Find the expected exchange rate, at the time the investment is to mature, such that the investor would be indifferent between investing with and without forward cover.

(b) Find the domestic interest rate and the real interest rate at home and abroad, if the purchasing power parity theory holds and the expected domestic rate of inflation over the period concerned is 2% *per annum*.

Answer

(a) If the investor invests one unit of domestic currency, with forward exchange rate cover, the proceeds of the investment, from equation (6.2), will be

$$\frac{E_s(1 + i_a)}{E_f}$$

Using the values stated in the example, this would give:

$$\frac{2 \times (1 + 0.06)}{2.03} = 1.0443$$

If the investor did not use forward cover, then using equation (6.8), the investment of one unit would be expected to give

$$\frac{E_s(1 + i_a)}{E_e}$$

Thus

$$\frac{2 \times 1.06}{E_e} = 1.0443 \quad \text{and} \quad E_e = 2.03$$

Although this may seem to be intuitively obvious, the tendency of expected exchange rates to equal forward rates can be seen here to be a consequence of risk neutrality and the actions of arbitrageurs and speculators.

(b) Investment in the domestic market can now be compared with either the covered interest arbitrage or the speculation transactions carried out in part (a). The investment of one unit in the domestic market would provide an accumulation of $(1 + i_d)$. Thus $(1 + i_d) = 1.0443$ and $i_d = 4.43\%$. This is lower than the foreign interest rate, reflecting the expected depreciation of the foreign currency against the domestic currency.

The domestic real interest rate is

$$\frac{i_d - f_d}{1 + f_d}$$

and using the domestic rate of inflation of 2% *per annum*, this gives a value for the domestic real interest rate of 2.38% *per annum*. The international Fisher effect suggests that the foreign real interest rate would also be 2.38% *per annum*. However, by using a different approach, it can be seen that this result is an implication of the other assumptions made in the question. Equation (6.10) gives a relationship between

exchange rates and inflation rates implied by purchasing power parity theory, as
follows:

$$\frac{E_e}{E_s} = \frac{(1+f_a)}{(1+f_d)}$$

Using the values for the expected exchange rate, the spot exchange rate and the
domestic inflation rate already obtained, we can calculate a value of 3.53% *per annum*
for the foreign inflation rate.

The real rate of interest in the foreign country is

$$\frac{i_a - f_a}{1 + f_a}$$

Using the value for the nominal rate of interest in the foreign country, we obtain a value
for the real rate of interest of 2.38%.

This example illustrates the fact that, if purchasing power parity theory holds, real
rates of interest are equalised in different countries. This arises because differences in
nominal rates reflect expected exchange rate movements, which themselves reflect
differences in the expected inflation rate in different countries. It should be emphasised
that if purchasing power parity theory was not expected to hold, real interest rates
would not, in general, be expected to tend to equality in different world markets. In
fact, we would expect the difference between real interest rates to reflect expected real
changes in the exchange rate.

6.9 INTERNATIONAL BOND INVESTMENT

A foreign currency fixed-interest bond would normally be regarded as a long-term
investment which guarantees a fixed return in foreign currency terms. Purchasing power
parity theory probably provides a more realistic explanation of currency movements
over the longer term than over the short term, and the ideas that lie behind purchasing
power parity theory can be useful for analysing longer-term foreign investments.

If purchasing power parity theory is believed to provide a good indicator of likely
future exchange rate movements, then all one needs to consider, when calculating the
return from a foreign currency bond in domestic currency terms, is expected relative
inflation rates. If, however, purchasing power parity theory is not thought likely to
provide a good indication of currency movements, a two-step approach to the analysis
is necessary.

The first step is to consider the likely change in real exchange rates between the
currencies of the domestic and foreign countries. That is, the likely change in exchange
rates over and above that predicted by purchasing power parity theory. For example,
an exchange rate may be temporarily high, in real terms, because the government is
pursuing a high interest rate or tight monetary policy. Investors may expect the
currency to fall, in real terms, as interest rates return to a more normal level.
Alternatively, a particular currency may be subject to speculation and thus may be
artificially high or low at any time. Having determined the expected movement in real
exchange rates, the expected relative inflation rates in the two countries can be
analysed. The expected change in real exchange rates can then be combined with the

movement predicted by purchasing power parity theory to produce the overall expected change in exchange rates.

The above approach has the advantage of isolating the fundamental factors which are expected to cause movements in exchange rates from the other factors which may affect exchange rate movements from time to time. The rationale for this is similar to the rationale underlying the analysis of equity investments, when it was suggested that real dividend growth should be predicted separately from future inflation rates, when predicting nominal dividend growth.

The following example considers a foreign currency bond investment in conditions when purchasing power parity theory is expected to hold.

Example 6.3

An analyst is considering the purchase of a Eurobond denominated in Euros. The bond pays an annual coupon of 6% and is redeemable at par in 10 years' time. The analyst expects Eurozone inflation to be at a level of 3% per year throughout the term to redemption. Find the purchase price, per €100 nominal of the bond for a sterling return of 5% *per annum*, if UK inflation is expected to be at a level of 2% *per annum*, throughout the term of the bond, and exchange rates adjust to reflect relative inflation rates. The current exchange rate is €1.45 per £1.

Answer

Every year, exchange rates adjust to allow for differences between the inflation rates of the two countries. Assume that £1 buys €X at the outset. At the end of the year, €$1.03 \times X$ buys the same amount of goods that €X bought at the beginning of the year. £1.02 is required to purchase the same quantity of goods at the end of the year as £1 bought at the beginning of the year. This means that £1.02 must purchase €$1.03 \times X$ at the end of the year, or £1 must purchase €$(1.03/1.02)X$; similarly €1 must purchase £$(1.02/1.03X)$. Another way of expressing this is to say that every year the number of £s a € can buy increases by a factor $1.02/1.03$ or 0.9903 (this of course represents a negative increase or decrease).

In this example, X, the initial exchange rate, is €1.45 per £. The payment of €6, therefore, at the end of the first year will purchase £$6 \times 0.9903/1.45$, the payment of €6 at the end of the second year will purchase £$6 \times 0.9903^2/1.45$, etc. There will then be a final redemption payment of €100 after 10 years. The present value of the payments, in sterling terms, at a rate of interest of 5%, is therefore

$$P = \frac{6 \times 0.9903}{1.06 \times 1.45} + \frac{6 \times 0.9903^2}{1.06^2 \times 1.45} + \frac{6 \times 0.9903^3}{1.06^2 \times 1.45} + \cdots + \frac{6 \times 0.9903^{10}}{1.06^{10} \times 1.45} + \frac{100 \times 0.9903^{10}}{1.06^{10} \times 1.45}$$

The first ten terms form a geometric progression with first term equal to $(6 \times 0.9903)/1.06 \times 1.45)$ and common ratio equal to $0.9903/1.06$; the present value is therefore

$$\frac{0.9903 \times 6}{1.06 \times 1.45} \times \frac{1 - (0.9903^{10}/1.06^{10})}{1 - (0.9903/1.06)} + \frac{100 \times 0.9903^{10}}{1.06^{10} \times 1.45} = £\frac{92.7205}{1.45} = £63.95$$

or £63.95 per €100 nominal.

6.10   INTERNATIONAL EQUITY INVESTMENT

Many further applications of the above ideas are possible. One could consider the valuation of a foreign equity where the dividends are anticipated to grow at a particular future rate. Returns could be calculated in real terms, in the domestic currency or in the foreign currency. No new mathematical principles are required, it is simply necessary to apply the above techniques consistently to the problem in hand.

One interesting feature of foreign equity investment, when purchasing power parity theory holds, relates to the inflation-hedging properties inherent in equity investment. A rise in the domestic rate of inflation will lead to a rise in the value of the foreign currency against the domestic currency, if purchasing power parity theory is assumed to hold. The fact that the foreign currency will purchase more units of the domestic currency will tend to offset the effect of the decline in the purchasing power of the domestic currency.

Furthermore, if the foreign country experiences a higher rate of inflation then, other things being equal, this should lead to higher nominal capital values and dividends from the equity investment in that country in the long term. However, if purchasing power parity theory is assumed to hold, there will be a devaluation of the foreign currency. The higher nominal capital values and dividends will be offset by the reduced value of the foreign currency.

The assumptions which underlie the above discussion are probably unrealistic in practice. However, purchasing power parity models do provide a starting point for the analysis of foreign investments. They also help us to understand the fundamental nature of foreign equity investment, as opposed to foreign currency fixed-interest investment, which is important when asset allocation decisions are taken.

6.11   FOREIGN CURRENCY HEDGING

It is possible to use a variety of derivative instruments to protect an investor against exchange rate movements if it is desired to invest in a particular international market without taking currency risk. Such an approach would be known as "currency hedging". Some of the instruments described in Chapter 7 will give protection over the long term from exchange rate movements. We will concentrate here on applying the forward currency transactions described earlier in this chapter. Such forward transactions might be used for shorter-term hedging purposes (say, 90 days). The principles of using currency swaps, for example, are similar.

Investors will take different approaches to deciding whether to hedge. As Lofthouse (2001) points out, there are cultural, empirical and theoretical issues to be considered. All of the following approaches would be valid in a different context:

(a) A policy never to hedge because a decision to invest in foreign markets is a decision to accept all aspects of economic exposure to those markets
(b) A policy always to hedge because an investor may wish to gain exposure to foreign investment markets but does not wish to be exposed to foreign currency risk
(c) A decision to hedge where statistical or economic models suggest that chosen foreign investment markets will outperform but currencies are at risk of underperforming (such an approach can lead to the logical separation of all currency and securities investment management)

(d) A decision to hedge in such a way that risk, relative to investment objectives, is minimised.

The importance of the last point may be why Davis and Steil (2001) have observed that international bond investments are often hedged whereas international equity portfolios are often left unhedged. For example, if a pension fund has a mixture of domestic currency fixed liabilities and salary-linked liabilities which are correlated with domestic inflation, it may be reasonable to hold domestic bonds and hedged foreign currency bonds to match the former and domestic and foreign currency equities to match the latter. If foreign exchange risk is hedged on a foreign currency bond portfolio, in effect, the returns are guaranteed in a domestic currency: the rate of exchange at which the foreign currency payments can be turned into domestic currency is fixed and known. If foreign currency equity investments are unhedged, then, for the reasons explained in Section 6.10, assuming purchasing power parity theory holds, those investment are, in effect, "real" investments that may be suitable for matching liabilities which are likely to increase with inflation. Hedging foreign currency equity portfolios leads to the creation of a financial asset which is, in fact, fundamentally rather complex. Notwithstanding the above, an investor may still wish to hedge foreign currency risk on an equity portfolio if it is desired to protect against a short-term fall in the value of the foreign currency or, perhaps, insure against a specific event such as a devaluation, interest rate change, etc. in the period before investments are realised.

Example 6.4

A pension fund holds £100m of US equities. The spot exchange rate is $1.65 per £1. The 91-day forward exchange rate is $1.63 per £1. The fund manager expects the spot exchange rate to be $1.50 per £1 in 91 days and therefore decides to hedge. The expected return from the US equity portfolio is 5% (in dollar terms) over the 91-day period.

(a) Calculate the fund manager's expected return if he hedges the equity portfolio by purchasing the sterling for dollars on the forward market, for settlement in 91 days time.
(b) The actual spot rate in 91 days time is $1.70 per 1. How much "better off" would the fund have been from not hedging?

Answer

(a) The foreign equity portfolio is worth $165m and is expected to be worth:

$$\$165(1.05) = \$173.25 \text{ in 91 days time}$$

If the fund manager hedges the total expected portfolio value, this will purchase £(173.25/1.63) = £106.29. The domestic currency expected return is therefore 6.29%.

It should be noted from this example that there is always some residual risk from hedging. In this case, the whole of the expected value of the portfolio has been hedged. If the portfolio underperformed expectations, the fund manager would have to make a forward purchase of sterling and immediate spot sale on which a profit or loss could arise. A more usual approach would be to hedge the current value of the equity portfolio (or depending on the currency strategy that had been determined, only part of the value). In this case, a residual exchange rate risk would remain.

(b) Using the strategy in (a) the fund manager has made a positive expected return over the period. It is also notable that a positive currency return has been made because of the forward discount that exists from purchasing sterling with dollars. However, the fund would still have been "better off" not hedging. If the fund had not hedged, the sterling value would have been:

$$£(173.25/1.5) = £115.5$$

thus giving rise to a 15.5% return. The success of hedging should be judged against the "opportunity cost" of not hedging.

   Examining this transaction more closely we can gain an interesting insight into the risks of hedging an equity portfolio, as a result of complicating the financial nature of the asset. The assumptions we make here are unrealistic but are useful in illustrating the point. Assume that purchasing power parity theory held over the short timescale of this investment. Assume therefore that the spot exchange rate change was caused by unanticipated UK inflation. Hedging through the forward market prevented the investor gaining protection from the falling purchasing value of sterling by fixing the rate at which dollars were to be exchanged for sterling. Hedged foreign equity investments are no longer a "real" asset.

REFERENCES

Argy, V. (1981), *The Post War International Money Crisis*, George Allen and Unwin.
Davis, E.P. and Steil, B. (2001), *Institutional Investors*, MIT Press.
Fisher, I. (1930), *The Theory of Interest*, Macmillan.
Lofthouse, S. (2001), *Investment Management*, John Wiley & Sons.
Pilbeam, K. (1998), *International Finance*, Macmillan.
Solnik, B.H. (1999), *International Investments*, Addison-Wesley.

7
Derivative Securities

7.1 INTRODUCTION

Derivative securities are financial instruments with a value dependent on the value of some other, underlying asset. They enable market operators to increase or reduce exposure to a market for a relatively modest outlay. The market in the underlying asset (on which the derivative security is based) is known as the *cash market*.

The best-known derivative securities are *futures* and *options*. These are actively traded on many exchanges throughout the world. *Forward contracts*, *swaps* and a variety of other option contracts are traded outside exchanges in *over-the-counter* markets.

Consideration is given to simple models for valuing forward and futures contracts. The essential differences between forward and futures contracts are discussed briefly and a general formula for theoretical pricing of forwards and futures is derived. Special attention is given to so-called *basis* relationships and to practical considerations in relation to index futures and bond futures.

Simple models for pricing swap contracts are also discussed in this chapter but consideration of option pricing models is deferred until Chapter 16. Readers could also consult specialist derivative texts such as those by Hull (2002) or Kolb (2003).

7.2 FORWARD AND FUTURES CONTRACTS

A forward contract is a legally binding contract to deliver/take delivery of a given quantity of an underlying asset at a fixed price on a specified future date. The contract is usually made between two financial institutions, or between a financial institution and one of its clients. It is a contract which is tailored to meet the needs of the two parties making the contract, and would not usually be traded on an exchange.

A futures contract is very similar to a forward contract in that it is a legally binding contract to deliver/take delivery of a given quantity of an underlying asset at a fixed price on a specified future date. In contrast to forward contracts, futures contracts are usually traded on an exchange which, by necessity, is properly regulated. For trading to be possible, futures contracts need to be standardised in terms of certain underlying features, such as the size of one contract, the delivery date and, in the case of commodities, the quality of the underlying asset. The underlying asset of a futures contract may be a commodity or a financial asset. There are many types of commodity, for example gold, wool and live cattle; types of financial asset include share indices, bonds and currencies.

A major difference between forward and futures contracts is the way in which settlement takes place. With forward contracts, settlement occurs entirely at maturity. With futures contracts, there is a *marking to market*, or daily settlement. The investor is required to place a deposit in a *margin account*. The amount that must be deposited at the time the contract is made is known as the *initial margin*. At the end of each trading day, the margin account is adjusted to reflect the gain or loss made by the investor based on the day's change in the futures price. The investor is entitled to withdraw any balance in the margin account in excess of the initial margin, and may be required to top up the margin account if it falls below a certain level, called the *maintenance margin*. Generally, interest is earned on the balance in the margin account.

Another difference between forwards and futures is that for most futures contracts, delivery of the underlying asset is not actually made. The holder of the contract usually closes the position prior to maturity by entering into an offsetting contract with the same delivery date as the original contract. All future cash flows therefore cancel each other out and the profit or loss to the investor is the difference between the futures price at the time the contract was taken out and the price of the future at the time the position was closed. With forward contracts, delivery is usually carried out in accordance with the terms of the contract.

7.2.1 Pricing of Forwards and Futures

The inherent similarity between forward and futures contracts means that they are normally considered to be the same in deriving valuation formulae for use in practice. The theoretical relationship between forward and futures prices was investigated independently by Cox, Ingersoll and Ross (1981) and by Jarrow and Oldfield (1981). Their results show that theoretical forward and futures prices are the same if interest rates are constant and the same for all maturities. If interest rates are variable, theoretical forward and futures prices are no longer the same. However, the differences between theoretical prices of forwards and futures are small enough to be ignored in most circumstances. Empirical research is consistent with this stance.

In this chapter, we assume that forward and futures prices are the same. We shall focus attention on forward prices, which are easier to derive since settlement occurs entirely at maturity. Some of the forward contracts considered are notional contracts in that they would not usually exist in practice, but they are useful in deriving theoretical pricing formulae.

In deriving simple valuation formulae, it is necessary to make the following assumptions: no transaction costs, no taxation, interest rates are constant and the same for borrowers and lenders.

When a forward contract is initiated, the forward price is, *by definition*, the delivery price which would make the contract have zero value, where the delivery price is the amount which must be paid upon settlement of the contract. The contract, when initiated, has the same value to both parties in the contract.

Let the time when the contract is initiated be t, the time when the contract is settled be T, the forward price at time t be F_t, and the price of the underlying asset at time t be S_t. Also, let the *risk-free* rate of interest be i, where the risk-free rate of interest is the annual redemption yield on a notional default-free bond of similar duration to the life of the forward contract. If the duration of the contract is short, the rate of interest on a Treasury Bill or similar security might be used.

7.2.2 Forward Pricing on a Security Paying no Income

Initially consider the forward price of an asset paying no income during the life of the forward contract. Consider two investors, A and B, at time t. Investor A holds one security, worth S_t. Investor B takes out a forward contract with investor A on the same security. An agreement is made between A and B that B takes delivery of the security at time T at the forward price F_t. To finance this, investor B sets aside an amount X at the risk-free rate, i, to accumulate to value F_t, at time T. Therefore, $X = F_t/(1 + i)^\tau$ where $\tau = T - t$, measured in years.

By definition, the contract has the same value to both A and B at time t. Therefore

$$S_t = \frac{F_t}{(1 + i)^\tau} \tag{7.1}$$

From equation (7.1), we see that the contract has zero value when it is initiated, since

$$S_t = \frac{F_t}{(1 + i)^\tau} = 0$$

Re-arranging equation (7.1),

$$F_t = S_t(1 + i)^\tau \tag{7.2}$$

Equation (7.2) gives the forward (or futures) price at time t for a contract maturing at time T on an asset paying no income over the life of the contract, given that the underlying asset is worth S_t at time t. This is a simple formula, showing that the forward (or futures) price at time t is simply the value of the underlying asset at time t accumulated at the risk-free rate of interest i.

It is important to realise that once the contract has been initiated, the delivery price is fixed and is equal to the forward price at the time the contract was initiated. The profit (or loss) to the party in the contract taking delivery of the asset is the difference between the underlying security price at the settlement date and the delivery price. If the value of the underlying asset at the settlement date is S_T, the settlement profit is $S_T - F_t$.

The forward price itself changes over time to reflect changes in the value of the underlying security and the effect of the passage of time on the accumulation factor $(1 + i)^\tau$. Consider time $t + \Delta t$, where $t + \Delta t$ is some time after t but before T. The theoretical forward price for a new contract initiated at time $t + \Delta t$ with the same maturity time T, using equation (7.2), is given by

$$F_{t + \Delta t} = S_{t + \Delta t}(1 + i)^{T - (t + \Delta t)} \tag{7.3}$$

The settlement profit or loss on this new contract at the settlement date T is given by $S_T - F_{t + \Delta t}$. $F_{t + \Delta t}$ will not equal F_t, except by chance.

Equation (7.3) shows that the forward (or futures) price converges on the underlying asset price with the passage of time. As $t + \Delta t$ approaches T, $T - (t + \Delta t)$ tends towards zero, $(1 + i)^{T - (t + \Delta t)}$ tends towards 1 and $F_{t + \Delta t}$ tends towards S_T. This is conceptually obvious. A forward contract initiated one week before the settlement date will be priced close to the price of the underlying asset. The price of a notional forward contract initiated one day prior to the settlement date will be (almost) identical to the price of the underlying asset.

If equation (7.2) is used to value a futures contract, the difference between $F_{t+\Delta t}$, and F_t is used as the theoretical basis for changes in the margin account over the period from t to $t + \Delta t$. At time T, we know from equation (7.3) that $F_T = S_T$; therefore, the overall change in the margin account since inception is equal to $S_T - F_t$.

Example 7.1

XYZ stock is currently trading at 300 pence.

(a) What is the theoretical price of a futures contract on this stock with a settlement date in 180 days' time if no dividends are payable on the stock over the next 6 months and the risk-free interest rate is 8% *per annum?*
(b) Suppose that after 50 days, the stock price has risen to 308 pence and the risk-free interest rate has remained unchanged. Calculate the theoretical change in the margin account for an investor holding the futures contract specified in part (a) over the 50-day period.

Answer

(a) From the information given, $S_t = 300$, $i = 0.08$ and $\tau = 180/365$ years. Using equation (7.2):

$$F_t = 300(1.08)^{180/365}$$

$$= 311.60 \text{ pence (to 2 decimal places)}$$

The theoretical futures price is therefore 312 pence per share (to the nearest penny).
(b) After 50 days, there are 130 days remaining before settlement, and the theoretical futures price of a contract initiated at time $t + 50$ days is given by

$$F_t = 308(1.08)^{130/365}$$

$$= 316.56 \text{ pence (to 2 decimal places)}$$

The theoretical change in the margin account is the difference between the theoretical futures price at time $t + 50$ days and the theoretical futures price at time t. Hence the theoretical change in the margin account is $316.56 - 311.60$ pence per share, that is $+4.96$ pence per share.

7.2.3 Forward Pricing on a Security Paying a Known Cash Income

Consider a forward contract on a security making known cash payments over the life of the contract. The cash payments may be coupon payments in the case of bonds or dividend payments in the case of shares. Suppose that over the life of the forward contract there are two cash payments c_1 and c_2 at times t_1 and t_2 respectively. Equation (7.2) is adjusted to allow for cash income by replacing the current underlying asset price, S_t, by S_t^*, where S_t^* is the current price of the asset less the discounted value of known cash payments payable over the life of the contract. That is,

$$S_t^* = S_t - \frac{c_1}{(1+i)^{\tau_1}} - \frac{c_2}{(1+i)^{\tau_2}} \tag{7.4}$$

where $\tau_1 = t_1 - t$
            $\tau_2 = t_2 - t$
            i = risk-free rate of interest

This approach is justifiable since the holder of the forward contract will not receive the cash income payable on the underlying security over the life of the contract.

Replacing S_t by S_t^* in equation (7.2) gives

$$F_t = \left(S_t - \frac{c_1}{(1+i)^{\tau_1}} - \frac{c_2}{(1+i)^{\tau_2}} \right)(1+i)^\tau \qquad (7.5)$$

Equation (7.5) gives the theoretical forward (or futures) price at time t of an asset paying two known cash payments c_1 and c_2 at times t_1 and t_2 over the life of the contract. It is important to remember that a cash payment is included in the calculations only if the payment date occurs during the life of the contract. If there are no cash payments over the life of the contract, then c_1 and c_2 both equal zero and equation (7.5) reduces to equation (7.2). The equation can be generalised to allow for more than two cash payments over the life of the contract. Suppose that there are n payments c_1, c_2, ..., c_n at times t_1, t_2, ..., t_n respectively. Then

$$S_t^* = S_t - \sum_{j=1}^{n} \frac{c_j}{(1+i)^{\tau_j}}$$

and

$$F_t = \left(S_t - \sum_{j=1}^{n} \frac{c_j}{(1+i)^{\tau_j}} \right)(1+i)^\tau \qquad (7.6)$$

Equation (7.6) gives a general formula for valuing forward or futures contracts on a security providing a known cash income.

Example 7.2

ABC stock is currently trading at 230 pence per share. A dividend payment of 10 pence is expected in 35 days' time, together with another dividend payment of 12 pence after a further 180 days. Calculate the theoretical price of a futures contract on this stock with a settlement date in 250 days' time if the risk-free rate of interest is 9% *per annum*.

Answer

From the information given,

$$S_t = 230 \qquad \tau = \frac{250}{365}$$

$$c_1 = 10 \qquad \tau_1 = \frac{35}{365}$$

$$c_2 = 12 \qquad \tau_2 = \frac{35 + 180}{365} = \frac{215}{365}$$

Using equation (7.5)

$$F_t = \left(230 - \frac{10}{(1.09)^{35/365}} - \frac{12}{(1.09)^{215/365}} \right)(1.09)^{250/365}$$

$$= 221.36 \text{ pence (to 2 decimal places)}$$

The theoretical futures price is therefore 221 pence per share (to the nearest penny).

7.2.4 Forward Pricing on Assets Requiring Storage

Certain commodities, for example gold and silver, may incur costs for the time that the commodity is stored prior to delivery at the settlement date of the contract. Theoretical pricing models for forward contracts can easily be adjusted to accommodate storage costs by treating the costs as *negative* income. In equation (7.6), cash income was allowed for by *reducing* the current value of the underlying asset by the present value of income received over the life of the contract. By treating storage costs as negative income, storage costs are allowed for by *increasing* the current value of the underlying asset by the present value of storage costs paid over the life of the contract. Suppose there are m storage costs $e_1, e_2, ..., e_m$ payable at times $d_1, d_2, ..., d_m$ respectively. Then the theoretical price of a forward contract on an underlying asset requiring storage is given by

$$F_t = \left(S_t + \sum_{k=1}^{m} \frac{e_k}{(1+i)^{\delta_k}} \right)(1+i)^\tau \tag{7.7}$$

where $\delta_k = d_k - t$.

Equation (7.7) is analogous to equation (7.6), except that the storage costs are considered as negative income. Notice that if there are no storage costs payable over the life of the contract, $e_k = 0$ for all k and equation (7.7) reduces to equation (7.2).

Consider a forward contract on a notional security paying cash income and incurring storage costs over the life of the contract. The theoretical forward price at time t is then given by

$$F_t = \left(S_t - \sum_{j=1}^{n} \frac{c_j}{(1+i)^{\tau_j}} + \sum_{k=1}^{m} \frac{e_k}{(1+i)^{\delta_k}} \right)(1+i)^\tau \tag{7.8}$$

where all symbols have been defined previously. Equation (7.8) is the most general formula for calculating the theoretical price of a forward or futures contract, assuming there are no transaction costs or taxes, and that interest rates are constant and the same for borrowers and lenders.

7.2.5 Stock Index Futures

Futures contracts are available on a variety of stock indices, for example the FT-SE 100, S&P 100, S&P 500 and NYSE indices (see Chapter 13). Futures contracts on stock indices are entirely cash settled. They can be considered as a contract to deliver/take delivery of the value of a basket of shares at a fixed price on a specified future date. Dividends payable on this basket of shares over the life of the contract need to be considered when deriving a theoretical index futures price. Theoretically, the present value of each dividend payment in terms of index points needs to be deducted from the current index level before accumulating at the risk-free rate of interest for a period of time equal to the life of the contract. Adjusting for dividends by calculating the present value of all dividends due to be paid may be difficult in practice and often a much simpler approach is adopted. For example, the London International Financial Futures Exchange (LIFFE) recommends the following formula for calculating the theoretical price at time t for the FT-SE 100 stock index future:

$$F_t = I_t \left(1 + \frac{i\tau}{365} \right) - I_t y \, \frac{d^*}{d} \tag{7.9}$$

where
F_t = theoretical futures price at time t
I_t = index level at time t
i = risk-free rate of interest
τ = number of days until settlement
y = annual dividend yield on FT-SE 100 index
d^* = dividend payments expected between time t and the settlement date
d = total dividend payments expected over the year ending on the settlement date

Equation (7.9) has a simple interpretation. The first part of the theoretical price, $I_t(1 + i\tau/365)$, represents the accumulated value of the index at the risk-free rate of interest, based on *simple* interest calculations. The second part of the theoretical price, $I_t y d^*/d$, represents the value of dividends expected between time t and the settlement date, expressed in terms of index points. Equation (7.9) therefore incorporates two simplifications. These are:

(i) simple interest methodology is used, rather than compound interest methodology;
(ii) dividends are not accumulated to the appropriate time.

Practitioners occasionally tailor equation (7.9) to suit their own requirements. For example, some practitioners assume that dividends are paid as a continuous stream and adjust equation (7.9) by incorporating a constant *dividend yield per annum*.

7.2.6   Basis Relationships

Futures traders often speak of *basis* relationships. Basis relationships are the relationships between the theoretical futures price, the actual futures price in the market and the market value of the asset underlying the contract. There are three types of basis: *simple* basis, *theoretical* basis and *value* basis.

Simple basis, also known as *crude* basis, is the difference between the value of the underlying asset in the market and the market price of the futures contract. Denoting the actual price of the futures contract in the market by $^A F_T$ and the market value of the asset underlying the contract by S_t, then

$$\text{Simple basis} = S_t - {}^A F_t \tag{7.10}$$

Theoretical basis is the difference between the value of the underlying asset in the market and the theoretical futures price. Denoting the theoretical futures price by F_t,

$$\text{Theoretical basis} = S_t - F_t \tag{7.11}$$

Value basis is the difference between the actual price of the futures contract quoted in the market and the theoretical futures price. That is,

$$\text{Value basis} = {}^A F_t - F_t \tag{7.12}$$

From equations (7.10), (7.11) and (7.12) we see that

$$\text{Simple basis} + \text{Value basis} = \text{Theoretical basis}$$

Basis relationships are used by traders to monitor the market and identify trading opportunities and strategies. It should be noted that as the settlement date of the contract approaches, all three basis relationships converge to zero.

7.2.7 Bond Futures

Bond futures contracts exist in a number of markets, including US, UK and Japanese government bonds. These contracts show some distinct differences from equity futures. First, each contract is not on a bond index, but on a notional bond (e.g. a 4% US Treasury Bond or a 5% Gilt). Second, delivery, when made, is in the form of physical bonds, rather than cash. For each futures contract, delivery of any bond within a specified maturity area can be made.

The seller of a future may deliver any one of the deliverable bonds, and will wish to determine which bond should be delivered by calculating which bond is *cheapest to deliver*.

Deliverable bonds cover a specified maturity zone and a wide range of coupon possibilities. *Price factors* provide a basis for comparison of different deliverable bonds. On delivery, the settlement amount, paid by the buyer of the future, is

(Bond futures price × price factor) + accrued interest

Price factors, which are officially calculated by the futures exchange, are in fact the discounted values of outstanding interest and capital payments, at the same rate of interest as the coupon rate on the notional bond (e.g. 9% *per annum* for UK Gilts).

For each deliverable bond, it is then possible to calculate

Clean bond price − (bond futures price × price factor)

In bond markets, this is known as the *gross basis*. It is analogous to the simple basis used in connection with equity futures contracts.

In practice, dealers also look at the *net basis*. This is the calculated profit or loss resulting from an arbitrage deal in which an investor buys a deliverable bond now, financing this purchase by borrowing at the *actual repo rate*, sells the bond future now, and subsequently delivering the bond against the future. The *actual repo rate* is the actual money market borrowing rate. In the calculations, the cost of futures margins is ignored. The *net basis* has some similarities to the *value basis* used in connection with equity futures contracts.

The *net basis* is calculated for each deliverable bond. The deliverable bonds can then be listed in order of the largest profit (or smallest loss). The bond at the top of the list is known as the *cheapest deliverable bond* and is likely to be the bond delivered by the seller of the futures contract at settlement.

A final statistic much used in connection with bond futures is the *implied repo rate*. This is calculated by determining the rate of interest at which the arbitrage trades discussed above produce zero profit.

Example 7.3

On 17 June 2002, the market price of the September German euro-Bobl future traded on the EUREX was €105.67 per €100 nominal, with a delivery date of 10 September 2002. Also on 17 June 2002, the market price (*clean price*) of the Bund 4% maturing on 7 February 2007 was €97.71 per €100 nominal for normal settlement two days later on 19 June 2002. If the official conversion factor of the Bund 4%, 7 February 2007, is 0.923400 and the shortest-term money market borrowing rate (actual repo rate) is 3.4625%, calculate (a) the *gross basis*; (b) the *net basis*; (c) the *implied repo rate*.

Answer

(a) The *gross basis* is simply:

$$\text{Clean price} - (\text{bond futures price} \times \text{conversion factor})$$

$$= 97.71 - (105.67 \times 0.923400)$$

$$= 0.134 \text{ (to 3 decimal places)}$$

(b) Consider buying the deliverable bond (Bund 4%, 2007) and financing this by borrowing at the *actual repo rate*. The total price of the bond is the clean price plus any accrued interest payable. By convention accrued interest is calculated using simple interest methodology. The number of days from the last coupon payment date (7 February 2002) to the settlement date (20 June 2002) is 133 days (Actual/Actual convention). Therefore, the accrued interest is:

$$\text{Accrued interest per } €100 \text{ nominal} = 100 \times 0.04 \times 133/365 = 1.458$$

This gives:

$$\text{Total price of the bond (\textit{dirty price})} = 97.71 + 1.458 = 99.168$$

The bond is held until delivery on 10 September 2002, after a further 82 days. By convention, euro interest rates are computed on a simple interest basis, dividing the actual number of days (here 82) by a notional 360 days in the year (Actual/360 convention). Therefore, the cost of borrowing, at the *actual repo rate*, to finance the purchase of the bond is:

$$99.168 \times 0.034625 \times 82/360 = 0.782$$

which is called the *cost of carry*. The total cost of purchasing the bond in the arbitrage transaction is:

$$\text{Dirty price (namely, market price + accrued interest) + cost of carry}$$

$$= 99.168 + 0.782$$

$$= 99.950$$

Now consider the settlement amount received in respect of delivery of the futures contract. The settlement price is:

(Deliverable bond price × conversion factor) + accrued interest

The time between the last coupon payment date and 10 September 2002 is 215 days, therefore:

Accrued interest on delivery date, per €100 nominal

$$= 100 \times 0.04 \times 215/365 = 2.356$$

And the futures contract settlement amount is:

$$105.67 \times 0.923400 + 2.356 = 99.932$$

The *net basis* is the profit or loss from the arbitrage transaction. That is,

$$Net\ basis = 99.932 - 99.950 = -0.018$$

The negative sign indicates that the arbitrage transaction incurs a loss.

(c) The *implied repo rate* is the rate of interest used to calculate the cost of borrowing for which the *net basis* equals zero. If the *implied repo rate* is i, then:

$$99.932 - (99.168 + cost\ of\ carry\ \text{at rate } i) = 0$$

That is,

$$99.932 - (99.168 + 99.168 \times i \times 82/360) = 0$$

giving $i = 0.03383$. The *implied repo rate* is therefore 3.38%.

7.3   SWAP CONTRACTS

A *swap* is a negotiated arrangement between two counterparties to exchange cash flows according to a pre-arranged formula. The most common type of swap is a *plain vanilla interest rate swap*, which involves an exchange of fixed payments for payments at a floating rate. The payments are based on a notional principal but only the interest payments are exchanged. We will concentrate on this type of swap. Other swap arrangements include currency swaps, equity swaps and commodity swaps.

Swaps first appeared in significant volume in the early 1980s. Since then, there has been very strong growth in the market for swaps. They are used extensively by trading companies and financial institutions in risk management (see Section 7.3.3) to change market exposure (e.g. to hedge interest rate risk).

7.3.1   Comparative Advantage Argument for Swaps Market

Take two companies, X and Y. If company X has a comparative advantage in the floating rate market, any interest rate premium (spread) it pays in the floating rate market is lower than any interest rate premium it pays in the fixed rate market, relative to company Y. If company Y wishes to borrow at floating rates and X at fixed rates, it would be more efficient for X to borrow at floating rates and Y at fixed rates and then conduct a swap (see Hull, 2002).

For example, suppose company Y wishes to borrow at a floating rate linked to three months London interbank offered rate (LIBOR) and company X wishes to borrow at a fixed rate for ten years. The efficient swap would involve Y borrowing at a fixed rate for ten years and X borrowing at a rate linked to three months LIBOR. They could do a swap arrangement whereby X agreed to pay Y a fixed rate (thus offsetting Y's borrowing commitments and exposing X to making a set of fixed payments). Y would agree to pay X a floating rate linked to LIBOR. This would offset X's borrowing commitment and commit Y to a series of LIBOR linked payments. This arrangement would be efficient because X and Y would be borrowing in their relatively cheapest markets and then exchanging. Any gains would be split.

A financial intermediary, such as a bank, usually arranges the swap. It aims to make a profit through the bid–ask spread and possibly a brokerage fee. The intermediary would make a separate swap arrangement with companies X and Y. For example, the arrangement between the intermediary and X would involve the intermediary paying X a floating rate and X paying the intermediary a fixed rate. The intermediary would pay Y a fixed rate and Y would pay the intermediary a floating rate. X and Y have both offset their payments, as required, and the intermediary has offset its position.[1] The risk to X and Y no longer depends on the solvency of each other but the solvency of the intermediary. X does not even need to know that Y exists and vice versa.

It may appear that swaps are always advantageous when there is comparative advantage. However, this is not necessarily the case. Why might X be paying a higher premium in the fixed rate market than in the floating rate market? A possible reason is that X is a risky client and thus has an apparent advantage in the floating rate market because the lender would be able to re-assess the credit risk every so often and change the terms of the loan. That risk does not disappear under the swap arrangement. The risk of the floating rate at which X can borrow being increased more than the floating rate agreed in the swap is still borne by X. If that happens, X will receive the floating payments from Y at a lower rate than X will pay them to the institution from which it has borrowed. If an intermediary is involved, any increase in the costs of borrowing at floating rates will still be borne by X. However, the intermediary would have a credit risk if market interest rates were such that the swap had a positive value. For example, if X paid floating and received fixed, market interest rates rose and then X defaulted, this would result in a loss to the intermediary.

7.3.2   Pricing Interest Rate Swap Contracts

When an interest rate swap agreement is negotiated, the net present value of the swap is approximately zero. In time, however, the swap can have either a positive value or a negative value, depending on the movement in interest rates.

The most common method for valuing an interest rate swap is to treat it as a long position in one bond combined with a short position in another bond. Suppose that the

---

[1] The intermediary incurs considerable interest rate risk if it does not offset its position. The intermediary retains both sides' credit risk throughout the life of the transaction.

swap arrangement is such that fixed payments are made at the same times as floating rate payments are received. Then we need to value a fixed-interest bond and take away the value of a floating-rate note. Valuation of the fixed-interest bond is straightforward if we are given the appropriate spot rates (see Section 2.20). If the fixed payments of f are made t_j years from now ($1 \leqslant j \leqslant n$), the value of the fixed-interest bond, B, is

$$B = \sum_{j=1}^{n} \frac{f}{(1 + {}_0i_{t_j})^{t_j}} + \frac{R}{(1 + {}_0i_{t_n})^{t_n}} \tag{7.13}$$

where ${}_0i_{t_j}$ is the annual spot rate between now and t_j years in the future and R is the notional principal involved in the agreement.

Immediately after a floating-rate payment, the value of the floating-rate payments is equal to the notional principal, R. Between payment dates, with the period before the next floating rate payment t_1 years away, the value of the floating-rate payments is simply the discounted amount of the nominal principal and the floating-rate payment, w. Thus, the value of the floating-rate note, N, is:

$$N = \frac{R + w}{(1 + {}_0i_{t_1})^{t_1}} \tag{7.14}$$

The value of the swap, S, is simply $B - N$. Thus, using equations (7.13) and (7.14),

$$S = \sum_{j=1}^{n} \frac{f}{(1 + {}_0i_{t_j})^{t_j}} + \frac{R}{(1 + {}_0i_{t_n})^{t_n}} - \frac{R + w}{(1 + {}_0i_{t_1})^{t_1}} \tag{7.15}$$

Example 7.4

Under the terms of a swap agreement, a company agreed to pay a floating rate and receive a fixed rate of 5.1% per annum, payable annually. The notional principal involved is $100 and the outstanding term of the swap is now exactly three years. The relevant spot rates for one, two and three years are now 5.250%, 5.378% and 5.642% respectively. Calculate the present value of the swap.

Answer

The present value of the fixed interest bond is:

$$\frac{5.1}{1.05250} + \frac{5.1}{(1.05378)^2} + \frac{105.1}{(1.05642)^3} = \$98.583$$

The present value of the floating rate note is simply $100 (because $w = 0$). Hence the present value of the swap $= -\$1.417$.

7.3.3   Using Swaps in Risk Management

Many commercial and industrial companies are subject to interest rate risk. For example, they may have borrowed at variable rates and are vulnerable to increases in short-term interest rates. By entering into a swap arrangement to receive variable-rate payments and pay fixed payments, such companies can obtain protection against changes in interest rates.

Swaps can also be used by a financial institution to change market exposure (e.g. change the duration of a fixed interest portfolio) in the same way as futures. For example, the holder of a long duration portfolio could reduce duration by agreeing to pay fixed and receive floating. The holder of a short duration portfolio could lengthen the duration by agreeing to pay floating and receive fixed. The portfolio duration can be lengthened considerably in this way (as with futures) as it is not necessary to have the cash that would be necessary to purchase the long securities.

7.4 OPTION CONTRACTS

An *option* is the right to buy (or to sell) a specified amount of an underlying asset at a fixed price (the *exercise price*) on (or before)[2] a specified date (the *expiry or expiration date*). Thus, an option is a right but *not* an obligation whereas a future is a right *and* an obligation. A *call* option gives the holder the right to buy. A *put* option gives the holder the right to sell.

Traded options give holders the choice of selling the option itself in an organised market. Thus, traded options may be:

(a) freely traded, quite independently of the underlying asset to which they relate;
(b) exercised i.e. the underlying asset may be purchased (or sold) at the fixed price;
(c) abandoned, to expire worthless with no delivery of the underlying asset taking place.

The market price of an option is often known as the *premium*. This is determined by the forces of supply and demand. Options are traded in standard units called *contracts*, say, for 100 shares.

A call option is described as *in-the-money* if the underlying asset price is above the exercise price (so that the option would be exercised if the asset price remained unchanged). If the underlying asset price is below the exercise price, a call option is *out-of-the-money*, as the holder would not exercise the option if the asset price remained at this level until expiry.

Put options are *out-of-the-money* when the underlying asset price is above the exercise price (because if the asset price remained unchanged until expiry, it would be better to sell the stock in the market). Put options are *in-the-money* when the asset price is below the exercise price (so that the option would be exercised if the asset price remained unchanged).

An investor who opens a position by selling a traded option is termed the *writer* of the option. The maximum profit to be made by an option writer is simply the premium received.

---

[2] An *American-style* option is continuously exercisable throughout its life. A *European-style* option may be exercised only on a specified date. These names are somewhat confusing because both American options and European options are traded in both Europe and America.

7.4.1   Payoff Diagrams for Options

Figure 7.1 shows the profit/loss (ignoring expenses) at expiry to a call option
holder against the underlying asset price at expiry. As it is possible for the share
price to rise to any level above the exercise price, the potential profit for a buyer is
unlimited. Ignoring expenses, a buyer breaks even if the asset price at expiry equals
the exercise price plus the premium paid. A buyer cannot lose more than the
premium paid.

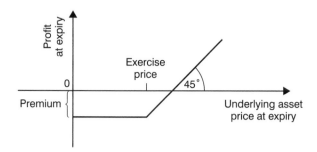

Figure 7.1   Profit/loss at expiry for a call option holder

As can be seen from Figure 7.2, the profit/loss diagram for the writer of a call option
is an inverted version of that for a call option holder. That is, it is the mirror image with
the mirror along the x-axis. For naked call writing (i.e. where the writer does not own
the underlying asset), the maximum loss is unlimited.

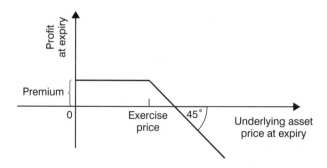

Figure 7.2   Profit/loss at expiry for a call option writer

Figure 7.3 shows the profit/loss at expiry for a put option holder. Ignoring expenses,
the buyer cannot lose more than the premium paid and cannot gain more than the
exercise price less the premium paid.

Again, the profit/loss diagram shown in Figure 7.4 for the writer of a put option is
an inverted version of that for a put option holder. The maximum loss is equal to the
exercise price less the premium (plus any expenses).

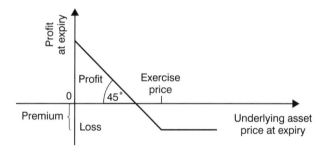

Figure 7.3   Profit/loss at expiry for a put option holder

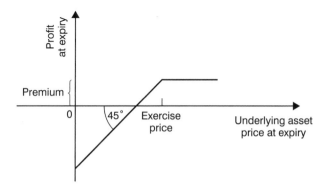

Figure 7.4   Profit/loss at expiry for a put option writer

7.4.2   Intrinsic Value and Time Value

An option price (premium) is made up of two parts — intrinsic value and time value. Splitting the value in this way is useful in discussing the factors that affect option prices.

The *intrinsic value* of an option is the difference between the underlying asset price and the exercise price for an in-the-money option. It is the benefit that could be obtained from exercising the option, if it could be exercised now. The intrinsic value of a call option is the amount by which the asset price exceeds the exercise price. For example, if the asset price is 217p and the exercise price of a call option is 200p, the intrinsic value is 17p. If a call option on the same asset had an exercise price of 220p, there would be no intrinsic value. A put option, on the other hand, has intrinsic value if the option exercise price is above the asset price; otherwise the intrinsic value is zero.

An option has *time value* because there is always a benefit in holding an option. Even if it is out-of-the-money, the asset price may change so that the option can be exercised favourably. If an option is in-the-money, it has a time value over and above the intrinsic value. In the case of a call option, for example, a rise in the asset price will benefit the investor (who can buy at a fixed price). A fall in the asset price is to the detriment of the investor only insofar as the asset price falls whilst being above the exercise price.

We know that:

$$\text{option price} = \text{intrinsic value} + \text{time value}$$

Thus:

$$\text{time value} = \text{option price} - \text{intrinsic value}$$

and we can take this as the definition of time value.

If the underlying asset price and other factors (e.g. volatility) remain unchanged, the time value of the option will gradually decrease until, at expiry, the time value is zero.

7.4.3 Factors Affecting Option Prices

A number of models have been formulated to value options, the best known being the Black–Scholes Model and the Binomial Model, which are discussed in Chapter 16. In this section we briefly discuss the factors that affect the value of an option in turn.

- *Exercise price*: This is part of the contract specification and mainly affects the intrinsic value. If the option is in-the-money, the higher the exercise price, the lower the intrinsic value of a call option and the higher the value of a put option.
- *Underlying asset price*: This is rather like the effect of the exercise price. If the underlying asset price is lower for a call option (higher for a put), the option will have a lower intrinsic value for a given exercise price.
- *Time to expiry*: Ignoring certain complications and other things being equal, the longer the time to expiry, the greater the time value. This holds for both calls and puts. The possibility of the underlying asset price rising (or falling) substantially during the outstanding period is greater the more time that remains before expiry. Option holders get the full benefits from favourable outcomes but avoid most of the loss from unfavourable outcomes, since the option may simply be abandoned.
- *Volatility of the underlying asset*: Other things being equal, the higher the volatility of the underlying asset, the higher the option price. This is because higher volatility increases the probability of making large gains whereas any losses are limited. Market operators often regard trading in options as trading in volatility as other variables are either known or easy to predict.
- *Interest rates*: A call option gives the holder exposure to the underlying assets for only a fraction of their full value. The surplus earns interest, and thus the higher the level of interest rates, the higher the call option price. In the case of puts, higher interest rates reduce the value of the option.
- *Income from the underlying asset*: Options do not receive income, so the higher the expected income from the underlying asset before the expiry date, the lower the value of a call option and the higher the value of a put option.

REFERENCES

Adams, A.T. (1989), *Investment*, Chapter 7, Graham & Trotman.
Benninga, S. (2000), *Financial Modeling*, Part III, The MIT Press.
Black, F. (1976), "The Pricing of Commodity Contracts", *Journal of Financial Economics*, 3, 167–79.
Cox, J.C., Ingersoll, J.E. and Ross, S.A. (1981), "The Relation Between Forward Prices and Futures Prices", *Journal of Financial Economics*, 9, 321–46.
Hull, J. (2002), *Options, Futures, and Other Derivative Securities*, Prentice-Hall International.

Jarrow, R.A. and Oldfield, G.S. (1981), "Forward Contracts and Futures Contracts", *Journal of Financial Economics*, 9, 373–82.

Kolb, R.W. (2003), *Futures, Options and Swaps*, Blackwell.

Lofthouse, S. (2001), *Investment Management*, Chapter 21, John Wiley & Sons.

Wilmott, P. (1998), *Derivatives: The Theory and Practice of Financial Engineering*, John Wiley & Sons.

PART II
Statistics for Investment

In Chapters 4 and 5 we discussed relationships between UK government bond yields, index-linked UK government bond yields, equity yields and inflation. In order to produce useful models of such relationships, data relating to these variables are required. In Chapter 12 in Part III we will introduce portfolio theory and the Capital Asset Pricing Model. To apply such models, we require estimates of expected returns, the variance of returns and the correlation between different asset classes. These estimates can be derived from historical data relating to the behaviour of investment variables and the relationships between them. Thus Part II will focus on summarising and presenting data, estimating parameters, testing hypotheses and looking at comovements of variables.

In Chapter 8 we discuss data sources, how data can be presented, and simple statistical measures. Chapter 9 shows how the concepts of probability theory apply to financial mathematics. The expected value of a distribution is discussed and some important probability distributions are introduced. Chapter 10 focuses upon estimating parameters and testing hypotheses. Chapter 11 is concerned with measuring and testing comovements in returns.

8
Describing Investment Data

8.1 INTRODUCTION

We can divide investment data into *cross-section* and *time series* data. For example, the dividend yield on the top 100 quoted companies would provide us with cross-section data. The average market dividend yield, at the close of trade in the UK equity market, on each day for the past ten years would provide a time series. We can calculate statistics to describe both cross-section and time series data (for example, to find the average dividend yield across top 100 quoted companies today, or the average dividend yield at the close of trade over the past ten years). We can also undertake further analysis to find relationships between different variables and to predict future patterns. The use of historical data to predict future patterns will be described in Chapter 17.

In this chapter we will discuss data sources, how data can be presented, and simple statistical measures.

8.2 DATA SOURCES

There are many sources of investment data that can be used in statistical analysis and modelling. Some of these sources are provided by government or quasi-governmental organisations and private sector data providers collate others. *Financial Statistics*, published by National Statistics (see Table 8.1), provides information on price inflation, institutional investment patterns, and so on. The Bank of England produces a statistical abstract with historical data relating to variables such as UK government bond yields, equity yields, exchange rates and short-term interest rates. A long historical study of investment markets has been undertaken by Barclays Global Investors. Each year they produce the results of their analysis in the *Equity Gilt Study*. This contains data relating to equity returns, UK government bond returns and cash returns on various different bases, as well as index levels and dividend yields. In many cases the data series go back to the end of the First World War. International data on variables relevant to investment markets are produced in *International Financial Statistics*, published by IMF (see Table 8.1). The OECD also publish various investment data as does the London Business School.

As we will see in Chapter 15, we often measure the general level of markets by reference to investment indices. FTSE International is a major index compiler and their data can be used to measure changes in equity dividend yields, UK government bond yields and equity and UK government bond market performance over a number of years. Data are also produced for international markets and for subsets of the UK equity market. The best source of information is found on their web page at http://www.ftse.com/. Indices measuring the level and performance of the property market are generally less reliable than their equity counterparts because of inevitable technical issues, such as the absence of any regular, objective measure of the value of properties. The most important UK provider of property indices is the Investment Property Databank (IPD). Their web page can be found at http://propertymall.com/ipdindex/.

Sometimes researchers and analysts have to engage in the laborious task of building up data from disaggregated sources. For example, it might be necessary to look at the average return on capital on a selection of public companies. Hemmington Scott is one source of data on individual companies, which permits free access to some data on their website at http://www.hemscott.com/. Other commercial data sources, such as Datastream or Bloomberg, are available only to subscribers. Away from the World-Wide Web, there are now many sources of data available on CD-ROM.

Examples of data sources and the type of data they provide are given in Table 8.1. Some of the commercial data sources are available at reduced prices for academic research, although data sold on such a basis may be slightly less timely than if the full subscription is paid. Some of the Internet services will also provide a limited service without subscription.

Table 8.1 Financial statistics

Provider	Web address	Type of data
Bloomberg	www.bloomberg.com	Wide range of international financial and investment data
Government Statistics	www.statistics.gov.uk	UK economic and financial statistics
Hemmington Scott	www.hemscott.com	UK company data
IMF	www.imf.org	International economic and financial analysis and statistics
OECD	www.oecd.org	Economic statistics from national accounts of OECD countries
Reuters	www.reuters.com	Business information and news

8.3 SAMPLING AND DATA TYPES

The set of all the data items in which we are interested is called the *population*. For example, if we wanted the average allocation of investment funds to different asset classes for UK pension funds, we would require the population of all UK pension funds. Any subset of the population is called a *sample*. It is not usually practical to perform statistical analyses on an entire population so, instead, a *sample survey* is conducted. The way in which the sample is chosen is very important because, if the sample is unrepresentative of the population, results from it will lack general validity. The results will be *biased*. One unbiased method of selecting a sample is *simple random sampling*. Using this method, every member of the population has an equal chance of being chosen.

Sometimes, it is possible to identify a number of distinct groups within the population, known as strata. Different size pension funds may invest differently from larger funds (for example, small pension funds may find it difficult to invest directly in property). In any sample, it may be desirable to ensure that each stratum is properly represented. *Stratified sampling* may be used to achieve this objective. The population is divided into strata and sub-samples are randomly selected within the strata.

Other types of sampling that are appropriate in particular circumstances include *cluster sampling* and *systematic sampling*.

In addition to considering the most appropriate type of sampling, the survey designer must also decide how large the total sample should be. This decision is constrained by the resources that are available and, furthermore, the designer has to consider the degree of accuracy required. In general, the larger the sample, the more accurate the deductions or *inferences* made about the population. However, the cost of collecting and processing a large amount of data may be more than the value of the information. Stratified sampling tends to lead to large total samples since it is necessary to ensure that each sub-sample is of a reasonable size.

The data which result from sampling may be numerical, such as the number of employees in each branch of a company. This is *quantitative data* and may be further subdivided into *discrete* and *continuous data*. Discrete data can take only a finite number of values, for example, the number of towns in which a company has a branch. A value such as 7.5 simply has no meaning in this context. Continuous data can take any value in a given range, for example, the daily maximum temperature.

Alternatively, data can describe a characteristic of the item or person being sampled, such as employment status. This is known as *categorical data*. Occasionally, categorical data may have numerical values, such as when tasters rank wines in order of preference, but the actual numbers only indicate order, they do not indicate anything about the size of the difference in preference and so the numbers cannot be added or multiplied in the way that ordinary numbers can.

8.4   DATA PRESENTATION

Having collected data, the next step in its analysis is to display it visually. A visual display should summarise the data to make it more manageable, whilst highlighting its main features. The following sections describe two types of tabular display and seven different types of graph. Section 8.4.10 considers some of the ways in which a misleading impression can be given by a poor graph.

8.4.1   Frequency Tables

Suppose that the figures in Table 8.2 represent the growth (% p.a.) of 50 small pension funds during the past year. Annualised growth is a *continuous variable* and the values in Table 8.2 have been quoted to the nearest 0.1%. Looking at the data in this form makes

Table 8.2   Growth (% p.a.) of 50 small pension funds

8.4	4.2	4.7	9.4	13.1	7.3	5.3	14.4	5.2	2.3
1.9	6.0	6.4	15.6	5.7	11.8	7.6	5.7	2.6	11.3
4.6	7.5	13.5	7.7	4.3	6.1	5.6	7.4	2.0	5.5
1.2	14.2	8.8	12.9	6.3	7.3	5.8	9.2	8.3	11.2
9.4	8.0	9.9	3.1	10.6	6.9	10.3	4.9	9.2	12.2

it very difficult to detect any pattern which may exist. Grouping the data in a *frequency table* will be helpful.

First, it is necessary to decide how many groups to use. Condensing the data into too few groups may obscure an important feature, but using too many groups will produce a table which is not much easier to read and interpret than the original data. Usually, between five and ten groups work well, but a large amount of data may need more groups.

Let us group the data in the intervals listed below.

$$0 \leqslant x < 4$$

$$4 \leqslant x < 6$$

$$6 \leqslant x < 8$$

$$8 \leqslant x < 10$$

$$10 \leqslant x < 12$$

$$12 \leqslant x < 14 \text{ and}$$

$$14 \leqslant x < 16\%$$

Defining the boundaries this way means that there is no doubt about which interval an observation belongs to. If we had written the intervals as: 0–4, 4–6, 6–8, etc., it would not have been clear to which interval an observation of 10% belonged. While defining the intervals as 0–3.9, 4–5.9, 6–7.9, etc., would have removed the problem of ambiguity, these intervals are discrete (there are gaps between them) and it is preferable to use continuous intervals for a continuous variable.

Now that the interval boundaries have been defined, each observation can be put into its interval and the frequency in each interval found as in columns (1) and (2) of Table 8.3. Notice that the table has been given a title, this is essential to allow readers to interpret what is displayed.

Frequency tables are suitable for all types of data.

Table 8.3 Frequency table for growth (% p.a.) of 50 small pension funds

(1)	(2)	(3)	(4)	(5)	(6)	(7)
Interval	Frequency	Cumulative frequency	Frequency density	Units	Adjusted frequency density	Adjusted relative frequency
$0 \leqslant x < 4$	6	6	1.5	2	3	0.06
$4 \leqslant x < 6$	12	18	6.0	1	12	0.26
$6 \leqslant x < 8$	11	29	5.5	1	11	0.23
$8 \leqslant x < 10$	9	38	4.5	1	9	0.19
$10 \leqslant x < 12$	5	43	2.5	1	5	0.11
$12 \leqslant x < 14$	4	47	2.0	1	4	0.09
$14 \leqslant x < 16$	3	50	1.5	1	3	0.06
Total	50				Total	1

8.4.2 Cumulative Frequency Tables

Cumulative frequency tables are suitable for discrete and continuous data and show the number of observations below the end (or less commonly above the beginning) of the current interval. This is demonstrated in column (3) of Table 8.3. Column (3) allows us to see, for example, that 29 funds (the majority) reported levels of growth below 8%.

8.4.3 Bar Charts

A *bar chart* is an effective way of displaying *discrete* or *categorical data*. Suppose that you have records showing the number of months in the past three years that each member of a sample of 100 UK higher income funds outperformed the index (see Table 8.4). These data are displayed in the frequency table, Table 8.4. The bar chart, Figure 8.1, is drawn so that the height of each bar represents *frequency*. Notice that the chart has a title and that each axis is labelled. To signify that the data are not continuous, the bars do not touch. A bar chart can be used with grouped data, but the groups (and bars) should be of equal width. Usually the label for each bar is placed at the centre of its base.

Table 8.4 Number of months each member of a sample of 100 UK equity higher income funds outperformed the FTSE 350 High Yield index over the past two years

months	0	1	2	3	4	5	6	7	8
frequency	0	0	0	1	0	2	4	8	12
months	9	10	11	12	13	14	15	16	17
frequency	14	18	15	10	8	3	3	1	0
months	18	19	20	21	22	23	24		
frequency	0	1	0	0	0	0	0	total	100

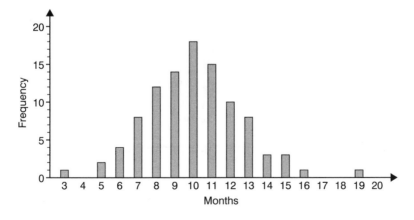

Figure 8.1   Funds outperforming the FTSE 350 High Yield index

The 100 funds could be divided by size and this information incorporated into a *component bar chart*, Figure 8.2. In Figure 8.2 it can be seen that smaller funds exhibit greater variability in performance. However, if there are too many components, the chart becomes difficult to read and a different form of presentation should be used.

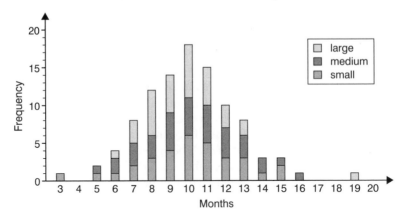

Figure 8.2 Funds outperforming the FTSE 350 High Yield index

One year's performance can be compared with another's using a *multiple bar chart*, Figure 8.3.

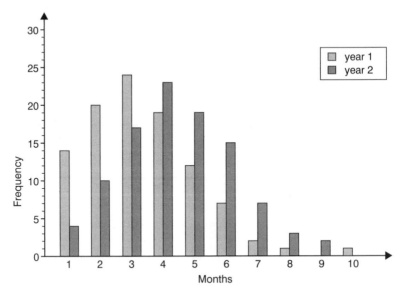

Figure 8.3 Comparison of fund performance, 2001, 2002

8.4.4 Histograms

Sometimes a histogram may appear to be the same as a bar chart, but there are important differences. In a histogram, frequency is represented by *area* rather than by

---

Excel Application 8.1

Bar charts can be constructed easily using the chart wizard within the insert pull-down menu.

Figure 8.1

- Enter the frequencies from Table 8.4 you wish to graph into the Excel spreadsheet.
- Select Chart ... from the Insert menu.
- Select chart type "column" and subtype "clustered column".
- Identify whether frequencies are listed in a column or a row, then identify the range of cells.
- The chart wizard expects two series of frequencies, but this figure only requires one so the range given included an adjacent blank row.
- Work through the chart options page of the wizard adding or removing labels, gridlines, etc. until the desired appearance is achieved. This can always be edited later by using the Chart pull-down menu and selecting Chart Options.
- Finally, decide whether to save your chart as an object within your spreadsheet or as a separate chart attached to the sheet.
- Subsequent editing may be undertaken via the Chart pull-down menu or by double clicking on a particular feature within the chart.

Figure 8.2

- Select chart sub-type Stacked Column from the chart wizard.
- When defining the data ranges for your three series it is useful to include the column heading cells from your Excel spreadsheet. The wizard then automatically selects these as series labels within the legend or key.

Figure 8.3

- As for Figure 8.1, select chart sub-type clustered column.
- As for Figure 8.2, include heading cells in data range to provide series labels.

---

height. For this reason it is not necessary to have intervals of equal width. Also, histograms nearly always depict continuous data, so the rectangles are drawn touching each other to signify the continuous horizontal scale. Figure 8.4 is a histogram of the data in Table 8.3.

Notice that the vertical scale of Figure 8.4 is *frequency density*; this is because in the histogram, area equals frequency. For example, the second rectangle has height 6 and the length of its base is 2 (since area of a rectangle = base × height).

$$\text{Frequency density} = \frac{\text{frequency}}{\text{class width}}$$

Calculating frequency density produces fractions which may not be convenient to work with. An alternative which leads to fewer fractions is to decide on a *standard class width* and call this one unit. Adjusted frequencies are then calculated by dividing by the number of standard units in each interval. This is shown in columns (5) and (6) of Table 8.3, using 2 as the standard class width.

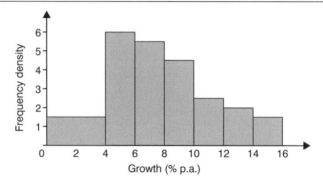

Figure 8.4   Histogram of growth of 50 small pension funds

The importance of using a relative frequency measure, rather than using actual frequencies is shown by Figure 8.5, which is unadjusted. The first, wide rectangle gives a visual impression of more low performing funds than were actually observed.

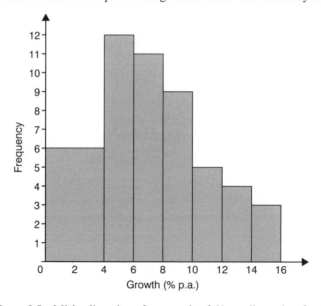

Figure 8.5   Misleading chart for growth of 50 small pension funds

Histograms representing different total frequencies are difficult to compare because the graphs have different areas. The solution is to scale the histograms so that each has a total *area* of one unit. This involves calculating relative frequencies and also making any necessary adjustments for unequal class widths (column (7), Table 8.3).

The dotted lines on the adjusted relative frequency histogram, Figure 8.6, join the midpoints of the tops of the rectangles. They meet the axis half a standard class width from the end of the last rectangle on each side. The shape thus formed is called a *frequency polygon*. Imagine collecting more and more data and therefore splitting it into narrower and narrower intervals; eventually the lines joining the points in the frequency polygon would become very short and would begin to look like a single curve

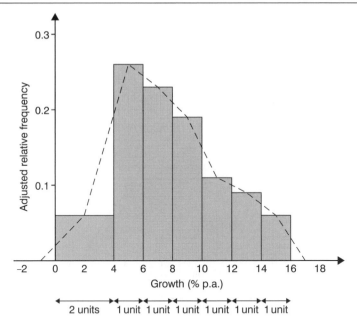

Figure 8.6   Adjusted relative frequency histogram with frequency polygon

---

Excel Application 8.2

Figures 8.5–8.8
The Excel software programme produces bar charts rather than histograms.
Although it is possible to build custom charts, it is very difficult to produce the
appearance and features of a histogram. If you are going to use histograms
frequently it may be worth investing time in creating a suitable template. For
occasional use, a fine pencil and graph paper will produce good results more quickly.

(Figure 8.7). Such a *frequency curve* can be thought of as the shape of the distribution
which would result if it were possible to observe all members of a large population.

8.4.5   Stem and Leaf Plots

A *stem and leaf plot* illustrates the distribution of data in a similar manner to a
histogram. However, it offers the advantage of retaining the value of each observation.
Figure 8.8a is a stem and leaf plot of the data from Table 8.2. It was constructed by
dividing the value of each observation into two parts, the stem (in this case the whole
number in the value) and the leaf (the remainder of the value). Each observation was
recorded by placing its leaf to the right of the appropriate stem. In Figure 8.8b the
leaves have been reordered within each stem branch to appear in order of magnitude.
This is an *ordered stem and leaf plot*.

   In instances when several stems have a large number of leaves, more may be revealed
about the distribution of the data by dividing each stem.

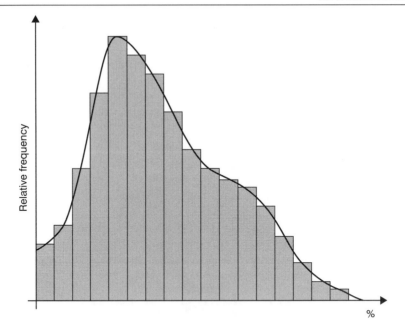

Figure 8.7   Frequency polygon becomes a frequency curve

15	6						
14	2	4					
13	5	1					
12	9	2					
11	8	3	2				
10	6	3					
9	4	9	4	2	2		
8	4	0	8	3			
7	5	7	3	3	6	4	
6	0	4	3	1	9		
5	7	3	6	8	7	2	5
4	6	2	7	3	9		
3	1						
2	6	0	3				
1	9	2					

15	6							Key:
14	2	4						8|7 = 8.7%
13	1	5						
12	2	9						
11	2	3	8					
10	3	6						
9	2	2	4	4	9			
8	0	3	4	8				
7	3	3	4	5	6	7		
6	0	1	3	4	9			
5	2	3	5	6	7	7	8	
4	2	3	6	7	9			
3	1							
2	0	3	6					
1	2	9						

Figure 8.8a   Stem and leaf plot   **Figure 8.8b**   Ordered stem and leaf plot
Annual growth (%) of 50 small pension funds

Stem and leaf plots offer some scope for comparing two data sets. Figure 8.9 demonstrates this.

8.4.6   Pie Charts

Pie charts are most suitable for categorical data and highlight how the total frequency is split between the categories. The pie (a circle) is cut into slices (sectors) so that the *area*

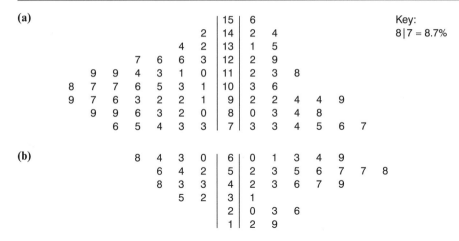

Figure 8.9 Back-to-back ordered stem and leaf plots: annual growth (%) of (a) large and (b) small pension funds

of a slice represents the frequency in that class. The angle at the centre of the sector is the same fraction of 360° (a full circle) as the class frequency is of the total frequency. The data in Table 8.5 have been displayed in Figure 8.10. Notice that the chart has a key to identify the sectors. An alternative is to place the labels in each sector, provided that the sectors are large enough to permit this. Pie charts become difficult to read if there are too many sectors or if several sectors are very small. When drawing one chart, the size of the circle is irrelevant.

Table 8.5 Asset allocation for UK pension funds

Asset class	Percentage	Angle
UK equities	52.8	$0.528 \times 360° = 190°$
UK fixed interest securities	7.3	$0.073 \times 360° = 26°$
Index-linked bonds	5.5	$0.055 \times 360° = 20°$
Overseas equities	19.6	$0.196 \times 360° = 71°$
Overseas bonds	3.3	$0.033 \times 360° = 12°$
Property	4.7	$0.047 \times 360° = 17°$
Cash and other	6.6	$0.066 \times 360° = 24°$

Sometimes an attempt is made to compare different-sized frequency distributions in drawing appropriately sized pie charts. Such diagrams are very difficult to read meaningfully and so a relative frequency or component bar chart is preferable. However, if pie charts are to be compared, it is essential to remember that frequency is represented by the *area*, not by the radius of the circle.

If a computer package is being used to draw a pie chart, it is usual to have the option of producing the diagram in three-dimensional perspective. Care should be taken with this since the result can be very misleading. This is demonstrated in

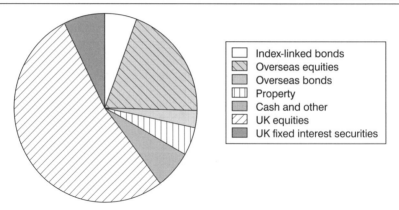

Figure 8.10   Asset allocation for UK pension funds

Excel Application 8.3

Figure 8.10

- As in Excel Application 8.1, use the chart wizard from the Insert pull-down menu.
- Select "Pie" for both the chart type and sub-type.
- The simplest way to enter the data range is to use the Collapse Dialogue Button at the right of the data range box, then select cells in the worksheet. If you are unsure about this (or any other part of a wizard or menu) right mouse click on the part in question and a help box will appear. Figure 8.12 shows the screen when the help box for the Collapse Dialogue Button has been opened.
- By including cells A4: A10 (see Figure 8.12) in those selected for the data range the labels seen in the key (legend) to the right of the pie chart are inserted automatically. This reduces the need for subsequent editing.

Figure 8.11, which displays the same data as Figure 8.10. The perspective makes the proportion allocated to overseas bonds (3.3%) appear to be substantially less than half the proportion allocated to "cash and other" (6.6%). Figure 8.12 shows the computer package.

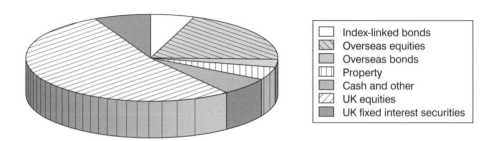

Figure 8.11   Misleading 3-D pie chart

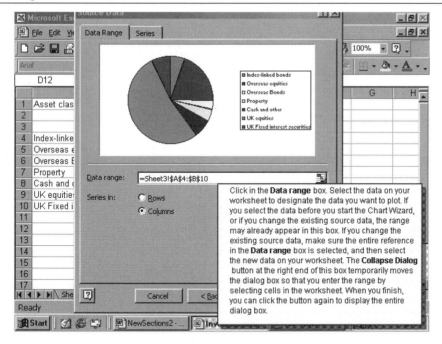

Figure 8.12   Creating a pie chart

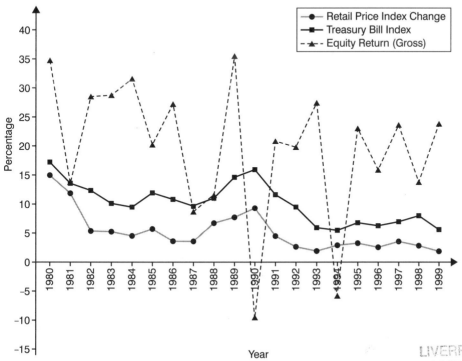

Figure 8.13   Multiple time series graph

8.4.7 Time Series Graphs

Time series graphs illustrate how a variable changes over time. The order of the
observations is of paramount importance and must not be destroyed in the handling of
the data. Several time series may be displayed together and Figure 8.13 shows an
example of this. Notice that both axes are labelled and that the graph has a key. It is
important to be very wary of extrapolating from time series data. For example, the
time series in Figure 8.13 has been truncated at 1999. Can you really predict the next

---

Excel Application 8.4

Figure 8.13

- Select Charts ... from the Insert pull-down menu.
- Select Chart type 'Line' and chart sub-type "Line with markers" displayed at each
  data value.
- After inserting the Data Range on page 2 of the wizard, don't forget to click on the
  Series tab to insert series labels. Otherwise these will need to be edited later using
  the Chart pull-down menu and selecting Source Data ... (Figure 8.14). This
  dialogue box can also be used to add or delete series.
- The labels on the x-axis were rotated from the default position by double clicking on
  this part of the saved chart, then using the Alignment page of the resultant menu.
- Similarly, default background shading and gridlines, visible in Figure 8.14, were
  removed to give the final appearance of Figure 8.13.

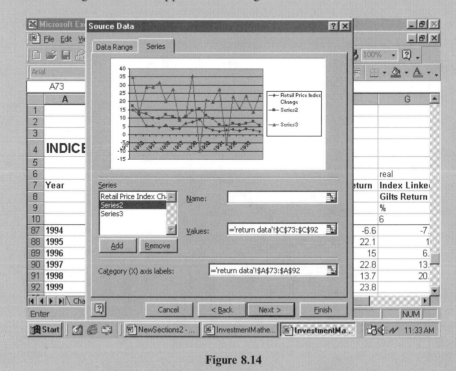

Figure 8.14

two years' figures? Your extrapolation can be checked against the figures quoted (see p. 152).

8.4.8 Cumulative Frequency Graphs

To construct the cumulative frequency curve in Figure 8.15, values from Table 8.3 were plotted against the appropriate interval end point and joined with a smooth curve. The *cumulative frequency curve* is also called an *ogive*.

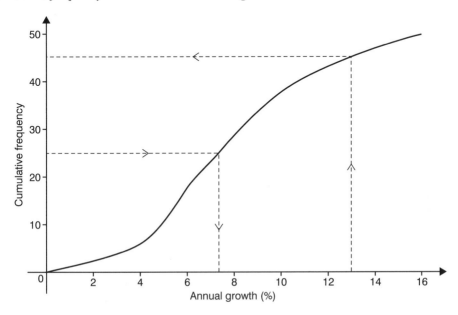

Figure 8.15   Cumulative frequence curve for data in Table 8.3

Estimates of intermediate values can be made by drawing a perpendicular line from the value in which you are interested on one axis, until it meets the curve. A second line is drawn perpendicular to the first at this point and the level at which it crosses the second axis is read off. For example, the lines drawn on Fig. 8.13 allow us to estimate that half the funds experienced an annual growth of less than 7.3%, or, reading in the opposite direction, five funds had growth exceeding 13%.

8.4.9 Scatter Diagrams

Scatter diagrams help us to look for a relationship between two variables. For example, Figure 8.16 shows two scatter diagrams for the 20-year period 1980–99. Each point on the diagram represents one year's returns.

The scatter diagrams give a general impression that perhaps high values of the variables plotted on the x-axis are associated with high values of the variables plotted on the y-axis at least for this time period. There is obviously quite a lot of variation in the data, particularly in Figure 8.16b, and there are a few obvious exceptions to the suggested relationship. We will return to scatter diagrams in Chapter 11.

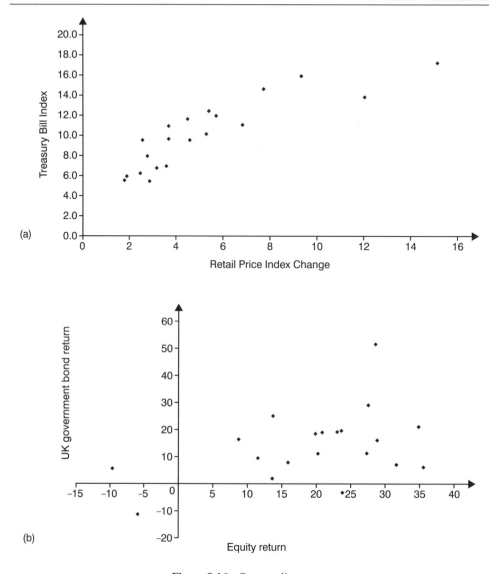

Figure 8.16 Scatter diagrams

Excel Application 8.5

Figure 8.16.

- Select chart type XY (Scatter) from chart wizard and chart sub-type "Scatter".
- You have the option to show more than one series on each scatter diagram, so Figure 8.16b could have been superimposed on Figure 8.16a. This makes sense in certain circumstances, but often just makes the graph difficult to read and interpret.

8.4.10   The Misrepresentation of Data

Earlier sections considered several ways in which data can be displayed to help us to read and interpret them. The aim was always to provide a simple summary which clearly showed the main features of the data. However, it is easy to mislead the reader (accidentally or intentionally) with poorly constructed diagrams. Misleading histograms and pie charts were noted in Sections 8.4.4 and 8.4.6. The dangers of extrapolation from time series were highlighted in Section 8.4.7. Further common misrepresentations are shown below to emphasise that one must always look very carefully before making inferences from a diagram.

In Figure 8.16a and b the same points have been plotted, but different scales have been used and in Figure 8.17a the vertical scale does not start from zero. The overall impression is quite different, as indicated in the figure captions.

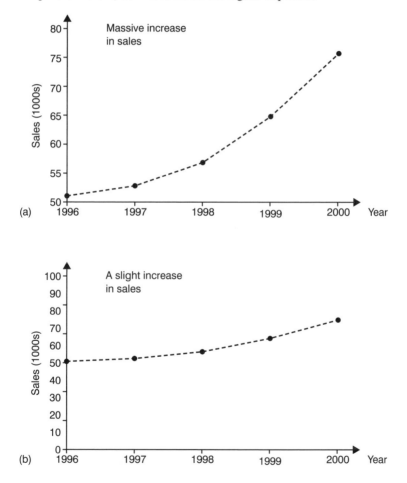

Figure 8.17   Sales of personal pension policies

The same scales have been used in Figure 8.18, but the use of the false zero in Figure 8.18b makes sales of policy D look more than twice as high as sales of policy A

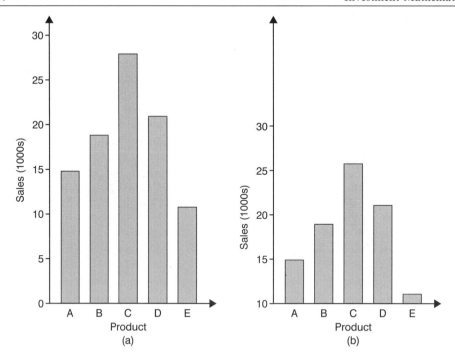

Figure 8.18 Sales of five different policies

and sales of product E almost insignificant. Despite the misleading visual impression of the diagram on the right, all the information we need to interpret it is actually given. However, had the vertical scale been missing, the diagram would have become meaningless.

Figure 8.19 "Improved production techniques double the output of olive oil in a decade."

Another type of distortion can occur in the use of three-dimensional diagrams. In Figure 8.19 the third bottle is indeed twice as high as the first, but most people will, at a glance, tend to interpret the bottle sizes in terms of the amount of liquid held. The third bottle has 8 times the capacity of the first, greatly exaggerating the increase in output.

The examples above illustrate that it is important to make sure that when diagrams are drawn they are meaningful and contain all the information that is necessary for interpretation.

8.5   DESCRIPTIVE STATISTICS

In the previous section we used tables, graphs and other diagrams to summarise data visually. The pictorial representations revealed important patterns in the data such as the most common values and whether observations were clustered together or widely spread. Observing these features and describing them qualitatively is useful. However, we often like to have quantitative measures of the data features which enable precise comparisons to be made between different data sets and which can also be manipulated mathematically. This section considers two types of numerical measure. Sections 8.5.1 to 8.5.6 describe measures which represent "typical" values in the distribution of observations, known as *measures of centrality* or *measures of location*. Sections 8.5.7 to 8.5.12 describe measures that indicate the extent to which the observations are spread out, known as *measures of dispersion*.

8.5.1   Arithmetic Mean

The *arithmetic mean* is a suitable measure of location for quantitative data. When one talks about "the average", it is usually the arithmetic mean which is being described. The arithmetic mean of n observations; $x_1, x_2, ..., x_n$ is

$$\bar{x} = \frac{1}{n} \sum_{i=1}^{n} x_i$$

In a grouped frequency table with k class intervals, where x_i refers to the *mid-point* of the ith interval and f_i to the frequency in that interval, the formula becomes

$$\bar{x} = \frac{\sum_{i=1}^{k} x_i f_i}{\sum_{i=1}^{k} f_i}$$

For the data in Table 8.3 this gives $\bar{x} = 7.64$, just a little lower than the true mean of 7.66 that can be calculated from the values in Table 8.2.

The arithmetic mean is the most important measure of location and we will be using it frequently in the following pages. Every observation makes a contribution to the calculation of the mean and this is usually regarded as an advantage. However, if there are a few very extreme observations the arithmetic mean can be badly distorted. This can be seen with the data in Figure 8.20. Column B shows the annualised growth of 12

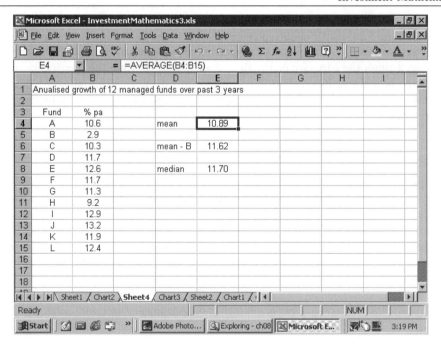

Figure 8.20   Calculating means

managed funds over the past three years. The arithmetic mean is 10.89% (shown in cell E4 of Figure 8.20).

There was one unusually small reported fund growth: fund B, 2.9%. This outlying value merits further attention. What were the circumstances that resulted in unusually small growth? Perhaps this is a data entry error and the correct annualised growth is

---

Excel Application 8.6

The calculation of the arithmetic mean within the Excel spreadsheet (Figure 8.20) is obtained as follows:

• Position cursor where the answer is required.
• Select the Insert from the top toolbar.
• Select Function ... from the drop-down menu.
• Select Statistical from the Function Category list in the "Post Function" dialogue box.
• Select AVERAGE from the function name list in the same dialogue box.
• Enter the array (B4:B15) containing the data (this can also be done by highlighting the area on the spreadsheet; or by entering individual observations separated by commas).

Next time you access the "Post Function" dialogue box the function AVERAGE will appear at the top of the "most recently used" list.

12.9%. Finding out more about this outlying value permits an informed decision on the appropriateness of including this observation in this and subsequent calculations. Removing this outlier from the calculation results in an arithmetic mean for the remaining 11 managed funds of 11.62%, shown in cell E6. The higher average may be a more meaningful summary statistic for managed fund growth in this period.

8.5.2 Median

The *median* is also a suitable measure of location for quantitative data and is the middle value when the observations have been arranged in order of size (or the arithmetic mean of the two middle values if there is an even number of observations). It has two important advantages over the mean: first, it is not badly distorted by extreme values and second, intervals without upper (or lower) limits do not give rise to difficulties. However, in normal circumstances the median is less important than the arithmetic mean because the amount of mathematical manipulation to which it can be subjected profitably is rather limited.

The median of the observations in Figure 8.20 is 11.7 (the arithmetic mean of the 6th and 7th values, after the 12 observations had been sorted by size). This can be obtained in an Excel spreadsheet by using the statistical function MEDIAN (list or array). When there are n observations the median is the $[(n+1)/2]$th observation.

When data have been summarised in a grouped frequency table, for example, Table 8.3, an estimate of the median can be found from the cumulative frequency. The median is the $[(50+1)/2] = 25\frac{1}{2}$th value, which clearly lies in the interval $6 \leqslant x < 8\%$. There are 18 observations up to the beginning of this interval, so the $25\frac{1}{2}$th value is $7\frac{1}{2}$th value in the interval. It is usual to assume that the 11 observations in the interval are evenly spread across its width of 2%, so the estimated median is:

$$6 + \frac{7.5}{11} \times 2 = 7.36\%.$$

This is close to the estimate of 7.3 obtained from the cumulative frequency curve in Section 8.4.8. In fact, the true median is 7.35. This can be calculated directly from Table 8.2.

It is very easy to find the median value in an ordered stem and leaf plot (Section 8.4.5) simply by counting the appropriate number of observations.

8.5.3 Mode

The *mode* is the most frequently occurring observation. There may be more than one value for the mode. This measure of location has the advantage of being suitable for both quantitative and categorical data.

The mode can be obtained in a Excel spreadsheet by using the statistical function MODE (list or array).

8.5.4 Link between the Mean, Median and Mode

In a symmetrical distribution of observations the mean, median and mode all occur at the same point (Figure 8.21a). If the distribution is not symmetrical, the three values

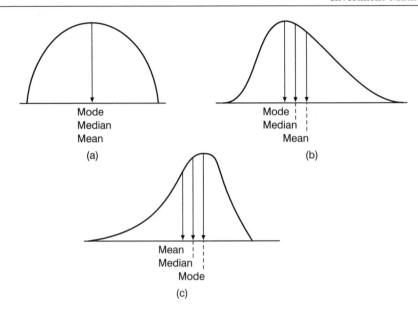

Figure 8.21 (a) Symmetrical distribution. (b) Positively skewed distribution. (c) Negatively skewed distribution.

are different and their order depends on whether the distribution is *positively skewed* (Figure 8.21b) or *negatively skewed* (Figure 8.21c).

8.5.5 Weighted Average

It may be the case that within a sample, some observations are more important than others and we would want to calculate an average which took this into account. The *weighted mean* facilitates this. Each sample observation x_i is associated with a weight w_i, where

$$\sum_{i=1}^{n} w_i = 1$$

and the weighted mean is

$$\bar{x} = \sum_{i=1}^{n} w_i x_i$$

Suppose we are constructing a new index for an emerging market, based on a small number of quoted companies in three sectors (see Table 8.6). It is desired to give more weight to larger sectors, so initial weights have been allocated. These total to 10, but for the calculation of a weighted mean must be adjusted to sum to one. The weighted mean is:

$$0.1 \times 60 + 0.3 \times 70 + 0.6 \times 50 = 51.6\%$$

Table 8.6

Sector	Total return x_i	Initial weight	Adjusted weight w_i
Agriculture and commodities	60%	1	0.1
Services	70%	3	0.3
Industrials	50%	6	0.6
Totals		10	1

This compares with an unweighted arithmetic mean of 60%. The unweighted arithmetic mean does not reflect the fact that the largest sector experienced the lowest returns.

8.5.6 Geometric Mean

The *geometric mean (G.M.)* is the nth root of the product of n numbers, that is

$$G.M. = (x_1 \times x_2 \times x_3 \times \ldots \times x_n)^{1/n}$$

It has two advantages over the arithmetic mean. First, it can be less affected by extreme values and, second, it is an intuitively better form of average when used to calculate the average rate of change per time period for quantities which grow over time.

Consider the growth of £100 invested at 10% p.a. for 4 years

Year	1	2	3	4
Accumulation factor	1.1	1.12	1.08	1.09

The geometric mean of the accumulation factor is:

$$\sqrt[4]{1.1 \times 1.12 \times 1.08 \times 1.09} = 1.097$$

implying an average annual return of 9.7% per annum. This is the most appropriate way to calculate the average rate of return (see Chapter 1). In some circumstances, the geometric mean can also be used to calculate investment indices (see Chapter 13).

The main drawback of the geometric mean is that it cannot be used if any of the observations are negative or zero.

The relevant Excel function is GEOMEAN (array or list).

We will now move on to discuss measures of dispersion.

8.5.7 Range

The *range* is simply the largest observation minus the smallest observation. Extreme values have a large effect on the range, which also tends to increase as the sample size increases.

The effect of an extreme observation is shown by the data in Figure 8.20. The range of all the observations is 10.3%, but if we discard the extreme observation, 2.9%, the range is only 4%.

To calculate the range of a set of observations within an Excel spreadsheet you might choose to sort the observations, then calculate the range by hand. Alternatively, use the statistical functions MAX and MIN, then subtract the latter from the former.

8.5.8   Inter-quartile Range

The *inter-quartile range (IQR)* is a measure of dispersion which is not affected by extreme values.

> The lower quartile is the value such that $\frac{1}{4}$ of the observations lie below it

> The upper quartile is the value such that $\frac{1}{4}$ of the observations lie above it

$$IQR = \text{upper quartile} - \text{lower quartile}$$

The inter-quartile range of the data in Table 8.2 is

$$9.9 - 5.3 = 4.6\%$$

The middle 50% of the small pension funds experienced growth within a range of 4.6%. Following on from the comments at the end of Section 8.5.2, stem and leaf plots (Section 8.4.5) facilitate the easy calculation of quartiles, or indeed any other subdivision of a set of ordered data. The interquartile range may also be read from a cumulative frequency curve (Section 8.4.8).

The relevant Excel function is QUARTILE (array or list, number). Entering number 1 returns the lower quartile, number 3 returns the upper quartile.

8.5.9   Mean Deviation (from the Mean)

The *mean deviation (M.D.)* is the arithmetic mean of the absolute differences between the sample mean, $\bar{x}$, and each observation, x_i. The reason for summing absolute differences is that some of the deviations $(x_i - \bar{x})$ will be positive and some will be negative. If we simply find the sum, it will produce a value of zero. Therefore, in the calculation of mean deviation we use the size of each deviation and ignore its sign.

$$M.D. = \frac{1}{n} \sum_{i=1}^{n} |x_i - \bar{x}|$$

or for grouped frequency table

$$\frac{1}{\sum_{i=1}^{k} f_i} \sum_{i=1}^{k} |x_i - \bar{x}| f_i$$

The mean deviation of the data in Figure 8.2 is 2.84%, obtained using the Excel statistical function AVEDEV (array or list).

This is the average deviation of the observed levels of fund growth from their average of 7.7%. Obtaining a large value for the mean deviation shows that the data are quite widely spread.

8.5.10 Sample Variance

The absolute values used in the calculations of the section above can be difficult to handle algebraically. An alternative approach to solving the problem of actual deviations summing to zero is to square the deviations and construct the following summation:

$$\frac{1}{n}\sum_{i=1}^{n}(x_i - \bar{x})^2 \qquad \text{or} \qquad \frac{1}{\sum_{i=1}^{k}f_i}\sum_{i=1}^{k}(x_i - \bar{x})^2 f_i$$

These formulae are then modified to give the *sample variance*, s^2:

$$s^2 = \frac{1}{n-1}\sum_{i=1}^{n}(x_i - \bar{x})^2 \qquad \text{or} \qquad s^2 = \frac{1}{\left(\sum_{i=1}^{k}f_i\right)-1}\sum_{i=1}^{k}(x_i - \bar{x})^2 f_i$$

The modification is necessary to ensure that the sample variance is *unbiased* and this point will be discussed further in Section 10.2. The modification is not important if n (or $\sum_{i=1}^{k}f_i$) is large, in which case a more convenient working form of the formula can be obtained by multiplying out the brackets and simplifying the resulting expression:

$$s^2 = \frac{1}{n}\sum_{i=1}^{n}x_i^2 - \bar{x}^2 \qquad \text{or} \qquad s^2 = \frac{1}{\sum_{i=1}^{k}f_i}\sum_{i=1}^{k}f_i x_i^2 - \bar{x}^2$$

The variance of the data in Table 8.2 is 12.5 obtained using the Excel function VAR (list or array).

8.5.11 Sample Standard Deviation

Since the deviations $(x_i - \bar{x})$ were squared in the calculation of the sample variance, the units of the sample variance are the square of the observation units, in the case above, $\%^2$. This is rather inconvenient and so we usually quote the square root of the sample variance, known as the *sample standard deviation*, which has the same units as the observations from which it was derived.

$$S = \sqrt{\text{Sample variance}}$$

This is the most important measure of dispersion and we will use it repeatedly in later chapters.

Thus, for the data of Table 8.2, $s = 3.5\%$.

8.5.12 Coefficient of Variation

The six monthly inflation rates for two regions

Region A:	1.1	1.4	1.6	1.2	1.5	1.3
Region B:	7.2	7.1	7.4	7.6	7.3	7.5

have the same range (0.6), IQR (0.4) and standard deviation (0.19). However, relative to the sizes of the numbers, the spread of A is greater than the spread of B. The *coefficient of variation* is a measure of spread which reflects this:

$$\text{Coefficient of variation} = \frac{\text{standard deviation}}{\text{mean}}$$

The coefficient of variation is usually expressed as a percentage. For A

$$\frac{s}{\bar{x}} \times \frac{100}{1} = \frac{0.19}{1.35} \times \frac{100}{1}$$

$$= 14\%$$

and for B

$$\frac{s}{\bar{x}} \times \frac{100}{1} = \frac{0.19}{7.35} \times \frac{100}{1}$$

$$= 2.6\%$$

Clearly the coefficient of variation is undefined if $\bar{x} = 0$. It may also be meaningless if the mean is close to zero. However, because the coefficient of variation has no units, it is a useful way of comparing the spreads of sets of observations which have been made in different units, without first having to convert the observations to a common unit.

Time Series Extrapolation Answers

The next data points for each of the time series displayed in Section 8.4.7 is:

Year	2000	2001
RPI change	2.1%	2.1%
Treasury Bill Index	3.2%	4.8%
Equity returns (gross)	−8.6%	−13.8%

Modelling Investment Returns

9.1 INTRODUCTION

As necessary background to understanding the stochastic approach to modelling investment returns, we begin by introducing important concepts and results from probability theory. Probability distributions and their properties are introduced, paying particular attention to three important distributions: the binomial distribution, the normal distribution and the lognormal distribution. These aspects of probability theory are then applied to modelling investment returns, focusing on the accumulation of investments under different circumstances.

9.2 PROBABILITY

Probability is a numerical measure, in the range 0 to 1, of the level of the uncertainty attached to an event. A probability of 0 means that there is no chance of the event occurring, while a probability of 1 means that the event is certain to occur. Thus the more likely the event, the higher its probability within this range of values. The sum of the probabilities relating to all possible outcomes of an experiment is 1.

The following subsections contain important definitions to aid understanding of subsequent sections describing the stochastic approach to modelling investment returns.

9.2.1 Relative Frequency Definition of Probability

The probability of an event is the *relative frequency* of its occurrence *in the long run:*

$$P(E) = \frac{\text{Number of times } E \text{ occurred}}{\text{Number of trials}}$$

Example 9.1

Suppose a company sells three insurance products, A, B and C. Inspection of company records for the past five years reveals that a third of claims relate to policies of type A, half arise from policies of type B, and a sixth from policies of type C.

Answer

The best estimate for the probability that the next claim received will arise from a type B policy is the historical relative frequency, 0.5.

9.2.2 Subjective Probability

Subjective probability is an opinion of the likelihood of an event. We all use this type of probability when we look out of a window before going outside, and decide whether to take an umbrella. Subjective probability may be used in investment because we do not have the knowledge required to determine the probability distribution of investment returns objectively. The subjective probability assigned is a professional opinion.

9.2.3 The Addition Rule

Consider the probability of event A or event B occurring in the *sample space* of Figure 9.1. Then, defining $n(A)$ as the number of observations in set A:

$$P(A \text{ or } B) = \frac{n(A \cup B)}{n(\mathscr{E})}$$

$$= \frac{n(A) + n(B) - n(A \cap B)}{n(\mathscr{E})}$$

$$= \frac{n(A)}{n(\mathscr{E})} + \frac{n(B)}{n(\mathscr{E})} - \frac{n(A \cap B)}{n(\mathscr{E})}$$

$$= P(A) + P(B) - P(A \text{ and } B) \qquad (9.1)$$

Thus the probability of event A or event B occurring is the sum of their individual probabilities, minus the probability of events A and B occurring together. This is called the *addition rule*.

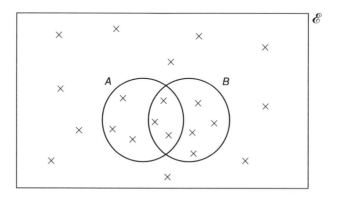

Figure 9.1   The sample space for a composite event

9.2.4 Mutually Exclusive Events

If the occurrence of one event implies that no other event in the sample space will occur, the events are said to be *mutually exclusive*. Now the set $\{A \cap B\}$ is empty, so the

addition rule reduces to

$$P(A \text{ or } B) = P(A) + P(B)$$

9.2.5 Conditional Probability

Conditional probability is the probability of an event occurring, given that another event is known to have already occurred.

Suppose that we have a sample space like the one in Figure 9.1. Then consider the probability that A occurs subject to the condition that B is known to have occurred already, written $P(A \mid B)$. The sample space is reduced to set B (Figure 9.2). Thus,

$$P(A \mid B) = \frac{n(A \cap B)}{n(B)}$$

$$= \frac{n(A \cap B)}{n(\mathcal{E})} \times \frac{n(\mathcal{E})}{n(B)}$$

$$= \frac{P(A \text{ and } B)}{P(B)}$$

Figure 9.2

This is the conditional probability of A given B, which can be rearranged to give the *multiplication rule*:

$$P(A \text{ and } B) = P(B)P(A \mid B) \tag{9.2}$$

or by symmetry

$$P(A \text{ and } B) = P(A)P(B \mid A)$$

9.2.6 Independent Events

Events A and B are *independent* if the probability that A will occur is not affected by the occurrence of B. In this case:

$$P(A \mid B) = P(A)$$

So the multiplication rule reduces to:

$$P(A \text{ and } B) = P(A)P(B) \tag{9.3}$$

This can be used as a test for independence, i.e. two events are independent if the probability of their joint occurrence is equal to the product of their individual probabilities.

Example 9.2

An analyst travels to work by train and feels that his train is late more often when it is raining than when the weather is dry. However, this impression may simply be due to the greater discomfort involved in standing in the rain. He decides to investigate whether the two events, "rain" and "train late", are independent. In 10 weeks he noted that the train ran late on 7 days and that it rained on 16 days. On 4 days it rained and the train was late. Thus,

$$P(\text{train late}) = \frac{7}{50} \quad \text{and} \quad P(\text{rain}) = \frac{16}{50}$$

Answer

If the events were independent the probability of their joint occurrence would be

$$\frac{7}{50} \times \frac{16}{50} = \frac{28}{625}$$

However, P(rain and train late) is $4/50 = 50/625$, which implies that the analyst's impression is correct, these two events are not independent.

9.2.7 Complementary Events

For any event E, there is a *complementary event* $\bar{E}$ or E', read "not E", such that $P(E) + P(E') = 1$. For example, if $P(E$: gilt returns $>$ inflation$) = 0.8$, then $P(E'$: gilt returns $\leqslant$ inflation$) = 0.2$. This relationship is useful when considering problems containing the words "at least".

Example 9.3

Let us consider the probability that at least one capitalisation change was announced in the US equity market during a trading day.

P(at least 1 capitalisation change) $= P(1$ change$) + P(2$ changes$) + P(3$ changes$) + \cdots$

Answer

The calculation is better approached in terms of the complementary event:

P(at least one capitalisation change) $= 1 - P$(no capitalisation changes announced)

Reference to historical records will reveal the relative frequency of the event "no capitalisation changes", enabling the required probability to be calculated.

9.2.8 Bayes' Theorem

Bayes Theorem states that if an event F is known to have occurred and is also known to be associated with one of a set of mutually exclusive events: $E_1, E_2 \ldots E_n$, then for a particular event, E_j

$$P(E_j \mid F) = \frac{P(E_j)P(F \mid E_j)}{\displaystyle\sum_{i=1}^{n} P(E_i)P(F \mid E_i)} \tag{9.4}$$

The values of $P(E_j)$ are called *prior probabilities*. They exist before anything is known about event F.

The probability is $P(E_j \mid F)$, calculated after the outcome F is known, is called a *posterior probability*. This is not as complicated as it looks, as is shown by the following example.

Example 9.4

In the last session of professional examinations 180 trainee investment analysts each took two subjects. Forty-five passed both exams and 72 passed just one. The local university runs revision courses in these subjects and 80% of those passing both subjects had attended both revision courses. Seventy-five per cent of those passing one subject had attended the revision courses, while only 46% of those failing both had done so. Calculate the probability that an individual selected at random from the register of those who attended the revision courses went on to pass both subjects.

Answer

Prior probabilities:

$$P(E_1 = \text{Pass 2}) = 0.25$$

$$P(E_2 = \text{Pass 1}) = 0.4$$

$$P(E_3 = \text{Pass 0}) = 0.35$$

Conditional probabilities of attending the revision courses (R):

$$P(R \mid E_1) = 0.8$$

$$P(R \mid E_2) = 0.75$$

$$P(R \mid E_3) = 0.46$$

So the posterior probability of passing two subjects, given that the revision courses were attended, is:

$$P(E_1 \mid R) = \frac{P(E_1)P(R \mid E_1)}{P(E_1)P(R \mid E_1) + P(E_2)P(R \mid E_2) + P(E_3)P(R \mid E_3)}$$

$$= \frac{0.25 \times 0.8}{0.25 \times 0.8 + 0.4 \times 0.75 + 0.35 \times 0.46}$$

$$= 0.303$$

9.3 PROBABILITY DISTRIBUTIONS

A *probability distribution* or *theoretical distribution* is a model for an *actual* or *empirical distribution*. The following subsections will describe important features of probability distributions, but, first, two examples of probability distributions.

Example 9.5

Consider an experiment in which three coins are tossed simultaneously and the number of heads which show is recorded. The number of heads, X, can take any one of the values 0, 1, 2, or 3 and thus, X is called a *discrete random variable*. There are 8 possible outcomes of the experiment: *TTT, TTH, THT, HTT, THH, HTH, HHT, HHH*.

Answer

Assuming the coins to be fair, each outcome is equally likely so in repeated trials we would expect X to take the value 0 in $\frac{1}{8}$ of them, the value 1 in $\frac{3}{8}$ of them, etc. Therefore, the probability distribution for the experiment is

x	0	1	2	3
$P(X=x)$	$\dfrac{1}{8}$	$\dfrac{3}{8}$	$\dfrac{3}{8}$	$\dfrac{1}{8}$

This distribution is illustrated in Figure 9.3. Actually performing the experiment would produce an empirical distribution which should grow closer to the theoretical distribution as the number of trials increases, provided the coin is fair.

Example 9.6

Long time series are readily available for UK inflation and Treasury Bill returns. Let us consider the 16 quinquennial periods since 1919, and define a variable X as the number of years in each quinquennial period that Treasury Bill returns were greater than inflation. Clearly, X is a discrete random variable, taking integer values in the range $[0, 5]$.

Answer

The frequency table and probability distribution for each event $X = x$ is as follows:

x	0	1	2	3	4	5
f	2	2	2	1	4	5
$P(X=x)$	$\dfrac{1}{8}$	$\dfrac{1}{8}$	$\dfrac{1}{8}$	$\dfrac{1}{16}$	$\dfrac{1}{4}$	$\dfrac{5}{16}$

This is an empirical distribution that can be recalculated as the passage of time permits more quinquennial periods to be added.

We might use a theoretical distribution as a model to approximate the ever-growing empirical distribution. Some important theoretical distributions are introduced later in this chapter (Sections 9.4, 9.5, 9.7) and statistical modelling applied to investment will be developed further in the chapters in Part III.

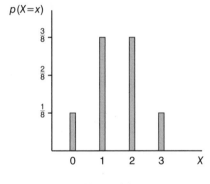

Figure 9.3

Examples 9.5 and 9.6 involve discrete random variables and therefore, result in *discrete probability distributions*. A continuous random variable will have a *probability density function*, $f(x)$ (see Section 9.3.9). In Sections 9.3.1 to 9.3.8 discrete variables will be used, but the results obtained hold for continuous variables, with summation being replaced by integration.

9.3.1 Cumulative Distribution Function (c.d.f.)

The *cumulative distribution function* gives the probability that an observation, X, is less than or equal to the value x; it is usually denoted by $F(x)$. For example 9.5 above, the c.d.f. is

$$
\begin{array}{c|cccc}
x & 0 & 1 & 2 & 3 \\
\hline
F(x) & \dfrac{1}{8} & \dfrac{4}{8} & \dfrac{7}{8} & 1
\end{array}
$$

This is illustrated in Figure 9.4.

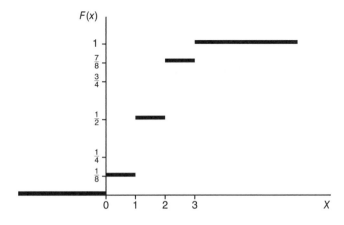

Figure 9.4

9.3.2 The Mean and Variance of Probability Distributions

The sample mean,

$$\bar{x} = \frac{\sum_{i=1}^{k} x_i f_i}{\sum_{i=1}^{k} f_i}$$

and the sample variance in its unmodified form,

$$s^2 = \frac{1}{\sum_{i=1}^{k}} \sum_{i=1}^{k} (x_i - \bar{x})^2 f_i$$

have theoretical equivalents, in which relative frequency, $f_i \Big/ \left(\sum_{i=1}^{k} f_i \right)$ is replaced by probability, $p(x_i)$. The mean becomes,

$$\mu = \sum_{i=1}^{k} x_i p(x_i) \tag{9.5}$$

and the variance is

$$\sigma^2 = \sum_{i=1}^{k} (x_i - \mu)^2 p(x_i)$$

$$= \sum_{i=1}^{k} x_i^2 p(x_i) - 2\mu \sum_{i=1}^{k} x_i p(x_i) + n\mu^2 \sum_{i=1}^{k} p(x_i)$$

$$= \sum_{i=1}^{k} x_i^2 p(x_i) - \mu^2 \tag{9.6}$$

noting that $\sum_{i=1}^{k} p(x_i) = 1$.

9.3.3 Expected Values of Probability Distributions

Suppose the random variable X must assume one of the values $x_1, x_2, ..., x_k$, with associated probabilities $p(x_i), p(x_2), ..., p(x_k)$ where

$$\sum_{i=1}^{k} p(x_i) = 1.$$

Then the expected value of the random variable is

$$E[X] = \sum_{i=1}^{k} x_i p(x_i) \tag{9.7}$$

Example 9.7

In a lottery 50,000 tickets are for sale at 25p each. The prizes to be won are as follows: 1 of £1000, 5 of £100, 10 of £50, 50 of £5 and 500 of £1. If you buy a ticket, what are your expected winnings?

Answer

$$E[X] = \sum_{i=1}^{k} x_i p(x_i)$$

$$= \left(1000 \times \frac{1}{50,000} \right) + \left(100 \times \frac{5}{50,000} \right) + \left(50 \times \frac{10}{50,000} \right) + \left(5 \times \frac{50}{50,000} \right)$$

$$+ \left(1 \times \frac{500}{50,000} \right)$$

$$= 0.055 \quad \text{i.e. } 5.5\text{p}$$

The expected value formula (9.7) is just the mean of the random variable X, but can be extended to the case where functions of a random variable are required.

In general, if $g(X)$ is a function of the random variable X,

$$E[g(X)] = \sum_{i=1}^{k} g(x_i)p(x_i) \tag{9.8}$$

9.3.4 Properties of the Expected Value

Let $g(X)$ and $h(X)$ be functions of a random variable, X, let Y be another random variable and let c and k be constants, then:

(i) $E[cg(x)] = cE[G(X)]$ \hfill (9.9)

(ii) $E[g(X) + c] = E[g(X)] + c$ \hfill (9.10)

(iii) $E[g(X) + h(X)] = E[g(X)] + E[h(X)]$ \hfill (9.11)

(iv) $E[cX + kY] = cE[X] + kE[Y]$ \hfill (9.12)

If X and Y are independent random variables,

(v) $E[XY] = E[X]E[Y]$ \hfill (9.13)

These properties are easily demonstrated with simple algebra, provided it is remembered that

$$\sum_{i=1}^{n} p(x_i) = 1.$$

These results are derived in Annex 9.1.

9.3.5 The General Linear Transformation

Let c and k be constants and let $g(x) = x$, then combining equations (9.9) and (9.10):

$$E[kx + c) = kE[x] + c$$
$$= k\mu + c \qquad (9.14)$$

This transformation can be useful when, for example, trying to calculate the mean of awkwardly large numbers.

9.3.6 Variance

Just as the mean, μ, is the expected value of the random variable X, the variance, σ^2 is the expected value of $(X - \mu)^2$. The following are important properties which are shown more fully in Annex 9.2. Let c and k be constants, then:

(i) $\text{var}(kX) = k^2\sigma^2$ \hfill (9.15)

(ii) $\text{var}(X + c) = \sigma^2$ \hfill (9.16)

Combining equations (9.15) and (9.16):

$$\text{var}(kX + a) = k^2\,\text{var}(X) = k^2\sigma^2 \qquad (9.17)$$

If X and Y are independent random variables:

(iii) $\text{var}(cX + kY) = c^2\,\text{var}(X) + k^2\,\text{var}(Y)$ \hfill (9.18)

The expectation form of the variance leads to a very convenient formula with which to calculate variances:

$$\sigma^2 = E[(X - \mu)^2]$$
$$= E[(X^2 - 2\mu X + \mu^2)]$$
$$= E[X^2] - 2\mu E[X] + \mu^2$$
$$= E[X^2] - \mu^2$$
$$= E[X^2] - (E[X])^2 \qquad (9.19)$$

Example 9.7 continued

Use equation 9.19 to find the standard deviation of winnings in the lottery example of Section 9.3.3.

Answer

$$\sigma = £4.64$$

9.3.7 Covariance

Let X and Y be random variables with means μ_X and μ_Y, then the *covariance* of X and Y is defined as

$$\text{cov}(X, Y) = E[(X - \mu_X)(Y - \mu_Y)] \qquad (9.20)$$

It can be seen that covariance is an extension of the form of variance defined in Section 9.3.6, since

$$\text{cov}(X, X) = \text{var}(X)$$

For the purpose of calculation, it is usually easier to first rearrange equation (9.20) as follows:

$$E[(X - \mu_X)(Y - \mu_Y)] = E[XY] - \mu_Y E[X] - \mu_X E[Y] + \mu_X \mu_Y$$
$$= E[XY] - \mu_X \mu_Y \qquad (9.21)$$

With this expression for covariance it is immediately obvious that if X and Y are independent random variables, $\text{cov}(X, Y) = 0$ since $E[XY] = E[X]E[Y]$. However, it should be noted that obtaining a covariance of zero does not imply that the variables are independent. This is different from the situation described in Section 9.2.6.

Covariance is a measure of association between variables. If X tends to be large when Y is large, and small when Y is small, the deviations $(X - \mu_X)$ and $(Y - \mu_Y)$ will tend to have the same sign. Thus their products will be positive, which will result in a positive covariance. If X tends to be large when Y is small and vice versa, the products $(X - \mu_X)(Y - \mu_y)$ will tend to be negative, yielding a negative covariance. This point will be taken up again in Chapter 11.

9.3.8 Moments of Random Variables

The expected values $E[X] = \mu$ (Section 9.3.3) and $E[(X - \mu)^2] = \sigma^2$ (Section 9.3.6) are particular cases of *moments* of the random variable X.

The *kth moment of X about the origin* is defined as $E[X^k]$. Thus, the mean is the first moment of X about the origin.

The *kth moment of X about the mean* is defined as $E[(X - \mu)^k]$. Thus, the variance is the second moment of X about the mean.

While the mean and the variance are moments which describe the location and dispersion of a random variable, other moments may help to describe other aspects of the distribution. For example, the third moment about the mean, $E[(X - \mu)^3]$, may be used to indicate how much the distribution is skewed. This moment will be zero for a symmetric distribution, positive when there is skew to the right and negative when there is skew to the left.

9.3.9 Probability Density Function (p.d.f.)

In Chapter 8, Section 8.4.4, relative frequency histograms and frequency polygons were discussed, including the situation in which more and more data are collected and therefore split into narrower and narrower intervals. Eventually the lines joining the points in the frequency polygon become very short and begin to look like a single curve, (Figure 8.7). That limiting curve is called *probability density function* and is usually written $f(x)$. It encloses an area of 1 unit and probabilities are represented by areas under the curve. Thus the probability of making an observation between a and b is found by finding the area of the shaded strip in Figure 9.5.

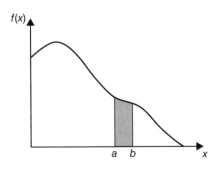

Figure 9.5

Example 9.8

A particular property mutual fund puts all unit realisations in a queue as a way of managing the liquidity of the fund.

Suppose that the time taken for the mutual fund to deal with liquidations has the following probability density function, where time is measured in weeks:

$$f(t) = 6\left(\frac{t}{25} - \frac{t^2}{125}\right) \qquad 0 \leqslant t \leqslant 5$$

What is the probability that a liquidation will take place between 3 and 4 weeks?

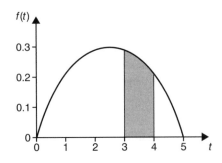

Figure 9.6

Answer

The probability required is the area of the shaded strip in Figure 9.6:

$$\frac{6}{125} \int_3^4 (5t - t^2) = \frac{6}{125} \left[\frac{5t^2}{2} - \frac{t^3}{3} \right]_3^4$$

$$= \frac{6}{125} \left(40 - \frac{64}{3} - \frac{45}{2} + 9 \right)$$

$$= 0.248$$

9.4 THE BINOMIAL DISTRIBUTION

The *binomial distribution* is a discrete probability distribution and is defined as follows: if there are n independent trials of an experiment with only the same two possible outcomes at each trial, usually denoted a "success" and a "failure", where p is the probability of "success" in a single trial, then the probability, $p(x)$, of obtaining x "successes" from the n trials is given by the binomial distribution:

$$p(x) = {}^n C_x p^x (1 - p)^{n-x}, \qquad x = 0, 1, \ldots, n$$

where ${}^n C_x = \dfrac{n!}{x!(n-x)!}$

The distribution has mean, $\mu = np$ and variance $\sigma^2 = np(1 - p)$ which is often written as $\sigma^2 = npq$ where $q = 1 - p$.

Example 9.9

Suppose that a particular fund manager defines "success" as being in the top quartile of comparable funds, ranked by performance. Thus, "failure" is to be in the bottom three quartiles. The fund managers working for a particular fund management company have a probability of 0.3 of "success". Find the probability that, over a period of 12 quarters, an individual fund manager will appear in the top quartile:

(a) on at least eight occasions
(b) at least once.

Answer

(a) Here, the variable X is the number of "successes" experienced, $n = 12$ and $p = 0.3$.

$$P(X \geqslant 8) = {}^{12}C_8 0.3^8 0.7^4 + {}^{12}C_9 0.3^9 0.7^3 + {}^{12}C_{10} 0.3^{10} 0.7^2 + {}^{12}C_{11} 0.3^{11} 0.7 + 0.3^{12}$$

$$= 0.00949$$

As mentioned in Section 9.2.7, the words "at least" should trigger inspection of whether it would be simpler to solve the problem in terms of the complementary event. In this case $1 - P(X < 8)$ would have had more terms to calculate. However, use of the complementary event is the best way to approach part (b).

(b) $P(X \geqslant 1) = 1 - P(X = 0)$

$\qquad\qquad = 1 - 0.7^{12}$

$\qquad\qquad = 0.986$

9.5 THE NORMAL DISTRIBUTION

The normal distribution is a continuous probability distribution with probability density function

$$f(x) = \frac{1}{\sqrt{2\pi\sigma^2}}\, e^{-(1/2)([x - \mu]/\sigma)^2}$$

A graph of this function is a bell-shaped curve which is symmetrical about the mean value, μ. The degree to which it is spread out is determined by the value of the standard deviation, σ (Figure 9.7) Although it is not practical to show it on the diagrams, the two tails of the curve extend indefinitely, never quite touching the x-axis.

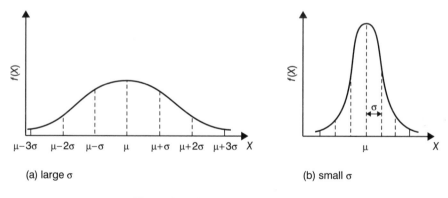

Figure 9.7   (a) Large σ (b) Small σ

For every normal distribution, regardless of how spread out it is, approximately 68% of the area under the curve is within one standard deviation of the mean, 95% of the area is within 1.96 standard deviations of the mean and about 99.7% of the area within three standard deviations. These properties enable a feel to be obtained for the likelihood of a particular observation being recorded. An observation more than, say, three standard deviations from the mean would be very rare and perhaps could be regarded with suspicion. If you are satisfied that the recording is accurate, perhaps the reading casts doubt on the value of μ or σ being used. This is discussed further in the next chapter.

The probability of an observation lying between a and b is found by calculating the area under the curve between these two values (Figure 9.8). Unfortunately it is not possible to evaluate

$$\int_a^b \frac{1}{\sqrt{2\pi\sigma^2}}\, e^{-(1/2)([x - \mu]/\sigma)^2}\, dx$$

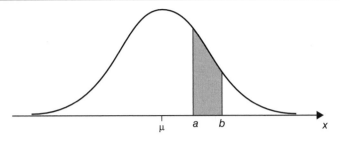

Figure 9.8

analytically. Instead, a numerical evaluation must be performed by computer. However, there are an infinite number of different normal distributions, depending on the values of μ and σ, and producing numerical evaluations for each required probability is not practical. Fortunately it is possible to convert observations from any normal distribution into equivalent values from the *standard normal distribution*.

9.5.1 The Standard Normal Distribution

The *standard normal distribution* is a special case of the normal distribution, having mean 0 and standard deviation 1. Probabilities from this distribution are available in published tables (see pp. 410–11). To use these tables to find probabilities for a normal distribution, mean μ and standard deviation σ, each observation x is transformed using the formula $z = (x - \mu)/\sigma$. This transformation is simply a change of scale:

$$P(X \leqslant A) = P\left(\frac{X - \mu}{\sigma} \leqslant \frac{A - \mu}{\sigma}\right)$$

and from equations (9.10) and (9.15) the distribution of $(X - \mu)/\sigma$ has mean 0 and standard deviation 1. Thus, a transformed value, z, belongs to the standard normal distribution and this we look up in the table on pp. 410–11.

The table gives areas in the right-hand tail of the standard normal distribution for positive values of z (Figure 9.9). Any required area can be calculated using symmetry, by subtracting from 1, or by adding or subtracting two areas with different values of z. It is advisable to sketch the required area, then it becomes clear how the values extracted from the table should be combined.

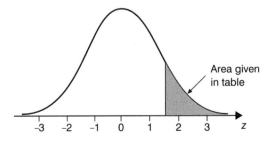

Figure 9.9

Example 9.10

Historically, the daily percentage price change of a particular share has been normally distributed with mean 0.032% and standard deviation 0.006%. Find the probability that on a specific day the price change is between 0.03 and 0.0325.

Answer

$$\text{Normal distribution: } \mu = 0.032, \qquad \sigma = 0.006$$

The required probability is

$$P(0.03 \leqslant X \leqslant 0.0325)$$

First, convert the lower limit to a value from the standard normal distribution:

$$x = 0.03 \qquad z = \frac{0.03 - 0.032}{0.006}$$

$$= -0.33$$

Looking up $z = 0.33$, since only positive values are given, we find $P(z > 0.33) = 0.3707$. By symmetry, this will be the left-hand tail area from $z = -0.33$ (see Figure 9.10).

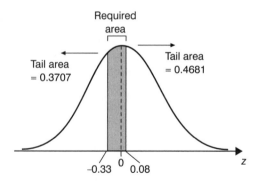

Figure 9.10

Then the upper limit:

$$x = 0.0325 \qquad z = \frac{0.0325 - 0.032}{0.006}$$

$$= 0.08$$

From the table, $P(z > 0.08) = 0.4681$. It can be seen from Figure 9.10 that the required probability is

$$1 - (0.3707 + 0.4681) = 0.1612$$

Other standard normal tables may give areas in the left-hand tail (Figure 9.11a) or the area between 0 and a positive z value (Figure 9.11b). It is essential to know which type of table you are working with.

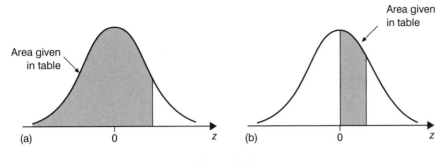

Figure 9.11

9.6 THE NORMAL APPROXIMATION TO THE BINOMIAL

If we have a binomial distribution for which the value of n is large and the value of p is not too extreme, a histogram of binomial probabilities would be shaped very much like a normal distribution (Figure 9.12), suggesting that the normal distribution could be used as an approximation to the binomial distribution.

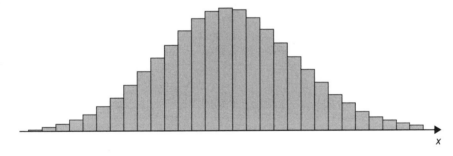

Figure 9.12

Since calculating binomial probabilities is tedious and may not be efficient, using the normal distribution with $\mu = np$ and $\sigma = \sqrt{npq}$ is usually preferable. The following rules of thumb are generally applied when deciding whether to use a normal approximation in order to ensure a satisfactory level of accuracy:

(i) $0.1 \leqslant p \leqslant 0.9$
(ii) $\mu = np > 5$

Additionally, discrete observations are converted into continuous intervals, for example, $x = 6$ becomes $5.5 \leqslant x < 6.5$.

Example 9.11

Returning to the fund management company of example 9.9, suppose it has 60 fund managers. Find the probability that for any given quarter between 20 and 26 (inclusive) of their funds lie in the top quartile of comparable funds.

Answer

First, using the normal approximation to the binomial:

$$\mu = np = 18 \qquad \sigma = \sqrt{npq} = \sqrt{12.6}$$

The required probability is $P(19.5 \leqslant X \leqslant 26.5)$

When $x = 19.5$: $z = \dfrac{19.5 - 18}{\sqrt{12.6}} = 0.42$

Looking this value up in the table on pp. 410 yields a probability of 0.3372.

When $x = 26.5$: $z = \dfrac{26.5 - 18}{\sqrt{12.6}} = 2.39$

Looking this value up in the table yields a probability of 0.00866.

 Figure 9.13 shows a sketch of these two probabilities. Thus, the required probability is

$$0.3372 - 0.00866 = 0.32854$$

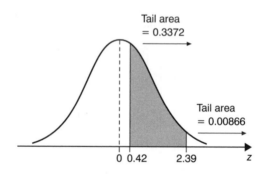

Figure 9.13

Let us compare this with the exact binomial solution for $n = 60$, $p = 0.3$:

$$P(20) \leqslant X \leqslant 26) = {}^{60}C_{20}0.3^{20}0.7^{40} + {}^{60}C_{21}0.3^{21}0.7^{39} + {}^{60}C_{22}0.3^{22}0.7^{38}$$

$$+ {}^{60}C_{23}0.3^{23}0.7^{37} + {}^{60}C_{24}0.3^{24}0.7^{36} + {}^{60}C_{25}0.3^{25}0.7^{35}$$

$$+ {}^{60}C_{26}0.3^{26}0.7^{34}$$

$$= 0.32088$$

 The accuracy of the normal approximation to the binomial is quite good, with far less scope for computational errors.
 The continuity correction is important. If it had been omitted in this example we would have calculated $P(20 \leqslant X \leqslant 26)$:

$$x = 20 \qquad z = 0.56 \qquad \text{table value} = 0.2877$$
$$x = 26 \qquad z = 2.25 \qquad \text{table value} = 0.01222$$

The calculated probability would have been $0.2877 - 0.01222 = 0.27548$, which is a very poor approximation to the exact binomial solution.

9.6.1 Binomial Proportions

When using the normal approximation to the binomial distribution, the transformation $z = (x - \mu)/\sigma$, discussed in Section 9.5.1, becomes $z = (x - np)/\sqrt{npq}$. Sometimes it is more convenient to work with the proportion of successes in n trials, rather than the actual number of successes, x. Let $\hat{p} = x/n$ denote that proportion, then dividing numerator and denominator by n, we obtain

$$z = \frac{\hat{p} - p}{\sqrt{\dfrac{pq}{n}}}$$

Thus

$$\mu_{\hat{p}} = p \qquad \text{and} \qquad \sigma_{\hat{p}} = \sqrt{\frac{pq}{n}}$$

9.7 THE LOGNORMAL DISTRIBUTION

The *lognormal distribution* is a continuous distribution, for a positive variable, with probability density function

$$f(x) = \frac{1}{\sqrt{2\pi}\sigma x} e^{-1/2([\ln(x) - \mu]/\sigma)^2}, \qquad x > 0$$

It has

$$\text{Mean} = e^{(\mu + 1/2\sigma^2)} \qquad \text{and} \qquad \text{Variance} = e^{(2\mu + \sigma^2)}(e^{\sigma^2} - 1) = m^2\alpha^2$$

where m is the mean and α is the coefficient of variation.

While this looks rather forbidding, it is not too difficult when stated as follows:

A random variable X has a lognormal distribution with parameters μ and σ, if $Y = \ln(X)$ has the normal distribution with mean μ and standard deviation σ.

Being positively skewed, with a range from 0 to ∞, the lognormal distribution is useful for modelling investment returns.

Example 9.12

An investment bank models the expected performance of its assets over a given period such that over that period, the rate of return on the bank's portfolio, i, has a mean value of 0.1% and standard deviation of 0.2%. Assume that $(1 + i)$ is lognormally distributed.
Calculate the value of j such that the probability that i is less than or equal to j is 0.05.

Answer

$(1 + i)$ is lognormally distributed with mean (1.001) and variance 4×10^{-6}. If $(1 + i)$ is lognormally distributed then $\ln(1 + i) \sim N(\mu, \sigma^2)$ and $E(1 + i) = \exp[(\mu + \sigma^2/2]$ and variance $\exp[2\mu + \sigma^2][\exp(\sigma^2) - 1]$. Therefore:

$$1.001 = \exp[\mu + \sigma^2/2] \quad \text{and} \quad 4 \times 10^{-6} = \exp[2\mu + \sigma^2][\exp(\sigma^2) - 1]$$

$$\therefore \quad \frac{4 \times 10^{-6}}{1.001^2} = \exp(\sigma^2) - 1 \quad \text{and} \quad \sigma^2 = 3.992 \times 10^{-6}$$

and using this value for σ^2 in the equation 9 for the mean we obtain $\mu = 0.0009975$.

We now have the mean and variance of the normal distribution for $\ln(1 + i)$
$\ln(1 + i) \sim N(9.9975 \times 10^{-4}, 3.992 \times 10^{-6})$.

We require a value for j such than $P(i < j) = 0.05$

$$\frac{\ln(1 + i) - 9.975 \times 10^{-4}}{\sqrt{3.992 \times 10 - 6}} \sim N(0, 1)$$

Probability that $Z \leqslant -1.645 = 0.05$ where $Z \sim N(0, 1)$

$$\therefore \quad P\left(\frac{\ln(1 + i) - 9.975 \times 10^{-4}}{\sqrt{3.992 \times 10^{-6}}}\right) \leqslant -1.645 = 0.05$$

$$\therefore \quad P(\ln(1 + j) \leqslant -2.28921 \times 10^{-3}) = 0.05$$

$$\therefore \quad j = -0.2287\%$$

9.8 THE CONCEPT OF PROBABILITY APPLIED TO INVESTMENT RETURNS

An analyst employing a deterministic approach to financial mathematics may well use a best estimate of the rate of interest over any time period, in order to calculate present values or accumulated values of future cash flows. If the stochastic approach is employed, more information can be used to calculate expected values and variances of cash flow accumulations, together with other useful statistics.

Rather than using a best estimate for the rate of interest, an analyst may be able to use information to form a probability distribution for the rate of interest, thus treating it as a random variable. Because the interest rate may change over time, it is appropriate to define a random variable I_t to be the rate of interest between time $t - 1$ and time t (where time is measured in suitable units, such as years). The assumed probability distributions for the random variable I_t may be either discrete or continuous distributions and can be defined by their probability or density functions respectively.

Example 9.13

At a particular time t, the rate of interest I_t (measured in percentage terms) is assumed to follow the probability distributions described below. In each case calculate (a) the mean value of I_t and (b) the variance of I_t.

(i) A binomial distribution with parameters $p = 0.5$, $n = 12$.
(ii) A distribution with density function $f(i_i) = 1/(10 - 3)$. (N.B. this is known as a uniform distribution with parameters 10 and 3).

Answer

(i) The probability function for a binomial distribution with parameters p and n is

$$P(I_t = i_t) = p^{i_t}(1-p)^{n-i_t}\,{}^{n}C_{i_t}$$

the mean value is np and the variance is $np(1-p)$ (see Section 9.4).

(a) The mean value of $I_t = 0.5 \times 12$
$$= 6.$$
(b) The variance of $I_t = 12 \times 0.5 \times 0.5$
$$= 3.$$

(ii) We are given a probability density function and, in order to find the expectation of the random variable, we must integrate the density function multiplied by the value of I_t, over all possible values of I_t (i.e. equation 9.8, modified for the continuous variable). In the case of this uniform distribution, the range of possible values of I_t is 3 to 10.

(a) The mean value of I_t is

$$E[I_t] = \int_3^{10} \frac{1}{10-3} \times i_t \, di_t$$

$$= \left[\frac{i_t^2}{14}\right]_3^{10}$$

$$= \frac{100}{14} - \frac{9}{14} = 6.5$$

(b) Equation 9.19 indicates that to find the variance we should first find $E[I_t^2]$

$$E[I_t^2] = \int_3^{10} \frac{1}{10-3} \times i_t^2 \, di_t$$

$$= \left[\frac{i_t^3}{21}\right]_3^{10}$$

$$= \frac{1000}{21} - \frac{27}{21} = 46.3$$

and the variance is

$$E[I_t^2] - [E[I_t]]^2 = 46.3 - 6.5^2 = 4.05$$

9.9 SOME USEFUL PROBABILITY RESULTS

Most of the probabilistic and statistical results which will be needed in later sections have already been presented in Section 9.3. It is worth reiterating these, however, using notation relevant to the random variable I_t, which has already been defined. These results will then be used in the derivation of moments of accumulated values.

Result 1

$$\text{var}(I_t) = E[I_t^2] - (E[I_t])^2$$

thus, if $E[I_t] = \iota_t$, then

$$\text{var}(I_t) = E[I_t^2] - \iota_t^2 \qquad \text{(cf. equation 9.19)}$$

Result 2   If $h(I_t)$ is a function of the random variable I_t and if k and c are constants, then

$$E[h(I_t)k + c] = kE[h(I_t)] + c$$

(combining equations 9.9 and 9.10)

Result 3a

$$\text{var}(I_t + c) = \text{var}(I_t) \qquad \text{(cf. equation 9.16)}$$

Result 3b

$$\text{var } k(I_t) = k^2 \text{ var}(I_t) \qquad \text{(cf. equation 9.15)}$$

Result 4   A further important result arises from the consideration of independent events. If a number of random variables are independent, the expectation of the product of the random variables is the product of the expectations of the random variables. For example, given a series of independent random variables $I_1, I_2, ..., I_n$, then

$$E[I_1 \times I_2 \cdots \times I_n] = E[I_1]E[I_2] \ldots E[I_n] \qquad \text{(cf. equation 9.13)}$$

Result 5   Adding the constant c to each random variable has no effect on their independence, so that

$$E[(I_1 + c)(I_2 + c) \ldots (I_n + c)] = (E[I_1] + c)(E[I_2] + c) \ldots (E[I_n] + c)$$

Result 6   Similarly, if a function of independent random variables is considered, the variables will remain independent, thus:

$$E\{[h(I_1) + c][h(I_2) + c] \ldots [h(I_n) + c]\} = E[h(I_1) + c]E[h(I_2) + c] \ldots E[h(I_n) + c]$$

It is also necessary to revisit the definition of a moment of a random variable (Section 9.3.8). The kth moment of the random variable I_t is defined to be

$$M_k(I_t) = E[I_t^k]$$

In other words, it is the expectation of the kth power of the random variable. For example, let $k = 1$, then $M_1(I_t) = E[I_t]$. This is the mean value of I_t. Let $k = 2$, then $M_2 = E[I_t^2]$.

Using Result 1, it can be said that, because $\text{var}(I_t) = E[I_t^2] - (E[I_t])^2$, variance of a random variable is equal to the second moment of the random variable minus the first moment squared.

Example 9.14

An analyst believes that the rate of return on equities during 2002 will take one of the following values:

$$6\% \text{ with probability } 0.2$$
$$8\% \text{ with probability } 0.3$$
$$10\% \text{ with probability } 0.3$$
$$12\% \text{ with probability } 0.1$$
$$14\% \text{ with probability } 0.1$$

For the percentage rate of interest calculate: (a) the first moment, (b) the second moment, (c) the variance.

Answer

(a) The first moment, the mean, is

$$E[I_{2002}] = [0.2 \times 6 + 0.3 \times 8 + 0.3 \times 10 + 0.1 \times 12 + 0.1 \times 14]\% = 9.2\%$$

(b) The second moment is $E[I_{2002}^2]$, thus we take each value, square it and multiply by the appropriate probability, i.e.

$$[0.2 \times 6^2 + 0.3 \times 8^2 + 0.3 \times 10^2 + 0.1 \times 12^2 + 0.1 \times 14^2] = 90.4$$

(c) The variance is

$$E[I_{2002}^2] - (E[I_{2002}])^2 = 90.4 - 9.2^2 = 5.76$$

9.10 ACCUMULATION OF INVESTMENTS USING A STOCHASTIC APPROACH: ONE TIME PERIOD

Having looked at the calculation of moments of rates of interest, it is now appropriate to move on to consider the accumulation of amounts of money using a stochastic rather than a deterministic approach to the theory of interest. In the case where money is accumulated over one time period, useful results can be derived easily. In particular, the mean and variance of the rate of interest can be used to calculate the mean, the second moment and hence, the variance of the accumulation of a sum of money over one time period.

The notation I_t will again be used to denote the rate of interest as a random variable for the period $t-1$ to t; the mean value of the rate of interest will be denoted by ι_t (that is by the Greek letter ι, pronounced iota, with the appropriate subscript) and the variance by s_t^2, for the period $t-1$ to t.

The expected value of the accumulation of a unit sum of money, over the period $t-1$ to t is $E[1 + (I_t)]$. Using Result 2 from Section 9.9, this is equal to $[1 + E[I_t]] = (1 + \iota_t)$. That is, the expected accumulation of a unit sum invested for one time period is equal to the accumulation of the sum at the expected interest rate.

Using Result 3a, the variance of the accumulation of a unit sum invested from time $t-1$ to t is $\text{var}[(1 + (I_t)] = \text{var}(I_t) = s_t^2$.

It is worth noting that the variance of I_t would probably be calculated using the probability function or density function, by calculating the second moment of the random variable I_t, i.e. $E[I_t^2]$ and subtracting the square of the first moment. Thus, using Result 1:

$$\text{var}(I_t) = E[I_t^2] - [E[I_t]]^2$$

Having calculated the variance of $(1 + I_t)$, the second moment can be calculated as follows:

$$E[1 + I_t]^2 = \text{var}(1 + I_t) + [E[1 + I_t]]^2 = s_t^2 + (1 + \iota_t)^2 \qquad (9.22)$$

Example 9.15

An investor is considering investing a sum of money for 1 year. The annual effective rate of interest is not known with certainty, but it is believed that it will take a value 0.08 with probability 0.3, 0.09 with probability 0.4, or 0.12 with probability 0.3. Calculate, for the accumulation of £10 for one year:

(a) the first and second moments of the rate of interest;
(b) the expected accumulation;
(c) the second moment of the accumulation;
(d) the standard deviation of the accumulation.

Answer

(a) The expected value of the rate of interest is

$$(0.3 \times 0.08 + 0.4 \times 0.09 + 0.3 \times 0.12) = 0.096$$

The second moment of the rate of interest is

$$(0.3 \times 0.08^2 + 0.4 \times 0.09^2 + 0.3 \times 0.12^2) = 0.00948$$

(b) The expected accumulation of £10 is

$$E[10(1 + I_t)] = 10 \times 1.096 = £10.96$$

(i.e. the expected accumulation is the accumulation at the expected rate of interest).

(c) The second moment is the expected value of the square of the accumulation, which can be calculated in two ways. First, it can be calculated directly as follows:

$$0.3 \times [10 \times 1.08]^2 + 0.4 \times [10 \times 1.09]^2 + 0.3 \times [10 \times 1.12]^2 = 120.148$$

Second, it can be calculated using the mean and variance of the rate of interest

$$\text{var}[10(1 + I_t)] = 100 \ \text{var}(1 + I_t)$$

$$= 100 \ \text{var}(I_t) = 100(0.00948 - 0.096^2)$$

$$= 0.0264$$

and

$$\{E[10(1 + I_t)]\}^2 = 10.96^2$$

therefore

$$E[10(1 + I_t)]^2 = 0.0264 + 10.96^2 = 120.148$$

(d) The variance of the accumulation has been calculated above. The standard deviation is the square root of the variance $= \sqrt{0.0264}$. Thus the required value is 0.1625.

9.11 ACCUMULATION OF SINGLE INVESTMENTS WITH INDEPENDENT RATES OF RETURN

Useful results can be obtained if the rate of return is regarded as a random variable which can take different values in each successive year, and it is assumed that the value it takes in one year is independent of the value taken in any other year. This is particularly the case if the rates of interest are assumed to follow the same probability distribution in each year. These results use standard results from probability theory. They are derived by a different method and discussed in the text by McCutcheon and Scott (1986), to which the interested reader may refer.

The accumulation of a single unit sum of money invested for n years will be defined as A_n. In general, it can be said that.

$$E[A_n] = E[(1 + I_1)(1 + I_2)(1 + I_3) \ldots (1 + I_n)]$$

If each of the I_t's are independent random variables then, using Result 4,

$$E[A_n] = E[1 + I_1]E[1 + I_2] \ldots E[1 + I_n] = (1 + \iota_1)(1 + \iota_2) \ldots (1 + \iota_n) \qquad (9.23)$$

where $\iota_t = E[I_t]$. Therefore, the expected value of the accumulation of a single investment is equal to the accumulation of the investment at the expected rates of interest in each year. Furthermore,

$$E[A_n^2] = E\{[(1 + I_1)(1 + I_2) \ldots (1 + I_n)]^2\}$$

If successive values of $(1 + i_t)$ are independent, then successive values of $(1 + i_t)^2$ must also be independent. Therefore,

$$E[A_n^2] = E[(1 + I_1)^2(1 + I_2)^2 \ldots (1 + I_n)^2]$$

$$= E[(1 + I_1)^2]E[(1 + I_2)^2] \ldots E[(1 + I_n)^2] \qquad (9.24)$$

Thus the second moment of A_n is the product of the second moments of the accumulations in the individual years.

If the variance of the rate of interest in the tth year is s_t^2, then the variance of the accumulation of a unit of money in the tth year is also s_t^2 (from Probability Result 3a). The second moment of the accumulation in the tth year (i.e. $E[1 + I_t]^2$) is the square of the mean of the accumulation, plus the variance, which is $(1 + \iota_t)^2 + s_t^2$ from Probability Result 1. Therefore the second moment of the accumulation, over n years is

$$[s_1^2 + (1 + \iota_1)^2][s_2^2 + (1 + \iota_2)^2] \dots [s_n^2 + (1 + \iota_n)^2]$$

and the variance is the second moment minus the square of the mean, which is

$$[s_1^2 + (1 + \iota_1)^2][s_2^2 + (1 + \iota_2)^2] \dots [s_n^2 + (1 + \iota_n)^2] - (1 + \iota_1)^2(1 + \iota_2)^2 \dots (1 + \iota_n)^2$$

Thus if the mean and variance, or else the first and second moments, of the rate of interest in each year can be estimated, it is possible to calculate the mean and the variance of the accumulation of a sum of money over any number of years.

If it is further assumed that the rate of interest is a random variable which is identically and independently distributed with mean ι and variance s^2 in each year, the results simplify still further. Equation (9.23) becomes

$$E[A_n] = (1 + \iota)(1 + \iota) \dots (1 + \iota) = (1 + \iota)^n \tag{9.25}$$

which is analogous to the simple compound interest results derived in Part I of this book. Equation (9.24) becomes

$$E[A_n^2] = [s^2 + (1 + \iota)^2][s^2 + (1 + \iota)^2] \dots [s^2 + (1 + \iota)^2]$$

Therefore,

$$E[A_n^2] = [1 + 2\iota + \iota^2 + s^2]^n \tag{9.26}$$

and the variance of the accumulation is

$$E[A_n^2] - (E[A_n])^2 = [1 + 2\iota + \iota^2 + s^2]^n - (1 + \iota)^{2n} \tag{9.27}$$

because $[(1 + \iota)^n]^2 = (1 + \iota)^{2n}$.

Example 9.16

The rate of interest is a random variable which is distributed with mean 0.08 and variance 0.01 in each of the next 15 years. The value taken by the rate of interest in any one year is independent of the values taken in any other year. Calculate:

(a) the expected accumulation, at the end of 15 years, if one unit is invested at the beginning of 15 years;
(b) the second moment of the accumulation;
(c) the variance of the accumulation.

How would the answers to (a) and (c) differ if 10 units had been invested for 15 years?

Answer

(a) The expected value of the rate of interest, $\iota = 0.08$. The expected accumulation is therefore (using equation (9.25))

$$(1.08)^{15} = 3.17$$

(b) The second moment of the accumulation is

$$[1 + 2\iota + \iota^2 + s^2]^n = [1 + 2 \times 0.08 + 0.08^2 + 0.01]^{15}$$

(where s^2 is the variance of the rate of interest)

$$= 11.437$$

(c) The variance is the second moment of the accumulation minus the square of the first moment:

$$11.437 - (3.17)^2 = 1.3881$$

The statistical results stated earlier can be used to calculate values for the expectation and variance of the accumulation of 10 units. Using Probability Result 2, the expected accumulation if 10 units are invested is ten times the expected accumulation if one unit is invested; therefore,

$$\text{Expected accumulation} = 10 \times 3.17 = 31.7$$

Using Probability Result 3, the variance is 10^2 times the variance if only one unit had been invested; therefore,

$$\text{Variance} = 100 \times 1.3881 = 138.81$$

9.12 THE ACCUMULATION OF ANNUAL INVESTMENTS WITH INDEPENDENT RATES OF RETURN

The next application of the stochastic approach to the theory of interest which will be considered is the accumulation of annual investments. There are two examples of this application which may be of particular interest: first, an investor may wish to make a series of annual investments (this may be an insurance company wishing to invest annual premiums from an insurance policy); second, an investor may purchase a security, such as a bond, and wish to accumulate the coupon payments from the bond until the maturity date. The coupon payments will then form a series of annual (or semi-annual) investments invested at an unknown rate of interest. We will again assume that the values taken by the rate of interest are independent of each other.

The accumulation of a series of annual investments of one unit *per annum*, for n years, will be denoted by P_n.

$$\begin{aligned}
P_n = &(1 + i_1)(1 + i_2) \ldots (1 + i_n) \\
&+ (1 + i_2)(1 + i_3) \ldots (1 + i_n) \\
&+ (1 + i_3)(1 + i_4) \ldots (1 + i_n) \\
&+ \cdots \\
&+ (1 + i_{n-1})(1 + i_n) \\
&+ (1 + i_n)
\end{aligned}$$

The annual investments can be seen merely as a series of single investments, invested at the beginning of each of the next n years.

If the accumulation of $(n-1)$ annual premiums is considered, then

$$\begin{aligned}
P_{n-1} = {} & (1+i_1)(1+i_2) \ldots (1+i_{n-1}) \\
& + (1+i_2)(1+i_3) \ldots (1+i_{n-1}) \\
& + (1+i_4)(1+i_5) \ldots (1+i_{n-1}) \\
& + \cdots \\
& + (1+i_{n-2})(1+i_{n-1}) \\
& + (1+i_{n-1})
\end{aligned}$$

The relationship between P_n and P_{n-1} is $P_n = (1+i_n)(1+P_{n-1})$. That is, the accumulation of n annual premiums is equal to the accumulation of $(n-1)$ annual premiums, further accumulated for one year plus an additional investment of one unit accumulated over the nth year. Therefore, $E[P_n] = E[(1+I_n)(1+P_{n-1})]$ using this relationship. P_{n-1} is dependent only on the values taken by the random variables $(I_1), (I_2), \ldots, (I_{n-1})$ which have all been assumed to be independent of the value taken by the random variable I_n. Therefore, using Probability Result 5:

$$E[P_n] = E[1+I_n]E[1+P_{n-1}]$$

This relationship can now be used to determine successive values of $E[P_n]$ Again, to simplify the notation, $E[I_t]$ will be defined as ι_t,

$$\begin{aligned}
E[P_1] &= E[1+I_1] = (1+\iota_1) \\
E[P_2] &= E[1+I_2]E[1+P_1] \\
&= (1+\iota_2)(1+1+\iota_1) = (1+\iota_1)(1+\iota_2)+(1+\iota_2) \\
E[P_3] &= E[1+I_3]E[1+P_2] \\
&= (1+\iota_3)[1+(1+\iota_1)(1+\iota_2)+(1+\iota_2)] \\
&= (1+\iota_1)(1+\iota_2)(1+\iota_3)+(1+\iota_2)(1+\iota_3)+(1+\iota_3)
\end{aligned}$$

In general:

$$\begin{aligned}
E[P_n] &= E[1+I_n]E[1+P_{n-1}] \\
&= (1+\iota_n)E[1+P_{n-1}] \\
&= (1+\iota_n)[1+(1+\iota_{n-1})(1+\iota_{n-2}) \ldots (1+\iota_1) \\
&\quad + (1+\iota_{n-1})(1+\iota_{n-2}) \ldots (1+\iota_2)+\cdots+(1+\iota_{n-1})] \\
&= (1+\iota_n)(1+\iota_{n-1}) \ldots (1+\iota_1)+(1+\iota_n)(1+\iota_{n-1}) \ldots (1+\iota_2) \\
&\quad +\cdots+(1+\iota_n)(1+\iota_{n-1})+(1+\iota_n)
\end{aligned} \tag{9.28}$$

It may be regarded as more desirable to keep the expression in the more general form

$$E[P_n] = (1+\iota_n)E[1+P\iota_{n-1}] \tag{9.29}$$

It is also of interest to derive the second moment of the accumulation of annual investments

$$E[P_n^2] = E[(1 + I_n)^2(1 + P_{n-1})^2] = E[(1 + I_n)^2]E[(1 + P_{n-1})^2] \quad \text{(due to independence)}$$

$$= E[1 + 2I_n + I_n^2]E[1 + 2P_{n-1} + P_{n-1}^2] \tag{9.30}$$

Again, the recurrence relationship can be used to find an expression for $E[P_n^2]$ in successive years; defining s_t^2 to be the variance of the rate of interest in year t

$$E[P_1^2] = E[(1 + I_1)^2]$$

$$= E[1 + 2I_1 + I_1^2]$$

$$= [1 + 2\iota_1 + s_1^2 + \iota_1^2], \qquad \text{as } E[I_1^2] = s_1^2 + \iota_1^2$$

Similarly,

$$E[P_2^2] = E[(1 + I_2)^2]E[(1 + P_1)^2]$$

$$= E[1 + 2I_2 + I_2^2]E[1 + 2P_1 + P_1^2]$$

$$= (1 + 2\iota_2 + s_2^2 + \iota_2^2)(1 + 2E[P_1] + s_1^2 + \iota_1^2)$$

$$\text{where } E[P_1] \text{ is calculated as above}$$

In general:

$$E[P_n^2] = E[(1 + I_n)^2]E[(1 + P_{n-1})^2]$$

$$= (1 + 2\iota_n + s_n^2 + \iota_n^2)[1 + 2E[P_{n-1}] + E[P_{n-1}^2]] \tag{9.31}$$

This recurrence relationship can be used to calculate successive values of the second moment of P_n.

The variance of P_n can then be found, in the usual way, by subtracting the square of the first moment. Therefore,

$$\text{var}(P_n) = (1 + 2\iota_n + s_n^2 + \iota_n^2)\{1 + 2E[P_{n-1}] + E[P_{n-1}^2]\}$$

$$- (1 + \iota_n)^2\{E[1 + P_{n-1}]\}^2 \tag{9.32}$$

Once again, convenient results can be obtained if it is assumed that $E[I_t] = \iota$ for all values of t and that $s_t^2 = s^2$ for all values of t: that is if we assume that the first and second moments of the distribution of I_t are the same for all t. Equation (9.28) then becomes

$$E[P_n] = (1 + \iota)^n + (1 + \iota)^{n-1} + \cdots + (1 + \iota) \tag{9.33}$$

In general, from equations (9.29) and (9.33) it can be seen that

$$E[P_n] = (1 + \iota)E[1 + P_{n-1}] = \ddot{s}_{\overline{n}} \qquad \text{(calculated at rate of interest } \iota) \tag{9.34}$$

Therefore, $E[P_n]$ is equal to the accumulation of a series of annual investments calculated at the expected rate of interest. This is analogous to the result, derived in the previous section that $E[A_n] = (1 + \iota)^n$. This result could also be derived by summing the expected accumulations of a series of annual premiums.

From equations (9.31) and (9.32):

$$E[P_n^2] = (1 + 2\iota + s^2 + \iota^2)\{1 + 2E[P_{n-1}] + E[P_{n-1}]^2\} \tag{9.35}$$

$$\text{var}(P_n) = (1 + 2\iota + s^2 + \iota^2)\{1 + 2E[P_{n-1}] + E[P_{n-1}^2]\} - (E[P_n])^2 \tag{9.36}$$

Clearly, unless computer methods are used, the calculation of second moments and variances of accumulations of annual investments will become difficult for large values of n.

Example 9.17

An investment manager purchases a bond on 1 January 2001 which has a maturity value of £100 and pays a coupon of £5 per £100 nominal at the end of every year. The bond is redeemed on 31 December 2006 and the investment manager wishes to invest the coupon payments, on deposit, until the bond is redeemed. It is assumed that the rate of interest at which the coupon payments can be reinvested is a random variable and the rate of interest in any one year is independent of the rate of interest in any other year.

  (i) Find the mean value of the total accumulated investment on 31 December 2006 if the rate of interest has an expected value of 8% in 2002, 7% in 2003, 6% in 2004, and 5% in 2005 and 2006.
 (ii) Calculate the mean value of the total accumulated investment on 31 December 2006 if the rate of interest has an expected value of 6.5% in each of the years from 2002 to 2006 inclusive.
(iii) State an expression in terms of moments of P_4 which would allow you to calculate the variance of the accumulated value of the investment, assuming that the variance of the interest rate is the same in each year and is equal to 0.01.

Answer

In this case, a series of five annual investments of £5 is being considered; if the expected value of these investments is found, the £100 maturity value plus the final £5 coupon payment can simply be added to this expected value to find the mean of the total, as the final payments are not random variables.

(i) Returning to equation (9.28) and using Probability Result 2:

$$E[5(P_5)] = 5 \times E[P_5] = 5[(1 + \iota_5)(1 + \iota_4)(1 + \iota_3)(1 + \iota_2)(1 + \iota_1)$$
$$+ (1 + \iota_5)(1 + \iota_4)(1 + \iota_3)(1 + \iota_2)$$
$$+ (1 + \iota_5)(1 + \iota_4)(1 + \iota_3)$$
$$+ (1 + \iota_5)(1 + \iota_4)$$
$$+ (1 + \iota_5)]$$

(where ι_1 is the rate of interest in 2002, ι_2 the rate of interest in 2003, etc.)

$$= 5[(1.05)^2(1.06)(1.07)(1.08) + (1.05)^2(1.06)(1.07)$$
$$+ (1.05)^2(1.06) + (1.05)^2 + (1.05)]$$
$$= 5[1.3505 + 1.2505 + 1.1687 + 1.1025 + 1.05]$$
$$= 29.611$$

The expected value of the final investment, at maturity, is therefore

$$100 + 5 + 29.611 = £134.61$$

This answer could also be found by using the recurrence relationship in equation (9.29) explicitly, i.e. $E[P_n] = (1 + \iota_n)E[1 + P_{n-1}]$, where ι_n is $E[i_n]$, and this approach is illustrated below.

$$E[P_1] = (1 + \iota_1) = 1.08$$

$$E[P_2] = (1 + \iota_2)E[1 + P_1] = (1.07)(1 + 1.08) \qquad = 2.2256$$

$$E[P_3] = (1 + \iota_3)E[1 + P_2] = (1.06)(1 + 2.2256) \qquad = 3.41914$$

$$E[P_4] = (1 + \iota_4)E[1 + P_3] = (1.05)(1 + 3.41914) = 4.64010$$

$$E[P_5] = (1 + \iota_5)E[1 + P_4] = (1.05)(1 + 4.64010) = 5.9221.$$

Therefore, the expected accumulated value of the coupon payments is

$$5 \times E[P_5] = 5 \times 5.9221 = 29.611$$

and the expected accumulated value of the whole investment is

$$100 + 5 + 29.611 = £134.61$$

(ii) If the interest rate has the same expected value in each year, equation (9.34) can be used to calculate the expected value of the accumulation of the coupons:

$$E[5(P_5)] = 5 \times E[P_5] = 5\ddot{s}_{\overline{5}|} \qquad \text{calculated at } 6.5\%$$

$$= \frac{(5 \times 1.065)(1.065^5 - 1)}{0.065} = 30.3186$$

Therefore the expected accumulated value of the total investment is

$$100 + 5 + 30.3186 = £135.319$$

(iii) It is now necessary to find an expression for the variance of a random variable $(5 \times P_5)$ plus a constant (105). Using Probability Result 3, this variance must equal $5^2 \operatorname{var}(P_5)$, as the addition of the constant does, not affect the variance. From equation (9.24)

$$E[P_5^2] = (1 + 2\iota + s^2 + \iota^2)[1 + 2E[P_4] + E[P_4^2]]$$

where ι is the expected value of the interest rate and s^2 is the variance of the rate of interest (both of which are the same in all years). Inserting these values for the parameters, the following expression is obtained:

$$(1 + 2 \times 0.065 + 0.01 + 0.065^2)[1 + 2\ddot{s}_{\overline{4}|} + E[P_4^2]]$$

$$\text{where } \ddot{s}_{\overline{4}|} \text{ is calculated at } 6.5\%$$

$$\ddot{s}_{\overline{4}|} = \frac{1.065(1.065^4 - 1)}{0.065} = 4.6936$$

Therefore,

$$E[P_5^2] = 1.4423E[10.3872 + E[P_4^2]] = 11.8853 + 1.4423 \times E[P_4^2]$$

Therefore

$$\text{var}(P_t) = 11.8853 + 1.14423E[P_4^2] - [E[P_5]]^2 \qquad \text{(using Probability Result 1)}$$

$$= 1.14423E[P_4^2] - 24.8834.$$

Thus the variance of the total investment is

$$25[1.14423E[P_4^2] - 24.8834] = 28.60575E[P_4^2] - 622.085$$

A further example of the application of the stochastic approach to financial mathematics arises from analysing the accumulation of a level annual deposit per year when the interest rate is assumed to be a random variable. This is illustrated below.

Example 9.18

In any year the yield on funds invested on deposit has a mean value ι and standard deviation s and is independent of yields in all previous years. Money is invested only at the beginning of the year. Find the mean and variance, at the end of 2 years, of the accumulation of an investment of one unit of money *per annum* at the beginning of each year if $\iota = 0.06$ and $s = 0.01$.

Answer

Using equation (9.34), the expected value, at the end of 2 years, of the annual investments is

$$E[P_2] = \ddot{s}_{\overline{2}|} \text{ calculated at } 6\% = \frac{(1.06)(1.06^2 - 1)}{0.06} = 2.1836$$

To obtain the variance of the deposit, it is required to establish successive values of $E[P_n^2]$. In this case, as the deposit is for only 2 years, it is only necessary to calculate $E[P_1^2]$ and then this value is used to calculate $E[P_2^2]$ Using equation (9.35)

$$E[P_1^2] = (1 + 2\iota + s^2 + \iota^2) = (1 + 2 \times 0.06 + 0.01^2 + 0.06^2) = 1.1237$$

$$E[P_2^2] = (1 + 2\iota + s^2 + \iota^2)[1 + 2E[P_1] + E[P_1^2]]$$

$$= 1.1237[1 + 2 \times 1.06 + 1.1237]$$

$$= 4.7686 \qquad (\text{as } E[P_1] = \ddot{s}_{\overline{1}|} = 1.06)$$

Therefore

$$\text{var}(P_2) = E[P_2^2] - [E[P_2]]^2$$

$$= 4.7686 - 2.1836^2$$

$$= 0.000\ 49.$$

More complex applications of the stochastic approach to the theory of interest will be discussed in Chapter 17.

Annex 9.1   Properties of the expected value

(i)
$$E[cg(X)] = \sum_{i=1}^{n} cg(x_i)p(x_i)$$

$$= c \sum_{i=1}^{n} g(x_i)p(x_i)$$

$$= cE[g(X)]$$

(ii)
$$E[g(X) + c] = \sum_{i=1}^{n} (g(x_i) + c)p(x_i)$$

$$= \sum_{i=1}^{n} g(x_i)p(x_i) + c \sum_{i=1}^{n} p(x_i)$$

$$= E[g(X)] + c$$

(iii)
$$E[g(X) + h(X)] = \sum_{i=1}^{n} \{g(x_i) + h(x_i)\}p(x_i)$$

$$= \sum_{i=1}^{n} g(x_i)p(x_i) + \sum_{i=1}^{n} h(x_i)p(x_i)$$

$$= E[g(X)] + E[h(X)]$$

(iv) Writing the joint probability $\{p(X = x_i)$ and $(Y = y_j)\}$ as $p(x_i, y_j)$:

$$E[cX + kY] = \sum_{i=1}^{n} \sum_{j=1}^{n} (cx_i + ky_j)p(x_i, y_j)$$

$$= c \sum_{i=1}^{n} \sum_{j=1}^{n} x_i p(x_i, y_j) + k \sum_{i=1}^{n} \sum_{j=1}^{n} y_j p(x_i, y_j)$$

$$= c \sum_{i=1}^{n} x_i p(x_i) + k \sum_{j=1}^{n} y_j p(y_j)$$

since for each x_i
$$\sum_{j=1}^{n} p(x_i, y_j) = p(x_i)$$

and for each y_j
$$\sum_{i=1}^{n} p(x_i, y_j) = p(y_j)$$

Thus,
$$E[cX + kY] = cE[X] + kE[Y]$$

(v) $$E[XY] = \sum_{i=1}^{n} \sum_{j=1}^{n} x_i y_j p(x_i, y_j)$$

$$= \sum_{i=1}^{n} \sum_{j=1}^{n} x_i y_j p(x_i) p(y_j) \text{ since the variables are independent}$$

$$= \sum_{i=1}^{n} x_i p(x_i) \sum_{j=1}^{n} y_j p(y_j)$$

$$= E[X]E[Y]$$

Annex 9.2   Properties of the variance

(i) For equation 9.15

$$\text{var}(kX) = E[(kX - k\mu)^2]$$

$$= k^2 \sum_{i=1}^{n} p(x_i)(x_i - \mu)^2$$

$$= k^2 \, \text{var}(X)$$

(ii) For equation 9.16

$$\text{var}(X + c) = E[\{(X + c) - (\mu + c)\}^2]$$

$$= E[(X - \mu)^2]$$

$$= \text{var}(X)$$

(iii) For equation 9.18

$$\text{var}(cX + kY) = E[(cX + kY)^2] - \{E[cX + kY]\}^2$$

$$= E[c^2 X^2 + 2ckXY + k^2 Y^2]$$

$$- \{c^2 E[X]^2 + 2ck E[X]E[Y] + k^2 E[Y]^2\}$$

and since X and Y are independent $E[XY] = E[X]E[Y]$ so,

$$\text{var}(cX + kY) = c^2(E[X^2] - E[X]^2) + k^2(E[Y^2] - E[Y]^2)$$

$$= c^2 \, \text{var}(X) + k^2 \, \text{var}(Y)$$

REFERENCE

McCutcheon, J. J. and Scott, W. F. (1986), *An Introduction to the Mathematics of Finance*, Heinemann.

Estimating Parameters and Hypothesis Testing

10.1 INTRODUCTION

In Chapter 8 we considered the collection of sample data in order to find out about the characteristics of a larger population. This was seen to be a more efficient use of resources than trying to collect data from the entire population in order to reveal its characteristics. The process of using sample data to estimate the values of population parameters is one aspect of *statistical inference*. We have already encountered estimators for the population mean and standard deviation in Chapter 8. These estimators ($\bar{x}$ and s) take single values and, therefore, the values obtained are termed *point estimates*. In this chapter we will consider a different type of estimate, an *interval estimate*, called a *confidence interval*. Later, we will consider another aspect of statistical inference, *hypothesis testing* which is also known as *significance testing*. This is the process of testing theories (hypotheses) about the values of population parameters. But, first, let us define an *unbiased estimator*.

10.2 UNBIASED ESTIMATORS

An *unbiased estimator* for a population parameter has an expected value which is the same as the actual value of that parameter. For example, suppose a sample is taken and the sample mean found as an estimate of the population mean:

$$E[\bar{X}] = E\left[\frac{1}{n}(X_1 + X_2 + X_3 + \cdots + X_n)\right]$$

$$= \frac{1}{n}\{E[X_1] + E[X_2] + E[X_3] + \cdots + E[X_n]\}$$

$$= \mu$$

The expected value of the sample mean is the population mean, so the sample mean is an unbiased estimator.

The first formula given in Section 8.5.10 for the sample variance was

$$\frac{1}{n}\sum_{i=1}^{n}(x - \bar{x})^2$$

The expected value of this formula is, using equations 9.8 and 9.9, $[(n-1)/n]\sigma^2$ not the population variance, σ^2. Thus, this is a biased estimate of the population variance. However, the expected value obtained indicates how to modify the formula in order to obtain an unbiased estimator. It is necessary to multiply by $n/(n-1)$. Thus,

$$s^2 = \frac{1}{n-1} \sum_{i=1}^{n} (x_i - \bar{x})^2$$

The factor $n/(n-1)$ is called Bessel's correction factor.

10.3 CONFIDENCE INTERVAL FOR THE MEAN

If a sample is taken from a population and its mean $\bar{x}_1$ is calculated, the value of $\bar{x}_1$ can be used as an estimate of the population mean, μ, but how good an estimate is this? How close to μ is $\bar{x}_1$ likely to be? Certainly, if we took another sample and calculated its mean, $\bar{x}_2$, we would expect the value to be different from the value of $\bar{x}_1$ obtained from the first sample. It can be shown that such sample means, provided that the sample size is reasonably large, are approximately normally distributed with mean μ and standard deviation $\sigma/\sqrt{n}$, regardless of the distribution of the underlying population. This is known as the *central limit theorem*. The standard deviation of the sample means, $\sigma/\sqrt{n}$, is called the *standard error of the mean* and Annex 10.1 shows how this expression arises.

Since the distribution of sample means is normal, 95% of sample means lie within 1.96 standard errors of the population mean (Figure 10.1). Thus,

$$P\left(\mu - 1.96\frac{\sigma}{\sqrt{n}} \leqslant \bar{x} \leqslant \mu + 1.96\frac{\sigma}{\sqrt{n}}\right) = 0.95$$

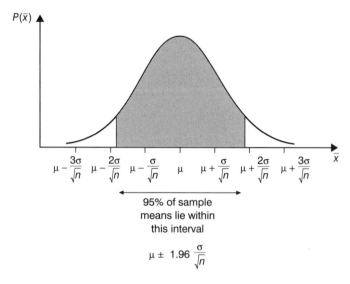

Figure 10.1 The distribution of sample means

Rearranging the first two parts of the inequality:

$$\mu - 1.96 \frac{\sigma}{\sqrt{n}} \leqslant \bar{x}$$

$$\mu \leqslant \bar{x} + 1.96 \frac{\sigma}{\sqrt{n}}$$

Similarly for the second two parts:

$$\bar{x} - 1.96 \frac{\sigma}{\sqrt{n}} \leqslant \mu$$

Combining these again:

$$P\left(\bar{x} - 1.96 \frac{\sigma}{\sqrt{n}} \leqslant \mu \leqslant \bar{x} + 1.96 \frac{\sigma}{\sqrt{n}} \right) = 0.95$$

Thus, there is a probability of 0.95 of the population mean lying in the interval $\bar{x} \pm 1.96\sigma/\sqrt{n}$. The expression $\bar{x} \pm 1.96\sigma/\sqrt{n}$ defines the limits of the 95% *confidence interval for the population mean*.

If many samples are taken from a population, their means found and confidence intervals constructed, 95% of the intervals will contain the population mean. However, 5% of the intervals will fail to capture the population mean. When a single sample is taken, there is no way of telling whether the resultant confidence interval actually contains the population mean, we can only say that it is much more likely that it does than that it is one of the 5% of intervals which do not (see Figure 10.2).

In order to calculate a confidence interval from sample data, the sample mean, the sample size and the population standard deviation should be known. In practice, the final requirement is unrealistic. If the population standard deviation was known, we would probably also know the value of the population mean and hence, would not be concerned with estimating it. However, the expression above remains approximately true if the sample standard deviation, s, is substituted for σ, provided the sample is reasonably large, say over 30.

Example 10.1

In a random sample of 100 bank customers with bad debts, the mean amount owed was £5000 and the standard deviation was £750. In order to estimate the mean value of all unsettled accounts we will construct a 95% confidence interval using the formula $\bar{x} \pm 1.96s/\sqrt{n}$.

Answer

We are 95% sure that the population mean lies in the range

$$5000 \pm 1.96 \frac{750}{\sqrt{100}} = 5000 \pm 147$$

Thus we are 95% confident that μ lies between £4853 and £5147.

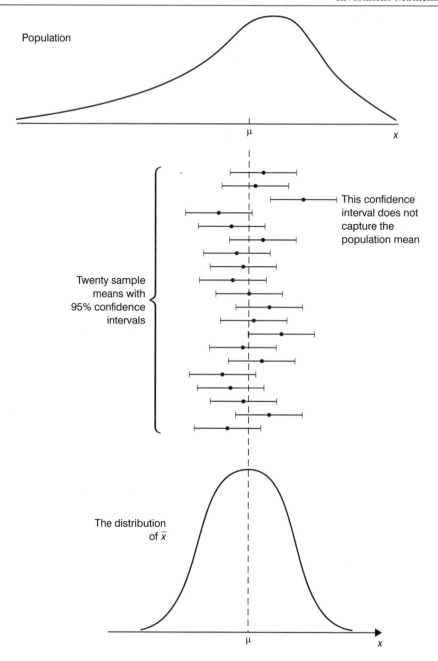

Population

Twenty sample
means with
95% confidence
intervals

This confidence
interval does not
capture the
population mean

The distribution
of $\bar{x}$

Figure 10.2

10.4   LEVELS OF CONFIDENCE

There is nothing special about 95% as a level of confidence when estimating the location of the mean, it just happens to be a commonly used value which is suitable for many purposes. If we wished to be more certain that the confidence interval contained the population mean, we might calculate a 99% confidence interval. In this case, if many samples were taken and confidence intervals found for each, 99% of the intervals would contain the population mean, but 1% would not. Failing to capture the mean within the confidence interval 1% of the time is, for most purposes, an easily acceptable risk. It may be the case that we are prepared to accept a much lower level of confidence, perhaps 90%. Whatever the degree of confidence required, the interval is calculated by using the formula $\bar{x} \pm z\sigma/\sqrt{n}$, where z is the appropriate point of the standard normal distribution:

$$\text{for 90\% confidence } z_{0.05} = 1.64$$
$$\text{for 95\% confidence } z_{0.025} = 1.96$$
and $$\text{for 99\% confidence } z_{0.005} = 2.58$$

Example 10.1 continued

Returning to the situation described in Section 10.3, the 99% confidence interval for the mean of all bad debts, using the original sample of 100 bank customers is

$$5000 \pm 2.58 \, \frac{750}{\sqrt{100}} = 5000 \pm 193.5$$

$$= \text{£}4806.50 \text{ to } \text{£}5193.50$$

It should be noted that the price to be paid for the higher level of confidence, given that the sample size remains the same, is a wider interval. Since the width of the confidence interval depends on the value of $s/\sqrt{n}$, a more precise interval may be obtained by increasing the sample size.

10.5   SMALL SAMPLES

Small samples present no difficulty if the underlying population is normal and its standard deviation is known: confidence intervals are calculated in the manner described in Section 10.3. However, life is seldom that simple. Suppose that it is known that the population under consideration has a normal distribution. Usually, it will be necessary to estimate the population standard deviation by finding the sample standard deviation.

The interval

$$\mu - 1.96 \, \frac{\sigma}{\sqrt{n}} < \bar{x} < \mu + 1.96 \, \frac{\sigma}{\sqrt{n}}$$

can be rewritten as

$$-1.96 < \frac{\bar{x} - \mu}{\sigma/\sqrt{n}} < 1.96$$

and the central term has a standard normal distribution.

If σ is replaced by s, normality is lost and $(\bar{x} - \mu)/(s/\sqrt{n})$ follows *Student's t distribution* with $n - 1$ degrees of freedom. This distribution, like the normal distribution, is a symmetrical, bell-shaped curve, but more spread out. Its precise shape is determined by the parameter ν, the number of *degrees of freedom*. In this situation there are $n - 1$ degrees of freedom since, for a fixed value of $\bar{x}$, only $n - 1$ of the n observations can be freely chosen. The nth value is then fixed because $\sum x = n\bar{x}$. Figure 10.3 shows the shape of the t distribution when $\nu = 4$; for comparison the standard normal distribution is also shown.

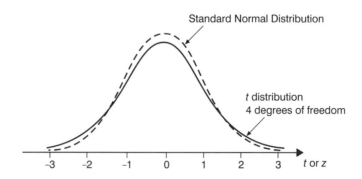

Figure 10.3   Student's t and standard normal distribution

As the value of ν increases, the t distribution gets closer and closer to the normal distribution, which is why Section 10.3 indicated that it is reasonable to calculate confidence intervals using $\bar{x} \pm zs/\sqrt{n}$ when n is large. For small samples the appropriate expression is $\bar{x} \pm ts/\sqrt{n}$ where the t value depends not only on the degree of confidence required, but also on the number of degrees of freedom. Critical values of the t distribution for values of ν between 1 and 30 are given in the table on p. 408.

Example 10.2

A particular index of commercial property values is used widely by investment analysts. It is calculated by looking at the valuation of a sample of properties within each town. The mean valuation change, calculated from 20 properties, is £70,000 in a particular town. The standard deviation is £10,000.

Answer

Assuming that the valuation changes follow a normal distribution, the 90% confidence interval for the mean valuation change in the whole town is:

$$\bar{x} \pm t_{19,\,005}\,\frac{s}{\sqrt{n}} = 70,000 \pm 1.729\,\frac{10,000}{\sqrt{20}}$$

$$= 70,000 \pm 3866$$

$$= £66,134 \text{ to } £73,866$$

So far, it has been stressed that in using the t distribution to calculate confidence intervals we are assuming that the population distribution is normal. In practice we need not be too concerned about this; such confidence intervals remain good approximations with non-normal populations, provided that the distribution is unimodal and not highly skewed.

10.6 CONFIDENCE INTERVAL FOR A PROPORTION

A stockbroker aims to dispatch cheques within three working days of receiving orders for share sales. In order to check whether the desired level of service is being upheld, a random sample of 100 sales is taken and 16 cheques are found to have taken more than three days to despatch. Let us consider the 95% confidence interval for the proportion of all cheques dispatched late.

A confidence interval is required for the population proportion, π, given a sample proportion of $\hat{p} = 0.16$. This is a binomial situation since a dispatch is either late or it is not. Remembering the normal approximation to the binomial (Section 9.6) the mean number of late dispatches is $\mu = n\pi$ and the standard deviation is $\sigma = \sqrt{n\pi(1 - \pi)}$.

Thus, $(x - n\pi)/\sqrt{n\pi(1 - \pi)}$ follows the standard normal distribution. Dividing each term by n,

$$\frac{\hat{p} - \pi}{\sqrt{\dfrac{\pi(1 - \pi)}{n}}}$$

follows the standard normal distribution. Thus, the confidence interval for π is given by

$$\hat{p} \pm z \sqrt{\frac{\pi(1 - \pi)}{n}}$$

which unfortunately contains the unknown value of π.

There are two ways of overcoming this problem. We could use our sample proportion as a point estimate of π, yielding a confidence interval of

$$\hat{p} \pm z \sqrt{\frac{\hat{p}(1 - \hat{p})}{n}}$$

Alternatively, we could use the worst possible case scenario of $\pi = 0.5$. This value of π yields the largest possible standard error and, hence, the widest (most cautious) confidence interval for a given level of confidence.

In this case let us use the sample proportion $\hat{p} = 0.16$ as a point estimate, then the 95% confidence interval for the population proportion π is

$$0.16 \pm 1.96 \sqrt{\frac{0.16 \times 0.84}{100}}$$

$$= 0.16 \pm 0.07$$

$$= 0.09 \text{ to } 0.23$$

We can be 95% confident that between 9% and 23% of cheques are being dispatched late.

10.7   CLASSICAL HYPOTHESIS TESTING

An hypothesis is simply a statement about the value of a population parameter, for example $\mu = 175$. Sample data are used to test whether this stated value is reasonable or not. If it is thought unreasonable, the hypothesis is rejected in favour of some alternative hypothesis. Thus, in every hypothesis test there will be two hypotheses: the *null hypothesis*, H_0 and the *alternative hypothesis*, H_1.

Suppose that a certain type of investment fund is marketed with the claim that, on average, it will outperform a comparable investment index by 0.005% per month, and that we wish to investigate the claim. For the present we will assume that the claim is true, thus the null hypothesis is H_0: $\mu = 0.005$. It is then necessary to decide on the alternative hypothesis that we wish to test H_0 against. The simplest alternative is H_1: $\mu \neq 0.005$.

The next stage is to gather some data. We could monitor the fund for 36 months and measure its outperformance. Let the data from the experiment be $\bar{x} = 0.0025$ and $s = 0.007$.

If H_0 is true, 95% of sample means will be within 1.96 standard deviations of 0.005: $0.005 \pm 1.96/\sqrt{n}$. Since σ is unknown, but n is large, we can use the sample standard deviation as a substitute for σ and under H_0 there is a probability of 0.95 that $\bar{x}$ lies in the range

$$0.005 \pm 1.96 \times \frac{0.007}{\sqrt{36}} = 0.0027 \text{ to } 0.0073$$

Thus, 95% of all sample means for this experiment would lie in the interval 0.0027% to 0.0073%, if H_0 were true (Figure 10.4). The value we obtained, $\bar{x} = 0.0025$ is outside this interval and we would expect to see such values on only 5% of occasions. While H_0 could be true, perhaps this extreme value of $\bar{x}$ casts doubt on the original hypothesis that $\mu = 0.005$. Therefore, we reject H_0: $\mu = 0.005$ in favour of the alternative hypothesis H_1: $\mu \neq 0.005$.

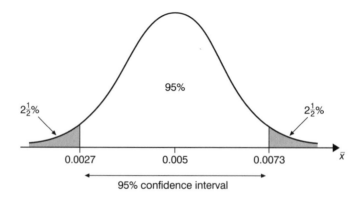

Figure 10.4   Two-tailed test

This is a *classical hypothesis test at the 5% significance level*. The significance level is the area of the "tails" of the distribution which lie outside the confidence interval $\mu \pm 1.96\sigma/\sqrt{n}$. It is the probability of rejecting the null hypothesis H_0, when in fact it is true (see Figure 10.4).

It is not necessary to go through the whole procedure of constructing the confidence interval, then checking whether the sample mean lies within the interval or out in a tail. We can simply say that the most extreme case in which we would retain the null hypothesis is when the sample mean lies at an endpoint of the confidence interval. That is

$$\bar{x} = \mu_0 \pm z \, \frac{s}{\sqrt{n}}$$

$$z = \left| \frac{\bar{x} - \mu_0}{s/\sqrt{n}} \right|$$

where μ_0 is the value of μ being tested in the null hypothesis (in our case $\mu_0 = 0.005$) and z depends on the significance level of the test (in our case 5%, so $z = 1.96$).

For our experiment

$$\left| \frac{\bar{x} - \mu_0}{s/\sqrt{n}} \right| = \left| \frac{0.0025 - 0.005}{0.007/\sqrt{36}} \right|$$

$$= 2.14$$

This is a more extreme value than the critical value $z_{0.025} = 1.96$, indicating that the sample mean lies in a tail of the distribution shown in Figure 10.4. Therefore, the null hypothesis H_0: $\mu = 0.005$ is rejected in favour of the alternative hypothesis H_1: $\mu \neq 0.005$, as before.

This is a *two-tailed test* and is useful for detecting whether the investment fund is deviating from its investment objectives. However, it might be the case that we are only anxious to detect underperformance. Then we would conduct a *one-tailed test*:

$$H_0: \mu = 0.005\% \qquad H_1: \mu < 0.005\%$$

The critical value then becomes $z = -1.64$ since only 5% of the standard normal distribution lies to the left of this value. The observed value of $z = -2.14$ in our example is more extreme than this, so the null hypothesis is rejected in favour of the alternative hypothesis, H_1: $\mu < 0.005\%$.

In our example the critical value of $\bar{x}$ is

$$\frac{-1.64 \times 0.007}{6} + 0.005 = 0.0031\%$$

any sample with mean outperformance below this level would cause the null hypothesis, H_0: $\mu = 0.005\%$, to be rejected.

The choice of 5% as the significance level is conventional, but arbitrary. If we wanted to be more cautious about rejecting the null hypothesis we could, for example, select a 1% significance level. In this case for a two-tailed test $z = \pm 2.58$, then our observed value of -2.14 would not lead to the rejection of the null hypothesis. In this case it is less likely that we will reject the null hypothesis when it is, in fact, true. However, it is more likely that we will accept the null hypothesis when it is false.

10.8   TYPE I AND TYPE II ERRORS

In the example above the null hypothesis will be rejected on 5% of occasions when it is true. This is called a *type I error* and the probability of making such an error is also called the significance level of the test, α.

It may be the case that the null hypothesis is retained when the alternative is true, this is called a *type II error*. The probability of making a type II error for the one-tailed test with null hypothesis H_0: $\mu = \mu_0$ and alternative hypothesis H_1: $\mu > \mu_0$, when in fact $\mu = \mu_1$, is marked β in Figure 10.5.

The probability of making a type II error for a two-tailed test with hypotheses H_0: $\mu = \mu_0$ and H_1: $\mu \neq \mu_0$, when in fact $\mu = \mu_1$, is illustrated in Figure 10.6.

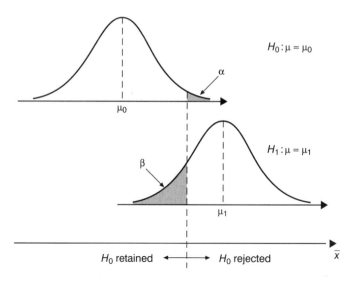

Figure 10.5   Type I and Type II errors

10.9   POWER

The probability of adopting the alternative hypothesis when it is correct is $(1 - \beta)$. This is called the *power* of the test.

For a more powerful significance test β must be reduced, but inspection of Figures 10.5 and 10.6 reveals that, with the same sample, this could only be done at the expense of increasing α. However, a larger sample would reduce the standard error, thus reducing β for a fixed value of α.

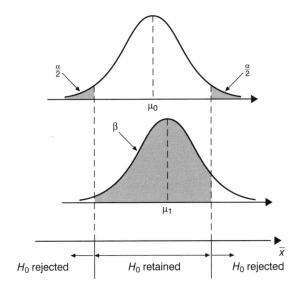

Figure 10.6 Type I and Type II errors

10.10 OPERATING CHARACTERISTIC

In Figure 10.5, relating to the one-tailed test, sliding μ_1 to the right will decrease the value of β and moving μ_1 to the left, will increase β. Figure 10.7 gives an idea of the relationship between μ_1 and β, although the precise shape of the curve depends on the standard error of the mean and, hence, on the sample size. The curve is called the *operating characteristic* of the test.

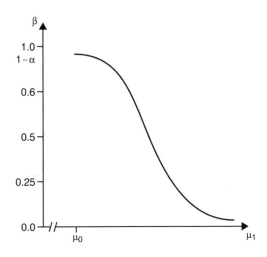

Figure 10.7 Operating characteristic

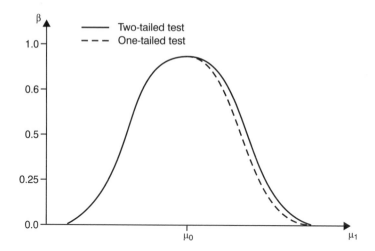

Figure 10.8 Operating characteristic

Figure 10.8 shows the operating characteristic of a two-tailed test and has superimposed the operating characteristic of a one-tailed test. In the appropriate half of the diagram, the latter lies below the former, which shows that the one-tailed alternative reduces the probability of a type II error. Thus, if it is feasible to formulate a one-sided alternative hypothesis, this is likely to be preferable.

10.11 HYPOTHESIS TEST FOR A PROPORTION

Suppose that the market share for a particular mutual fund provider has averaged 30%, as measured by the number of people purchasing units, for a long period. Following a special advertising campaign, it was discovered that of a random sample of 100 people who had recently bought mutual fund units, 37 had bought the brand in question. Let us consider whether these data indicate that the market share has increased.

The null hypothesis, expressing the idea of no change, is H_0: $\pi = 0.3$. The alternative hypothesis will be one-sided since we are investigating whether the market share has increased, rather than just whether it has changed: H_1: $\pi > 0.3$.

We must now choose a significance level for the test, say 5%, so the critical z value is $z_{0.05} = 1.64$. The test statistic is

$$z = \frac{\hat{p} - \pi}{\sqrt{\dfrac{\pi(1 - \pi)}{n}}}$$

In this case, $\hat{p}$ from the sample is 0.37, π from the null hypothesis is 0.3 and the sample size, n, is 100:

$$z = \frac{0.37 - 0.3}{\sqrt{\dfrac{0.3 \times 0.7}{100}}}$$

$$= 1.528$$

Since the test statistic is less extreme than the critical value (Figure 10.9) we retain the null hypothesis and say that there is insufficient evidence to claim that the market share has increased. The wording of this statement is important: it does not mean that the null hypothesis is true. It only means that this sample does not provide enough evidence to justify rejecting the null hypothesis at this level of significance. Many tests of economic and financial data meet this problem. We may have some evidence that the market share has risen, but it is insufficient as the basis of such a claim since the probability of being wrong exceeds 5%. If further testing of the market share was desired, a larger sample would be advantageous.

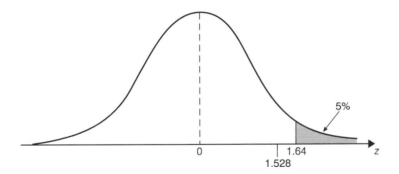

Figure 10.9   One-tailed test

10.12   SOME PROBLEMS WITH CLASSICAL HYPOTHESIS TESTING

Classical hypothesis testing has a number of drawbacks, three of which will be discussed. First, the choice of significance level is largely arbitrary, but has a great effect on the outcome of the test.

Suppose that the mutual fund company in Section 10.11 decided that it is appropriate to test at the 10% significance level (which is equivalent to constructing a 90% confidence interval around the population proportion). The appropriate test statistic is then $z_{0.1} = 1.28$. The calculated value of 1.528 is more extreme than this, so the null hypothesis would be rejected in favour of the alternative that the market share has increased. Thus, the advertising company would now be able to claim success with its campaign. This is not a fault with hypothesis testing *per se*. It is merely a warning that unqualified statements based on statistics can be misleading.

Second, a small sample will have a large standard error, making it difficult to achieve a significant result. Then the null hypothesis may be retained when intuitively, the alternative is better. The effect of sample size is easily demonstrated, even with the fairly large sample of Section 10.11. With a sample of 100 and $\hat{p} = 0.37$ the null hypothesis H_0: $\pi = 0.3$ was retained. However, if 119 customers had been surveyed and 44 found to have bought the fund in question, which is the same proportion as previously ($\hat{p} = 0.37$), the result would have been different. The new test statistic is

$$z = \frac{\hat{p} - \pi}{\sqrt{\dfrac{\pi(1 - \pi)}{n}}}$$

$$= \frac{0.37 - 0.3}{\sqrt{\dfrac{0.3 \times 0.7}{119}}}$$

$$= 1.67$$

This is more extreme than the critical value of $z = 1.64$ so the null hypothesis would be rejected in favour of the alternative, H_1: $\pi > 0.3$.

Third, the alternative hypotheses used in classical hypothesis testing only indicate significant differences (in one or both directions) from the value of the parameter stated in the null hypothesis. It is not possible to test an alternative hypothesis which gives an alternative value for the parameter. For example, H_0: $\pi = 0.3$ and H_1: $\pi = 0.35$ cannot be tested, we must instead test H_0: $\pi = 0.3$ and H_1: $\pi > 0.3$.

10.13 AN ALTERNATIVE TO CLASSICAL HYPOTHESIS TESTING: THE USE OF *p*-VALUES

This approach alleviates all the difficulties outlined in the previous section, but particularly addresses the third drawback. With hypotheses such as H_0: $\pi = 0.3$ and H_1: $\pi = 0.35$, and the sample data of Section 10.11 ($\hat{p} = 0.37$, $n = 100$), it is reasonable to calculate the probability that $\hat{p}$ will be at least as large as 0.37 in the case where H_0 is true and where H_1 is true. These probabilities are called *p-values*. The results of the test can be reported by presenting both *p*-values and then leaving the reader to make the accept or reject decision.

The *p*-value for H_0 is:

$$P(\hat{p} \geqslant 0.37 \text{ if } \pi = 0.3) = P(z \geqslant 1.528)$$

$$= 0.0630, \quad \text{about } 6\%.$$

The p-value for H_1 is

$$P(\hat{p} \geqslant 0.37 \text{ if } \pi = 0.35) = P\left(z \geqslant \dfrac{0.37 - 0.35}{\sqrt{\dfrac{0.35 \times 0.65}{100}}}\right)$$

$$= P(z \geqslant 0.419)$$

$$= 0.3372, \quad \text{about } 34\%.$$

This approach may still be used with the original hypotheses of Section 10.11, H_0: $\pi = 0.3$ and H_1: $\pi > 0.3$. It is simply a matter of calculating the single p-value relating to the null hypothesis (0.0630). Quoting this value removes the need to fix an arbitrary level of significance in order to report an accept or reject decision and the responsibility for interpreting the results of the test passes to the reader. The statistical analysis is essentially the same but the methodology automatically leads to the relevant information being given to the reader.

If the alternative hypothesis had been two-sided, H_1: $\pi \neq 0.3$, a two-sided p-value would be required. This is the probability of obtaining a sample result at least as extreme as the one observed. In our case this is $P(\,|z| \geqslant 1.528)$, which is simply twice the one-sided value, i.e. 0.126. If you read p-values without accompanying hypotheses, it is usual to assume that they are one-sided.

10.14   STATISTICAL AND PRACTICAL SIGNIFICANCE

It is easy to assume that when a statistically significant result is obtained it is important. However, the following example will illustrate a case with a high level of statistical significance, but questionable practical significance.

Example 10.3

The market exposure limit for a particular trader in a given market is £60,000. However, for a long period of time, the trader's exposure was not properly monitored. When the system records were analysed it was discovered that his average exposure was £64,700. As a result, it was decided to reduce his exposure limit to £50,000. One hundred days after the change, records showed a new mean exposure of £62,900 with a standard deviation of £5200. Has the reduction in exposure limit reduced his average exposure? (Units below are £000's.)

Answer

$$H_0\text{: } \mu = 64.7 \qquad H_1\text{: } \mu < 64.7$$

The p-value for H_0 is

$$P(\bar{x} \leqslant 62.9 \mid \mu = 64.7) = P\left(z \leqslant \dfrac{62.9 - 64.7}{\dfrac{5.2}{10}}\right)$$

$$= P(z \leqslant -3.46)$$

$$= 0.00023$$

This is very strong evidence against the null hypothesis and we can say that the observed reduction in mean exposure is highly significant in the statistical sense. However, in practical terms, it is difficult to view a reduction in mean exposure from £64,700 to £62,900 as significant. We might describe the observed change as significant but not substantial. There is little doubt that there has been improvement, but the change has not been as great as might have been hoped. It may be more relevant to test whether the average exposure is greater than £50,000.

The opposite can also happen. We can sometimes see a substantial change in the mean value of a variable but, because the standard deviation is so large, the change is not statistically significant (i.e. there is still a reasonable probability that there has been no underlying change).

Annex 10.1   Standard error of the sample mean

The variance of the sample means drawn from a population with variance σ is

$$\mathrm{var}(\bar{X}) = \mathrm{var}\left\{ \frac{1}{n}(x_1 + x_2 + x_3 + \cdots + x_n) \right\}$$

$$= \frac{1}{n^2}\left\{ \sum_{i=1}^{n} \mathrm{var}(x_i) \right\}$$

$$= \frac{1}{n^2}\left\{ \sum_{i=1}^{n} \sigma^2 \right\}$$

$$= \frac{n\sigma^2}{n^2}$$

$$= \frac{\sigma}{n}$$

The standard error of the mean is the square root of this: $\sigma/\sqrt{n}$.

11

Measuring and
Testing Comovements in Returns

11.1 INTRODUCTION

Frequently, it is desired to consider relationships between financial and investment variables. For example, is there an association between equity returns and bond returns? If such a relationship exists, is it possible to predict the value of one variable from a known value of the other? *Correlation* and *regression* are techniques which may be used to address these questions.

11.2 CORRELATION

If two variables move in step they are said to be *correlated*. However, finding correlation between two variables does not necessarily imply that changes in one *cause* changes in the other. It is possible that a causal relationship exists, but it may be that both variables are moving in step with a third variable. For example, US equity returns may be correlated with appreciation of the US dollar. High US equity returns may not cause the US dollar to be strong but both may be related to a strong US economy. Alternatively, correlation may be purely coincidental, such as would most likely be the case if correlation were found between equity returns and the phase of the moon. Both of these are examples of *spurious correlation*.

11.3 MEASURING LINEAR ASSOCIATION

The first stage in detecting whether a linear relationship exists between two variables is to plot a scatter diagram. Look back to Figure 8.16. There is obviously quite a lot of variation in the data, but nevertheless, a positive correlation between the two variables is discernible in each case. Figure 11.1 is a scatter diagram for the data set in Figure 11.3. This data set will be used throughout the chapter.

A priori one might expect Treasury Bond Returns to be strongly correlated with inflation and the retail price index. However, there are a number of factors that would affect equity values other than bond yields, so one might expect weaker correlation between equity returns and UK government bond returns (Table 11.2 and Figure 11.1).

When all the points on the scatter diagram lie on a straight line, with large values of one variable being associated with large values of the other variable, there is perfect positive correlation (Figure 11.2a). If the line is such that large values of one variable are associated with small values of the other variable, there is perfect negative correlation (Figure 11.2b). In each case, the slope of the line is irrelevant when considering the *strength* of the association between the two variables. How steeply the line slopes simply indicates how large a change would be produced in one variable by a fixed change in the other variable.

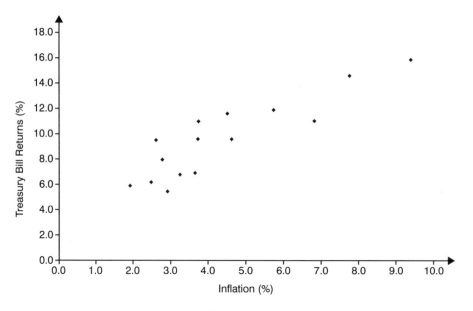

Figure 11.1

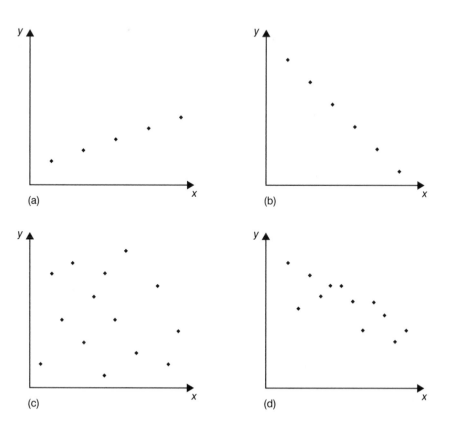

Figure 11.2 (a) Perfect positive correlation, (b) perfect negative correlation, (c) no correlation, (d) moderate negative correlation

If points appear all over the scatter diagram, without a discernible pattern, (Figure 11.2c), there is no correlation between the variables. Independent variables (Section 9.2.6) are always uncorrelated. Figures 11.1 and 11.2d show positive and negative correlations respectively which lie between the extremes described above.

It is imprecise to talk about strong or weak correlation, so various methods have been devised to produce a numerical measure of the association between variables. We will consider two: Pearson's Product Moment Correlation Coefficient, r, for when the data have numerical values and Spearman's Rank Correlation Coefficient, r_s, for when the data are defined by their position. In each case, the value of the correlation coefficient will always lie in the range -1 to $+1$: $+1$ signifying perfect positive correlation, -1 signifying perfect negative correlation, and 0 indicating no correlation.

11.4   PEARSON'S PRODUCT MOMENT CORRELATION COEFFICIENT

Pearson's Product Moment Correlation Coefficient detects the extent to which the data points lie on a straight line and may be defined as

$$r = \frac{\text{Covariance of } x \text{ and } y}{\sqrt{(\text{variance of } x)(\text{variance of } y)}}$$

Thus,

$$r = \frac{\sum_{i=1}^{n}(x_i - \bar{x})(y_i - \bar{y})}{\sqrt{\sum_{i=1}^{n}(x_i - \bar{x})^2 \sum_{i=1}^{n}(y_i - \bar{y})^2}} \tag{11.1}$$

By multiplying out the brackets and simplifying, equation (11.1) can be rearranged into the following equivalent forms, where n is the number of data points.

$$r = \frac{n\sum_{i=1}^{n}x_i y_i - \sum_{i=1}^{n}x_i \sum_{i=1}^{n}y_i}{\sqrt{\left(n\sum_{i=1}^{n}x_i^2 - \left(\sum_{i=1}^{n}x_i\right)^2\right)\left(n\sum_{i=1}^{n}y_i^2 - \left(\sum_{i=1}^{n}y_i\right)^2\right)}} \tag{11.2}$$

or

$$r = \frac{\sum_{i=1}^{n}x_i y_i - n\bar{x}\bar{y}}{\sqrt{\left(\sum_{i=1}^{n}x_i^2 - n\bar{x}^2\right)\left(\sum_{i=1}^{n}y_i^2 - n\bar{y}^2\right)}} \tag{11.3}$$

Excel Application 11.1

The calculation of the Pearson product moment correlation coefficient within the Excel spreadsheet (Figure 11.3) is obtained as follows:

- Position cursor where the answer is required.
- Select the Insert from the top toolbar.
- Select Function... from the drop-down menu.
- Select Statistical from the Function Category list in the "Post Function" dialogue box.
- Select PEARSON from the function name list in the same dialogue box.
- Enter the data arrays B2:B16 and C2:16 (this can also be done by clicking the spreadsheet symbol on the right of each array box, then highlighting the area on the spreadsheet).

Next time you access the "Post Function" dialogue box the function PEARSON will appear at the top of the "most recently used" list.

0.888 is a high level of positive correlation, as expected.

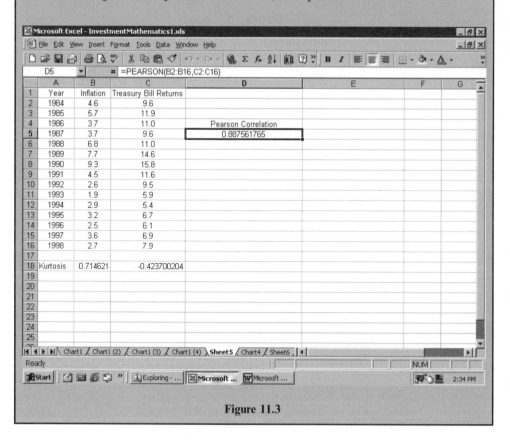

Figure 11.3

Equations (11.2) and (11.3) make the calculation of r more straightforward if hand calculations are to be performed, but this is not a concern if a spreadsheet package is available.

Figure 11.3 and Excel application 11.1 demonstrate the calculation of Pearson's Product Moment Correlation coefficient for the data shown in Figure 11.1.

11.5   COVARIANCE AND THE POPULATION CORRELATION COEFFICIENT

The covariance of the random variables X and Y is defined as

$$\text{cov}(X, Y) = E[(X - \mu_X)(Y - \mu_Y)]$$

If we had a sample of n observations $(x_1, y_1), (x_2, y_2), ..., (x_n, y_n)$, the *sample covariance* would be:

$$\frac{1}{n} \sum_{i=1}^{n} (x_i - \bar{x})(y_i - \bar{y})$$

This is almost the same as the numerator of equation (11.1), the correlation coefficient for that sample. Using the unadjusted form of the sample variance, equation (11.1) can be rewritten as

$$r = \frac{\text{sample covariance}}{\sqrt{s_x^2 s_y^2}}$$

In this way we define the *population correlation coefficient*, ρ_{xy} as

$$\rho_{xy} = \frac{\text{cov}(X, Y)}{\sqrt{\text{var}(X)\text{var}(Y)}}$$

which is more often written as

$$\rho_{xy} = \frac{\sigma_{xy}}{\sigma_x \sigma_y} \tag{11.4}$$

The Excel function for a population correlation coefficient is CORREL (array1, array2).

11.6   SPEARMAN'S RANK CORRELATION COEFFICIENT

When the data can be placed in order, but not given an absolute size, Spearman's Rank Correlation Coefficient, r_s, is used:

$$r_s = 1 - \frac{6 \sum_{i=1}^{n} d_i^2}{n(n^2 - 1)}$$

where d is the paired difference in ranks and n is the number of pairs of observations.

Table 11.1

Fund manager	January rank	February rank	d	d^2
A	1	5	−4	16
B	5	3	2	4
C	8	6	2	4
D	7	4	3	9
E	2	7	−5	25
F	3	2	1	1
G	10	9	1	1
H	4	8	−4	16
I	6	1	5	25
J	9	10	−1	1
			$\sum d = 0$	$\sum d^2 = 102$ $n = 10$

Note: The d column will always add up to zero, which is a means of checking for errors.

Example 11.1

Ten fund managers are ranked by performance in January and February (Table 11.1). Do the ranks indicate that fund managers who are successful in January are also successful in February?

Answer

Calculating Spearman's Rank Correlation Coefficient:

$$r_s = 1 - \frac{6 \sum_{i=1}^{n} d_i^2}{n(n^2 - 1)}$$

$$= 1 - \frac{6 \times 102}{10 \times 99}$$

$$= 0.382$$

There is very little correlation between the two sets of ranks, which suggests that relative performance in the second month is not closely related to performance in the first month.

11.7   PEARSON'S *VERSUS* SPEARMAN'S

It is possible to use Spearman's Rank Correlation Coefficient with quantitative data. It is left to the reader to check that for the data in Figure 11.3 $r_s = 0.9098$. N.B. where there is a tie in 7th place, each is given a rank of 7.5, the mean of 7 and 8.

The number obtained is different from the Pearson's Product Moment Correlation Coefficient calculated in Section 11.4 ($r = 0.888$). This is because the formulae detect different patterns. As stated in Section 11.3, Pearson's formula detects the extent to which the points lie on a straight line. Spearman's formula detects the extent to which the ranks increase (or decrease) together and does not take into account the size of the observations.

11.8 NON-LINEAR ASSOCIATION

Figure 11.4 certainly shows a definite relationship between the two variables, (in fact it is $y = x^4$) but since it is not linear, $r = 0.562$, which is a fairly low value. Since Spearman's Coefficient only considers the ranks of the variables it is much higher, $r_s = 0.957$, which is a fairer representation of reality than Pearson's Coefficient. Thus, if a visual inspection of the data suggests a curved relationship, it may be more sensible to use Spearman's Rank Correlation Coefficient rather than Pearson's Product Moment Coefficient. However, Spearman's Coefficient does not indicate the type of curvilinear relationship present, whereas knowing that the data are close to lying on a straight line enables us to predict the value of one variable, given a value for the other variable (Section 11.12). This is often desirable and leads to the strategy of transforming the data.

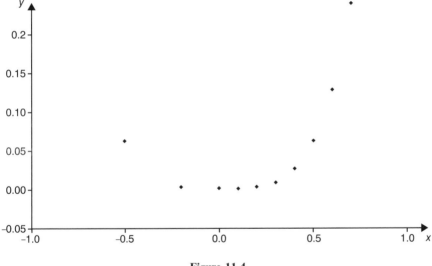

Figure 11.4

Figure 11.5a indicates that there may be a curvilinear relationship between the variables x and y. In Figure 11.5b the data have been transformed by plotting x against $\log(y)$. This has straightened out the graph and yields a correlation coefficient of $r = -0.913$; there is a strong linear association between x and $\log(y)$.

In other circumstances, the graph may be straightened out more effectively by plotting $\log(x)$ against y, or $\log(x)$ and $\log(y)$, or by trying a different function such as $1/x$. Discovering the best transformation for a particular data set involves trial and error, but this is fairly painless with the aid of an appropriate computer package.

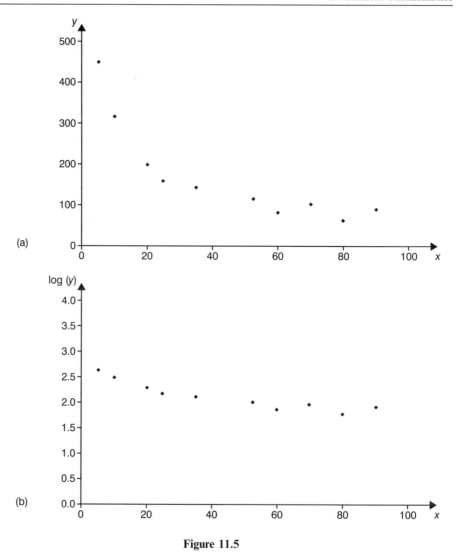

(a)

(b)

Figure 11.5

An alternative to transforming the data is to fit an appropriate curve, such as a polynomial. The interested reader should refer to a more advanced statistical text and employ appropriate statistical software.

11.9 OUTLIERS

Outlying values can severely affect the value of Pearson's Coefficient, so it should be checked that such values are not mistakes, before proceeding with calculations. The outlier in Figure 11.6a decreases the value of r from 0.940 to 0.343, while the outlier in Figure 11.6b increases the value of r from 0.385 to 0.717. The effect on Spearman's Rank Coefficient will not be so dramatic.

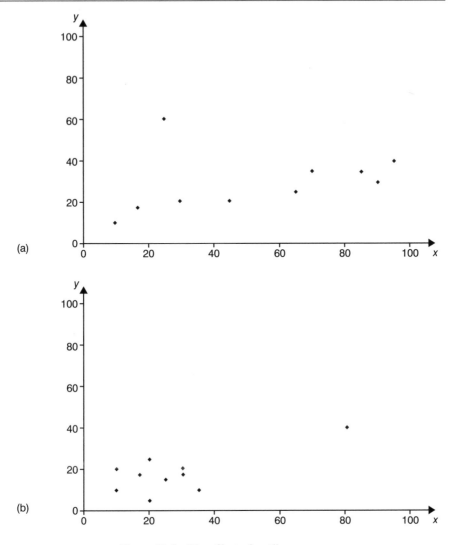

Figure 11.6   The effect of outliers

11.10   SIGNIFICANCE TEST FOR *r*

The data used to calculate the correlation coefficient are a sample from the larger population of possible observations, so r is subject to sampling fluctuations. The population correlation coefficient, ρ, is generally unknown. Thus r acts as a point estimate for ρ, just as $\bar{x}$ is a point estimate for μ (Section 10.1). It is possible to carry out significance tests on the value of r, just as we tested values of $\bar{x}$ in Section 10.3. However, the following test assumes that both variables have a normal distribution and it should not be used if this is clearly not the case. We will use the data from Figure 11.3 again.

Excel Application 11.2

Tests for normality suitable for the data in Figure 11.3 include the *Lilliefors test* and the *Shapiro-Wilks test*. However, these are not available within Excel (the interested reader should refer to a more advanced statistical text and specialist statistical software). A guide to normality can be obtained within Excel by using the statistical functions KURT(array) to calculate the kurtosis of each data set (shown in row 18 of Figure 11.3), and SKEW(array) to calculate the skewness of the data set.

The kurtosis function compares the shape of a data set with the normal distribution. A value of zero represents a perfectly normal distribution, but this will rarely happen in practice. Positive values represent a distribution that is more peaked than the normal distribution, while negative kurtosis values indicate a distribution that is flatter than the normal distribution.

The values in row 18 of Figure 11.3 are not too large and separate calculation of Lilliefors and Shapiro-Wilks statistics confirmed that the assumption of normality was reasonable in this case.

With a larger data set it might be possible to conduct a rough visual check of normality with Excel by constructing a bar chart (Section 8.4.3). However, using a statistical software package to produce *normal plots* would be better.

The null hypothesis that will be tested is

$$H_0: \rho = 0$$

against the alternative hypothesis

$$H_1: \rho \neq 0$$

The first step is to calculate the value of the test statistic:

$$T = r\sqrt{\frac{n-2}{1-r^2}}$$

which, under the null hypothesis of there being no correlation present, follows a t distribution with $(n-2)$ degrees of freedom, $r = 0.888$. So,

$$T = 0.888\sqrt{\frac{15-2}{1-0.888^2}}$$

$$= 6.963$$

Next we look up the critical points in the table on p. 408 for $\nu = 13$ and find that the calculated test statistic is much larger than the most extreme value in the table, $t_{0.005,13} = 3.012$. Therefore we reject the null hypothesis and conclude that there is significant correlation between inflation and Treasury Bill returns, as might be expected.

Of course we could have chosen a one-sided alternative hypothesis in view of the large, positive value of r, that is

$$H_1: \rho > 0$$

but with a value as high as $T = 6.963$, the outcome would be the same. We would reject the null hypothesis and conclude that there is significant positive correlation between the two variables in question.

11.11 SIGNIFICANCE TEST FOR SPEARMAN'S RANK CORRELATION COEFFICIENT

If there is a sufficiently large number of observations, Spearman's Rank Correlation Coefficient may also be tested in the manner described in Section 11.10.

$$H_0: \rho = 0$$

$$H_1: \rho \neq 0$$

(or, if appropriate, a one-sided alternative hypothesis).

$$T_s = r_s \sqrt{\frac{n-2}{1-r_s^2}}$$

However, T_s only *approximately* follows Student's t distribution with $n - 2$ degrees of freedom and in order to retain reasonable accuracy, we reserve the test for occasions when $n \geqslant 20$.

11.12 SIMPLE LINEAR REGRESSION

If a scatter plot and the value of a correlation coefficient indicate a linear association between two variables, we may wish to be able to predict the value of one variable from the value of the other. A regression line facilitates this.

The variable for which we choose known values which we then use to make predictions about the other variable is called the *independent* or *explanatory variable*. The variable for which we predict values is called the *dependent variable*, since its value depends on the value chosen for the independent variable. In general, we plot the dependent variable on the y axis.

It is not always easy to decide which is the independent variable, Prior theory (see Chapters 4–6) would generally lead us to believe that high inflation would lead to higher equilibrium nominal investment returns. We will therefore plot inflation on the x-axis and Treasury Bill returns on the y-axis.

The high value of r obtained in Section 11.4 (0.888) indicates that it would be reasonable to describe the relationship between the two variables with a straight line. Figure 11.7 shows a scatter diagram of the data in Figure 11.3 and a possible regression line has been added. This was drawn by moving a straight edge around on the graph until the line which seems to be the best fit for the data was obtained.

This method of constructing a regression line is very imprecise and if several different people were asked to find the line of best fit they would probably all draw different lines. Therefore, we require a formal method of finding the best line so that everyone

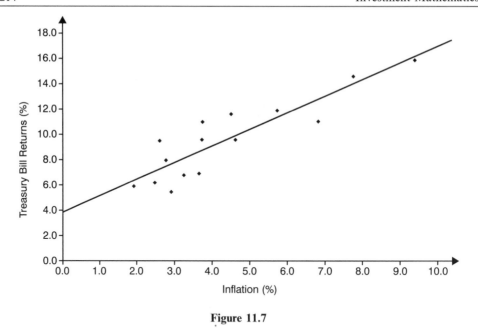

Figure 11.7

will produce the same answer and so that the estimates obtained can be tested statistically. The most common method used is the *method of least squares.*

11.13   THE LEAST-SQUARES REGRESSION LINE

The least-squares regression line y on x is placed on the scatter diagram so that the sum of the squared vertical distances from the points to the line is minimised (Figure 11.8). The line is positioned so that

$$\sum_{i=1}^{n} d_i^2$$

is the smallest value possible for these particular points. We sum squared distances because some points lie above the line and some below. Those above have positive deviations from the line and those below have negative deviations. If the deviations were simply added together they would tend to cancel each other out. There would be more than one position of the line for which the total was zero, and some of these would not look like a good fit for the data at all; summing squared deviations removes this difficulty.

The regression line has equation $\hat{y} = a + bx$ and enables predicted values of y to be obtained from known values of x ($\hat{y}$ is read "y hat").

The constants a and b have to be calculated in reverse order using

$$b = \frac{\sum_{i=1}^{n} x_i y_i - n\bar{x}\bar{y}}{\sum_{i=1}^{n} x_i^2 - n\bar{x}^2}$$

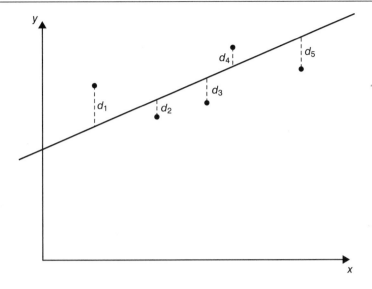

Figure 11.8

and

$$a = \bar{y} - b\bar{x}.$$

An important property of the least-squares regression line is that it always passes through the point $(\bar{x}, \bar{y})$. This fact provides a quick check for the accuracy of calculations carried out to find the position of the line.

Let us now find the least-squares regression line y on x for the data in Figure 11.3. The formulae for a and b require us to know the values of:

$$\bar{x}, \bar{y}, \sum_{i=1}^{n} x_i y_i, \sum_{i=1}^{n} x_i^2 \text{ and } n$$

most of which are already known from the calculation of r in Section 11.4, the rest being easy to calculate from Figure 11.3.

If we wish to plot the regression line we must calculate the position of two points and join them using a straight edge. The calculations should be checked by finding the position of a third point and ensuring that it does lie on the line which has been drawn. For the first two points, it is usual to choose values of x that are towards the extremes of the x range and which keep the calculations as simple as possible.

Let $x = 2$,

$$\hat{y} = -3.87 + 1.31 \times 2$$

$$= 6.49$$

Let $x = 9$,

$$\hat{y} = -3.87 + 1.31 \times 9$$

$$= 15.66$$

Excel Application 11.3

Employing the statistical functions SLOPE(known y-values, known x-values) and INTERCEPT(known y-values, known x-values) to obtain the values of a and b, respectively, removes the need for hand calculation. In our example, $a = 1.31$ and $b = 3.87$.

An alternative is to use LINEST(known y-values, known x-values, true). This is an array formula so must be entered into a block with two columns and five rows. To do this, select (highlight) a range of cells, say, D2:E6, type $=$ LINEST(B2:B16, C2:C16, , TRUE) and then simultaneously press Ctrl-Return. It will return the array:

a	b
standard error of a	standard error of b
r^2	standard error of y
F	degrees of freedom
the regression sum of squares	the residual sum of squares

We will return to the interpretation of rows 3–5 of this array later in this chapter.

To add a conventional linear regression line to a scatterplot using Excel, one can click on the chart to select it, then click on the Chart dropdown menu. One of the options is Add Trendline. Select this and on the Type tab select Linear. Excel will then add the regression line to the scatterplot.

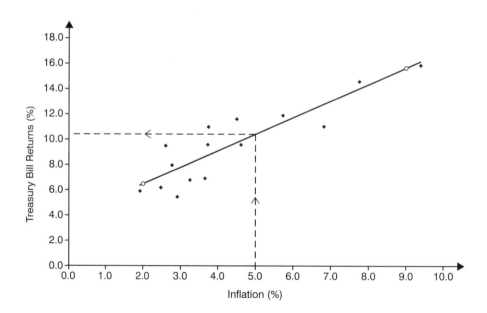

Figure 11.9

These two points have been plotted (o) and the regression line drawn on the scatter diagram in Figure 11.9. The easiest point with which to check the calculations is $(\bar{x}, \bar{y})$ which must lie on the regression line. The point $(4.4, 9.6)$ does indeed lie on the line which has been drawn.

The regression line may now be used to make predictions. For example, what Treasury Bill return will we predict when inflation is 5%? The answer of approximately 10.5% can be read off the graph by following the dashed lines in the direction of the arrows. Alternatively, an answer may be calculated directly from the regression equation without the need to draw the graph:

$$x = 5 \qquad \hat{y} = 3.87 + 1.31 \times 5$$
$$= 10.42$$

It is important to remember that this regression line only facilitates the prediction of y values for given values of x. It is not correct to reverse the direction of the arrows and predict values of x from given values of y (see Section 11.14 below, for two solutions to this problem). Also, notice that the regression line has been drawn so that it does not extend beyond the range of available data points. This is because we have no reason to believe that the relationship between two variables will continue to be linear beyond the range $x = 1.9$ to $x = 9.3$. Therefore, it would not be wise to make predictions outside this range (such predictions would be known as *extrapolation*).

11.14 THE LEAST-SQUARES REGRESSION LINE OF x ON y

In some cases it will not be immediately obvious which is the dependent variable. Table 11.2 shows UK equity returns and UK government bond returns in successive

Table 11.2

Year	UK government bond returns (gross) x	UK equity returns (gross) y
1984	6.8	31.6
1985	10.8	20.2
1986	11.0	27.3
1987	16.2	8.7
1988	9.4	11.5
1989	5.9	35.5
1990	5.6	−9.6
1991	18.9	20.8
1992	18.4	19.8
1993	28.8	27.5
1994	−11.3	−5.9
1995	19.0	23.0
1996	7.7	15.9
1997	19.5	23.6
1998	25.0	13.7

years. Certainly, a case can be made that changes in bond yields are a cause of changes in equity values (see Chapter 3 for a discussion of how a change in the discount rate affects equity values). However, more generally, UK equity and UK government bond returns can be regarded as being linked by a range of different factors which may not lead to direct causality from one market to another. As a result, we may wish to predict bond returns from equity returns (x from y) and vice versa (y from x). Let us construct a regression line

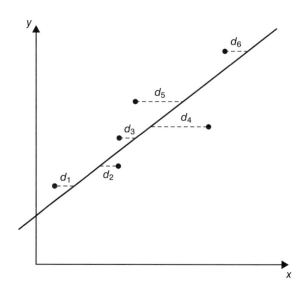

Figure 11.10

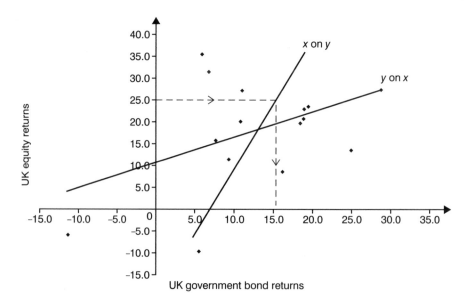

Figure 11.11

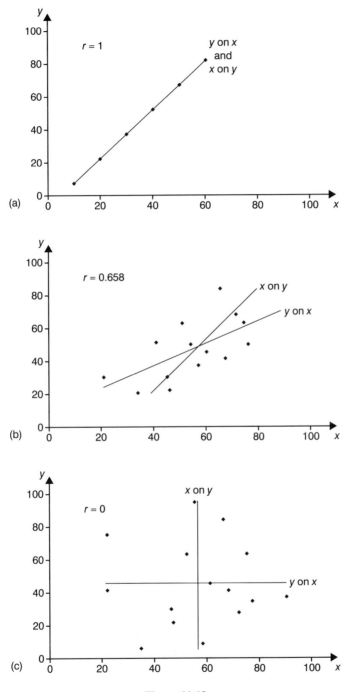

Figure 11.12

which will allow us to predict UK government bond returns (x) from UK equity returns (y). This will be the least-squares regression line of x on y. The only difference between its construction and that described in Section 11.13 above is that horizontal distances from data points to the line will be minimised, rather than vertical differences (see Figure 11.10).

The formulae for this line are the same as those in Section 11.11, except for the interchange of x and y:

$$\hat{x} = c + dy$$

where

$$d = \frac{\sum\limits_{i=1}^{n} x_i y_i - n\bar{x}\bar{y}}{\sum\limits_{i=1}^{n} y_i^2 - n\bar{y}^2}$$

and

$$c = \bar{x} - d\bar{y}$$

This regression line also passes through the point $(\bar{x}, \bar{y})$ and values can be read off by following the dashed lines in the direction of the arrows shown in Figure 11.11.

Figure 11.11 shows the two regression lines for the data in Table 11.2. They are not the same, which is usually the case. Only when $r = 1$ or $r = -1$ are the lines identical. As $|r|$ decreases they pivot about the point $(\bar{x}, \bar{y})$ until, when $r = 0$ they are at right angles (see Figure 11.12). We could interpret Figure 11.12c by saying that if no linear relationship exists between the two variables the best estimate we can make for the value of y is its mean value, regardless of the value taken by x, and vice versa.

The calculation of the x and y regression line was not strictly necessary. Since it is unclear which should be regarded as the dependent variable in this case we could just as easily have plotted the data the other way round, thus predicting UK government bond returns by using a y on x regression line, utilising the formulae of Section 11.13. Therefore, for the rest of the chapter we will only consider the y on x regression line. However, it is important to remember that it is not always meaningful to predict in both directions: common sense should be exercised before calculating predicted values.

11.15   PREDICTION INTERVALS FOR THE CONDITIONAL MEAN

Regression lines are constructed from sample data and are, therefore, subject to sampling variation. Thus, two samples may result in two different regression lines:

$$\hat{y} = a_1 + b_1 x \qquad \text{and} \qquad \hat{y} = a_2 + b_2 x$$

Linear regression theory assumes that there is a "true" regression line.

$$\mu_{y|x} = \alpha + \beta x$$

We may wish to use a predicted value $\hat{y}$ to construct a confidence interval for the value of $\mu_{y|x}$, in a similar way to constructing a confidence interval for a sample mean, $\bar{x}$. This is called a *prediction interval for the conditional mean*, $\mu_{y|x}$. The values of $\hat{y}$ follow

Student's t distribution with $(n-2)$ degrees of freedom and the interval at a particular point on the regression line $(x_0, \hat{y}_0)$ is constructed using

$$\hat{y}_0 \pm ts_{y|x} \sqrt{\frac{1}{n} + \frac{(x_0 - \bar{x})^2}{\displaystyle\sum_{i=1}^{n} x_i^2 - n\bar{x}^2}}$$

where $s_{y|x}$ is the standard error of the estimate $\hat{y}$, given by

$$s_{y|x} = \sqrt{\frac{\displaystyle\sum_{i=1}^{n} (y_i - \hat{y}_i)^2}{n-2}}$$

$$= \sqrt{\frac{\displaystyle\sum_{i=1}^{n} y_i^2 - a \sum_{i=1}^{n} y_i - b \sum_{i=1}^{n} x_i y_i}{n-2}}$$

which is more convenient for calculations. Returning to the example in Section 11.13, suppose we construct a 95% prediction interval for the conditional mean $\mu_{y|x_0}$ corresponding to the value $x_0 = 5\%$. Recall that $\hat{y}_0 = 10.42\%$. The other values which we need to calculate the prediction interval are available from either the calculation of $\hat{y}$, Section 11.13, or the calculation of r, Section 11.10:

$$a = 3.868, \qquad b = 1.306, \qquad n = 15, \qquad \bar{x} = 4.36, \qquad \sum_{i=1}^{n} x_i^2 = 348.8$$

$$\sum_{i=1}^{n} y_i = 143.5, \qquad \sum_{i=1}^{n} y_i^2 = 1512 \qquad \text{and} \qquad \sum_{i=1}^{n} x_i y_i = 709.$$

Also, $t_{13, 0.025} = 2.160$. Thus,

$$s_{y|x} = \sqrt{\frac{1512 - 3.868 \times 143.5 - 1.306 \times 709}{13}}$$

$$= 1.544$$

N.B. This standard error is part of the array returned by the Excel function LINEST, see Excel Application 11.3.

The prediction interval is

$$10.42 \pm 2.160 \times 1.544 \sqrt{\frac{1}{18} + \frac{(5 - 4.36)^2}{348.8 - 15 \times 4.36^2}}$$

$$= 10.42 \pm 2.160 \times 1.544 \times 0.249$$

$$= 9.59\% \text{ to } 11.25\%.$$

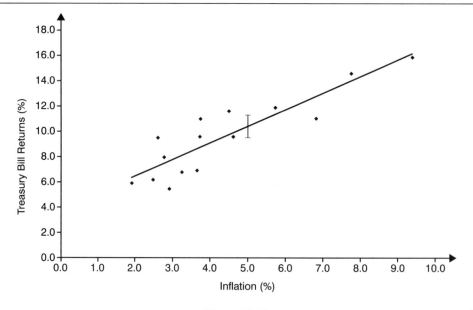

Figure 11.13

That is, the 95% prediction interval for Treasury Bill returns when inflation is 5% is between 9.59% and 11.25%. This interval is marked as a vertical bar on Figure 11.13.

In these calculations, the term $(x_0 - \bar{x})^2$ gets bigger as x_0 moves away from $\bar{x}$. As this term gets larger, the prediction interval becomes wider. This means that the prediction interval is narrowest at the point $(\bar{x}, \bar{y})$ and diverges from the line, in both directions, from this point.

11.16   THE COEFFICIENT OF DETERMINATION

The coefficient of determination is the amount of variation in the variable Y which is explained by the regression line y on x, divided by the total amount of variation in the variable Y. The coefficient of determination lies in the interval [0, 1]. It has value 1 when there is perfect correlation and there is no difference between predicted y values and actual y values. The coefficient of determination has value 0 when the regression line is not helpful for describing the relationship between the variables x and y because it accounts for none of the variation between predicted and actual y values. In practice, your data sets will yield coefficients of determination between these extreme values.

The point which is highlighted in Figure 11.14 deviates from the mean of all Y values by the amount $(y_i - \bar{y})$. A measure of the amount of variation in all the y values of Figure 11.14 can be obtained by considering the total

$$\sum_{i=1}^{n} (y_i - \bar{y})^2.$$

(The deviations were squared before summing to prevent positive and negative ones cancelling each other out.)

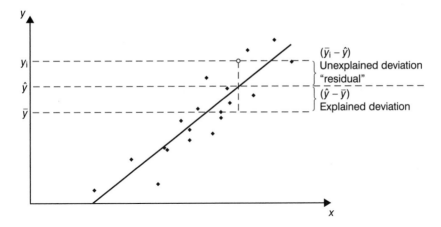

Figure 11.14

Some of each deviation $(y_i - \bar{y})$ is expected because of the regression line which has been calculated. This is the quantity $(\hat{y}_i - \bar{y})$, the *explained variation*. The remaining deviation $(y_i - \hat{y}_i)$ is not explained by the regression relationship and can be thought of as a kind of error term. It is called a *residual*. In the same manner as above, a measure of the total explained variation in Figure 11.14 can be obtained by finding the total

$$\sum_{i=1}^{n} (\hat{y}_i - \bar{y})^2.$$

Then the coefficient of determination is

$$\frac{\text{Explained variation}}{\text{Total variation}} = \frac{\displaystyle\sum_{i=1}^{n} (\hat{y}_i - \bar{y})^2}{\displaystyle\sum_{i=1}^{n} (y_i - \bar{y})^2}$$

$$= \frac{\displaystyle\sum_{i=1}^{n} (a + bx_i - \bar{y})^2}{\displaystyle\sum_{i=1}^{n} (y_i - \bar{y})^2}$$

By multiplying out the brackets and substituting in expressions for a and b, we obtain

$$\frac{\left(\displaystyle\sum_{i=1}^{n} x_i y_i - n\bar{x}\bar{y}\right)^2}{\displaystyle\sum_{i=1}^{n} (x_i - \bar{x})^2 \sum_{i=1}^{n} (y_i - \bar{y})^2} = r^2$$

Excel Application 11.4

Returning to the array produced by the statistical function LINEST (see Excel Application 11.3), the coefficient of determination is shown in the first column, row three.

The significance of the value of this coefficient can be tested using the F value and degrees of freedom (d.f.), also produced within the array. The F value is simply {d.f. × regression sum of squares ÷ residual sum of squares} from rows 4 and 5.

In our example $F = 48.25$ and d.f. $= 13$. Checking published tables reveals that the critical value of F with 1 d.f. in the numerator and 13 d.f. in the denominator is 9.07 at the 5% significance level. The observed value of 48.25 is substantially in excess of this. Therefore, we can be confident that the regression line calculated is useful for predicting Treasury Bill returns from inflation levels.

So the coefficient of determination is equal to the square of Pearson's Product Moment Correlation coefficient. Therefore considerable effort is saved as $(\hat{y}_i - \bar{y})$ and $(y_i - \bar{y})$ do not have to be calculated for each data point. Once the correlation coefficient has been found it is a simple matter to obtain the coefficient of determination by squaring. Returning to the data of Figure 11.3, we found r to be 0.8876, thus $r^2 = 0.788$. This means that almost 80% of the variation in the y values observed is explained by the regression relationship calculated in Section 11.11. The remaining 20% of the variation observed must be due to other factors.

11.17   RESIDUALS

Residuals were defined in the previous section as $e_i = y_i - \hat{y}_i$. That is, residuals represent the variation of the Y values around the regression line. The *population errors*, ε_i are the differences between the observed values y_i and the "true" regression line:

$$\varepsilon_i = y_i - (\alpha + \beta x_i)$$

Linear regression as described in Section 11.12 makes the following assumptions about the population error structure:

(i) The errors are independent random variables.
(ii) The mean of the errors is zero.
(iii) The variance of the errors is constant, independent of the value of X.
(iv) The errors are normally distributed.

A simple linear regression model will not be appropriate for the data if these assumptions are clearly violated. The data-based residuals, e_i, *estimate* the population error structure, ε_i, and a scatter plot of the residuals may help to identify occasions when the model is inappropriate. Figure 11.15 shows three such scatter plots. In Figure 11.15a, linear regression has been applied when the underlying relationship was not linear. This has resulted in a definite curve within the residual plot. In Figure 11.15b, the increasing scatter as the value of X increases indicates that the residuals do not have a constant variance. The model is said to suffer from *heteroskedasticity*. In Figure 11.15c, the

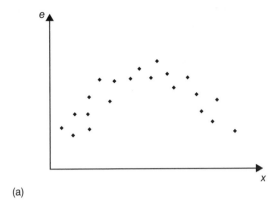

(a)

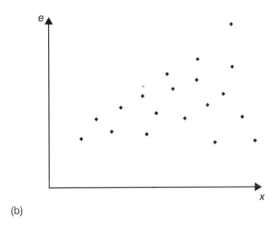

(b)

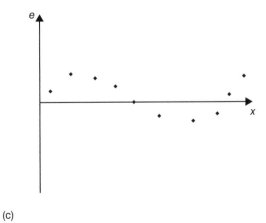

(c)

Figure 11.15

residuals are not independent of each other. This is known as *autocorrelation*. In addition, a histogram of the residuals should be plotted to check assumption (iv).

11.18   MULTIPLE REGRESSION

In many models of financial data, simple linear regression is not adequate since several factors are influencing change in the dependent variable. For example, the sales of a product might be affected by its price, the level of income, the level of advertising, the existence of competing products, etc. Therefore it may be desirable to extend the simple linear regression model to include additional explanatory variables. A *multiple linear regression model* has the form

$$\hat{y} = a + b_1 X_1 + b_2 X_2 + \cdots + b_n X_n$$

Although the mathematics required to extend the regression model in this way is relatively straightforward, the amount of calculation required increases dramatically. The hand calculation of multiple regression coefficients is not practical and an appropriate computer package should be used. It is then necessary to interpret the computer printout, and for this the reader is referred to the appropriate computer software manual.

Excel Application 11.5

The statistical function LINEST(known *y*-values, known *x*-values, const, stats) will return an array containing the parameters of a multiple regression line:

$$y = a_1 x_1 + a_2 x_2 + \cdots + a_k x_k + b$$

The critical value of F for testing the significance of r^2 will have degrees of freedom $\nu_1 = k$ and $\nu_2 = n - (k + 1)$.

11.19   A WARNING

It is important to remember, throughout, that a high value of r does not imply cause and effect. The relationship between X and Y may be spurious.

Part III
Applications

This final part of this book considers applications of the material covered in Parts I and II. Chapter 12 discusses the ideas underlying modern portfolio theory (MPT) and neo-classical asset pricing. Chapter 13 describes the construction of market indices that are integral to the topic of Chapter 14, portfolio performance measurement. Chapter 15 covers further topics in bond analysis, building on the material in Chapter 2. Chapter 16 provides some introductory insights into option pricing and investment strategies. A broad description of the issues and techniques used in stochastic investment models is given in Chapter 17.

Part III
Applications

Modern Portfolio Theory and Asset Pricing

12.1 INTRODUCTION

In 1952, H.M. Markowitz published a paper entitled "Portfolio Selection". This marked the beginning of a new type of investment research and analysis, based on the idea of using statistical measures of dispersion as measures of risk.

Investors are assumed to be risk averse, meaning that they wish to bear as little risk as possible for a given level of expected return. Furthermore, as investors normally hold *portfolios*, it is an individual investment's contribution to the overall risk of the *portfolio* which is the prime concern, not the risk associated with the investment itself in isolation.

In the original theory, risk was defined as the standard deviation (or variance) of return from an investment. This measure quantifies the extent to which single-period monetary returns from an investment fluctuate. Having quantified risk, it was possible to build models which concentrated on risk as well as expected return, and to provide an understanding of the process of diversification.

After developing the two-parameter portfolio analysis model, researchers began to examine what the implications would be if all investors used this approach. This led to the development of the Capital Asset Pricing Model, which has far-reaching implications.

It is important to mention at the outset that although academic text books generally emphasise the above approach to risk, it has been heavily criticised by many practitioners. They argue that for many purposes it is wrong to concentrate on the fluctuations in investment returns in developing a concept for risk. The investor's perception of risk depends on many other factors, which can be difficult to quantify. For example, if an investment portfolio is held in respect of liabilities which must be paid when they fall due, "risk" is related to variations between the value of investments and the value of liabilities. "Risk" in this context therefore has more to do with the *mismatching* of investments to liabilities (see Section 15.7). However, the *market prices* of investments are determined by the risk perceptions of investors in *aggregate*. It is the consensus view that matters, not the view of particular investors. Thus, it is still possible for the market as a whole to treat risk in a manner which is broadly consistent with modern portfolio theory as regards the market pricing of investments.

We first look at the Markowitz model for portfolio selection in Sections 12.2 to 12.6. This leads to the Capital Asset Pricing Model, which will be discussed in Section 12.11.

12.2 EXPECTED RETURN AND RISK FOR A PORTFOLIO OF TWO INVESTMENTS

In developing the Markowitz model, we will take "risk" to mean standard deviation of return.

The standard statistical formulae for the expected value and variance of the linear combination of two random variables (equations (9.12) and (9.18)) lead to the following formulae for the expected (rate of) return and the corresponding variance of return of a portfolio of two investments, A and B.

$$E(R_p) = \alpha E(R_A) + (1 - \alpha)E(R_B) \tag{12.1}$$

$$\sigma_p^2 = \alpha^2\sigma_A^2 + (1 - \alpha)^2\sigma_B^2 + 2\alpha(1 - \alpha)\sigma_{AB} \tag{12.2}$$

where $E(R_p)$ = the expected return of the portfolio
$E(R_A)$ = the expected return of investment A
$E(R_B)$ = the expected return of investment B
σ_p^2 = the variance of the portfolio return
σ_A^2 = the variance of return for investment A
σ_B^2 = the variance of return for investment B
σ_{AB} = the covariance between the returns of investment A and the returns of investment B
α = the proportion of the portfolio's value invested in investment A

The parameter α has a value between 0 and 1. When $\alpha = 0$, the funds are invested entirely in B. When $\alpha = 1$, the funds are invested entirely in A. When $0 < \alpha < 1$, the funds are invested partly in A and partly in B.

Using equation (11.4), we can replace σ_{AB} in equation (12.2) by $\sigma_A\sigma_B r_{AB}$, where r_{AB} is the correlation coefficient between the returns of investment A and the returns of investment B, to give

$$\sigma_p^2 = \alpha^2\sigma_A^2 + (1 - \alpha)^2\sigma_B^2 + 2\alpha(1 - \alpha)\sigma_A\sigma_B r_{AB} \tag{12.3}$$

Note that the expected return of the portfolio is simply the value-weighted average of the expected returns of the individual investments (equation (12.1)). But this is not generally the case with the risk measure, as can be seen from equation (12.3). The variance of return and hence the standard deviation of return (risk) of the portfolio depends not only on the risk of the individual investments, but also on the extent to which their returns are correlated. The lower the degree of correlation, the greater the benefits of diversification and the lower the overall level of risk incurred. We illustrate this point by considering three situations:

(a) The returns of A and B are perfectly positively correlated ($r_{AB} = +1$).
(b) The returns of A and B are uncorrelated ($r_{AB} = 0$).
(c) The returns of A and B are perfectly negatively correlated ($r_{AB} = -1$).

(a) Returns of A and B are Perfectly Positively Correlated

Substituting $r_{AB} = +1$ into equation (12.3),

$$\sigma_p^2 = \alpha^2\sigma_A^2 + (1 - \alpha)^2\sigma_B^2 + 2\alpha(1 - \alpha)\sigma_A\sigma_B$$
$$= \{\alpha\sigma_A + (1 - \alpha)\sigma_B\}^2$$
$$\sigma_p = \alpha\sigma_A + (1 - \alpha)\sigma_B \tag{12.4}$$

Thus, in this case the risk of the portfolio as measured by the standard deviation of portfolio return is simply the value-weighted average of the individual risks of the component investments. Note that the form of equation (12.4) is similar to that of equation (12.1).

The expected return and risk of the portfolio in this case, for the range of values of α, are shown in Figure 12.1. There is a straight line joining A and B, indicating that there is risk averaging, but no benefits of diversification in terms of risk reduction. Expected return and risk both decrease as α increases because B has a higher expected return and a higher risk than A.

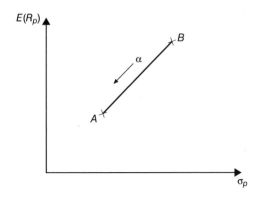

Figure 12.1   Expected return and risk for portfolios of A and B with $r_{AB} = +1$

(b)   Returns of A and B are Uncorrelated

Substituting $r_{AB} = 0$ into equation (12.3),

$$\sigma_p^2 = \alpha^2 \sigma_A^2 + (1 - \alpha)^2 \sigma_B^2$$

$$\sigma_p = \sqrt{\alpha^2 \sigma_A^2 + (1 - \alpha)^2 \sigma_B^2} \qquad (12.5)$$

This is less than $\alpha \sigma_A + (1 - \alpha)\sigma_B$ except when $\alpha = 1$ or $\alpha = 0$, in which case the whole investment is undertaken in a single asset.

Figure 12.2 shows that again a single line is obtained, but in this case the line is curved. As α decreases from 1, the portfolio risk is reduced initially, even though B is a more risky investment than A, illustrating the benefits of diversification.

What is the value of α for which the portfolio risk is minimised? This is the same as the value of α for which the variance of portfolio return is minimised. Differentiating equation (12.5) with respect to α,

$$\frac{\partial \sigma_p^2}{\partial \alpha} = 2\alpha \sigma_A^2 - 2(1 - \alpha)\sigma_B^2$$

Setting $\partial \sigma_p^2 / \partial \alpha = 0$ for minimum, we obtain

$$0 = 2\alpha \sigma_A^2 - 2(1 - \alpha)\sigma_B^2$$

$$0 = 2\alpha(\sigma_A^2 + \sigma_B^2) - 2\sigma_B^2$$

$$\alpha = \frac{\sigma_B^2}{\sigma_A^2 + \sigma_B^2} \qquad (12.6)$$

This value of α gives the minimum risk portfolio.

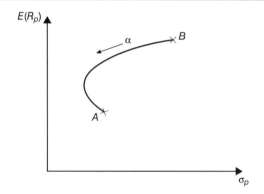

Figure 12.2   Expected return and risk for portfolios of A and B with $r_{AB} = 0$

(c)   Returns of A and B are Perfectly Negatively Correlated

Substituting $r_{AB} = -1$ into equation (12.3),

$$\sigma_p^2 = \alpha^2 \sigma_A^2 + (1 - \alpha)^2 \sigma_B^2 - 2\alpha(1 - \alpha)\sigma_A \sigma_B$$

$$= \{\alpha\sigma_A - (1 - \alpha)\sigma_B\}^2$$

$$\sigma_p = \alpha\sigma_A - (1 - \alpha)\sigma_B$$

Figure 12.3 shows that in this extreme and generally unrealistic situation, it is possible to choose a value of α for which $\sigma_p = 0$. For this value of α, the return from the portfolio is known with certainty because the variations in return from the two investments will exactly offset each other. The value of α for which $\sigma_p = 0$ is given by:

$$0 = \alpha\sigma_A - (1 - \alpha)\sigma_B$$

$$0 = \alpha(\sigma_A + \sigma_B) - \sigma_B$$

$$\alpha = \frac{\sigma_B}{\sigma_A + \sigma_B} \tag{12.7}$$

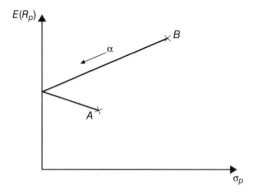

Figure 12.3   Expected return and risk for portfolios of A and B with $r_{AB} = -1$

Example 12.1

An investor intends to construct a portfolio consisting entirely of the shares of Company A and Company B. Short-selling is not allowed. The prospects for the shares are as follows

	Share A	Share B
Expected return (E)	10%	20%
Standard deviation of return (σ)	20%	30%

(a) Assuming that the objective is the minimisation of σ_p, what proportion of available funds should be invested in A and what proportion in B if the returns of A and B are:
  (i) perfectly positively correlated ($r_{AB} = +1$);
  (ii) uncorrelated ($r_{AB} = 0$);
  (iii) perfectly negatively correlated ($r_{AB} = -1$)?
(b) Assuming that the objective is the maximisation of the function $E(R_p) - \sigma_p^2$, what proportion of available funds should be invested in A and what proportion in B if the returns of A and B are uncorrelated?

Answer

(a) (i) Short-selling is not permitted and, therefore, to minimise risk, all available funds should be invested in A (see Figure 12.1).
  (ii) Substituting $\sigma_A = 0.2$ and $\sigma_B = 0.3$ into equation (12.6),

$$\alpha = \frac{0.09}{0.04 + 0.09}$$

$$= 0.692$$

So 69.2% of funds should be invested in A and 30.8% of funds should be invested in B.
  (iii) Substituting $\sigma_A = 0.2$ and $\sigma_B = 0.3$ into equation (12.7),

$$\alpha = \frac{0.3}{0.2 + 0.3}$$

$$= 0.6$$

So 60% of funds should be invested in A and 40% of funds should be invested in B.

(b) With $r_{AB} = 0$,

$$E(R_p) - \sigma_p^2 = \alpha E(R_A) + (1 - \alpha)E(R_B) - \alpha^2 \sigma_A^2 - (1 - \alpha)^2 \sigma_B^2$$

Substituting $E(R_A) = 0.1$, $E(R_B) = 0.2$, $\sigma_A = 0.2$ and $\sigma_B = 0.3$,

$$E(R_p) - \sigma_p^2 = 0.1\alpha + 0.2(1 - \alpha) - 0.44\alpha^2 - 0.09(1 - \alpha)^2$$

$$= -0.13\alpha^2 + 0.08\alpha + 0.11$$

$$\frac{\partial\{E(R_p) - \sigma_p^2\}}{\partial\alpha} = -0.26\alpha + 0.08$$

Setting $\partial\{E(R_p) - \sigma_p^2\}/\partial\alpha = 0$, we obtain

$$0 = -0.26\alpha + 0.08$$

$$\alpha = \frac{0.08}{0.26}$$

$$= \underline{0.308}$$

This value of α gives a maximum because $\partial^2\{E(R_p) - \sigma_p^2\}/\partial\alpha^2$ is negative. So 30.8% of funds should be invested in A and 69.2% of funds should be invested in B.

12.3   EXPECTED RETURN AND RISK FOR A PORTFOLIO OF MANY INVESTMENTS

We now generalise to consider the expected return and risk of a portfolio of n investments. The general formulae for the expected return and variance of return of a portfolio of n investments are

$$E(R_p) = \sum_{i=1}^{n} x_i E(R_i) \tag{12.8}$$

$$\sigma_p^2 = \sum_{i=1}^{n} x_i^2 \sigma_i^2 + \sum_{i=1}^{n} \sum_{\substack{j=1 \\ j \neq i}}^{n} x_i x_j \sigma_{ij} \tag{12.9}$$

where $E(R_p)$ = the expected return of the portfolio
             $E(R_i)$ = the expected return of the ith investment
             σ_p^2 = the variance of the portfolio return
             σ_i^2 = the variance of return for the ith investment
             σ_{ij} = the covariance between the returns of the ith and jth investments
             x_i = the proportion of the portfolio's value invested in the ith investment

$$\sum_{i=1}^{n} x_i = 1$$

and $x_i \geqslant 0$ if no short-sales are allowed.

The reader may wish to check that when $n = 2$, equations (12.8) and (12.9) lead to equations (12.1) and (12.2) (with A, B and α replaced by 1, 2 and x_i respectively).

For $n = 3$, we obtain

$$E(R_p) = x_1 E(R_1) + x_2 E(R_2) + x_3 E(R_3)$$

$$\sigma_p^2 = x_1^2 \sigma_1^2 + x_2^2 \sigma_2^2 + x_3^2 \sigma_3^2 + 2x_1 x_2 \sigma_{12} + 2x_1 x_3 \sigma_{13} + 2x_2 x_3 \sigma_{23}$$

where $x_1 + x_2 + x_3 = 1$.

There are now three variance terms and three covariance terms in the formula for the variance of portfolio return. Figure 12.4 shows the expected return and risk of all possible portfolios consisting of three investments A, B and C, with each pair

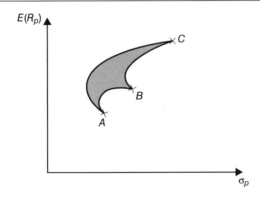

Figure 12.4 Expected return and risk for portfolios of A, B and C

having small positive correlation, as is typical. Unlike the two-investments case, where the possible portfolios lie on a single line, the possible portfolios cover the shaded area.

For $n = 4$, there are four variance terms and six covariance terms; for $n = 5$ there are five variance terms and ten covariance terms; in the general case with n investments, there are n variance terms and $(n^2 - n)/2$ covariance terms, as will be clear from Table 12.1, remembering that $x_i x_j \sigma_{ij} = x_j x_i \sigma_{ji}$.

Table 12.1 Variance–covariance matrix (with weights) for n investments.

Investment	1	2	3	4	$\rightarrow n$
1	$x_1^2 \sigma_1^2$	$x_1 x_2 \sigma_{12}$	$x_1 x_3 \sigma_{13}$	$x_1 x_4 \sigma_{14}$	
2	$x_2 x_1 \sigma_{21}$	$x_2^2 \sigma_2^2$	$x_2 x_3 \sigma_{23}$		
3	$x_3 x_1 \sigma_{31}$	$x_3 x_2 \sigma_{32}$	$x_3^2 \sigma_3^2$		
4	$x_4 x_1 \sigma_{41}$				
$\downarrow$					
n					

Note that for portfolios which are spread over a large number of investments, the number of covariance terms dominates the number of variance terms. Thus, the risk of the portfolio will depend more on the average covariance between investments than on the riskiness of the investments themselves. The covariances tend to be smaller than the variances, so the portfolio variance will fall as investments are added to the portfolio.

12.4 THE EFFICIENT FRONTIER

The shaded area in Figure 12.5 shows the expected return and risk of all possible portfolios available to an investor, with different proportions of the different potential investments. Those portfolios which lie on the line ST offer a higher return for the same amount of (or less) risk than those which lie below and/or to the right of the line. They

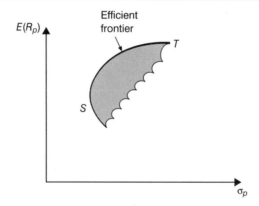

Figure 12.5   Expected return and risk for all possible portfolios

are therefore of particular interest to investors. The assumption that investors are "risk-averse" means that the investor will wish to bear as little risk as possible for a given level of expected return. The line ST is therefore known as the *efficient frontier*, as it is the locus of points which minimise risk for different levels of expected return. The risk-averse investor will only consider portfolios (the efficient portfolios) on the efficient frontier because those falling to the right of it are inferior.

12.5   INDIFFERENCE CURVES AND THE OPTIMUM PORTFOLIO

An *indifference* curve is the locus of points at which the investor gets a particular level of satisfaction or *utility* from any combination of expected return and risk. For a risk-averse investor, indifference curves are concave, moving upward and to the right, indicating that the greater the amount of risk incurred by the investor, the greater the added expected return necessary to keep the investor equally satisfied. The steeper the slope of the curve, the more risk-averse the investor, because it

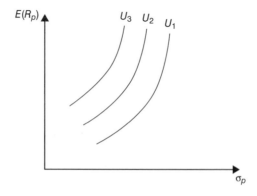

Figure 12.6   Indifference curves

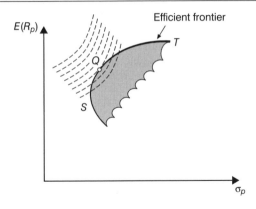

E(R_p) Efficient frontier

Figure 12.7

indicates that a greater amount of extra return is required to compensate for an increase in risk. Clearly, investors will have their own set of indifference curves, depending on their individual trade-off between expected return and risk (i.e. their own utility functions).

Figure 12.6 shows three indifference curves U_1, U_2 and U_3. Curve U_1 gives the least amount of utility because it provides the highest risk for a given level of expected return or, alternatively, the lowest expected return for a given level of risk. Curve U_3 gives the greatest amount of utility.

Figure 12.7 shows the efficient frontier, together with the investor's set of indifference curves. The optimum portfolio, determined by the investor's indifference curves, is at the point of tangency Q because no possible portfolio lies on a higher indifference curve.

12.6 PRACTICAL APPLICATION OF THE MARKOWITZ MODEL

Application of the basic portfolio selection model requires knowledge of the expected return and variance of return for every available investment, together with the covariance between every pair of investments. In general, such information is not obtainable and the application of the model has therefore tended to concentrate on the stock market. Historic rates of return are used to estimate the distribution of returns in the future, the assumption being that the successive past rates of return are individual representatives of the same underlying distribution and that the distribution will remain unchanged into the future. Even then, the large number of securities available to an investor makes the amount of calculation necessary to determine an efficient frontier unmanageable. If there are a thousand securities to choose from, nearly half a million covariances are required!

12.7 THE MARKET MODEL

We now turn to the work of Sharpe (1963) in modifying the basic portfolio selection model. This is concerned with both reducing the mass of information required in applying the model and also providing further insights into the process of diversification.

It is well known that when a stock market goes up, most securities tend to increase in price, and when a stock market goes down, most securities tend to decrease in price. Sharpe suggested that this common response to market changes could be written mathematically as

$$R_{it} = a_i + b_i R_{mt} + e_{it} \tag{12.10}$$

where R_{it} = the return on the ith security in period t
                 R_{mt} = the return on the market index in period t
                 a_i = the constant return unique to security i
                 b_i = a measure of the sensitivity of the return of security i to the return on
                          the market index
                 e_{it} = the random residual error in period t, assumed to be independently and
                          normally distributed with zero mean and constant variance

Equation (12.10) describes what is known as the *Market Model*. It requires that the only common factor affecting all securities is the return on the market index. All securities, to a greater or lesser extent, tend to move with the market.

Assuming that the return process is stationary, it follows from equation (12.10) that:

$$E(R_i) = a_i + b_i E(R_m) \tag{12.11}$$

$$\sigma_i^2 = b_i^2 \sigma_m^2 + \sigma^2(e_i) \tag{12.12}$$

and

$$\sigma_{ij} = b_i b_j \sigma_m^2 \tag{12.13}$$

where σ_m^2 is the variance of return on the market index, $\sigma^2(e_i)$ is the variance of the error term and σ_{ij} is the covariance between the return on security i and the return on security j.

It is possible to estimate a_i, b_i and $\sigma^2(e_i)$ by studying the historical relationship between the return on security i and the return on the market index. R_i is plotted against R_m for a number of periods (say every month for 5 years) and a "best fit" line is drawn through the points, as in Figure 12.8. The gradient of the line is an estimate of b_i and the intercept with the y-axis is an estimate of a_i. The scatter of points about the regression line represents the residual variation in returns after removing the market effect. In practice, a_i, b_i and $\sigma^2(e_i)$ are often estimated using regression analysis (see Chapter 11).

For a portfolio of n securities, where x_i is the proportion of the portfolio's value invested in the ith security,

$$E(R_p) = a_p + b_p E(R_m)$$

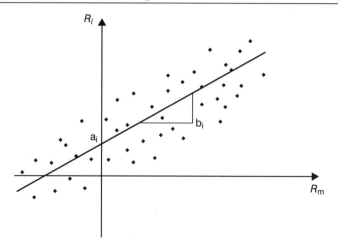

Figure 12.8

where

$$a_p = \sum_{i=1}^{n} x_i a_i$$

$$b_p = \sum_{i=1}^{n} x_i b_i$$

$$\sum_{i=1}^{n} x_i = 1$$

and $x_i \geqslant 0$ if no short-sales are allowed.

Also, substituting the results for σ_i^2 and σ_{ij} given by equations (12.12) and (12.13) into equation (12.9), we obtain

$$\sigma_p^2 = \sum_{i=1}^{n} x_i^2 b_1^2 \sigma_m^2 + \sum_{i=1}^{n} x_1^2 \sigma^2(e_i) + \sum_{i=1}^{n} \sum_{\substack{j=1 \\ j \neq i}}^{n} x_i x_j b_i b_j \sigma_m^2$$

The missing terms in the double summation (given by $j \neq i$) are equal to

$$\sum_{i=1}^{n} x_i^2 b_i^2 \sigma_m^2.$$

But this is simply the first expression on the right-hand side. Hence,

$$\sigma_p^2 = \sum_{i=1}^{n} \sum_{j=1}^{n} x_i x_j b_i b_j \sigma_m^2 + \sum_{i=1}^{n} x_i^2 \sigma^2(e_i)$$

$$\Rightarrow \quad \sigma_p^2 = \left(\sum_{i=1}^{n} x_i b_i \right) \left(\sum_{j=1}^{n} x_j b_j \right) \sigma_m^2 + \sum_{i=1}^{n} x_i^2 \sigma^2(e_i)$$

or

$$\sigma_p^2 = b_p^2 \sigma_m^2 + \sum_{i=1}^{n} x_i^2 \sigma^2(e_i)$$

An important implication of the above is that the need to estimate large numbers of covariances in applying the portfolio selection model has been removed. Now we only need to estimate a_i, b_i and $a^2(e_i)$ for each security. Thus, if there are a thousand shares to choose from, only a thousand regressions would be required.

12.8   ESTIMATION OF EXPECTED RETURNS AND RISKS

One of the critical issues in actually implementing modern portfolio theory (MPT) is the calibration of the model, that is, assigning numbers to the parameters in the model such as the expected returns, risks and correlations. The efficient frontier, for example, is extremely sensitive to the values used and shifting the expected return of an asset even marginally lower can often result in the asset falling out of the efficient frontier altogether. Therefore, the estimation of the parameters takes on great practical importance.

The conventional approach to calibration is to find an appropriate set of historical data and estimate sample means, variances and correlations, which are then used in the model. The fact that appropriate datasets are not always available, and that the sample statistics will vary hugely depending on the particular time period used, makes this approach highly unsatisfactory. Furthermore, the data from many years ago is likely to be inappropriate for use in the future.

Most users of MPT therefore prefer to combine data analysis with economic and financial theory to obtain more satisfactory estimates. One approach to formalising the aggregation of theory and empiricism is to be found in "Bayesian" statistical theory (see Black and Litterman (1992), or Satchell and Scowcroft (2001), but note that the mechanics of Bayesian statistics are beyond the scope of this book). These approaches also permit the investor's views to be combined with theory to produce efficient portfolios which are tilted to take these views into account.

An alternative approach is based on "resampling" and is described by Michaud (2001).

12.9   PORTFOLIO SELECTION MODELS INCORPORATING LIABILITIES

Most institutional holdings of assets back a portfolio of liabilities. For example, pension funds eventually have to be used to pay the benefits to the members of the pension scheme and the funds held by life insurance companies are held in respect of future claims. The "risks" associated with the investment strategy are therefore defined with respect to the liabilities and not necessarily relative to cash (the asset most often regarded as the risk-free asset).

The conventional approach to extending portfolio theory to incorporate liabilities is to model liabilities as negative holdings in "liability" assets. Without liabilities, the emphasis is to understand how terminal wealth, W_1 defined by

$$W_1 = W_0 \sum_{i=1}^{n} x_i(1 + R_i)$$

varies with different investment proportions specified by the x_is and where R_i is the (random) rate of return on security i.

With liabilities, we might consider

$$S = W_1 - \sum_{j=1}^{m} y_j L_j,$$

where S is the surplus (deficit) or profit (loss) at the end of the investment horizon; y_j is the exposure to liability j ($j = 1$ to m) and L_j is the value of liability j at the end of the investment horizon. In many practical cases, $m = 1$, i.e. there is only one type of liability to be paid off.

Another common case is when the value of that liability at the end of the period can be expressed in terms of the returns of existing assets. For example, if the liability is the accumulated value of a lump sum investment of £1,000 in a unit-linked policy, then L is approximately £1,000 $(1 + R_k)$ where R_k represents the return on the equity market. For asset managers, the "liability" is often specified as a market index or some combination of indices. For example, the asset manager may be asked to invest the money in order to outperform a benchmark portfolio of 40% invested in the bonds that make up the British Government All Stocks Index and 60% in the shares that make up the FTSE Actuaries All Share Index. The liability in this case is usually referred to as a "benchmark". There is rarely any legal liability for the asset manager to deliver better than benchmark return, but if they perform worse than benchmark for a prolonged period of time, they are likely to lose the mandate.

The optimal portfolio is calculated by considering the expected value and variance of the surplus, S (instead of terminal wealth, W_1), with respect to the x_is. For example, if we consider the example above in which the asset manager is attempting to outperform the benchmark of 40% bonds, 60% equities, then the zero-risk portfolio is to invest in 40% bonds and 60% equities. This is quite different from the conventional risk-free portfolio of 100% invested in cash. Indeed, relative to the liability, a portfolio of 100% invested in cash is very risky indeed.

If the liability is a fixed nominal amount, the statistical properties of S and W_1 are identical, except for the expected value. The mean-standard deviation plot of S will therefore be exactly the same as for W_1, but with a different scale on the y-axis (the returns will all be reduced by L). For example, suppose that an investor with £10,000 in initial wealth has decided (after using a mean-variance approach) that their optimal portfolio is 80% invested in equities and 20% invested in cash. Suppose further that the expected rate of return and standard deviation of that portfolio are 10% p.a. and 15% p.a., respectively, so that the expected value and standard deviation of wealth at the end of the year are £11,000 and £1,500. If the investor now discovers that they have to pay £5,000 at the end of the year, the current portfolio is still efficient, but the surplus (assets minus liability at the end of the year) has a mean of £6,000 and standard deviation of £1,500. Of course, the investor may decide that the 80% equity/20% cash portfolio is no longer optimal, but it does still remain an efficient portfolio, i.e. there is no other portfolio that offers an expected surplus of £5,000 with lower standard deviation.

When the liabilities are random, their correlation with the asset classes and their volatility and expected size are among the inputs that are required for the new run of the optimiser. When the liability is a combination of the assets (as in the case of the benchmark referred to earlier) that are already under consideration, the incorporation of the correlations is relatively easy. This is because the correlations are just linear combinations of the assets for which we have already calculated correlations. So the correlations between the liabilities and assets can easily be calculated using the results of Chapter 9. Indeed, this case is so common that a whole jargon has emerged to describe the parameters. The surplus, S, is referred to as the "excess" or "relative" return and the standard deviation of the relative return is referred to as the "tracking error" although that term is also used to refer to other, closely related, statistics or "active risk".

Suppose that the rate of increase in the liabilities can be written as

$$L = \sum_{i=1}^{n} l_i R_i$$

and that the rate of return on the assets can be written as

$$A = \sum_{i=1}^{n} a_i R_i.$$

The surplus, S, is then given by:

$$S = A - L = \sum_{i=1}^{n} a_i R_i - \sum_{i=1}^{n} l_i R_i = \sum_{i=1}^{n} (a_i - l_i) R_i$$

Straightforward application of the properties of the mean and variance (see Section 9.13) to the definition of A yields:

$$E[A] = \sum_i a_i E[R_i]$$

and

$$Var[A] = \sum_i \sum_j a_i a_j \sigma_i \sigma_j \rho_{ij}$$

where σ_i represents the variance of the returns on asset i and ρ_{ij} represents the correlation between the returns on assets i and j.

Similarly, the mean and variance on S are given by

$$E[S] = \sum_i s_i E[R_i]$$

and

$$Var[S] = \sum_i \sum_j s_i s_j \sigma_i \sigma_j \rho_{ij}$$

where $s_i = a_i - l_i$.

Example 12.2

An investment manager is given the task of outperforming a benchmark of 50% equities and 50% bonds. The expected returns on the asset classes are 10% and 8%, respectively, and the standard deviations of the returns are 20% and 12%. The correlation between the returns is 0.5.

The manager decides to invest 70% in equities and 30% in bonds.
Calculate the expected relative return and the tracking error of the portfolio.

Answer

Using the notation from earlier:

$$s_{equity} = 0.2$$

$$s_{bond} = -0.2$$

$$E[R_{equity}] = 0.1$$

$$E[R_{bond}] = 0.08$$

$$\sigma_{equity} = 0.2$$

$$\sigma_{bond} = 0.12$$

$$\rho_{equity, bond} = 0.5$$

The relative performance ("surplus") of the manager versus the benchmark will therefore have a distribution which has a mean of $0.2 \times 0.1 + (-0.2) \times 0.08 = 0.004$ and a standard deviation of $(0.2^2 \times 0.2^2 + (-0.2)^2 \times 0.12^2 + 2 \times (0.2) \times (-0.2) \times 0.12 \times 0.2 \times 0.5)^{0.5} = 0.035$. This means that the likely rate of outperformance is 0.4% and the standard deviation (tracking error) is 3.5%.

If the liabilities depend on other random variables (such as mortality rates, inflation, or the weather in the case of non-life insurance liabilities), it is more difficult to establish the means, variances and correlations. In these cases it may be necessary to consider building an asset liability model to estimate the necessary parameters. Asset liability models are discussed further in Chapter 17.

When analysing surplus rather than terminal wealth, it is also quite common to use metrics other than volatility to measure risk. Alternatives that are often encountered are value at risk (VaR), probability of shortfall and expected shortfall. If the distributions of all the assets and liabilities are from the normal family, these alternative metrics can usually be derived from the variance and will tend to rank portfolios in the same order. The advantages in using them include that they may be easier to interpret and that they can deal with non-normal distributions. These alternative risk measures are explained in a little more detail in Section 12.13, Chapter 14 and Chapter 17.

12.10 MODERN PORTFOLIO THEORY AND INTERNATIONAL DIVERSIFICATION

It is becoming increasingly common for investors to hold an international portfolio, i.e. they wish to hold assets that are denominated in a currency other than their domestic currency. The desire to hold international (global) portfolios is driven partly by investors having liabilities spread globally and/or wanting international diversification and partly by investment managers who are increasingly finding it more relevant to research companies across sectors. For example, many of the large pharmaceutical, telecommunications and resource companies are very obviously global in their operations and profit bases. The country in which the company is listed or headquartered is arbitrary from the point of view of many investors.

From a theoretical perspective, it would also seem desirable that investors diversify their investment risks across as large a base as possible. If all the securities in the world are accessible to investors, their risk should be measured in the context of the global market.

However, the fact that "international" assets are quoted in currencies other than the domestic currency adds a layer of complication. For an investor with liabilities or wealth expectations denominated in a particular currency, the fact that the assets are currency mismatched can have significant implications. For example, an investor investing €1000 in a euro-denominated portfolio of shares and selling the portfolio for €1050 six months later would have enjoyed a rate of return of 5% per half year. However, an investor based in the UK who measures their wealth in £-sterling, might have seen £600 leave their account at the date that the portfolio was purchased and only £540 return to their account six months later, i.e. a rate of return of -10% per half year. This would have been the case if the exchange rate at the time of purchase were 0.6000£/€ and had moved to 0.5143£/€ at the time of sale.

Changes in the value of the domestic currency versus other currencies are typically as volatile as the changes in value of the underlying assets. Investing in an overseas market is therefore a joint decision about the likely returns from the securities listed in that market and the likely change in exchange rate between the domestic currency and that of the overseas market.

Some investors regard the currency decision as an integral part of investing overseas. According to the theory of purchasing power parity (PPP), currency rates will eventually change so that the cost of a good is the same in all countries for all consumers. One light-hearted example of this theory is the Big Mac Index produced by UBS and *The Economist*. The idea is that a Big Mac hamburger from McDonald's is a well-defined, standard item. If the cost of the hamburger is £1.99 in the UK and $2.70 in the US and the exchange rate between the two countries is £1 for $1.50, then the hamburger in the US looks "cheap" relative to the UK burger (or, the UK burger looks expensive). Theoretically it would be worth a UK consumer buying their burger direct in the US since it would cost them £2.70/1.50 = £1.80 which is cheaper than the £1.99 quoted in UK stores. In practice, individuals will not be able to take advantage of this difference. Nevertheless, if enough goods exhibit the same sort of discrepancy over a period, capital flows will force the exchange rate to equalise the prices.

The empirical evidence for PPP is very weak (see Rogoff, 1996). The price differentials appear to exist for many years, if not decades. Since the investment horizon for many investors is far shorter than this, most international investors prefer to take either an active view on currency, or to "hedge" out the impact of the currency. The currency hedging does not altogether remove a currency effect; what it does remove is most of the unpredictability associated with changes in exchange rates.

Currency hedging is usually achieved by entering into forward contracts, i.e. investors agree with a counter-party to buy back their own currency at a fixed rate at some time in the future. The rate at which they agree to buy back their currency is the forward rate and is (largely) determined by the interest rates in the two countries.

The forward currency rate (i.e. the rate at which the two parties agree to exchange currencies in the future), is determined by the principle of no-arbitrage. The principle of no-arbitrage is that an investor should not be able to buy something at one price and sell it simultaneously at another, so locking in a profit, or any potential for a profit. The way this principle applies to currencies is that investors should not be able to exchange their currency for another, invest it in a risk-free rate and exchange it back after some time and thereby lock in a different return from that which they might get from investing in the domestic risk-free rate.

To make the above more specific: suppose that the current exchange rate is such that £1 will buy \$1.50 and that the risk-free rate in the UK is 5% p.a. and in the US is 10% p.a. and that a UK investor is wanting to enter a one-year forward currency contract. Suppose further that the investor borrows £100 in the UK market and so becomes obliged to pay back £105 in one year's time. The investor then takes the £100, converts it to \$150 and invests it in the risk-free US asset. The investor also enters a forward rate contract to convert the dollars back to sterling at an exchange rate of X (expressed as how many dollars one pound can buy) in one year's time.

At the end of one year, the investor will receive \$165 back (the \$150 plus the risk-free rate) and will convert it back to sterling at an exchange rate X, i.e. the investor will receive £165/X. The principle of no-arbitrage states that this amount, £165/X, must be equal to £105 and hence that $X = 165/105 = 1.57$. Otherwise, the investor will lock in a profit (or loss) despite having taken no risk.

When it comes to investing in an overseas stock market, buying a forward currency contract cannot hedge out all the currency impact since the amount of money to be converted back to the domestic currency is not known in advance.

For an investor in any particular country, optimal portfolio construction can be thought of as a simple exercise in expanding the number of risky assets in which he or she can invest. These assets can be hedged or unhedged. So, for example, a UK-based investor can invest in the domestic markets and can also invest in the hedged US stock market and the unhedged US market. This approach is advocated by Meese and Dales (2001) as a means of deciding how much to invest overseas and how much of that overseas investment should be currency hedged.

Any of these approaches lead to investors (even those with the same level of risk aversion) holding different portfolios. Much of the difference arises because the risk-free rate in each country is different. This makes the development of an international asset pricing theory difficult.

12.11   THE CAPITAL ASSET PRICING MODEL

Investors have different views of the future, so their estimates of expected return and risk for a given security are bound to differ. However, in developing a model for the *market pricing* of securities, we need to consider the aggregate of investors.

The Capital Asset Pricing Model (CAPM) gives a simple relationship between expected return and risk in a competitive market. It is built on a number of assumptions which concern investor behaviour and market conditions. The following is a set of underlying assumptions which allows the derivation of the model.

(1) All investors are risk-averse and measure risk in terms of standard deviation of portfolio return (as for the Markowitz Model).
(2) All investors have a common time horizon for investment decision making (e.g. one month or two years).
(3) All investors have identical subjective estimates of future returns and risks for all securities.
(4) There exists a risk-free asset and all investors may borrow or lend unlimited amounts at the risk-free nominal rate of interest.
(5) All securities are completely divisible, there are no transaction costs or differential taxes, and there are no restrictions on short-selling.
(6) Information is freely and simultaneously available to all investors.

Much courage is required to develop a model on the basis of these assumptions! Many of them are clearly unrealistic. However, the final test of a model is how good it is at forecasting, not whether the assumptions are strictly valid.

Given the above assumptions, all investors face the same risk–return diagram as shown in Figure 12.9, and hence the same efficient frontier. As before, they can choose different optional portfolios according to their indifference curves. Thus, investor X would choose portfolio C and investor Y would choose portfolio D.

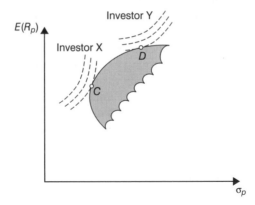

Figure 12.9

Let us now introduce the concept of lending at the risk-free rate, R_f. Furthermore, if the condition $x_i \geqslant 0$ is relaxed, borrowing at the risk-free rate also becomes possible. This opens up new alternatives. First, consider the case in which either borrowing or lending at the risk-free rate (with $\sigma = 0$) is combined with investment in security (or portfolio) A. Suppose that α is the proportion of funds invested in A. The ability to borrow at the risk-free rate means that there is no limit to the amount which may be invested in A, so that α may be greater than 1. Then using equation (12.3),

$$\sigma_p^2 = \alpha^2 \sigma_A^2 + (1-\alpha)^2 \cdot 0 + 2\alpha(1-\alpha) \cdot 0$$

$$= \alpha^2 \sigma_A^2$$

So

$$\sigma_p = \alpha \sigma_A$$

We also know that

$$E(R_p) = \alpha E(R_A) + (1 - \alpha)R_f$$

A straight line is therefore obtained on the risk–return diagram.

Figure 12.10 shows the opportunity set of risky portfolios together with the risk-free asset, F. Rather than invest in portfolio C, investor X would now do better investing in portfolio M, and then lending at the risk-free rate to reach a higher indifference curve at M_1 on the line FM. Similarly, rather than invest in portfolio D, investor Y would do better borrowing at the risk-free rate and investing in portfolio M to reach a higher indifference curve at point M_2 on the line FM.

In fact, all investors maximise their utility by choosing M and moving up or down the line FM until they are at a tangent to their highest available indifference curve. The set of *efficient portfolios*, which give the maximum expected return for given levels of risk, becomes the whole of the straight line through F and M. This particular *separation theorem* was first developed by Tobin (1958).

The question arises as to the content of the portfolio M. Since no investors will hold risky portfolios other than M and since all securities are held by one or other investor, it follows that M must contain all securities in proportion to their market capitalisations. The expected rate of return from M, denoted by $E(R_m)$, is thus the value-weighted average of the expected returns of all securities in the market.

FM, which is known as the *Capital Market Line*, is a straight line with gradient $\{E(R_m) - R_f\}/\sigma_m$ and intercept R_f. The equation of the *Capital Market Line* is therefore

$$E(R_e) = R_f + \left\{ \frac{E(R_m) - R_f}{\sigma_m} \right\} \sigma_e \qquad (12.14)$$

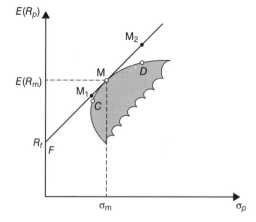

Figure 12.10

where e denotes an efficient portfolio. Equation (12.14) gives the expected return for efficient portfolios only. It does not give the expected return for non-efficient portfolios or for individual securities.

Consider now a portfolio, S, consisting of a single risky security i and the market portfolio, M. Suppose that α is the proportion of the value of S invested in i and $1 - \alpha$ is the proportion of the value of S invested in M.

If the possible combinations of i and M (which form S) are plotted, the gradient of the line in risk-return space is

$$\frac{\partial E(R_s)}{\partial \sigma_s}$$

or alternatively,

$$\frac{\partial E(R_s)/\partial \alpha}{\partial \sigma_s/\partial \alpha} \tag{12.15}$$

Now

$$E(R_s) = \alpha E(R_i) + (1 - \alpha)E(R_m)$$

and

$$\sigma_s = \{\alpha^2 \sigma_i^2 + (1 - \alpha)^2 \sigma_m^2 + 2\alpha(1 - \alpha)\sigma_{im}\}^{1/2}$$

so

$$\frac{\partial E(R_s)}{\partial \alpha} = E(R_i) - E(R_m)$$

and

$$\frac{\partial \sigma_s}{\partial \alpha} = \tfrac{1}{2}\{\alpha^2 \sigma_i^2 + (1 - \alpha)^2 \sigma_m^2 + 2\alpha(1 - \alpha)\sigma_{im}\}^{-1/2}$$

$$\times \{2\alpha \sigma_i^2 - 2(1 - \alpha)\sigma_m^2 + 2\sigma_{im} - 4\alpha\sigma_{im}\}$$

If we set $\alpha = 0$,

$$\frac{\partial E(R_s)}{\partial \alpha}\bigg|_{\alpha = 0} = E(R_i) - E(R_m) \tag{12.16}$$

$$\frac{\partial \sigma_s}{\partial a}\bigg|_{\alpha = 0} = \frac{\sigma_{im} - \sigma_m^2}{\sigma_m} \tag{12.17}$$

Notice also that at $\alpha = 0$, S is the market portfolio M.

Substituting equations (12.16) and (12.17) into (12.15), we obtain that the gradient at M in risk-return space is

$$\frac{E(R_i) - E(R_m)}{(\sigma_{im} - \sigma_m^2)\sigma_m}$$

However, we already know that the gradient of the Capital Market Line and hence the gradient at M is $[E(R_m) - R_f]/\sigma_m$. So

$$\frac{E(R_i) - E(R_m)}{(\sigma_{im} - \sigma_m^2)/\sigma_m} = \frac{E(R_m) - R_f}{\sigma_m}$$

$$E(R_i) - E(R_m) = \frac{\{E(R_m) - R_f\}(\sigma_{im} - \sigma_m^2)}{\sigma_m^2}$$

$$= \{E(R_m) - R_f\} \frac{\sigma_{im}}{\sigma_m^2} - E(R_m) + R_f$$

Hence

$$E(R_i) = R_f + \frac{\sigma_{im}}{\sigma_m^2} \{E(R_m) - R_f\}$$

or

$$E(R_i) = R_f + \beta_i\{E(R_m) - R_f\} \tag{12.18}$$

where

$$\beta_i = \frac{\sigma_{im}}{\sigma_m^2}$$

Equation (12.18), known as the *Securities Market Line*, is the main result of the CAPM and is of great importance. It gives a relationship between the expected return from a security and the risk of the security, as measured by β. The higher the β value, the higher the expected return necessary to attract investment. Notice that it is the covariance of the security's return with that of the market which is rewarded, not its total risk as measured by the standard deviation of return. The expression $\{E(R_m) - R_f\}$ is known as the *market risk premium*. In practice, R_f is normally taken to be the annualised rate of interest on a short-term government-backed security for the appropriate country, e.g. a 90-day Treasury bill.

Credit for the formulation of equation (12.18) is due to Sharpe (1964) and Lintner (1965).

Neither of the mainstream asset pricing models (the CAPM and the arbitrage pricing theory (APT), described in Sections 12.12 and 12.13) are particularly well supported by the existing empirical tests. However, there has been almost as much criticism of the tests themselves as there has been of the models. Some of the major problems with testing the CAPM are (a) that the CAPM is stated in terms of investor expectations rather than historic returns; and (b) Roll's critique (1977) in which he noted that the common assumption (see Stambaugh (1982) for supporting evidence) that a market index was a reasonable proxy for the true market (that strictly contains *all* assets) was in fact a potentially significant flaw in any test or application of CAPM. He proved that the CAPM was in fact identical to the hypothesis that the (unobservable) market portfolio was mean-variance efficient.

Therefore, for example, if the expected returns, variances and correlations between assets were calibrated in such a way that the market proxy (often an index) was on the estimated mean-variance efficient frontier, then researchers would find support for the CAPM. If the market proxy was not on the estimated efficient frontier, then the researcher would reject the CAPM. The insight is that neither conclusion necessarily says anything about the true market portfolio or the pricing of assets. It might be that if covariances and expectations are accurate, but the market proxy is off the efficient frontier, then the CAPM will be falsely rejected. On the other hand, the true parameters may put the market proxy on the efficient frontier, but the actual market portfolio off it and so the CAPM will be falsely accepted.

Despite this, early evidence, e.g. Fama and Macbeth (1973), was largely supportive of the CAPM. However, subsequent research has uncovered anomalies inconsistent with the CAPM, such as the "small firm effect" and "calendar effects" (see Dimson, 1988). In a widely reported empirical study published in 1992, Fama and French reported that beta had no explanatory power in the pricing of assets on the US market and that size (market capitalisation) and the book-value to market-value ratio were more important characteristics. The study and its findings have been replicated in other markets as well and have led to the hypothesis of a three-factor CAPM which is often used in empirical work:

$$E[R_i] = R_f + \beta_i(E[R_m - R_f) + \gamma_i SMB + \delta_i HML$$

where SMB is the difference between expected returns on "small" and "big" stocks and HML is the difference between the expected returns of stocks with high book-to-market ratios and stocks with low book-to-market ratios.

Kothari et al. (1995), using annual rather than monthly data, over the same historical period as the Fama–French study, found that beta was still significant. They suggested that the other factors were time-period specific features since there is very little theoretical support for their inclusion in a pricing model. They argued that the use of annual data was more appropriate than monthly data for testing the CAPM since it was less affected by market micro-structure effects and functions.

Dimson and Mussavian (1998, 1999) provide a more extensive review of other developments and enhancements to the CAPM. Hawawini and Keim (2000) provide a recent synthesis of the literature on testing of the CAPM. Key amongst these developments are the work of Merton (1973) and Breeden (1979) who moved the CAPM from its static, one-period horizon framework into continuous time, which permits more dynamic pricing.

Despite its many detractors, the CAPM remains an important theoretical framework. This is not least because it provided the fundamental insight that non-diversifiable risk (however measured) determines investors' return expectations and hence asset pricing.

Equation (12.18) can be rearranged to give

$$E(R_i) = (1 - \beta_i)R_f + \beta_i E(R_m) \tag{12.19}$$

A comparison between equation (12.19) and equation (12.11) reveals a similarity of structure. But there are important differences. Sharpe's Market Model is not supported by an asset pricing theory; it is simply a statistical model designed to reduce the mass of information required in applying the Markowitz Model. In addition, the market proxy need not be the true market for the Market Model still to be useful.

Furthermore, the intercept a_i in equation (12.11) can take on any value, whereas the equivalent term $(1 - \beta_i)R_f$ in equation (12.19) is precisely specified, given values for β_i and R_f. According to the CAPM, β is the only characteristic of an individual security which influences the expected return for that security.

If a security tends to move in line with the market, σ_{im} is equal to σ_m^2 so that the security has a β value equal to 1. A security with β value greater than 1 is sometimes said to be *aggressive*, whereas a security with β value less than 1 is said to be *defensive*. Securities are unlikely to have negative βs as this would imply a tendency to move against the trend of the market.

The β of a security is usually obtained by estimating the regression line of R_m on R_i, known as the *characteristic line*, just as was done for b in the Market Model — see Section 12.6. As β values are generally calculated from historical data, they may be very different from current β values. Thus, although the CAPM may be useful in understanding security price behaviour generally, its main use lies in the management of well-diversified portfolios where variations over time in the βs of individual securities tend to cancel out.

Since a portfolio has a return that is linked to the market just like an individual security, the β value of a portfolio is simply the weighted average of the β values of securities held in the portfolio, where the weights are equal to the value of the individual holdings. A diversified portfolio with β value less (or greater) than 1 should be less (or more) volatile than the market portfolio.

Equation (12.18) leads to the following relationship between a portfolio's expected return and its β value:

$$E(R_p) = R_f + \beta_p\{E(R_m) - R_f\}$$

Thus, over the years, high-β portfolios can be expected to give high returns; but the phrase "over the years" should be emphasised. In a falling market, portfolios with high β values will tend to underperform. There is the expectation of high returns from high-β portfolios but no guarantee that this will be achieved — after all, high-β portfolios are more "risky".

Equation (12.19) may be transformed from its expectational form into an *ex post* form by assuming that, on average, the expected rate of return on a security is equal to its realised rate. Thus,

$$R_{it} = (1 - \beta_i)R_f + \beta_i R_{mt} + e_{it} \tag{12.20}$$

The e_{it} are interpreted as *abnormal returns* since they represent returns in excess of those predicted by the CAPM. Rearranging equation (12.20), we obtain

$$e_{it} = R_{it} - (1 - \beta_i)R_f - \beta_i R_{mt} \tag{12.21}$$

The expression $(1 - \beta_i)R_f + \beta_i R_{mt}$ is known as the *benchmark return* so that the abnormal return in period t is equal to the actual return in period t less the benchmark return in period t.

Using an approach similar to that adopted for the Market Model in Section 12.7, equation (12.20) leads to the following formula for σ_i^2:

$$\sigma_i^2 = \beta_i^2 \sigma_m^2 + \sigma^2(e_i)$$

$$\Rightarrow \quad \sigma_i = \sqrt{\beta_i^2 \sigma_m^2 + \sigma^2(e_i)} \tag{12.22}$$

Equation (12.22) shows that the *total* risk of a security as measured by its standard deviation of returns σ_i, is dependent upon:

(i) $\beta_i\sigma_m$ — *systematic* or *market* risk that is related to fluctuation of the market as a whole and cannot be eliminated by diversification; and
(ii) $\sigma(e_i)$ — *non-systematic* or *specific* risk which can be eliminated by diversification. This type of risk is unique to the company or its industry (e.g. management competence or shifts in demand for the company's products) or is related to other factors such as company size or dividend yield. It is represented by the scatter around the regression line.

Again, using an approach similar to that adopted for the Market Model, the variance of portfolio returns for a portfolio of n securities is given by

$$\sigma_p^2 = \beta_p^2\sigma_m^2 + \sum_{i=1}^{n} x_i^2\sigma^2(e_i)$$

where x_i = the proportion of the portfolio's value invested in the ith security

$$\sum_{i=1}^{n} x_i = 1$$

$$\beta_p = \sum_{i=1}^{n} x_i\beta_i$$

and σ_m = the standard deviation of return on the market index

Example 12.3

One year ago, an investor in the UK who pays no tax or transaction costs put 45% of his money in share X, 35% in share Y and 20% in share Z. Share dividends have been re-invested in the same share but no other deals have been carried out. Actual returns over the last year, together with the risk characteristics of the three shares, are given below:

Share	Annual return (%)	β	Specific risk (%)
X	0	0.6	30
Y	30	1.2	60
Z	10	0.8	25

The standard deviation of returns on the market index is 20%, the return on the market index over the last year was 5% and the risk-free rate was 10% per annum.

(a) What were the actual return and abnormal return of the portfolio over the last year?
(b) What are the β, specific risk and total risk of the portfolio at present?
(c) Stating any assumptions that you make, what return would you expect for the portfolio over the next year?

Answer

(a) *Actual return*

Share	Fraction of portfolio	Annual return (%)	Fraction × annual return (%)
X	0.45	0	0
Y	0.35	30	10.5
Z	0.20	10	2.0
			12.5

So the actual return over the last year = 12.5%.

Abnormal return: Portfolio β one year ago is calculated as follows:

Share	Fraction of portfolio	β	Fraction × b
X	0.45	0.6	0.27
Y	0.35	1.2	0.42
Z	0.20	0.8	0.16
			0.85

Abnormal return = Actual return − Benchmark return

where

$$\text{Benchmark return} = (0.15 \times 10) + (0.85 \times 5)$$
$$= 1.5 + 4.25$$
$$= 5.75\%$$

Hence

$$\text{Abnormal return} = 12.5\% - 5.75\%$$
$$= 6.75\%$$

(b) It is first necessary to calculate the fraction of the portfolio currently invested in each share:

		Fraction of portfolio
Share X	45 × 1.0 = 45	40%
Share Y	35 × 1.3 = 45.5	40.4%
Share Z	20 × 1.1 = 22	19.6%
	112.5	100%

Value of β

Share	Fraction of portfolio	β	Fraction × β
X	0.400	0.6	0.24
Y	0.404	1.2	0.4848
Z	0.196	0.8	0.1568
			0.8816

So the portfolio β at present = 0.882.

Specfic risk

Share	Fraction of portfolio	Specific risk (%)	$\left(\dfrac{Fraction}{\times sp.\ risk}\right)^2$
X	0.400	30	144.00
Y	0.404	60	587.58
Z	0.196	25	24.01
			755.59

$$\text{Portfolio specific risk} = \sqrt{755.59}\%$$

$$= \underline{27.5\%}$$

Total risk

$$(\text{Total risk})^2 = (\text{Market risk})^2 + (\text{Specific risk})^2$$

$$= (0.882 \times 20)^2 + 755.59$$

$$= 311.17 + 755.59$$

$$\text{Total risk} = \sqrt{1066.76}\%$$

$$= \underline{32.7\%}$$

(c) Assume that dividends are reinvested in the same share; risk-free rate over the next year = 10%; and historic β is applicable over the next year.

In the UK, the market risk premium for equities compared with Treasury bills has historically averaged around 9% per annum since the 1920s although many academics and practitioners would now regard this figure to be far higher than what should be expected for the future. Simply substituting this figure of 9% into the CAPM avoids having to assess directly the expected return on the equity market index. Then using the CAPM,

$$E(R_p) = R_f + \beta_p(E(R_m) - R_f)$$

$$= 10 + (0.882 \times 9)\%$$

$$= \underline{17.94\%}$$

12.12   INTERNATIONAL CAPM

Several researchers have attempted to construct International Capital Asset Pricing Models (sometimes referred to as ICAPMs, although this should not be confused with the continuous-time Intertemporal CAPMs).

As an exposition of the considerations involved in constructing such a model, we outline Solnik's (1974) model. He makes two main assumptions about currency risk and how investors deal with it in pricing assets internationally. He assumes, first, that currency risk is eliminated by hedging and, second, that investors consume (or measure wealth) only in their own domestic currency. Investors are additionally assumed to have homogeneous expectations about security returns and exchange rate variations so that they would agree about expected returns whether they are denominated in local or foreign currency.

The hedging strategy that Solnik envisages depends on investors being able to borrow in each country at the risk-free rate of that country. The idea is that investors will borrow the same amount of money as they have invested in risky securities in that foreign country. That money will then be invested in the domestic risk-free asset. At the end of the investment horizon, the gain or loss due to currency in the risk-free transaction should approximately (because it is not possible to hedge the currency impact on the risky returns, only the capital invested) offset the loss or gain due to currency incurred in the risky securities.

Because of the homogeneity of assumptions, all investors in any one country will behave and price assets as if a form of the CAPM held within that country. In mathematical notation, they would price assets so that

$$E[HR_{ik}] - r_{fk} = \beta_{ik}(E[HR_{\cdot k}] - r_{fk}) \tag{12.23}$$

where HR_{ik} is the hedged return on security i for an investor in country k; r_{fk} is the risk-free rate in country k; $HR_{\cdot k}$ is the hedged "market" portfolio for country k and the beta coefficient is similar to the conventional beta coefficient, but defined using hedged returns, i.e.

$$\beta_{ik} = \frac{\text{cov}[HR_{ik}; \, HR_{\cdot k}]}{\text{var}[HR_{\cdot k}]}. \tag{12.24}$$

If security i's local market is itself country k, then the hedged return and the local return, LR_i, are the same. If we denote the local return in excess of the local risk-free rate by $LER_i = LR_i - r_{fk}$ then:

$$E[LER_i] = \beta_{ikL}(E[HR_{\cdot k}] - r_{fk}) \tag{12.25}$$

with

$$\beta_{ikL} = \frac{\text{cov}[LR_i; \, HR_{\cdot k}]}{\text{var}[HR_{\cdot k}]} \tag{12.26}$$

will be true within each country k.

What we have done so far is simply to specify that a series of CAPMs would hold in each country if investors did not invest abroad. The introduction of "hedged" and "local" returns is there to help ease the development of the model as the restriction about investing only locally is removed. To move from a collection of local CAPMs to an international pricing model, we now need to convert all the hedged returns to returns denominated in the local (home) currency.

Denote country k's market portfolio returns, when each security's returns is measured in local currency, by $LR_{\cdot k}$. At this point you should recall how the hedging strategy was defined: investors are assumed to sell (borrow) foreign currency at the risk-free rate to the same extent as they will invest overseas and then these borrowings are invested in the local cash market. Let W_j be the proportion of total wealth invested in country j and W_{jk} represent the proportion of the wealth of investors in country k invested in country j; the expected hedged returns can then be written

$$E[HR_{\cdot k}] = E[LR_{\cdot k}] - \sum_{j \neq k} W_{jk} r_{fj} + \sum_{j \neq k} W_{jk} r_{fk} \tag{12.27}$$

The hedged return is the local return less the interest owed on their foreign borrowings plus the interest earned on their local cash deposits. Noting that the total proportion of wealth invested by the investors of each country must add up to one, equation (12.27) can be simplified to

$$E[HR_{\cdot k}] = E[LR_{\cdot k}] - \sum W_{jk}r_{fj} + r_{fk} \qquad (12.28)$$

In other words, the expected hedged return on the market portfolio of country k is equal to the expected return on the optimal portfolio as calculated in local returns plus the difference between the local risk-free rate and a weighted average of all the risk-free rates worldwide.

If we combine the above expression with equation (12.25), we find

$$E[LER_i] = \beta_{ikL}\left(E[LR_{\cdot k}] - \sum W_{jk}r_{fj}\right) \qquad (12.29)$$

We can also see that because $HR_{\cdot k}$ and $LR_{\cdot k}$ differ only by a constant and so will not affect covariances or variances of the random variables, the beta coefficient can equally well be defined in terms of the local currency returns as in the hedged returns, that is

$$\beta_{ikL} = \frac{\text{cov}[LR_i;\ LR_{\cdot k}]}{\text{var}[LR_{\cdot k}]} = \beta_{ik}$$

We now have a set of "CAPMs" for each country expressed in local currency terms, i.e. in terms that all investors can agree on because they do not depend on the currency of the investor. To find an International CAPM, we need to aggregate the local CAPMs to find a pricing model in terms of a global market portfolio.

Dividing both sides of equation (12.29) by $(E[LR_{\cdot k}] - \sum W_{jk}r_{fj})$ and multiplying both sides by $\text{var}[LR_{\cdot k}]$, we obtain

$$E[LER_i]\frac{\text{var}[LR_{\cdot k}]}{\left(E[LR_{\cdot k}] - \sum W_{jk}r_{fj}\right)} = \text{cov}[LR_i, LR_{\cdot k}] \qquad (12.30)$$

Now define the return on the global market portfolio to be $LR_M = \sum W_k LR_{\cdot k}$. If we then multiply both sides of equation (12.30) by W_k and sum over all k we get

$$E[LER_i]\sum W_k \frac{\text{var}[LR_{\cdot k}]}{\left(E[LR_{\cdot k}] - \sum W_{jk}r_{fj}\right)} = \text{cov}[LR_i, LR_M] \qquad (12.31)$$

The above must hold for all risky assets, in particular the global market portfolio, LR_M. That is

$$(E[LR_M] - r_{fM})\sum W_k \frac{\text{var}[LR_{\cdot k}]}{\left(E[LR_{\cdot k}] - \sum W_{jk}r_{fj}\right)} = \text{cov}[LR_M, LR_M]$$

where r_{fM} is a weighted average of the r_{fk}, with weights equal to W_k. This implies that

$$\frac{(E[LR_M] - r_{fM})}{\text{var}[LR_M]} = \left[\sum W_k \frac{\text{var}[LR_{\cdot k}]}{\left(E[LR_{\cdot k}] - \sum W_{jk}r_{fj} \right)} \right]^{-1}$$

Finally, we can use this equivalence in equation (12.31) to obtain Solnik's CAPM:

$$E[LER_i] = E[LR_i] - r_{fk} = \frac{\text{cov}[LR_i, LR_M]}{\text{var}[LR_M]} (E[LR_M] - r_{fM})$$

Other researchers have produced similar models that differ in the way in which investors are assumed to deal with currency risk. The Black (1989) model is perhaps the most widely cited because it produces an analytic result that holds for all investors. In particular, all investors should hedge a fixed proportion, the universal hedging ratio, of their non-domestic assets. However, the assumptions required to describe this result imply highly unrealistic investment behaviour.

12.13   ARBITRAGE PRICING THEORY

The CAPM requires strong assumptions either about the way in which investors behave or the distribution of asset returns in order to derive a pricing formula. The APT of Ross (1976) provides a quite different approach to finding the equilibrium pricing of the assets in the market. It differs from the CAPM in both derivation and implicit assumptions, although the CAPM can be constructed as a special case of the APT.

The APT takes as its starting point a return generating function:

$$R_i = \sum_{k=0}^{K} \beta_{ik} F_k + \varepsilon_i \tag{12.32}$$

where the F_k are interpreted as common risk factors and the ε_I represent the idiosyncratic or firm-specific components of return and have zero expected value. We also assume that F_0 is always equal to one, but that all the other factors are random variables with a zero expectation. The firm-specific components are assumed to be independent of each other and of the common factors. The common factors may be correlated with each other and will generally have different standard deviations.

The return-generating function is very similar in structure to the multiple index model often used to help reduce the statistical estimation problems associated with MPT. One important difference is that in the APT the factors are completely unspecified and may indeed be unobservable directly.

The APT does not help us very much in terms of what the common risk factors might be, or indeed how many factors there should be. This is not in itself a failing of the theory. It can, though, help in understanding the principles involved to have a concrete model in mind.

We suppose there are four factors: short-term interest rates, long-term interest rates, the change in the price of oil and the change in consumer confidence. In each case the average value is subtracted out so that each factor has a mean of zero. Each share price will therefore change in response to a change in one of the underlying four factors, or because of a firm-specific impact, e.g. the news that the firm has registered a patent for a drug. Some companies will be more sensitive to the factors than others. For example, an oil company or a transportation company will be highly sensitive to changes in the price of oil. Other types of companies may not be very sensitive to the changes in oil prices, but may depend crucially on short-term borrowing and thus will react strongly to changes in short-term interest rates.

It is also conceptually important to note that the APT starts off by specifying a return-generating function. The CAPM has no such associated function. The single-index model (the Sharpe Model, or Market Model) is theoretically unrelated to the CAPM despite many apparent and statistical similarities. Sharpe (1964) and Harrington (1987) provide more detailed discussions about the similarities, differences and tests of the models. Using the return-generating function in equation (12.32), the return-generating function for a portfolio, p, that comprises weights in the securities of w_i, can be written

$$R_p = \sum_{k=0}^{K} \left(\sum_{i=1}^{n} w_i \beta_{ik} \right) F_k + \sum_{i=1}^{n} w_i \varepsilon_i$$

If the number of securities in the portfolio is large, i.e. n is large, the last term will be approximately zero. This approximation is true because of the law of large numbers, i.e. the average of a large number of drawings of a random variable converges to the expected value of the random variable. This in turn implies that the return on a portfolio is equal to the weighted sum of the underlying risk factors.

It should be noted that a large number of portfolios can be created, each having a return that is a weighted average of the underlying random factors. As a simple example, suppose that the number of factors is one. Then a portfolio's return is (approximately) given by

$$R_p = a_p + \beta_{\cdot p} F$$

where $a_p = \sum_{i=1}^{n} w_i \beta_{i0}$ (remembering that we have assumed that F_0 is one) and

$$\beta_{\cdot p} = \sum_{i=1}^{n} w_i \beta_{i1}$$

The expected return on p is given by α_p. The standard deviation (which we will interpret as risk) of the portfolio is equal to $\beta_{\cdot 1} \sigma_F$, where σ_F is the standard deviation of the factor.

Suppose now that we are able to find another portfolio, q, with weights v_i which has the same standard deviation as p. Put into mathematics, we are therefore supposing that

$$R_q = \sum_{k=0}^{K} \left(\sum_{i=1}^{n} v_i \beta_{ik} \right) F_k + \sum_{i=1}^{n} v_i \varepsilon_i$$

and that

$$\beta_{\cdot p} = \sum_{i=1}^{n} w_i \beta_{i1} = \sum_{i=1}^{n} \nu_i \beta_{i1} = \beta_{\cdot q}$$

We have again assumed that the law of large numbers applies and the residual term,

$$\sum_{i=1}^{n} \nu_i \varepsilon_i,$$

is negligibly small.

If a_q is bigger than a_p then it will be profitable to construct an "arbitrage portfolio" by short-selling the portfolio p and buying q. We could do this by borrowing the amount of money required to buy portfolio p and promising to pay back whatever portfolio p is worth in, say, one year's time. We would then use the borrowed money to buy portfolio q. Because the two portfolios have the same risk (the same exposure to each common factor) and will be perfectly correlated, every time p goes down, q will also go down by the same magnitude LESS the extra return. And when p goes up, q will also go up by the same amount PLUS the extra return. At the end of the year, we would sell q and use the money to pay our promise of the value of p. Because q is guaranteed to return more than p, it means we have generated a profit without taking any risk.

A market with persistent arbitrage opportunities will be characterised by some investors who have limitless wealth. As envious as we may be of some investors' levels of wealth, we do not observe individuals with infinite wealth. Hence it is reasonable to assume that there are, at best, fleeting arbitrage opportunities in the market and that all portfolios with the same risk profiles will have the same expected return. Alternatively, if we assume that investors are non-satiated and that the market is in equilibrium, then no risk-free, excess return opportunities will exist since the investors will have continued trading until they had disappeared. We will encounter arbitrage arguments later in Chapter 16 on option pricing models.

It has been demonstrated above that if we can construct a combined portfolio that uses no wealth (borrowing the value of p and selling q involves no additional wealth) and generates no risk (q and p have the same betas), the market will enforce an expected return on the combined portfolio that is also zero.

Again, putting this into mathematics we have that

$$\sum w_i = \sum \nu_i = 1, \text{ which can be expressed as}$$

$$\sum_{i=1}^{n} (w_i - \nu_i) = 0$$

and

$$a_p - a_q \qquad = 0$$

$$\Longrightarrow \quad \sum_{i=1}^{n} w_i \beta_{i0} - \sum_{i=1}^{n} \nu_i \beta_{i0} = 0$$

$$\Longrightarrow \quad \sum_{i=1}^{n} (w_i - \nu_i) \beta_{i0} \quad = 0$$

and

$$\beta_{.p} - \beta_{.q} = 0$$

$$\Rightarrow \quad \sum_{i=1}^{n} w_i \beta_{i1} - \sum_{i=1}^{n} v_i \beta_{i1} = 0$$

$$\Rightarrow \quad \sum_{i=1}^{n} (w_i - v_i)\beta_{i1} = 0$$

Rephrasing the above, the weighted average of the risk exposures, β_{i1}, the weighted average of the expected returns, β_{i0}, and a weighted average of unity are all equal to zero. An algebraic consequence of the above three facts is that the expected returns must be a linear combination of the risk exposures and a constant. For each security, therefore

$$\beta_{i0} = \lambda_0 + \lambda_1 \beta_{i1}$$

If there were more than one factor, say k of them, then

$$\beta_{i0} = \lambda_0 + \lambda_1 \beta_{i1} + \lambda_2 \beta_{i2} + \cdots + \lambda_k \beta_{ik}$$

Example 12.4

Consider a highly simplified market with only three securities and a single common risk factor. Assume that the firm-specific factors are negligibly small (in this small market we cannot rely on the law of large numbers to eradicate specific risk in portfolios so we have to assume that the specific risks themselves are small in order to have an illustrative example). The three securities, denoted A, B and C, have risk exposures of 0.6, 1.0 and 1.8 to a common factor, respectively.

Show how the principle of no-arbitrage will imply that the expected return on each security can be written as a linear function of its risk exposure.

Answer

We consider two portfolios. The first portfolio is a combination of A and C, which we will denote p; the second portfolio is a single holding in B, which we will denote q. For p and q to have common factor risk exposures of 1.0, p would need to be composed of two-thirds of A and one-third of C because $0.67 \times 0.6 + 0.33 \times 1.8 = 0.4 + 0.6 = 1.0$. Portfolio q would of course just have a risk exposure of 1.0 because it was composed entirely of B, which itself has an exposure of 1.0.

Because we are assuming that there are no arbitrage opportunities, the expected return on A multiplied by two-thirds plus the expected return on C multiplied by one-third must equal the expected return on B, which has the same risk. For example, if B has an expected return of 10% p.a., A may have an expected return of 6% and C an expected return of 18% per annum. Another possibility is that A offers an expected return of 3% per annum and C an expected return of 24% per annum.

We could form the following rule for the first case: the expected return is equal to 0% plus 10% times the risk exposure, i.e.

for A, $0\% + 10\% \times 0.6 = 6\%$
for B, $0\% + 10\% \times 1.0 = 10\%$ and
for C, $0\% + 10\% \times 1.8 = 18\%$

For the second case, the rule could be minus 7.5% plus 17.5% times the risk exposure, i.e.

for A, $-7.5\% + 17.5\% \times 0.6 = -7.5\% + 10.5\% = 3\%$
for B, $-7.5\% + 17.5\% \times 1.0 = 10\%$ and
for C, $-7.5\% + 17.5\% \times 1.8 = 24\%$

The key point is that, no matter what values the risk exposures and the expected return on B are, we will always be able to find a common rule that expresses the expected return on each asset to be X% plus Y% times the risk exposure of the asset.

The ability to write expected returns as a linear function of the risk exposure may initially appear a little abstract: why should it be important to know that the expected returns can always be written in a particular mathematical form? It is when we try to interpret the formula that we get some important financial insights: the expected return is equal to a constant plus multiples of its risk exposures.

In theory, therefore, it is possible to price any asset provided that you know how sensitive the return is to the various risk exposures. It also means that a portfolio of risky assets will have risk exposures that are weighted averages of the risk exposures of the individual assets in the portfolio. This is a powerful insight, because if you know the risk exposures of the individual assets then you can build a portfolio with exactly the risk exposures that you want.

As noted earlier, the APT does not depend on knowing what the factors are or even how many factors there are. However, this is a practical stumbling block which has led to much criticism, e.g. Dhrymes (1984) and Shanken (1982). Empirical researchers have tried two main approaches. The first could reasonably be called a pure statistical approach: The idea is to use an applied statistical technique called factor analysis to analyse the correlations between securities to discover if there are common factors in the return series of securities. Factor analysis does not help directly in interpreting what the factors are, but can help in determining how many factors there are. Further, it gives an approximation to the values of the factors in the data set used to perform the analysis. These estimates are given as weighted averages of the individual securities. It is possible to use knowledge of the securities (e.g. their sectors, or their business exposures, etc.) to try to interpret what the weights might be implying about the underlying factors.

The second method is to use (financial) economic theory to try to specify which economic factors, e.g. the price of oil, or interest rates, etc., might affect security prices to different extents. Having specified the possible factors, one can then test to see whether or not the securities are sensitive to the hypothecated factors and that there is no correlation across securities except through the hypothecated factors. If there is any statistically significant "residual" correlation, then that implies that a further common factor exists that should be included in the model.

The APT has generally fared a little better than the CAPM in empirical testing (Roll and Ross (1980), Roll *et al.* (1983)), although this is far from representing unequivocal confirmation (Reinganum, 1981).

12.14 DOWNSIDE MEASURES OF RISK

One the frustrations often expressed about theories such as MPT is that the measure of risk is "symmetric" in the sense that both large positive and large negative returns contribute to a high risk estimate. You will recall from Section 8.5.11 that each observation's contribution to the estimated standard deviation depends on how different it is from the average of the observations and not whether it is above or below the average.

Since most people associate risk with undesirable outcomes, this feature of standard deviation is sometimes seen as a hindrance to its use as a measure of risk. Before discussing some of the alternative measures that make explicit the link between the measure of risk and undesirable outcomes, it is worth emphasising the distinction between the theoretical concept of a standard deviation (or, indeed, any statistic) and an estimated or sample standard deviation. The well-known formula for a standard deviation given in Section 8.5.11 is an estimator of the actual underlying standard deviation. When we take a history of share returns and compute the standard deviation, we only have an estimate. The use of mean-variance analysis as used in MPT depends not only on means and variances, but also on the fact that the mean and variance tell us ALL that is relevant (to an expected utility maximising investor) about the WHOLE distribution of returns.

One important case that enables MPT to be used with all conventional utility functions to find an optimal portfolio is the normal distribution. In this case the mean and the variance not only correspond with our data analytic interpretations of mean (as the location) and variance (as the spread of the data around the mean), but they are also the parameters for the distribution. In other words, if we knew the true mean and variance and could assume that the returns followed a normal distribution, we would know exactly what the probabilities were that the return would be above or below every single level.

On the other hand, there are other distributions for which the theoretical mean and variance can be easily calculated, but are less useful in summarising the distribution. For example, consider the following distribution with density function

$$f(x) = 2.0(1 - x), \qquad 0 \leqslant x \leqslant 1$$

Using the techniques from Chapter 9 we can derive the mean of this distribution to be $\frac{1}{3}$ and the variance to be $\frac{1}{18}$. A picture of this distribution is shown in Figure 12.11.

It is clear that this distribution has a very different shape from a normal distribution with the same mean and variance. Different investors will choose the one distribution over the other depending on their risk tolerances. For example, the above distribution may appeal to an investor who wishes to have an absolute minimum return of zero, but wants some upside potential. Another investor may be willing to accept a negative return (which is possible for a normal distribution with the same mean and variance) in return for a greater probability of obtaining a rate of return greater than 33% and indeed a greater likelihood of getting a very high return.

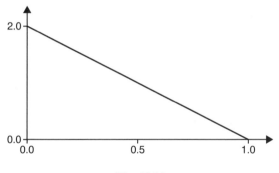

Fig. 12.11

It should be noted that there is one type of investor who would be indifferent between the above distribution and the normal distribution with the same mean and variance. This type of investor has a quadratic utility function. Unfortunately quadratic utility functions are not very good at predicting the behaviour of investors and contain some extremely implausible features. For example, they would suggest that an investor would prefer less wealth to more wealth at high levels of wealth and that investors exhibit increasing levels of relative and absolute risk aversion.

The above example demonstrates that if we just observed a set of historical returns and calculated the sample mean and sample variance, we have little to go on in terms of constructing optimal portfolios. We also need to make some assumption about the underlying distribution. Only then can we use the historical data to "calibrate" the MPT framework.

When it comes to the normal distribution, the mean and variance correspond to the two unknown parameters in the density function and hence determine everything there is to know about the distribution. That means that every other measure of risk will just be some combination of the mean and variance. Once we have estimates for the mean and variance, these can be used to estimate all the other measures of risk. For example, suppose we want the measure of risk to be a downside measure such as the probability that the return will be less than some target minimum value. We can then use our estimates of the mean and variance to estimate this alternative risk measure by replacing the parameters for the normal distribution by the sample statistics, i.e.

$$\Pr[R < r_{\min}] = \Phi\left(\frac{r_{\min} - \bar{x}}{s}\right) \tag{12.33}$$

where $\bar{x}$ is the sample mean, s is the sample standard deviation (square root of the sample variance), $r_{\min}$ is the target minimum return and $\Phi(\cdot)$ is the distribution function for the standard normal distribution.

This estimator for the measure of downside will also be efficient since to estimate the sample mean and sample variance ALL the data are used. This is in contrast to, for example, the estimator

$$\Pr[R < r_{\min}] = \frac{\#(R < r_{\min})}{n}$$

where the numerator represents the number of times in the sample that the return was less than the target minimum and the denominator is the size of the sample. As an example of this inefficiency, suppose that in the sample none of the observations was below the minimum. In this case the second estimator would produce a measure of risk of zero. The parametric estimator given in equation (12.33) would at least produce a positive number.

12.15   MARKOWITZ SEMI-VARIANCE

Markowitz proposed semi-variance as an alternative measure of risk. Semi-variance is the same as variance, except that the riskiness (as measured by a typical deviation from the average return) is calculated using only the points below the mean.

For a continuous distribution, such as is usually appropriate for return distributions, with distribution function $F(x)$ and mean μ, the semi-variance is defined as

$$Semi\text{-}var[X] = \int_{-\infty}^{\mu} (x - \mu)^2 dF(x)$$

An estimator, given a data set $\{x_i\}$, for semi-variance is given by

$$d^2 = (1/n^-) \sum_{i:\, x_i \leqslant \bar{x}} (x_i - \bar{x})^2,$$

where n^- is the number of observations below the mean.

Another parametric estimator could be constructed by fitting a density function to the empirical data and then estimating the d^2 statistic by integration. For example, we might suppose that the distribution is a normal distribution and use the sample mean and sample standard deviation as estimators for the unknown parameters. A possible estimator for d^2 is then given by

$$d^2 = \int_{-\infty}^{\bar{x}} (x - \bar{x})^2 (2\pi s^2)^{-0.5} \exp\left\{ -0.5 \left(\frac{x - \bar{x}}{s} \right)^2 \right\} dx$$

For most distributions, the above integration procedure would have to be performed numerically. The advantages of the parametric estimator over the first-mentioned estimator are as outlined in the previous section which referred to estimators of shortfall probability.

The square root of d^2, d, can be referred to as the semi-standard deviation. For example, suppose that we observe the following returns on the market and calculate the estimated mean, standard deviation and semi-standard deviation, see Table 12.1.

The standard deviation is larger than the semi-standard deviation. If we are interpreting risk as the size and likelihood of a return below the mean, then the semi-standard deviation is telling us that the share with these returns is not as risky as we might have estimated from the conventional standard deviation.

In this case, one of the main reasons that the standard deviation is larger is the return of 40.50% in quarter 4 of 1999. The semi-standard deviation is completely robust to how far above the mean a particular return is because it effectively ignores them when estimating the risk; after all, for the proponents of semi-standard deviation, a large or very large positive return are not signs of risk. Downside measures of risk have been

Table 12.1

Quarter	Return (%)
1998 Q1	5.50
1998 Q2	−6.25
1998 Q3	17.50
1998 Q4	12.50
1999 Q1	6.50
1999 Q2	5.50
1999 Q3	9.50
1999 Q4	40.50
2000 Q1	20.50
2000 Q2	22.50
2000 Q3	−15.50
2000 Q4	8.50
2001 Q1	3.50
2001 Q2	19.50
Average	10.73
Standard deviation	13.46
Semi-sd	11.77

extended by many authors Bawa and Lindenberg (1977), Harlow and Rao (1989), Sortino and Price (1994). The following popular and more general definition of downside risk (downside deviation) is given by the square root of the following

$$D^2 = \int_{-\infty}^{MAR} (x - MAR)^2 dF(x)$$

where MAR stands for "minimal acceptable return". The MAR will differ from investor to investor depending on what constitutes "risk" for that investor.

12.16   MEAN SEMI-VARIANCE EFFICIENT FRONTIERS

In one sense efficient frontiers are simply a convenient way of summarising all the possible expected return and risk combinations that are possible from a set of assets. Any measure of risk, such as semi-variance, can be calculated and the portfolio with the highest expected return at each level of risk can be recorded thereby giving an "efficient" frontier.

If investors know which measure of risk is important to them and are able to choose between portfolios on the basis of expected return and this measure of risk, this approach is entirely appropriate. It is often difficult, however, to know what the appropriate measure of risk is, or whether using that measure of risk is rational and coherent (this is discussed in Section 17.10).

The original Markowitz approach showed that the mean and variance of the returns could be used unambiguously to find efficient portfolios for all (subject to some fairly mild assumptions) investors if the return distributions on the assets could be assumed to be multivariate normal (or from a class of related distributions referred to as elliptically symmetric). There is an alternative interpretation of Markowitz that we noted: the mean and variance are also the appropriate statistics to consider if the investors have a particular type of utility function: a quadratic utility.

Because quadratic utility functions are unrealistic (for example, investors do not always prefer more to less and also exhibit increasing absolute and relative risk aversion), we can discard mean-variance as an appropriate way of deciding upon efficient investments unless, of course, the alternative assumption of multivariate normality (or one of very few other distributions with appropriate statistical qualities) is appropriate.

If it is assumed that investors want to use semi-variance as the measure of risk and we do not want to impose strong distributional assumptions on the returns, it is useful (for interpretation purposes) to know the investor's type of utility function. Fishburn (1977) has shown that this measure of risk accords with an expected utility theory provided that investors have a fairly plausible utility function that is linear in return above the MAR (that is, no risk aversion above MAR), but exhibits increasing aversion to returns below MAR.

$$U(r) = \begin{cases} r & r > MAR \\ r - \tau(MAR - r)^2 & r \leqslant MAR \end{cases}$$

where τ is a measure of risk aversion.

The expected utility of an investor with such a utility function is then given by $E[U(R)] = E[R] - \tau D^2$, where R is a random variable representing the rate of return on the asset. This has much the same form as more common (approximations to) expected utility functions, viz.

$$E[U(R)] = E[R] - \tau \, Var[R]$$

The importance of this fact is that it is only if we can link the statistics used to measure risk and return with how investors choose investments (for example, using expected utility maximisation) that we can devise a portfolio selection theory. Simply stating that downside deviation is a "better" risk measure than standard deviation is rather empty unless it can be shown that investors will choose assets using that measure of risk.

Annex 12.1   Using Excel to calculate efficient frontiers

Solver solution
Several commercial providers have developed software that enable one to construct efficient frontiers based on various definitions of risk and with a variety of constraints. But it is helpful to be aware that one of the standard Add-Ins that accompanies Excel, namely Solver, provides a method for calculating efficient portfolios.

You first have to check that Solver has been installed with your version of Excel as it is often not installed in a "typical installation". You can check by looking in the \Tools dropdown menu and see if Solver appears as one of the options. If not, you can try to include the Add-In yourself: click on the \Tools\Add-Ins menu. You should see a pop-up box with various Add-Ins and check boxes that indicate whether or not they have been loaded. If the Solver Add-In is one of the options, then check the appropriate box. If Solver does not appear in the list, then you will need to load it from the original Excel Installation CD-ROM.

Solver is a program that "optimises" a solution. It finds the set of parameters (in this case portfolio weights) that either maximises or minimises some function of the weights (for example, the risk of the portfolio). You can also include constraints, such as forcing the weights to be greater than zero.

As an example of how to use Solver, we will consider the following asset classes with the appropriate expected returns, standard deviations and volatilities.

			Correlations		
Asset class	Mean	Std Dev	Equity	Bond	Cash
Equity	10%	20%	1	0.5	0
Bond	8%	10%	0.5	1	0
Cash	4%	0%	0	0	1

The way in which we demonstrate how Solver can deal with the problem is by no means the most efficient, but it is the most direct and hopefully understandable.

We now need to set up the problem in Excel. We suppose that we enter the mean returns in cells A1, A2 and A3. The covariances and variances of the asset classes are conveniently stored in a "covariance matrix". In cells B1, C2 and D3, we enter the three variances 0.04, 0.01 and 0. In cell B2, we enter the covariance between Equity and Bond returns: $0.2*0.1*0.5 = 0.01$. In cell B3 we enter the covariance between Equity and Cash, i.e. 0, and in cell C3, the covariance between Cash and Bond returns, i.e. 0.

We can now enter a possible starting portfolio, i.e. the proportions invested in each asset class. This starting portfolio can be any valid portfolio. For example, suppose that we are going to constrain our portfolio to have only positive holdings in the asset classes. We also know that the proportions must add to one. So, for example, we enter 0.50, 0.25 and 0.25 in cells E1, E2 and E3. And in cell E4, we enter $=SUM(E1:E3)$ to check that our proportions will add to unity.

The expected return on this portfolio is the weighted average of the expected returns on the asset classes. We put this in cell F1 as $=A1*E1+A2*E2+A3*E3$. An alternative formula is $=SUMPRODUCT(A1:A3,E1:E3)$. Other alternative formulae can include matrix algebra, which is possible in Excel, but that is beyond the scope of this book. The value in cell F1 should be 0.08 for this portfolio.

The variance on the portfolio is put into cell F2 as $=E1^2*B1+E2^2*C2+2*E1*E2*B2$. For the portfolio above, the value should be 0.013125.

Having set up the information in the spreadsheet, we are now in a position to do some optimisation. In this simple example, we are going to find the portfolio that offers the highest expected return given that the standard deviation is equal to 7%.

Use the dropdown menus \Tools\Solver to start Solver. Using the "radio buttons", make sure that "Max" is selected for "Equal to" and enter F1 as the Target Cell. In the "By changing cells" input box, enter E1:E3, i.e. the cells that define the make-up of the portfolio. We now need to enter all our constraints.

Click the Add button next to the "Subject to constraints" box. This produces a dialog box. Our first constraint is that the variance of the portfolio must be equal to 0.0049 (i.e. 0.07^2). Enter F2 as the "cell reference" and select " = " from the list box of operators and enter 0.0049 in the right-hand "constraint" box.

Then click Add on the dialog box so that we can enter the next constraint, i.e. that the proportions must add to one. This is done is a similar way: enter E4 as the cell to be constrained and set the relation to be " = " and the constraint to be 1.

Then click Add so that we can enter the final constraint, i.e. that the proportions are all positive. Enter E1:E3 as the cells to be constrained. Set the relationship to be " > = " and enter the value 0 in the constraint box.

Then click "OK" on the dialog box and you should be returned to the main Solver dialog box. Now just click "Solve". After a few moments, Solver should have changed the values in cells E1:E3 to 0.1127, 0.5596 and 0.3277 respectively and have offered you the option to retain this solution or go back to the portfolio you originally entered. The Solver solution is the efficient solution, i.e. about 11% invested in equities, 56% invested in bonds and 33% invested in cash delivers the highest return (0.069) for the given risk of 0.07.

To find a whole efficient frontier in this way can be a little tedious as you have to proceed by entering a range of possible risk values and finding the maximum return for each, but it does provide a simple and quite quick (when you are used to it) way of solving small efficiency problems.

REFERENCES

Bawa, V.S. and Lindenberg, E.B. (1977), "Capital market equilibrium in a mean-lower partial moment framework", *Journal of Financial Economics*. 5, 2, 189–200.

Black, F. (1989), "Universal hedging: optimizing currency risk and reward in international equity portfolios", *Financial Analysts Journal*, July/August, 45, 4.

Black, F. (1990), "Equilibrium exchange rate hedging", *Journal of Finance*, July, 45, 3.

Black, F. and Litterman, R. (1992), "Global portfolio optimization", *Financial Analysts Journal*, Sept./Oct., 28–43.

Breeden, D. (1979), "An intertemporal asset pricing model with stochastic consumption and investment opportunities", *Journal of Financial Economics*, 7, 265–96.

Dhrymes, P. (1984), "The empirical relevance of arbitrage pricing models", *Journal of Portfolio Management*, 10.

Dimson, E. (ed.) (1988), *Stock Market Anomalies*, Cambridge University Press.

Dimson, E. and Mussavian, M. (1998), "A brief history of market efficiency", *European Financial Management*, 4, 1.

Dimson, E. and Mussavian, M. (1999), "Three centuries of asset pricing", *Journal of Banking and Finance*, 23, 12.

Elton. E.J. and Gruber, M.J. (1987), *Modern Portfolio Theory and Investment Analysis*, 3rd Edition, Wiley.

Fama, E. and French, K.J. (1992), "The cross section of expected stock returns", *Journal of Finance*, 47, 2, 427–65.

Fama, E. and Macbeth, R. (1973), "Risk, return and equilibrium: empirical tests", *Journal of Political Economy*, 81, 607–35.

Fishburn, P.C. (1977), "Mean-risk analysis with risk associated with below target returns", *American Economic Review*, 66, 115–26.

Harlow, W.V. and Rao, K.S. (1989), "Asset pricing in a generalised mean-lower partial moment framework: theory and evidence", *Journal of Financial and Quantitative Analysis*, 24, 285–311.

Harrington, D.R. (1987), *Modern Portfolio Theory, The Capital Asset Pricing Model and Arbitrage Pricing Theory: A User's Guide*, 2nd Edition, Prentice-Hall.

Hawawini, G. and Keim, D.B. (2000), "The cross-section of common stock returns: a review of the evidence and some new findings" in *Security Market Imperfections in Worldwide Equity Markets* (eds Keim, D.B. and Ziemba, W.T.), Cambridge University Press.

Kothari, S.P., Shanken, J. and Sloan, R.G. (1995), "Another look at the cross section of expected stock returns", *Journal of Finance*, 50, 2.

Lintner, J. (1965), "The valuation of risky assets and the selection of risky investments in stock portfolios and capital budgets", *Review of Economics and Statistics*, 47, 13–37.

Markowitz, H.M. (1952), "Portfolio selection", *Journal of Finance*, 7, 77–91.

Markowitz. H.M. (1991), *Portfolio Selection, Efficient Diversification of Investments*, Basil Blackwell.

Meese, R. and Dales, A. (2001), "Strategic currency hedging", *Journal of Asset Management*, 2, 1.

Merton, R.C. (1973), "A rational theory of option pricing", *Bell Journal of Economics and Management Science*, Spring.

Michaud, R. (2001), *Efficient Asset Management: A Practical Guide to Stock Portfolio Optimization and Asset Allocation*. Oxford University Press.

Reinganum, M.R. (1981), "Abnormal returns in small firm portfolios", *Financial Analysts Journal*, 37, 2.

Rogoff, K. (1996), "The purchasing power parity puzzle", *Journal of Economic Literature*, 34, 2, 647–668.

Roll, R. (1977), "A critique of the asset pricing theory's tests, Part I: On past and potential testability of the theory", *Journal of Financial Economics*, 4, 129–76.

Roll, R. and Ross, S.A. (1980), "An empirical investigation of the arbitrage pricing theory", *Journal of Finance*, 35, 5, 1073–103.

Roll, R., Ross, S.A. and Chen, N. (1983), "Some empirical tests of theory of arbitrage pricing", *Journal of Finance*, 18, 5.

Ross, S.A. (1976), "The arbitrage theory of capital asset pricing", *Journal of Economic Theory*, 13, 2, 341–60.

Satchell, S. and Scowcroft, A. (2001), "A demystification of the Black–Litterman model: managing quantitative and traditional portfolio construction", *Journal of Asset Management*, 1, 2, 138–50.

Shanken, J. (1982), "The arbitrage pricing theory: is it testable?", *Journal of Finance*, 37, 5.

Sharpe, W.F. (1963), "A simplified model for portfolio analysis", *Management Science*, 9, 227–93.

Sharpe, W.F. (1964), "Capital asset prices: a theory of market equilibrium under conditions of risk", *Journal of Finance*, 19, 425–42.

Solnik, B. (1974), "An equilibrium model of the international capital market", *Journal of Economic Theory*, 8, 500–25.

Sortino, F. and Price, L. (1994), "Performance measurement in a downside risk framework", *Journal of Investing*, 59–65.

Stambaugh, R.F. (1982), "On the exclusion of assets from tests of the two-parameter model: a sensitvity analysis", *Journal of Financial Economics*, 10, 3, 237–68.

Tobin, J. (1958), "Liquidity preference as behaviour towards risk", *Review of Economic Studies*, 26, 65–86.

13
Market Indices

13.1 INTRODUCTION

A characteristic of developed investment markets is the availability of indices which chart aggregate changes in market levels. These indices usually relate to price but may also relate to other statistics such as total return or yield. Some of the fundamental questions to be addressed in constructing an index are:

(a) How many constituents will be in the index and how should they be chosen?
(b) Will the index be representative of the market as a whole?
(c) Is the index to be an arithmetic average or a geometric average?
(d) Are the constituents to be given equal weighting or are they to be weighted in some way?
(e) How frequently is the index to be calculated?

The answers to these questions are largely determined by the proposed uses for the index. Possible uses include:

(i) measurement of short-term changes in the level of the market;
(ii) decision-making (in respect of the whole market, sectors of the market and individual stocks within sectors);
(iii) historical studies; and
(iv) portfolio performance measurement.

In addition, an index may:

(v) form the basis of derivative instruments, such as futures and options, which provide a means of hedging against movements in the market or speculating on such movements; and
(vi) allow the construction of index funds which are designed to track the index with the minimum of dealing costs.

13.2 EQUITY INDICES

Investors can measure the price performance of an individual share by comparing the current price with the price at some base date. More precisely, they could monitor the *price relative* P_t/P_0 where P_t is the price at time t and P_0 is the price at time 0 (the *base date*) adjusted for any intervening capital changes such a rights issues. But with thousands of shares listed on a stock market, it is difficult to get an idea of how that market has moved by considering individual shares. Furthermore, the market values of some companies are much larger than those of others, and it is usually necessary to take this into account when constructing an index.

We now consider how to construct various types of equity indices, concentrating on those which are used in practice in equity markets around the world.

Simple Aggregate Price Index

An index for m shares can be constructed by simply adding the share prices of the constituents together and dividing by a *divisor*. Thus, the index at time t is

$$I_t = \frac{K \sum_{s=1}^{m} P_{st}}{D_t}$$

where K = the index number at the base date e.g. 100
          P_{st} = the share price of constituent s at time t
and D_t = the value of the divisor at time t after adjusting for past capital and constituent changes to ensure continuity.

The divisor at the base date, D_0 is set equal to

$$\sum_{s=1}^{m} P_{s0}$$

thus giving a value of K for the index at the base date.

If there is a capital or constituent change at time t, the new divisor D'_t is calculated from the former divisor D_t using the formula:

$$D'_t = \frac{\sum_{s=1}^{m} P'_{st}}{\sum_{s=1}^{m} P_{st}} D_t$$

where P'_{st} is the share price of constituent s immediately after the change and P_{st} is the share price of constituent s immediately before the change. This ensures that the index immediately after the change is equal to the index immediately before the change.

This type of index performs like an investment portfolio in which the price of a stock determines its weighting in the portfolio. It would only normally be used to measure short-term changes in the level of an equity market.

The *Dow Jones Industrial Average* (US) and the *Nikkei Stock Average* (Japan) are both examples of simple aggregate price indices.

The *Dow Jones Industrial Average* is based on the prices of 30 large market value stocks traded on the New York Stock Exchange and was first published in 1928. The limited number of stocks is a function of its age, since it predates the age of computers. In recent years it has included some non-industrial stocks among its constituents.

The *Nikkei Stock Average* is based on the prices of 225 stocks quoted on the First Section of the Tokyo Stock Exchange, and was first published in 1950. Issues that do not have a par value of 50 yen are converted into 50-yen par value in computing the sum of stock prices. Stock selection is intended to achieve a well-balanced industry spread so as to represent the overall performance of the market.

Geometric Index

This type of index is obtained by multiplying together the price relatives of m shares, taking the mth root of the product and multiplying by the index number at the base date. In mathematical terms, a geometric index is defined as

$$I_t = K \left[\left(\frac{P_{1t}}{P_{10}} \right) \left(\frac{P_{2t}}{P_{20}} \right) \cdots \left(\frac{P_{mt}}{P_{m0}} \right) \right]^{1/m}$$

where P_{s0} = the share price of constituent s at the base date ($s = 1, ..., m$)
       P_{st} = the share price of constituent s at time t ($s = 1, ..., m$)
       K = the index number at the base date

A geometric index has the following important characteristics:

(a) A percentage change of a given amount in the price of any of the constituents affects the index to the same extent. For example, suppose a geometric index consists of 30 shares. If 29 of the shares show no change in price over a given period, whereas the price of the 30th share increases by 34.8%, then the index would increase by 1% (1.01 is the 30th root of 1.348).
(b) It "damps down" the impact of large rises in the price of individual constituents.
(c) It does not correspond to a feasible portfolio. In particular, a portfolio consisting of equal amounts (by value at the base date) of the constituent shares in a geometric index will always show the same performance as or better performance than the index over the period from the base date. This follows from the fact that the unweighted arithmetic mean of m non-negative numbers (not all equal) is always greater than the geometric mean of the same numbers.
(d) If one constituent falls to zero, the whole index falls to zero. In practice, however, a constituent which appears to be heading for financial collapse is removed before it can distort the index too severely, and is replaced by a new constituent.

The above characteristics may be illustrated by considering the behaviour of a geometric index based on only two shares (Table 13.1). For convenience, it is assumed that both shares have a price of 100p at time 0. The index number at the base date is taken to be 100. The value of a portfolio based on the purchase of £50 worth of share X and £50 worth of share Y at time 0 is also shown. Note that the index and the portfolio have the same numerical value only when the two share prices are equal. At other times, the portfolio has shown better performance than the index since the base date.

It should be clear from the above that a geometric index has undesirable characteristics for many of the possible uses of indices mentioned earlier. In particular, it should not be used for portfolio performance measurement purposes because it does not represent an attainable portfolio.

A practical advantage of a geometric index is that it is easy to adjust for technical changes, such as scrip issues and rights issues, by adjusting the base price of the individual share in question rather than having to "rebase" the whole index.

The *Financial Times Ordinary Share Index* (UK) and the *Value Line Composite Average* (US) are examples of geometric indices.

Table 13.1

	Price (in pence)		Geometric	Portfolio
Time	Share X	Share Y	index	£
0	100	100	100.0	100
1	100	110	104.9	105
2	110	100	104.9	105
3	100	150	122.5	125
4	125	75	96.8	100
5	125	125	125.0	125
6	150	100	122.5	125
7	5	100	70.7	75
8	0	1800	0	900

The *FT Ordinary Share Index* is based on 30 large market value stocks which cover a wide range of British industry and has a history going back to 1935. It is now calculated every minute of the working day. The Index was originally designed to measure short-term movements in the UK equity market, but this role has now largely been taken over by the *FT-SE 100 Index*, which is a capitalisation-weighted arithmetic index (see below).

The *Value Line Composite Average* is based on the prices of over 1,500 companies from the New York and American Stock Exchanges and the US over-the-counter market. It is calculated daily by multiplying the previous day's index by the geometric mean of the daily price relatives (today's price divided by yesterday's price) of the stocks in the index.

Capitalisation-weighted Arithmetic Index

This type of index combines the concept of a weighted arithmetic average of price relatives (equivalent to a Laspeyres index[1]) with the concept of *chain linking* to ensure

---

[1] Economists distinguish between a *Laspeyres* index and a *Paasche* index. The former is a base weighted index of a basket of goods whereas the latter is a current weighted index of a basket of goods. Thus, if P_t is the price of a good at time t and q_t is the quantity of the good at time t,

$$\text{Laspeyres index at time } n = \frac{\sum P_n q_0}{\sum P_0 q_0} \times 100$$

$$= \frac{\sum P_0 q_0 \left(\frac{P_n}{P_0} \right)}{\sum P_0 q_0} \times 100$$

$$\text{Paasche index at time } n = \frac{\sum P_n q_n}{\sum P_0 q_n} \times 100$$

continuity of the index when capital or constituent changes occur. A large number of shares are normally included in the index since otherwise the index can be heavily influenced by a large change in the price of a single constituent.

Prior to the first capital (or constituent) change, the index reflects the weighted-average price performance of the constituents, the weights being the market capitalisations at the base date (time 0). Thus, the index at time t is given by

$$I_t = \frac{K \sum_{s=1}^{m} N_{s0} P_{s0} \left(\dfrac{P_{st}}{P_{s0}} \right)}{\sum_{s=1}^{m} N_{s0} P_{s0}}$$

where K = the index number at the base date
N_{st} = the number of shares in issue for constituent s at time t
P_{st} = the share price of constituent s at time t

Since there have been no capital changes since the base date, N_{st} is equal to N_{s0} and thus

$$I_t = \frac{K \sum_{s=1}^{m} N_{st} P_{s0} \left(\dfrac{P_{st}}{P_{s0}} \right)}{\sum_{s=1}^{m} N_{s0} P_{s0}}$$

$$= \frac{K \sum_{s=1}^{m} N_{st} P_{st}}{\sum_{s=1}^{m} N_{s0} P_{s0}}$$

Example 13.1

A capitalisation-weighted arithmetic index consists of the shares of three companies X, Y and Z. If the index number was 100 at the base date, calculate the index at the end of years 1 and 2, given the following share prices (in pence). The number of shares in issue for X, Y and Z have been 200, 2000 and 400 respectively throughout the period.

	Company		
	X	Y	Z
Base date	150	50	100
End of Year 1	180	45	125
End of Year 2	250	25	150

Answer

$$\text{Index at end of year 1} = \frac{100(200 \times 180 + 2000 \times 45 + 400 \times 125)}{200 \times 150 + 2000 \times 50 + 400 \times 100}$$

$$= \underline{103.5}$$

$$\text{Index at end of year 2} = \frac{100(200 \times 250 + 2000 \times 25 + 400 \times 150)}{200 \times 150 + 2000 \times 50 + 400 \times 100}$$

$$= \underline{94.1}$$

In general, to allow for capital changes, the index at time t is defined as

$$I_t = \frac{K \sum_{s=1}^{m} N_{st} P_{st}}{B_t}$$

where B_t is the *index base* at time t.

The value of the index base at the base date is equal to the market capitalisation of the constituents at the base date, i.e.

$$B_0 = \sum_{s=1}^{m} N_{s0} P_{s0}$$

thus giving a value of K for the index at the base date.

To ensure continuity, the value of the index base is changed whenever there is a capital change so that the index is unaltered. This is known as *chain linking*.

Suppose there is a capital change C_t at time t. The index and the index base immediately before the change are I_t and B_t respectively. Let the new index and the new index base immediately after the change be I'_t and B'_t respectively. We know that

$$I_t = \frac{K \sum_{s=1}^{m} N_{st} P_{st}}{B_t} \qquad (13.1)$$

and

$$I'_t = \frac{K \left(\sum_{s=1}^{m} N_{st} P_{st} + C_t \right)}{B'_t}$$

To ensure continuity,

$$I_t = I'_t$$

$$\Rightarrow \quad \frac{K \sum_{s=1}^{m} N_{st} P_{st}}{B_t} = \frac{K \left(\sum_{s=1}^{m} N_{st} P_{st} + C_t \right)}{B'_t} \quad ,$$

$$B'_t = \frac{B_t \left(\displaystyle\sum_{s=1}^{m} N_{st} P_{st} + C_t \right)}{\displaystyle\sum_{s=1}^{m} N_{st} P_{st}}$$

$$B'_t = B_t + \frac{KC_t}{I_t} \qquad \text{using equation (13.1) above.}$$

There are many examples of capitalisation-weighted arithmetic indices around the world including the *FTSE Actuaries All-Share Index* (UK), the *FTSE 100 Index* (UK), the *Standard and Poors 500 Index* (US), the *Tokyo Stock Exchange New Index* (Japan), the *Morgan Stanley Capital International Indices* and the *FTSE All-World Indices*.

The *FT-Actuaries All-Share Index* is widely used in the UK for investment decision-making and portfolio performance measurement. The index is published daily, based on closing middle prices for the previous business day. Companies are classified into industry subsections, each with its own index. Most UK equity fund managers use this index as their performance yardstick as it closely represents the whole UK listed equity market, covering large, medium and small UK companies.

The *FTSE 100 Index* is, broadly speaking, an index of the 100 largest UK companies. It was introduced in 1984 to enable stock index futures and traded options to be created in the UK, and is calculated every minute of the working day.

The *Standard and Poors 500 Index* is based on the prices of 500 actively traded US stocks spread proportionately over all market sectors. As with the *FTSE Actuaries All-Share Index*, construction proceeds from industry groups to the whole index, so that a major use of the index is to study the performance of stocks relative to their industry group. It is generally regarded as an appropriate index for performance measurement of US equity portfolios.

The *Tokyo Stock Exchange New Index* consists of all shares listed on the First Section of the Tokyo Stock Exchange. Sub-indices are calculated for specific industry groups. Although some stocks in the index suffer from lack of availability, it is generally accepted to be the most appropriate index for performance measurement of Japanese equity portfolios.

The *Morgan Stanley Capital International Indices* and the *FTSE All-World Indices* are global equity indices which are widely used by international fund managers for asset allocation decisions and portfolio performance measurement. They both give price indices, together with total return indices in which dividends are reinvested, for many countries and regions as well as a "world" index. They also both give a breakdown of the world index by industry and economic sectors as separate indices. Indices are available in any currency but arc often published in dollars, sterling, yen or deutschmarks.

Suppose that I_t is the index in local currency terms for a particular country at time t. Then the dollar index for that country is simply given by

$$\$I_t = I_t \frac{X_t}{X_0}$$

where X_t is the value in dollars of each unit of local currency at time t, and the base date for the index is time $t = 0$.

The index for that country expressed in any other currency can be obtained in a similar manner. That is, any one currency index moves according to the movement in the local currency index combined with the exchange rate movement.

One of the most significant changes to the construction of the major world equity indices in recent years has been the change to free-float weighting. Prior to this change, the "market capitalisation" of the individual shares was based on all issued shares multiplied by market price. However, there are many companies where significant proportions of the issued capital are virtually never traded, e.g. firms where the government holds and has held some of the shares since inception, or cross-holdings with other companies or restricted employee share schemes or significant long-term holdings by founder families or directors. In order to make the index more representative of actual trading, the market caps are now weighted by the proportion of issued capital that is considered "free".

The application of the free-float adjustments is on a banded basis. So, for example, for the *FTSE All-World Series*, shares with at least 75% of issued capital "free" are included at 100% of the market cap; shares with a free float between 50% and 75% are included at 75% of market cap; shares with a free float of between 40% and 50% are included at 50%; etc.

The banding approach is intended to reduce frequent changes in weights and to help reduce the initial impact of the introduction of the free-float adjustment.

Dividend Yield Index

The most common method of constructing a dividend yield index, corresponding to a capitalisation-weighted arithmetic price index, is to divide the total dividends payable in the last year[2] for the constituents by the total market value of those constituents.

Dividend yield at time t is

$$\frac{\sum_{s=1}^{m} N_{st} D_{st}}{\sum_{s=1}^{m} N_{st} P_{st}} \times 100\%$$

where D_{st} is the dividend per share at time t of constituent s. This can be written as

$$\frac{\sum_{s=1}^{m} N_{st} P_{st} \left(\dfrac{D_{st}}{P_{st}} \right)}{\sum_{s=1}^{m} N_{st} P_{st}} \times 100\%$$

---

[2] In the *FT-Actuaries All-Share Index*, dividends used are the most up-to-date annual rates adjusted for any interim changes and also updated for any firm and precise forecasts.

In other words, the dividend yield of the index is the capitalisation-weighted average of the dividend yields, where the weights are the market capitalisations of the constituents.

13.3 BOND INDICES

Bond price indices receive less attention than equity price indices, partly because the direction and magnitude of movements in a bond market are usually gauged by studying changes in yields. However, total-return bond indices, which take into account both price movements and income earned, are widely used for performance measurement purposes.

Particular problems that arise with bond indices are the variety of coupons and terms to maturity, and often a lack of official trading price. Furthermore, a particular institutional investor may need an index appropriate to its liabilities, not an index representing the market as a whole.

As with equity markets, there are national bond market indices and world bond market indices. The *FTSE-Actuaries British Government Securities Indices* (UK) and the *Lehman Brothers Government/Corporate Bond Indices* (US) are examples of national bond market indices calculated by domestic institutions.

The *FTSE-Actuaries British Government Securities Indices* are the most widely used indices for UK government bonds, and are published daily in the *Financial Times*. The price indices are weighted arithmetic indices of dirty prices (i.e. including accrued interest), with weights given by the nominal amount outstanding. The method of construction is essentially the same as for the *FTSE-Actuaries All-Share Index* (see Section 13.2). The whole gilt-edged market (excluding index-linked gilts) is included in the main *all stocks* index and four separate sector price indices – *up to 5 years, 5–15 years, over 15 years* and *irredeemables* – are also produced. Stocks transfer from one sector index to another as their term shortens. The indices were designed to act as far as possible like individual stocks, so that discontinuities occur as prices fall whenever a constituent goes ex-dividend. To compensate for this, *accrued interest* for each index is shown together with the cumulative total of such interest for each calendar year to date. This allows investors to calculate the return on the index after allowing for the income elements as they wish – either reinvested in the index or invested in money market instruments.

In addition to the price indices, the *FTSE-Actuaries British Government Securities Indices* give average gross redemption yield statistics.

The yield indices for redeemable UK gilt stocks are calculated by fitting a curve with the following formula to the observed yields

$$\hat{i}_t = A + Be^{-Ct} + De^{-Ft}$$

where $\hat{i}_t$ represents the fitted yield at duration t and the parameters A, B, C, D and F are found by minimising

$$SS = \sum_j w_{t_j}(\hat{i}_{t_j} - i_{t_j})^2$$

and w_{t_j} is the market capitalisation of stock with maturity t_j.

The *Lehman Brothers Government/Corporate Bond Indices*, which have been published monthly since 1973, are probably the best known indices for the US domestic bond market. To qualify for inclusion, issues must be fixed-rate debt with at least one year to maturity, must have a market value outstanding in excess of $50 million and must, broadly speaking, be rated investment grade or higher by Moody's Investor Service or Standard and Poor's. The main statistic given is *total return*, defined for an investment as the price appreciation/depreciation plus any income received, expressed as a percentage of the initial investment, inclusive of accrued interest paid. The indices are capitalisation-weighted and are evaluated on a month-end to month-end basis. Total returns are published monthly for both the US government and corporate bond markets, and also for subsectors comprising securities with maturities ranging from 1 to 10 years and those with maturities ranging from 10 to 30 years. Within the corporate bond market, total returns are calculated for industrial, utility and finance sectors, as well as for various quality classes (*Aaa*, *Aa*, *A* and *Baa*).

International investors find national bond indices difficult to use because they must be obtained from different sources and their construction and frequency of calculation make them difficult to compare. As a result, a number of world bond indices have been developed. The oldest such index, first published in 1986, is *Salomon Smith Barney's World Government Bond Index*, which is widely used for international performance measurement purposes. It gives the capitalisation-weighted monthly total rate of return of all major domestic fixed-interest government bond markets together with the combined *world* government bond market. These returns are published in local currency and US dollar terms, and are also available in other major base currencies. Other global indices include the *JP Morgan Government Bond Indices* and the *Merrill Lynch International Bond Indices*.

Although world bond indices have been well accepted by most international investors, Thomson Financial Networks, a Boston-based investment advisory firm, has developed an alternative method of tracking bond performance, based upon benchmark issues. These are published in the *Financial Times* and the *Nihon Keizai Shinbun* (Japan). Advantages of using benchmark issues rather than indices for calculating global and bond performance are that benchmarks are always the most actively traded security in each sector of the yield curve, and that they are generally the lowest-yielding security for whatever level of credit quality. This compares with a much larger universe for a global bond index which can suffer not only from inherent credit quality considerations but also from varying degrees of market supply and liquidity.

13.4   EX-DIVIDEND ADJUSTMENT

All other things being equal, on the day that a dividend is paid by a company, the market value of the company will fall by the total amount of the dividend paid out. This is because if an investor were prepared to pay a price P_s for share s immediately before the dividend D_s per share were paid out, they would only be prepared to pay $P_s - D_s$ immediately after the dividend were paid out. This at least would be true if the size of D_s did not contain a signal about the future prospects of the share. We will ignore any signalling issues.

Recall from Section 13.2 that the value of a (simplified) capital-only market index is given by

$$I_t = \frac{\sum_{s=1}^{m} P_{st} N_{st}}{B_t}$$

where I_t is the value of the index at time t, N_{st} is the number of shares in issue for constituents security s at time t and B_t is the divisor that scales the market values so that changes in capital structure, do not affect the index.

For illustrative purposes, we shall assume that there are no changes to the divisor B over time, so that the index value is simply a function of the price of the securities. The size of the dividend to be paid by a company is usually declared well in advance of it actually being paid. But the effect of a dividend payment on the share price takes place at the start of the day that the share goes ex-dividend (xd).

Index compilers often collect information on xd effects. The extent to which the market value of a security will drop on the declaration of a dividend is the dividend per share multiplied by the number of shares in issue, $D_s \times N_s$. The total effect is the sum across all constituents and is conventionally divided by the same divisor as used in the index at the same time

$$X_t = \frac{\sum_{s=1}^{m} D_{st} N_{st}}{B_t}$$

The xd adjustments are normally collected on a cumulative basis over a calendar year, for example

$$C_t = \sum_{k=t_0}^{t} X_t$$

and the difference between the cumulative xd adjustment factors on two different dates represents the aggregate market value (expressed as index points) returned to investors between the two dates.

13.5 CALCULATING TOTAL RETURN INDICES WITHIN A CALENDAR YEAR

One of the primary purposes of an xd adjustment is to compute a total return index that is, an index that shows the aggregate return arising from both changes in price and dividends that are assumed to be reinvested back into the share.

Suppose that for constituent s, the price at yesterday's close is denoted by P_y and that today the stock went xd in respect of a declared dividend of D per share. The price per share of the stock at the end of today is denoted by P_t. Per share, the capital return for today is given by P_t/P_y.

The dividend D would enable an investor to purchase $D/(P_y - D)$ shares at the start of today. A shareholder holding one share at yesterday's close would therefore have $1 + D/(P_y - D)$ shares at the end of today. The total value of these holdings is equal to

$$P_t \left(1 + \frac{D}{P_y - D} \right)$$

At yesterday's close, the value per share to the shareholder was P_y. The total return per share at the end of today is therefore equal to

$$R = \frac{P_t \left(1 + \dfrac{D}{P_y - D} \right)}{P_y} = \frac{P_t}{P_y} \frac{P_y}{P_y - D} = \frac{P_t}{P_y - D}.$$

A similar line of argument can be applied to indices, so that a total return index, R_t, is given by

$$R_t = R_{t-1} \frac{I_t}{I_{t-1} - X_t} = R_{t-1} \frac{I_t}{I_{t-1}(C_t - C_{t-1})}$$

Example 13.2

The market price of a share at yesterday's close was 50p and at the start of today the share went xd in respect of a declared dividend of 5p per share. Calculate the total return over the course of the day to an investor who bought ten shares just before yesterday's close at a cost of 500p.

Answer

Because the purchase is just before the share goes xd, the investor will, in effect, immediately receive a "dividend" of 50p (5p × 10). At the start of today, the dividend could be used to buy 50p/45p = 1.11 new shares. At the end of today, the shareholder will therefore have $(10 + 1.11) \times 50\text{p} = 555.56\text{p}$ from an initial investment of 500p (50p * 10). The total return to the investor is therefore 555.56/500 = 1.111, or a rate of total return of 11.1% over the course of the day.

13.6 NET AND GROSS INDICES

Indices can be calculated on a gross (before tax) or net (after deduction of tax) basis. For example, dividends in the UK are paid net of tax at the basic rate of taxation. The xd adjustment uses these net dividends as the basis for calculation.

It would be possible to calculate a gross index by rating the net dividends back up to what they would have been had tax not been deducted at source. For example, if the basic rate of tax were 20%, then the gross xd adjustment would be calculated as the net xd adjustment divided by 0.8.

The use of gross indices can be useful when some investors are able to claim back the tax deducted at source.

13.7 COMMERCIAL REAL ESTATE INDICES

In the securities markets, indices can be constructed from published prices which, for actively traded stocks, are based upon actual transactions. It is much more difficult to produce meaningful indices for real estate for a number of reasons.

As sales are only carried out infrequently, published indices are by necessity compiled from valuations which are subjectively determined. In thin markets, current valuations are heavily influenced by previous valuations, which gives the erroneous impression of a slow adjustment in prices when looking at an historic data series. Construction of real estate indices is further confounded because valuations of the constituent properties in an index are seldom carried out at a single point in time, with the technical implication that further smoothing is introduced. Thus, real estate indices tend to understate the volatility of the underlying market.

As there is a centralised market place for securities, data are readily available, thus enabling the construction of up-to-date indices which reflect the particular market as a whole. The absence of a central market place for real estate means that only sample data are available, so that the indices may not be representative of the population at large. Given the heterogeneity of real estate, it is also difficult to define categories clearly, especially for secondary property.

There are two main types of real estate index: *portfolio-based* indices, which are the most common, and *barometer* indices. Both types of index are useful but are designed for different purposes.

Portfolio-based indices measure rental values, capital values or total returns of actual rented properties. Different indices of this type will give different results because the underlying portfolio of real estate included in the index will vary in size, regional spread and sector weighting (office, retail, etc.). Valuations rely heavily upon comparable evidence of sales of similar properties in the same area. Thus, there may be some delay in reflecting market movements as there may be little comparable evidence on which to base valuations. Furthermore, as the current rental income is fixed until the next rent review, any response to movements in rental values will be sluggish. The main use of this type of index is portfolio performance measurement.

The *barometer* type of index aims to track movements in the market by estimating the maximum full rental values (and/or yields) of a number of selected properties. Being based on valuers' estimates of rental value, the indices should provide an earlier indicator of changes in rentals than indices based on actual rents. The main use of this type of index is to highlight short-term changes in the level of the market in terms of rents and yields. But an index of this type is unsuitable for portfolio performance measurement since an investor could not closely match its movement with an actual portfolio of real estate holdings.

13.7.1 US real estate indices

One commercial real estate index frequently used in the United States is the *NCREIF Property Index* (NPI). This was originated by the National Council of Real Estate

Investment Fiduciaries (NCREIF) and the Frank Russell Company. The index produces a value-weighted average return, reported before the deduction of management fees. The first full year of performance data that can be derived directly from the index is that from 1979. There are a number of sub-indices, based on the normal US property classifications. These include: apartments, warehouses, retail and regional shopping malls. The market valuation of the NPI is less than 2% of the total value of institutionally held US real estate (Pagliari *et al.* 2001). Like the IPD index, the NPI is based on self-reporting (that is, the sample is made up of holdings by real estate advisory firms which choose to contribute to the index). The aggregate index is also affected by changes in the sectoral and geographical composition of the index over time.

Property performance can also be measured by tracking the performance of property investment companies in the UK or real estate investment trusts (REITS) in the US. To facilitate this, in the UK, the sectoral indices of FTSE All Share index can be used and, in the US, the NAREIT index can be used. However, both of these indices relate to the performance of geared real estate investments and, in addition, the prices of REIT and property company shares can fluctuate for reasons not always connected with the performance of the underlying real estate assets. However, such indices have the advantage of being based on the transaction prices of underlying shares, rather than on subjective valuations.

REFERENCE

Pagliari, J.L. Jnr, Lieblich, F., Schaner, M. and Webb, J.R. (2001), "Twenty Years of the NCREIF Property Index", *Real Estate Economics*, 29, 1–27.

Portfolio Performance Measurement

14.1 INTRODUCTION

An investor's ultimate objective is the construction and maintenance of portfolios of investments which show good performance. Furthermore, the remuneration of individual portfolio managers is often linked to the performance of the funds under their control. It is therefore essential that methods are available by which portfolio performance can be assessed. Information required in assessing portfolio performance might include:

(a) the achieved rate of return;
(b) performance of the portfolio compared with similar funds or with some yardstick such as a notional fund based on a market index (or a number of market indices); and
(c) consideration of the portfolio's risk profile.

For funds with long-term liabilities, sufficient time should be allowed for the wisdom or otherwise of investment decisions to become apparent. Short-term performance is an unreliable indicator of the manager's expertise as it is difficult to distinguish between short-term performance due to expertise from that due to luck.

There would seem to be no practical alternative to basing performance measurement on calculations which allow for changes in market values, even though a portfolio probably could not be realised for its full current market value. With quoted securities, there is a market price available to all investors, but it may not be possible to sell large holdings at this price. In the case of real estate, market values are subjective and it can take many months to complete a sale.

Real estate portfolios present many difficulties in performance measurement. The sensitivity of the results to a small change in valuation assumptions means that real estate performance measurement over periods of less than five or ten years has little meaning. The fact that real estate needs to be managed also gives rise to special problems — redevelopment, refurbishment or restructuring of leases can dramatically improve performance. On the other hand, negative factors such as depreciation and unforeseen capital expenditure need to be monitored.

We first consider three methods which are widely used for calculating rates of return — money-weighted rate of return, time-weighted rate of return, and linked internal rate of return.

14.2 MONEY-WEIGHTED RATE OF RETURN

The *money-weighted rate of return* for a fund over a period is simply the internal rate of return over that period. It is a satisfactory measure of the individual fund's performance taken in isolation, but as a test of the fund manager's investment skill it is not meaningful. The timing and magnitude of cash flows, which are beyond the control of the manager, influence the results.

The internal rate of return i for a fund over a period of one year is given by

$$M_0(1 + i) + \sum_{j=1}^{k} C_{t_j}(1 + 1)^{1 - t_j} = M_1$$

where M_0 = the initial value of the fund
          M_t = the final value of the fund
          C_{t_j} = the cash flow at time t_j
and k = the number of cash flows during the year.

Example 14.1

The following table gives details of the market values of Fund X at the beginning and end of a year together with the market values for the fund when cash flows arise during the year. Calculate the money-weighted rate of return.

Time (years)	Market value of Fund X	Cash flow
$\frac{1}{4}$	110	+10
$\frac{1}{2}$	140	+5
$\frac{3}{4}$	150	+10
1	150	

Answer

The money-weighted rate of return i is given by

$$100(1 + i) + 10(1 + i)^{3/4} + 5(1 + i)^{1/2} + 10(1 + i)^{1/4} = 150$$

The solution to this equation is $i = 22.3\%$ as can be seen by substituting $i = 0.223$ in the left-hand side of the equation:

$$100(1.223) + 10(1.223)^{3/4} + 5(1.223)^{1/2} + 10(1.223)^{1/4} = 149.98$$

Note that in calculating the money-weighted rate of return, the market value of the fund is only required for the beginning and end of the period.

As previously mentioned, the main problem with the use of money-weighted rates of return in performance measurement is that the results are influenced by the timing and magnitude of cash flows. This can be seen from the following illustration.

Suppose that Fund A and Fund B both have assets of 100 at the beginning of a year. Each fund shows a return of 2% in the first half of the year and a return of 20% in the second half. There is a positive cash flow for Fund A and Fund B of 50 and 10 respectively, occurring exactly half-way through the year in each case.

The value of Fund A at the end of the year will be

$$[100(1.02) + 50](1.20) = 182.4$$

Thus the money-weighted rate of return i for Fund A is given by

$$100(1 + i) + 50(1 + i)^{1/2} = 182.4$$

$i = 26.2\%$ satisfies this equation.

The value for Fund B at the end of the year will be

$$[100(1.02) + 10](1.20) = 134.4$$

Thus, the money-weighted rate of return for Fund B is given by

$$100(1 + i) + 10(1 + i)^{1/2} = 134.4$$

$i = 23.3\%$ satisfies this equation.

The calculations show that Fund A has a higher money-weighted rate of return than Fund B over the year. This was to be expected as Fund A had a higher proportion of funds invested when the return was high. But it would be wrong to say that Fund A had been better managed than Fund B. The rates of return for the funds were identical in respect of both the first half and the second half of the year.

For performance measurement purposes, it would be better to measure the rate of return for both Fund A and Fund B as being

$$(1.02)(1.20) - 1 = 0.224 \text{ or } 22.4\%$$

That is, the rate of return should give equal weight to the results achieved in each period of time.

14.3 TIME-WEIGHTED RATE OF RETURN

The *time-weighted rate of return* seeks to eliminate the distorting effects of cash flows so that more valid comparisons of fund managers' investment skills can be made. It is not a true rate of return. The method is dependent on the market value of the fund being available whenever there is a cash flow. Thus, more information is required in calculating the time-weighted rate of return as compared with calculating the money-weighted rate of return. It should be noted, however, that various methods have been developed for calculating the approximate market value of the fund where the actual market value is unknown.

The first step in calculating the time-weighted rate of return is to split the period under review into a number of shorter periods, each of which starts when there is a cash flow. Rates of return (based on the ratios of successive valuations) for these shorter periods are then combined to give the time-weighted rate of return for the whole period.

Thus, the time-weighted rate of return i over a period of one year is given by

$$(1 + i) = \frac{M_{t_1}}{M_0} \times \frac{M_{t_2}}{M_{t_1} + C_{t_1}} \times \cdots \times \frac{M_1}{M_{t_n} + C_{t_n}}$$

where M_0 = the initial value of the fund
         M_1 = the final value of the fund
         M_{t_r} = the value of the fund at time t_r $(r = 1, 2, ..., n)$
and C_{t_r} = the cash flow at time t_r $(r = 1, 2, ..., n)$.

Consider again Fund X in Example 14.1. The time-weighted rate of return is calculated as follows:

$$1 + i = \frac{110}{100} \times \frac{140}{120} \times \frac{150}{145} \times \frac{150}{160}$$

i.e.

$$i = 0.245 \qquad \text{or} \qquad 24.5\%$$

This compares with a money-weighted rate of return of 22.3% calculated in Example 14.1.

Where cash flows are large in comparison with the size of the fund and/or returns over the shorter periods vary greatly, the time-weighted rate of return may be significantly different from the money-weighted rate of return.

Comparison of the time-weighted rate of return of a fund with the time-weighted rates of return of a "peer group" of other similar funds is a simple statement of how well the fund has performed and relates to the real competitive world. If the constituents of the peer group are similar in terms of size, liability structure, constraints on the fund manager and the acceptable level of risk, this is an effective method of performance appraisal.

The comparison of time-weighted rates of return is usually quantified in terms of a *relative return*. The relative return of a portfolio against its benchmark is usually defined as follows:

$$r_p = \frac{1 + R_p}{1 + R_b} - 1$$

where r_p is the relative return for the portfolio p
         R_p is the time-weighted rate of return for portfolio p
and R_b is the time-weighted rate of return for the benchmark, b.

The above form of the relative return is known as the geometric relative return. The relative return can be compounded with the benchmark return to get the original rate of return, i.e.

$$(1 + R_b)(1 + r_p) = (1 + R_p).$$

In many practical cases, r_p is small compared with R_b and R_p and the arithmetic difference between R_p and R_b can be used to approximate the relative rate of return, i.e.

$$r_p^* = R_p - R_b$$

where r_p^* is the arithmetic relative rate of return.

Example 14.2

A portfolio generates a rate of return of 11.3% over a year in which its benchmark generates a rate of return of 10.8%. Calculate the geometric and arithmetic rates of return.

Answer

$$r_p = \frac{1 + R_p}{1 + R_b} - 1$$

$$= \frac{1.113}{1.108} - 1$$

$$= 0.0045$$

$$= 0.45\%$$

$$r_p^* = 11.3\% - 10.8\%$$

$$= 0.5\%$$

The use of the arithmetic version of relative return has more than just ease of calculation as justification. It also greatly facilitates a process known as *attribution* in which the sources of any relative performance are identified and quantified.

Suppose that the benchmark comprises a weighted average of several indices, for example, so that

$$R_b = \sum_{i=1}^{k} W_{b_i} R_{b_i}$$

where W_{b_i} is the weight in the ith asset class
         R_{b_i} is the benchmark return on the ith asset class
and k is the number of asset classes.

For example, the two asset classes may be equities and bonds; the weights may be 60% equities and 40% bonds and the benchmark returns may be the returns on the FTSE Actuaries All Share Index and the FTSE Actuaries British Government Securities All Stocks Index.

The portfolio's return can be similarly written as

$$R_b = \sum_{i=1}^{k} W_{p_i} R_{p_i}$$

where w_{p_i} is the proportion of the portfolio in asset class i
and R_{p_i} is the rate of return earned on asset class i.

The arithmetic relative return is then equal to

$$r_p^* = R_p - R_b$$

$$= \sum_{i=1}^{k} w_{p_i} R_{p_i} - \sum_{i=1}^{k} w_{b_i} R_{b_i}$$

$$= \sum_{i=1}^{k} [(w_{p_i} - w_{b_i})R_{b_i} + w_{p_i}(R_{p_i} - R_{b_i})]$$

$$= \sum_{i=1}^{k} (w_{p_i} - w_{b_i})R_{b_i} + \sum_{i=1}^{k} w_{p_i}(R_{p_i} - R_{b_i})$$

$$= \sum_{i=1}^{k} (w_{p_i} - w_{b_i})(R_{b_i} - R_b) + \sum_{i=1}^{k} w_{p_i}(R_{p_i} - R_{b_i})$$

(noting that $\sum_{i=1}^{k} (w_{p_i} - w_{b_i})R_b = 0$)

The first term on the right-hand side would be zero if the portfolio weights, w_{p_i}, were all the same as the benchmark weights, w_{b_i}. We would normally expect the term to be different from zero if the weights are different. This term is therefore usually referred to as the *asset allocation* component of the relative return. A skilful investor will have a positive weight, i.e. $w_{p_i} > w_{b_i}$ when $(R_{b_i} - R_b)$ is positive and a negative weight $w_{p_i} < w_{b_i}$ when $(R_{b_i} - R_b)$ is negative. Skilful asset allocators will therefore have positive asset allocation contributions.

The second term will be zero if $R_{p_i} = R_{b_i}$ for all i. In other words, if the returns in each asset class are the same as the benchmark returns, then the second term will be zero. A non-zero value indicates that the investor has chosen to invest differently from the benchmark in terms of the individual securities selected. It is therefore often referred to as the *stock selection* component of the relative return. Skilful stock selectors will have a positive *stock selection* component.

Example 14.3

An investor holds 50% of her assets in equities and 50% in bonds. Her benchmark portfolio is 60% FTSE Actuaries All Share Index and 40% FTSE Actuaries British Government Securities All Stocks Index. The returns are summarised as follows:

	Portfolio	*Benchmark*
Equities	12.0%	10.5%
Bonds	10.6%	11.25%
Total	11.3%	10.8%

Calculate the stock selection and asset allocation components of the relative return.

Answer

Asset allocation component:

$$(50\% - 60\%) \times (10.5\% - 10.8\%) + (50\% - 40\%) \times (11.25\% - 10.8\%)$$

$$= (-10\%) \times (-0.3\%) + 10\% \times 0.45\%$$

$$= 0.075\%$$

Stock selection component:

$$50\% \times (12\% - 10.5\%) + 50\% \times (10.6\% - 11.25\%) = 0.425\%$$

Most of the 0.5% relative outperformance came from better stock selection in equities. Asset allocation provided a small contribution because the investor held an underweight position in equities which performed relatively badly and an overweight position in bonds, which performed relatively well.

The advantage of the geometric calculation of relative return is that the relative returns on successive periods can be compounded to calculate the relative return over a longer period. So, if we denote the relative return over a period t_i to t_{i+1} by $r_p(t_i, t_{i+1})$ then

$$r_p(t_1, t_n) = (1 + r_p(t_1, t_2))(1 + r_p(t_2, t_3)) \ldots (1 + r_p(t_{n-1}, t_n)) - 1.$$

There is no equivalent result for arithmetic relative returns.

14.4   LINKED INTERNAL RATE OF RETURN

Suppose that a fund is valued at regular intervals but is not valued each time there is a cash flow. This means that there is insufficient information to calculate the time-weighted rate of return. In these circumstances, a practical compromise is to calculate the *linked internal rate of return*. Money-weighted rates of return for inter-valuation periods are calculated and are then combined (using a time-weighted approach) to give the rate of return for the whole period.

For example, suppose quarterly valuations are available. If the money-weighted rates of return for each quarter are 1%, 2%, 5% and 3%, the linked internal rate of return would be

$$(1.01)(1.02)(1.05)(1.03) - 1 = 0.114 \text{ or } 11.4\%$$

Excel Application 14.1

Excel provides two functions XIRR (values, dates, guess) and IRR (values, guess) that enable internal rates of return to be calculated quickly.

IRR (values, guess) calculates the internal rate of return based on a set of cash flows that occur at regular intervals, e.g. annually. The cash flows are contained in the array "values" and an initial estimate at what the IRR might be is given in "guess".

Suppose, for example, that a fund was £1.5m at the start of year 1 (1997) and that cash flows into (positive) or out of (negative) the fund at the end of years 1 to 5 were £0.1m, £0.2m, £0.8m, −£0.3m and −£0.1m.

Suppose finally that the value of the fund was £2.5m at the end of five years just after the last cash flow. The IRR function interprets all values as cash flows and we convert the fund values to cash flows by imagining that we start off by paying in £1.5m at the start of year 1 and then withdraw £2.5m at the end of year 5. The cash flows can then be entered into cells A1, A2, ..., A6 as

$$1.5, 0.1, 0.2, 0.8, -0.3, -2.6$$

Note that the final "cash flow" is given as the sum of the genuine −£0.1m and the imagined withdrawal of £2.5m.

If we enter $=$IRR(A1:A6, 0.1) in cell B1, Excel calculates the internal rate of return of 2.9% per annum. The guess used in this case (0.1) is the default value. This works in most cases, but it is useful to change it to several different values, including negative values, if the cash flows are large relative to the initial and final values, or if the answer is expected to be a negative IRR.

XIRR (values, dates, guess) is a more general version of IRR (values, guess) in that it allows for cash flows at particular dates irrespective of their regularity.

For example, suppose that the cash flows in the example above occurred in the middle of each year. We would then need to set up two columns in Excel. The first column could contain the dates; the second, the values. So, in our example, we would enter 1 Jan 1997, 30 Jun 1997, 30 Jun 1998, 30 Jun 1999, 30 Jun 2000, 30 Jun 2001 and 31 Dec 2001 in cells A1 to A7 and the values 1.5, 0.1, 0.2, 0.8, −0.3, −0.1, −2.5 in cells B1 to B7.

If we enter $=$XIRR(B1:B7, A1:A7, 0.1) in cell C1, then Excel computes the annualised IRR as 2.8%. As might be expected, this value is slightly lower than the case when the cash flows (which are positive overall) are applied at the end of the year as they have had longer to accumulate.

14.5 NOTIONAL FUNDS

A method of performance measurement which may be used when assets are held to meet specific liabilities is to compare the performance of the actual fund with that of a specially constructed notional fund, known as a *benchmark portfolio*, which has a specified mix of asset categories, e.g. 70% in equities and 30% in fixed-interest securities. The asset mix of the benchmark portfolio is chosen with a long-term view of risks and returns in mind, taking into account the liability structure of the fund. In constructing the benchmark portfolio, the initial value of the actual fund and the cash flow of the actual fund are deemed to be invested according to the specified asset mix. Each asset category is then assumed to move in line with an appropriate market index in which income is reinvested. Expenses involved in investing initial cash balances, cash flow and the notional investment income should be taken into account explicitly. The final value of the benchmark portfolio, at the end of the period of measurement, is then compared with that of the actual fund.

Constructing a second notional fund in which the asset categories move in line with the market indices but which has an initial asset mix and asset allocation of cash flow identical to those of the actual fund, enables an attribution analysis to be carried out and thus helps to explain the reasons for superior or inferior performance. Comparison of the final values of the second notional fund and the benchmark portfolio indicates the extent to which divergence from the benchmark asset mix affected performance. Comparison of the final values of each asset category within the second notional fund with those of the actual fund shows the extent to which stock selection within each asset category affected performance.

Suppose that the benchmark portfolio and the actual fund both contain three asset categories, a, b, and c; F is the final value of the actual fund; F^a, F^b and F^c are the final values of the a, b and c asset categories of the actual fund respectively; N_1 is the final value of the benchmark portfolio; N_2 is the final value of the second notional fund; and N_2^a, N_2^b and N_2^c are the final values of the a, b and c asset categories of the second notional fund respectively. Then the total performance of the actual fund is

$$F - N_1 = (F - N_2) + (N_2 - N_1)$$

$N_2 - N_1$ is the reward for strategic departures from the benchmark asset mix.

$F - N_2$ is the reward for the stock selection and may be broken down into the three asset categories as follows:

$$F - N_2 = (F^a - N_2^a) + (F^b - N_2^b) + (F^c - N_2^c)$$

Example 14.4

The total value of a UK pension fund at the beginning of a particular year was £500m. The pension fund trustees measure the performance of the fund against a benchmark portfolio invested 70% in the *FTSE Actuaries All Share Index* and 30% in the *FTSE Actuaries British Government All Stocks Index*; for benchmark purposes cash flows during the year are assumed to be invested or disinvested in the same proportions.

At the beginning of the year, the actual fund is invested in line with the asset mix of the trustees' benchmark portfolio and no rebalancing of assets is carried out during the year. Equity dividends are reinvested into equities and gilt interest payments are reinvested into gilts. However, the fund receives one cash flow of £100m on 1 July which is invested entirely in equities. At the end of the year, the equity portfolio is valued at £500m and the gilt portfolio is valued at £162m.

The *FTSE Actuaries All Share Index* (with gross dividends reinvested) gives time-weighted returns of −20% and +30% in the first and second halves of the year respectively. The *FTSE Actuaries British Government All Stocks Index* (with gilt interest reinvested) gives time-weighted returns of +10% and 0% in the first and second halves of the year respectively.

Analyse the performance of the fund, breaking down the results into asset allocation, equity stock selection and gilt stock selection. Ignore expenses.

Answer

Final value of the benchmark portfolio (£m) is

Equities:	$\{350(0.8) + 70\} \times 1.3 = 455$
Gilts:	$\{150(1.1) + 30\} \times 1.0 = \underline{195}$
	650

The final value of the actual fund was £662m so the actual fund outperformed the benchmark portfolio by £12m.

Final value of a second notional fund with actual allocation of cash flow, i.e. entire
cash flow on 1 July invested in equities (£m), is

$$
\begin{aligned}
\text{Equities:} \quad & \{350(0.8) + 100\} \times 1.3 = 494 \\
\text{Gilts:} \quad & 150 \times 1.1 \times 1.0 = \underline{165} \\
& 659
\end{aligned}
$$

We therefore have the results (£m):

$$
\begin{aligned}
\text{Asset allocation:} \quad & 659 - 650 = +9 \\
\text{Equity stock selection:} \quad & 500 - 494 = +6 \\
\text{Gilt stock selection:} \quad & 162 - 165 = \underline{-3} \\
& +12
\end{aligned}
$$

In practice, a common approach is to calculate time-weighted rates of return for the
asset categories of the actual fund and for the appropriate market indices, and then to
proceed as illustrated in the following example.

14.6 CONSIDERATION OF RISK

Adjustment for risk in portfolio performance measurement requires risk to be defined and
quantified, and also requires a model which gives a risk–return relationship. Attempts to
do this have concentrated on equity funds and have used the CAPM, which was discussed
in Chapter 12, as the basis for risk adjustment. This approach to portfolio performance
measurement, which is becoming more popular, will be discussed in this section.

However, it is first necessary to stress the reservations that have been voiced by many
practitioners, concerning the somewhat simplistic approach often adopted. They argue
that risk associated with an investment portfolio depends not only upon the investments
held but also upon the investor's liabilities, objectives, etc. Furthermore, the risk
associated with investments held in a particular asset category (e.g. domestic equities)
cannot be assessed fully in isolation. The risk characteristics of all other asset categories
and their correlations with the asset category being measured held by the investor (e.g.
real estate, overseas equities) should be taken into account.

Returning now to the use of the CAPM in adjusting for risk, the three most
commonly used measures of risk-adjusted performance are those of Treynor (1965),
Sharpe (1966) and Jensen (1968). Each of these measures is briefly described below.
Definitions of symbols employed in Chapter 12 will be used again.

(a) The *Treynor ratio*, T, assumes that the portfolios under consideration are fully
diversified or represent part of a fully diversified portfolio, so that the β value of the
portfolio is the appropriate measure of risk. The rate of return earned above the risk-
free rate is related to the portfolio β during the period of measurement, to give a
measure of reward per unit of risk. Thus

$$
T = \frac{R_p - R_f}{\beta_p}
$$

This simply measures a manager's ability to choose investments with higher rates of
return than others with similar β values.

(b) The *Sharpe ratio*, S, is similar to the Treynor measure but uses standard deviation of returns (total risk) during the period of measurement for the denominator. Thus

$$S = \frac{R_p - R_f}{\sigma_p}$$

This measures a manager's ability not only to pick winners but also to diversify efficiently.
(c) The *Jensen alpha*, α, is used when the β value of a portfolio is pre-specified. To measure performance in this situation, what is required is a comparison between the return from the actual portfolio in question and that of a passive *benchmark portfolio* which has the same β value as the actual portfolio. Using the CAPM, the return from the benchmark portfolio, R_b, is given by

$$R_b = R_f + \beta_p(R_m - R_f)$$

Then

$$\alpha = R_p - R_b$$

If α is positive, the fund manager has outperformed the market. This could be due to superior stock selection skills, good luck, or a combination of both.

Example 14.5

The records of three tax-free US equity funds and the *Standard and Poors 500 Index* over the last five years are as follows:

Fund	Total 5-year return (%)	Annualised return (% p.a.)	β	Specific risk (% p.a.)
X	129	18	1.2	7
Y	139	19	1.8	13
Z	101	15	0.5	20
S&P 500	119	17	1	0

Assuming that the risk-free rate of interest was 10% p.a. and that the standard deviation of returns on the S&P 500 was 25% p.a., rank the performance of the funds over the period using the Treynor, Sharpe and Jensen measures.

Answer

Treynor ratio

$$T_X = \frac{0.18 - 0.10}{1.2} = 0.067$$

$$T_Y = \frac{0.19 - 0.10}{1.8} = 0.050$$

$$T_Z = \frac{0.15 - 0.10}{0.5} = 0.100$$

Sharpe ratio

$$S_X = \frac{0.18 - 0.10}{\sqrt{1.2^2 \times 0.25^2 + 0.07^2}} = 0.260$$

$$S_Y = \frac{0.19 - 0.10}{\sqrt{1.8^2 \times 0.25^2 + 0.13^2}} = 0.192$$

$$S_Z = \frac{0.15 - 0.10}{\sqrt{0.5^2 \times 0.25^2 + 0.20^2}} = 0.212$$

Jensen alpha

$$\alpha_X = 0.18 - \{0.10 + 1.2(0.17 - 0.10)\} = -0.004$$

$$\alpha_Y = 0.19 - \{0.10 + 1.8(0.17 - 0.10)\} = -0.036$$

$$\alpha_Z = 0.15 - \{0.10 + 0.5(0.17 - 0.10)\} = -0.015$$

We therefore have the following ranking of the funds for each of the three measures.

	X	Y	Z
Treynor	2	3	1
Sharpe	1	3	2
Jensen	2	3	1

Notice that Fund X, which has low specific risk, does better when the Sharpe measure is used to measure performance.

The *active* or *relative* risk of a portfolio is defined as the standard deviation of the relative returns. It can be interpreted as representing the extent to which the investor is "betting" in trying to beat his or her benchmark. A high active risk suggests that the investor is taking large asset allocation or stock selection bets. A small active risk suggests that the investor is hugging their benchmark.

Active risks are also popularly referred to as "tracking errors" and are key measures of risk in the investment management community. Broadly speaking, there are two main approaches to estimating active risks. The first entails measuring historical relative returns and estimating their standard deviation. The second is to observe the proportions of each asset held in the portfolio and the benchmark and then use other estimates of the correlations and standard deviations of the individual assets to produce a measure of risk.

Mathematically, the second approach can be motivated as follows:

$$\text{active risk} = [\text{Var}\{R_p - R_b\}]^{1/2}$$

$$= \left[\text{Var}\left\{ \sum_{i=1}^{n} (w_i - b_i)R_i \right\} \right]^{1/2}$$

$$= \left[\sum_{i=1}^{n} \sum_{j=1}^{n} (w_i - b_i)(w_j - b_j)\text{Cov}(R_i, R_j) \right]^{1/2}$$

$$= \left[\sum_{i=1}^{n} \sum_{j=1}^{n} t_i t_j \sigma_{ij} \right]^{1/2}$$

where w_i = proportion of portfolio invested in security i
          b_i = benchmark proportion in security i
          $t_i = w_i - b_i$ = "bet" on security i
          R_i = random return on security i
          $\sigma_{ij} = \text{Cov}(R_i, R_j)$
          n = total number of securities
          $R_p = \sum w_i R_i$; $R_b = \sum b_i R_i$

If we assume that σ_{ij} is known from other data, then the active risk can be estimated without having observed any relative returns in the past.

Example 14.6

Consider the following portfolio and benchmark:

	Portfolio	Benchmark	Standard deviation
Security 1	90%	50%	15%
Security 2	10%	50%	20%

The correlation between the two securities is known to be 0.5.
   Estimate the tracking error (TE) as well as the standard deviations of the portfolio and benchmark.

Answer

$$\text{TE}^2 = (90\% - 50\%)^2 \times (15\%)^2 + (10\% - 50\%)^2 \times (20\%)^2$$
$$+ 2 \times 0.5 \times 15\% \times 20\% \times (90\% - 50\%) \times (10\% - 50\%)$$
$$= 0.0148$$
$$\text{TE} = 12.16\%$$

$$\text{Var(portfolio)} = (90\%)^2 \times (15\%)^2 + (10\%)^2 (20\%)^2$$
$$= 0.0213 + 2 \times 0.5 \times 90\% \times 10\% \times 20\% \times 15\%$$
$$\text{Std(portfolio)} = 14.60\%$$
$$\text{Var(benchmark)} = (50\%)^2 \times (15\%)^2 + (50\%)^2 \times (20\%)^2$$
$$+ 2 \times 0.5 \times 50\% \times 50\% \times 20\% \times 15$$
$$= 0.0231$$
$$\text{Std(benchmark)} = 15.21\%$$

Note that portfolios with betas close to unity will typically have small systematic components and the tracking error will be dominated by the unique component. Noting that the unique component *could* be diversified away, the investor must be expecting to exploit some perceived informational advantage over the market in these cases.
   The tracking error can be further decomposed into "systematic" and "unique" components much the same as total risk using the single index model.

If we can assume that

$$R_i = \alpha_i + \beta_i R_b + e_i$$

then the arithmetic relative return of a portfolio p is given by:

$$r_p = R_p - R_b = \sum_{i=1}^{n} w_i R_i - R_b$$

$$= \sum_{i=1}^{n} w_i(\alpha_i + \beta_i R_b + e_i - R_b)$$

$$= \sum_{i=1}^{n} w_i \alpha_i + \sum_{i=1}^{n} w_i(\beta_i - 1)R_b + \sum_{i=1}^{n} w_i e_i$$

$$= \alpha_p + R_b(\beta_p - 1) + e_p$$

Hence,

$$\text{Var}(r_p) = \text{Var}(R_b)(\beta_p - 1)^2 + \text{Var}(e_p)$$

$$= \frac{\text{systematic component}}{\text{of active risk}} + \frac{\text{unique}}{\text{component}}$$

Example 14.7

A portfolio has a total tracking error of 10% and a "beta" of 1.05. The benchmark has a standard deviation of 20%. Calculate the two components of the square of the tracking error.

Answer

$$\text{Systematic component} = (1.05 - 1)^2 \times (0.2)^2$$

$$= 0.0001 = (0.01)^2$$

$$\text{Unique component} = (0.1)^2 - 0.0001$$

$$= 0.0099 = (0.0995)^2$$

14.7 INFORMATION RATIOS

A measure of risk-adjusted *relative* return (or "skill") is the information ratio. This is a generalisation of the Sharpe ratio and is indeed referred to as such on occasion. Perhaps the most common form of the information ratio, IR, is given by

$$\text{IR} = \frac{r_p}{TE}$$

where r_p is the relative return of portfolio p and TE is the tracking error.

Another version of the information ratio, which we denote IR^{α}, is given by

$$\text{IR}^{\alpha} = \frac{\alpha}{\sqrt{\text{Var}(e_p)}}$$

where α is Jensen's alpha and $\sqrt{\text{Var}(e_p)}$ is the standard deviation of the unique component.

This second form is intended to be a truer measure of skill since it is not affected at all by the systematic risk and return. Any tracking error generated by a different level of systematic risk would (in theory at least) be accompanied by a different level of return. This has nothing to do with the "skill" of the investor and hence should not be reflected in a measure which purports to represent "skill".

14.8 SURVIVORSHIP BIAS

Performance measurement is used not only as part of the monitoring of existing investments, but also as an input to future investment decisions. Although most experts and regulators will advise that past performance is a poor guide to the future, it is also true that good performance is an important part of retaining business and winning new business. In addition, if an investor is considering a new type of asset for his or her portfolio, or just reviewing strategy, he or she will want to know what returns, risks and correlations might be delivered. Historical data is usually an important element of the evidence. However, the mere existence of historical data (particularly long-term data) is a potential source of bias, namely survivorship bias. Survivorship bias arises when the characteristic that is being measured is also critical to the existence of the data set.

An important example of where and how survivorship bias arises is investment management. Investment managers compete for business by implying that they are able to earn superior returns than their competitors. One of the ways in which they typically do this is by showing long-term historical performance measurement figures that are higher than a common benchmark. Even ignoring some rather underhand practices that might exist, survivorship bias will usually have distorted the evidence. The investment managers who underperformed are more likely to have been fired by their clients than those who performed well. The investment managers who have "survived" because of their past good performances are therefore the ones more likely to have long past performance histories. The database is therefore "biased" by exactly the characteristic that is of interest to the investor.

Various standards (such as the Global Investment Performance Standards) have been instituted to try to reduce survivorship bias influences and particularly any deliberate manipulation of past performance through survivorship bias. Nevertheless survivorship bias will remain in most datasets and the analyst will need to satisfy him or herself that it is either not too significant or not important in the particular context.

Example 14.8

A very simple example can be created (using a spreadsheet, for example) to demonstrate how pernicious survivorship bias can be. Suppose that 256 random variables from a standard normal distribution have been generated. For the purposes of illustration, we suppose that these represent the relative performance of 256 investment managers in year 1. We then repeat this process five more times so that we have the relative performances of the imaginary managers for six consecutive years.

In order to mimic a process that will induce survivorship bias, we order the performance figures depending on the performance of the managers in year 1, from largest to smallest. We then discard the performance figures for years 2 to 6 that correspond to the worst 50% (128) of the year-1 performance figures. We then re-order all the performance figures depending on the performance of the manager in year 2, from largest to smallest. The performance figures in years 3 to 6 that correspond to the worst 50% (64) of the year 2 figures are then discarded. The process is then repeated, each time dropping performance in subsequent years from the worst 50% so that we end up with six years of performance figures with 256, 128, 64, 32, 16 and 8 numbers in each.

Since all the numbers were generated randomly from a standard normal, the sample mean and standard deviation from each of the six sets of numbers are not significantly different from zero and unity, respectively. However, if we calculate "long-term" performance figures by calculating the average across years 1 to 6, 1 to 5, 1 to 4, etc., then a very different pattern emerges. An example of one such simulation is given in the table.

	Year 1	Year 2	Year 3	Year 4	Year 5	Year 6
Number of observations	256	128	64	32	16	8
Average performance in individual year	0.00	0.07	0.10	0.00	−0.10	0.28
Standard deviation	1.24	0.97	1.15	1.21	1.09	1.10
Average cumulative performance	0.00	0.48	0.60	0.73	0.70	0.76
Standard deviation of cumulative performances	1.24	0.57	0.48	0.31	0.33	0.23

The performances in the individual years could not be used to reject the hypothesis that they cannot produce positive relative performance, on average. This is not surprising since the numbers were generated with a mean of zero. However, when we look at the cumulative average levels of performance, allowing for survivorship bias, we can see that the average appears to be significantly above zero.

Unfortunately empirical studies in finance and economics are plagued by survivorship bias. The datasets that are available are available only because they have survived to be studied. Sometimes, the survivorship bias may be deliberately induced. Unscrupulous investment managers, for example, may offer a large number of different portfolios in which investors may invest. Over time, some of the better-performing portfolios will be retained and the less-good portfolios will be closed, or merged into others. The surviving portfolios will then look as if they have a good long-term record, even though this is entirely by chance.

At a macro-level, it is only the economies and markets that have survived that can produce long-term information. For example, the equity markets in the US and the UK are typically those with the longest readily available return histories. Average equity returns and risks calculated from the data from those markets will therefore be tainted by survivorship bias. The markets that have disappeared or closed at some point, e.g. the Russian market, will not have long data histories.

Empirical studies and information therefore have to be treated with considerable caution. The unqualified use of sample means and covariances for efficient-frontier modelling, or calibrating stochastic investment models is not usually appropriate and some combination of theory and empirical evidence will often provide more robust estimates.

14.9 TRANSITIONS

One of the uses of performance measurement is to decide whether to retain an investment manager or to switch to a different manager. The process of switching manager (the transition) will itself impact the performance of the portfolio. Because the new manager will usually hold different underlying securities from the old manager, there is usually a lot of buying or selling over a short period of time during the transition. The intensity of the trading gives rise to costs (and opportunities) that can be measured. As with any trading, a transition generates transaction costs including tax, commission and spreads. A fourth component, market impact, is often much more pronounced in a transition than at other times. Market impact is the effect whereby the sale (or purchase) of an asset causes the price of the asset to fall (or rise) because of the trade itself. In a transition it is often the case that large amounts of stock are being sold or purchased in a short period of time. This is different from "normal" trading when a manager can dispose of, or acquire stock in small chunks over several weeks. The effect is particularly pronounced on small or irregularly traded assets.

Any attempt to alleviate market impact by delaying purchase or sale of assets gives rise to "opportunity costs". By not transitioning quickly, the fund is exposed to possible underperformace during the period of the delay.

Market impact can be assessed after the fact by measuring the price of the asset during the course of the transition and observing whether or not the price moves "against" the fund at the times of the sales or purchases.

REFERENCES

Adams, A.T. (1989), *Investment*, Graham and Trotman.
Adams, A.T. and Matysiak, G.A. (1991), "Constructing UK property market barometers", Discussion Paper in *Property Research* No. 5, City University Business School.
Curwin, J. and Slater, R. (1985), *Quantitative Methods for Business Decisions*, Van Nostrand Reinhold (UK).
Dobbie, G.M. and Wilkie, A.D. (1978), "The FT-Actuaries fixed interest indices", *Journal of the Institute of Actuaries*, 105, 15–26.

Financial Times Business Information (1985), *A Guide to Financial Times Statistics*.

Financial Times, County NatWest WoodMac and Goldman, Sachs (1991), *FT-Actuaries World Indices: Construction and Maintenance Rules*.

Godfrey, A.I. (1977), *Quantitative Methods for Managers*, Edward Arnold.

Haycocks, H.W. and Plyman, J. (1964), "The design, application and future development of the Financial Times-Actuaries Index", *Journal of the Institute of Actuaries*, 90.

Holbrook, J.P. (1977), "Investment Performance of Pension Funds", *Journal of the Institute of Actuaries*, 104.

Hymans, C. and Mulligan, J. (1980), *The Measurement of Portfolio Performance — An Introduction*, Kluwer.

Jensen, M.C. (1968), "The performance of mutual funds in the period 1945–1964", *Journal of Finance*, 23, 389–415.

Morgan Stanley (1987), *Capital International Perspective: Investor's Guide*.

Pensions Research Accountants Group (1989), *Investment Performance Measurement for UK Pension Funds*.

Saloman Brothers (1986), *Introduction to the Saloman Brothers World Government Bond Index*.

Sharpe, W.F. (1966), "Mutual fund performance", *Journal of Business*, 39, 119–38.

Shearson Lehman Brothers (1992), *The Lehman Brothers Indices*.

Solnik, B. (1991), *International Investments*, 2nd Edition, Addison-Wesley.

Temple, P. (1991), "Was it good for you too?", *Professional Investor*, May, 20–4.

Treynor, J.L. (1965), "How to rate management of investment funds", *Harvard Business Review*, 43, 63–75.

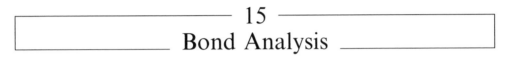

15
Bond Analysis

15.1 INTRODUCTION

Some of the mathematical techniques which may be used to manage a portfolio of fixed-interest bonds are discussed in this chapter. The following aspects will be given particular attention: the importance of duration and its relationship with volatility; the use of duration and volatility in the analysis of policy switching; the concept of matching; the concept of immunisation and its use in the management of a bond portfolio. The reader is referred back to the discussion of duration and yield curves in Chapter 2, which is directly relevant to this chapter; the examples in Chapter 2 are also relevant to this chapter. The reader is also referred back to the discussion of the real yield gap in Chapter 5, a concept which is also useful in the management of a bond portfolio.

15.2 VOLATILITY

The change in the price of a bond, for a given change in yield, can be measured by looking at the *volatility* or *modified duration* (see Section 2.10). We will now develop this concept further and discuss the importance of volatility for an investor who is investing to meet predetermined liabilities.

Volatility (V) is defined as the differential of the bond price, with respect to a change in the redemption yield, divided by the price, thus:

$$V = -\frac{1}{P}\frac{dP}{di}$$

As was mentioned in Section 2.10, taking a differential, rather than considering changes in price for a finite change in redemption yield, avoids the difficulty that the proportionate change in price corresponding to a rise in yields may be different from that corresponding to a fall in yields.

The differential could be taken with respect to the annual effective yield from the bond, to the yield *per annum* convertible half-yearly (the redemption yield quoted for a gilt-edged security in the UK) or to the force of interest. The annual effective yield, the yield *per annum* convertible half-yearly and the force of interest will be denoted by i, $i^{(2)}$ and δ respectively.

The second and third of these possibilities are of particular interest: the second because it is the measure of volatility used in most world bond markets and the third because it leads to some convenient mathematical results. The two forms of volatility in which we are interested could be defined as

$$V_\delta = -\frac{1}{P}\frac{dP}{d\delta} \tag{15.1}$$

and

$$V_{i^{(2)}} = -\frac{1}{P}\frac{dP}{di^{(2)}} \tag{15.2}$$

Although volatility is defined in terms of the differential of the present value of an investment with respect to yield, when volatilities are quoted in practice, the percentage change in the price of a bond caused by a finite change in the redemption yield is calculated. Market practice is to calculate volatility as the average of the percentage changes in the bond price caused by a small increase and decrease in the yield to maturity. If the bond is a gilt-edged security, so that the yield quoted is a yield *per annum* convertible half yearly (defined as $i^{(2)}$), volatility would be calculated using

$$-\frac{1}{P}\frac{\Delta P}{\Delta i^{(2)}}$$

The calculation would be carried out for a small increase and decrease in $i^{(2)}$ of, say, 0.0001 or 0.01%.

If it is desired to consider the proportionate change in the present value of a portfolio of bonds for a 1% change up or down in the yield basis, in order to make comparisons with the volatility of other bond portfolios under different interest rate scenarios, the result of the following calculation may be useful:

$$\frac{[\text{Present value @ } i\% - \text{Present value @ } (i + \text{or} - 1)\%]}{\text{Present value @ } i\%}$$

15.3 DURATION

A concept which is related to that of volatility is *discounted mean term*, often called *duration*. Duration was defined in Chapter 2 as a weighted average of the times of payments where the weights are the present values of the payments (hence *discounted mean term*).

Assume that a security is held which pays half-yearly cash flows at times $t_1, t_2, ..., t_n$ (n is the number of half-years until the investment is redeemed). A specific example of such an investment is a gilt-edged security, the duration of which was derived in Chapter 2. The cash flows are of amounts $C_{t_1}, C_{t_2}, ..., C_{t_n}$ respectively. Using a time unit of half a year, the discounted mean term is

$$\frac{1 C_{t_1} v + 2 C_{t_2} v^2 + \cdots + n C_{t_n} v^n}{C_{t_1} v + C_{t_2} v^2 + \cdots + C_{t_n} v^n} \tag{15.3}$$

where $v = (1 + i^{(2)}/2)^{-1}$ (i.e. the discounting factor over one effective time period) and $i^{(2)}$ is the redemption yield *per annum* convertible half-yearly. The duration, as shown above, would be measured in half-years. The duration or discounted mean term will generally be required in years; this is found simply by dividing the duration in half-years by 2 to give

$$\frac{0.5C_{t_1}v + 1C_{t_2}v^2 + \cdots + (n/2)C_{t_n}v^n}{C_{t_1}v + C_{t_2}v^2 + \cdots + C_{t_n}v^n} \tag{15.4}$$

If it is desired to measure duration in years, using an *annual* effective rate of interest, but still with half-yearly payments, this can be done by replacing the powers of v, v^2, etc. by $v^{1/2}$, v, etc., where v is now calculated as $(1+i)^{-1}$ (the discounting factor over our new effective time period) with i as the effective annual rate of return. This must give an identical result to the duration in years using an effective half-yearly return.

The assumptions that the next payment is exactly half a year away and that there is exactly half a year between successive payments can be dropped and the expression for duration can be written as

$$\frac{t_1 C_{t_1}v^{2t_1} + t_2 C_{t_2}v^{2t_2} + \cdots + t_n C_{t_n}v^{2t_n}}{C_{t_1}v^{2t_1} + C_{t_2}v^{2t_2} + \cdots + C_{t_n}v^{2t_n}} \tag{15.5}$$

where time is measured in years and the rth cash flow takes place at time t_r and is of amount C_{t_r}. A half-yearly effective interest rate is used, so that $v = (1 + i^{(2)}/2)^{-1}$.

It may also be desired to calculate the duration in years for a given force of interest δ. In Chapter 1, it was stated that, if time is measured in years and δ is the annual force of interest, the present value of a sum of money, C_t, due in t years is equal to

$$C_t e^{-\delta t} \qquad \text{where} \qquad e^{\delta t} = (1+i)^t = \left(1 + \frac{i^{(2)}}{2}\right)^{2t}$$

giving

$$\delta = \ln(1+i) = 2 \ln\left(1 + \frac{i^{(2)}}{2}\right)$$

Therefore equation (15.5) can be written

$$\frac{t_1 C_{t_1}e^{-\delta t_1} + t_2 C_{t_2}e^{-\delta t_2} + \cdots + t_n C_{t_n}e^{-\delta t_n}}{C_{t_1}e^{-\delta t_1} + C_{t_2}e^{-\delta t_2} + \cdots + C_{t_n}e^{-\delta t_n}} \tag{15.6}$$

where time is measured in years and there are n payments from the investment.

This must give an identical result to equation (15.5) in which the nominal yield per annum convertible half-yearly was used.

15.4 THE RELATIONSHIP BETWEEN VOLATILITY AND DURATION

It is useful to develop a relationship between volatility and duration by deriving an expression for the differential of the present value with respect to the force of interest δ.

The present value of an investment, for a given force of interest δ, is the denominator of the expression for the discounted mean term, thus:

$$P = [C_{t_1}e^{-\delta t_1} + C_{t_2}e^{-\delta t_2} + \cdots + C_{t_n}e^{-\delta t_n}] \tag{15.7}$$

In general, the differential coefficient of e^{ax}, with respect to x is ae^{ax} and thus, differentiating equation (15.7) with respect to δ,

$$\frac{dP}{d\delta} = -[t_1 C_{t_1}e^{-\delta t_1} + t_2 C_{t_2}e^{-\delta t_2} + \cdots + t_n C_{t_n}e^{-\delta t_n}]$$

Therefore

$$V_\delta = -\frac{1}{P}\frac{dP}{d\delta}$$

is equal to

$$\frac{t_1 C_{t_1}e^{-\delta t_1} + t_2 C_{t_2}e^{-\delta t_2} + \cdots + t_n C_{t_n}e^{-\delta t_n}}{C_{t_1}e^{-\delta t_1} + C_{t_2}e^{-\delta t_2} + \cdots + C_{t_n}e^{-\delta t_n}}$$

Consequently volatility, calculated by taking the differential with respect to the force of interest δ, is equal to discounted mean term:

$$V_\delta \equiv Duration$$

It is also useful to consider volatility calculated by taking a differential of the present value with respect to the gross redemption yield convertible half-yearly ($i^{(2)}$). By the chain rule for differentiation:

$$\frac{dP}{di^{(2)}} = \frac{dP}{d\delta} \times \frac{d\delta}{di^{(2)}}$$

$$\delta = 2 \ln\left(1 + \frac{i^{(2)}}{2}\right)$$

so that

$$\frac{d\delta}{di^{(2)}} = \left(1 + \frac{i^{(2)}}{2}\right)^{-1}$$

since the differential of the logarithm of a function is the differential of the function divided by the function. Therefore,

$$V_{i^{(2)}} = -\frac{1}{P}\frac{dP}{di^{(2)}} = -\frac{1}{P}\frac{dP}{d\delta}\left(1 + \frac{i^{(2)}}{2}\right)^{-1}$$

and

$$V_{i^{(2)}} = V_\delta \left(1 + \frac{i^{(2)}}{2} \right)^{-1}$$

Given that $V_\delta \equiv Duration$

$$V_{i^{(2)}} \equiv Duration \left(1 + \frac{i^{(2)}}{2} \right)^{-1} \qquad (15.8)$$

With $v = (1 + i^{(2)}/2)^{-1}$, and defining $V_{i^{(2)}}$ as modified duration:

$$Modified\ Duration = Duration \times v \qquad (15.9)$$

Modified duration and volatility are terms which can be used interchangeably; the term modified duration is often used by market practitioners.

Relationship (15.9) also holds if an annual effective rate of interest is used when calculating volatility, but with v calculated as $(1 + i)^{-1}$, where i is the annual effective rate of interest.

Therefore. it can be seen from the above analysis that duration is equal to the volatility of a bond, if volatility is calculated by differentiating with respect to the force of interest. Duration is approximately equal to the volatility of a bond if volatility is calculated by differentiating either with respect to the gross redemption yield *per annum* convertible half-yearly or with respect to the effective yield *per annum*. It is important to note that, however volatility is defined, an increase in duration implies an increase in volatility.

Excel Application 15.1

Excel provides a significant number of useful functions for bond analysis. If the functions are not available, you will need to run the Setup program, install the Analysis Tool Pak and enable it using Tools/Add-Ins. Two of the relevant Excel functions are Yield (settlement, maturity, rate, pr, redemption, frequency, basis) which returns the yield on a security that pays periodic interest and MDuration (settlement, maturity, coupon, yld, frequency, basis) which returns the Macauley modified duration for a security with an assumed par value of 100.

In the yield formulae:

settlement	refers to the settlement date when the security was bought
maturity	refers to the maturity date of the security
rate	is the annual coupon rate
pr	is the price per 100 nominal paid
redemption	is the redemption value per 100 nominal
frequency	is the number of coupon payments per year
basis	is the type of day count basis to use (important mainly for calculating accrued interest)

Basis	Day count basis
0 or omitted	30 days per month, 360 days in a year (US, NASD)
1	actual number of days between coupon payments/actual number of days in the year
2	actual days between payments/360 days in a year
3	actual days between payments/365 days in a year
4	30 days per month/360 days per year (European)

So, for example, if a 5% US bond with semi-annual payments maturing on 30 Sept 2005 priced on a 30/360 basis is bought on 1 March 1999 for 90 per 100 nominal, the yield to maturity can be calculated by putting

1 Mar 1999	in cell A1
30 Sep 2005	in cell A2
0.05	in cell A3
90	in cell A4
100	in cell A5
2	in cell A6
0	in cell A7

$$= \text{Yield (A1, A2, A3, A4, A5, A6, A7) in cell B1.}$$

This should give a value of 0.069162.

In the MDuration formula:

coupon	is the annual coupon rate
yld	is the annual yield

So, for example, the Macauley modified duration for the bond above at the date of purchase in 1997 can be calculated by putting the following formula in cell D1

$$= \text{MDuration (A1, A2, A3, B1, A6, A7)}$$

This should give a value of 5.3184 (years).

15.5   FACTORS AFFECTING VOLATILITY AND DURATION

Because an increase in duration implies an increase in volatility, the factors which affect volatility will have a similar impact on duration. The way in which volatility and discounted mean term as particular financial factors vary can be seen by differentiating equation (15.6), the general formula for discounted mean term, with respect to the variable in question.

Studying the way in which volatility varies if the pattern of payments changes is of particular interest. For example, if a fixed-interest bond is being considered, the variation of volatility with coupon could be examined. If a bond pays a coupon of D per annum, annually in arrears, and is redeemable at 100 in n years time, equation (15.6) for the discounted mean term can be simplified to:

$$\frac{Dv + 2Dv^2 + 3Dv^3 + \cdots + nDv^n + n100v^n}{Dv + Dv^2 + Dv^3 + \cdots + Dv^n + 100v^n}$$

assuming that the first coupon is payable in exactly one year from now. This can be written as

$$\frac{D(Ia)_{\overline{n}|} + n100v^n}{Da_{\overline{n}|} + 100v^n} \tag{15.10}$$

An increase in the coupon rate, D, will increase the weighting of those payments which are made earlier in the life of the bond and will therefore reduce the discounted mean term; this is true whatever the rate of interest. The problem can be analysed more formally if equation (15.10) is differentiated with respect to the coupon rate D. The argument should be clear intuitively and the reader is left to illustrate the idea by calculating the volatility of bonds with different coupon rates.

Volatility, or duration, also varies with the term of a bond. In general, volatility increases with term to redemption. However, at a rate of interest which is higher than the coupon rate, the volatility of a bond will not continue increasing indefinitely as the term to redemption increases. As the term of a bond increases, additional payments are received and the redemption payment is deferred. The increase in the time of payment (by which each payment is multiplied) is eventually outweighed by the reduction in the present value factor; in particular, the weighting of the present value of the relatively large redemption payment is reduced as the term of the bond increases.

The duration of a low-coupon bond will therefore increase with term to redemption and then reduce from its peak, as the bond tends towards a perpetuity. It will be found, for example, that if a bond has a coupon rate of 5% and the yield is 10%, a 25-year bond will have a higher duration than an irredeemable bond.

If the coupon rate is higher than the rate of interest, the duration of a bond will continue increasing towards its limiting value as the term tends towards infinity. The tendency of the present value of the later payments (including the redemption payment) to reduce is not as great if the rate of interest is lower. Again, these results can be found by differentiating equation (15.10) with respect to the term to redemption.

The third factor which affects duration or volatility is the general level of yields. As the rate of interest at which payments are discounted reduces, the redemption proceeds become more important as a proportion of the total present value. Duration will therefore increase as the rate of interest falls. This concept is developed further in the following section.

15.6 CONVEXITY

Just as modified duration (volatility) measures the rate at which the price of a bond varies as its yield changes, so convexity measures the rate at which the modified duration itself is altered as the yield changes. Mathematically, convexity is therefore the second derivative of price with respect to yield, divided by price:

$$\text{convexity} = -\frac{1}{P}\frac{d^2P}{d_i^2}$$

To get a feel for why convexity is important in analysing bond prices, it is worth considering again the approximate formula for duration, but now making the dependence of price on yield specific:

$$\text{modified duration} \approx -\frac{1}{P(i)}\frac{\Delta P(i)}{\Delta i}$$

$$= -\frac{1}{P(i)}\frac{P(i + \Delta i) - P(i)}{\Delta i}$$

We can then re-arrange the above expression so that:

$$P(i + \Delta i) = P(i)[1 - \Delta i \times \text{modified duration}]$$

Indeed, this is one of the most common uses of modified duration, to estimate how the price changes as yield changes. For example, if the price of a bond is 100 and its duration is 10, say, at a given yield of 5% p.a. and the yield changes to 5.1% p.a., we might estimate the new price to be

$$P(5.1\%) = 100[1 - 0.1\% \times 10]$$

$$= 99$$

This estimation procedure is effective only if (a) there is no optionality (e.g. variability in redemption date) in the bond; and (b) the change in yield is very small. If the yield were to shift significantly, say, from 5% p.a. to 6% p.a., the approximation would be significantly incorrect for many bonds. This can easily be demonstrated by considering the simple example of a zero-coupon bond of term 30 years. If the yield were 5%, the price is easily calculated as

$$P(5\%) = 1.05^{-30}$$

$$= 0.2314$$

If the yield were to shift instantly to 3%, the price would be

$$P(3\%) = 1.03^{-30}$$

$$= 0.4120.$$

The (modified) duration of the zero-coupon bond is

$$\text{modified duration (5\%)} = \frac{30}{1.05} = 28.57$$

An estimated price at 3% would then have been

$$\hat{P}(3\%) = 0.2314[1 + 2\% \times 28.57]$$

$$= 0.3636$$

which is unacceptably different from the actual price.

The problem with the approximation can be demonstrated graphically in Figure 15.1. The curved line represents the price–yield relationship. The dashed line

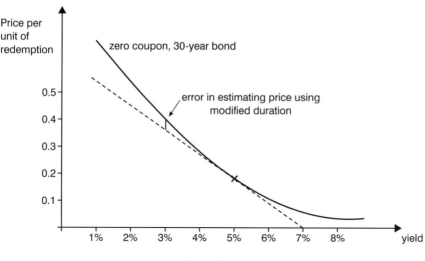

Figure 15.1

is the modified duration of the bond at a yield of 5%, i.e. the slope of the price–yield relationship at that point. The difference between the dashed line and the solid line represents the "error" of the approximation. In our example, this is $0.4120 - 0.3636 = 0.0484$.

The "problem" with the approximation is that the slope of the price–yield relationship itself has changed at the lower yield of 3% and is much steeper. Because the price–yield relationship is a curve, rather than a straight line, we have to take into account the rate of change in the duration, i.e. the convexity.

For some bonds the price–yield relationship is much less curved.

Example 15.1

Consider a two-year bond with coupons payable annually in arrear of 10%. Calculate:

(a) the price of the bond at a yield of 5%;
(b) the modified duration of the bond at a yield of 5%;
(c) the approximate price of the bond if the yield moves to 3%;
(d) the true, theoretical price of the bond at a yield of 3%.

Answer

(a) $P(5\%) = \dfrac{0.1}{1.05} + \dfrac{1.1}{1.05^2} = 1.0930$

(b) modified duration $(5\%) = \dfrac{1}{1.0930} \times \dfrac{1}{1.05} \times \left[\dfrac{0.1}{1.05} + \dfrac{2.2}{1.05^2} \right]$

$$= 1.8218$$

(c) $\hat{P}(3\%) = 1.0930 \times [1 + 2\% \times 1.8218]$
$\qquad = 1.1328$

(d) $P(3\%) = \dfrac{0.1}{1.03} + \dfrac{1.1}{1.03^2} = 1.1339$

This example in which the approximate value is close to the actual value highlights a more general fact that high coupon, short maturity bonds will have low convexity. Low coupon, long-term bonds will have significant convexity, which in turn means that more sophisticated approximation methods are needed.

The convexity of a zero-coupon bond of term n years at a yield of i is given by

$$\text{convexity} = \frac{-1}{P} \frac{d^2 P}{di^2}$$

$$= \frac{-1}{P} \frac{d^2}{di^2} (1+i)^{-n}$$

$$= \frac{-1}{P} n(n+1)(1+i)^{-(n+2)}$$

$$= \frac{-1}{(1+i)^{-n}} n(n+1)(1+i)^{-(n+2)}$$

$$= \frac{-n(n+1)}{(1+i)^2}$$

In the more general case

$$\frac{d^2 P}{di^2} = \frac{-1}{(1+i)^2} \left[\sum_{j=1}^{n} C_{t_j}(t_j^2 + t_j) v^{t_j} \right]$$

Example 15.2

What is the convexity of a zero-coupon, 30-year bond priced to yield of 5% p.a.?

Answer

$$\text{Convexity} = \frac{-30 \times 31}{1.05^2} = -843.54$$

An improved approximation to how the price of a bond changes with changes in yield can be derived by assuming that the price–yield relationship is quadratic, i.e.

$$P(i) = ai^2 + bi + c$$

and also

$$P(i + \Delta i) = a(i + \Delta i)^2 + b(i + \Delta i) + c$$
$$= ai^2 + 2ai\Delta i + a\Delta i^2 + bi + b\Delta i + c$$

It follows that

$$P(i + \Delta i) - P(i) = 2ai\Delta i + a\Delta i^2 + b\Delta i. \tag{15.11}$$

If we recognise the following

$$\frac{dP}{di} = 2ai + b$$

and

$$\frac{d^2P}{di^2} = 2a$$

then equation (15.11) can be written as

$$P(i + \Delta i) - P(i) = \Delta i \times \frac{dP}{di} + \Delta i^2 \times \frac{1}{2}\frac{d^2P}{di^2}$$

If we now divide both sides by $P(c)$,

$$\frac{P(i + \Delta i) - P(i)}{P(i)} = \frac{dP}{di}\frac{1}{P}\Delta i + \frac{d^2P}{di^2}\frac{1}{P} \times \frac{1}{2}\Delta i^2$$

$$= -(D_i\Delta i + \tfrac{1}{2}C_i\Delta i^2)$$

where D_i is the duration at yield i and C_i is the convexity at yield i.
   Hence,

$$P(i + \Delta i) = P(i)[1 - (D_i\Delta i + \tfrac{1}{2}C_i\Delta i^2)]$$

Example 15.3

Use the improved approximation above to estimate the price of a zero-coupon, 30-year bond at a yield of 3%, if its price at a yield of 5% is 0.2314; its modified duration at this yield is 28.57 and its convexity is −843.54.

Answer

$$P(3\%) = 0.2314\left[1 + 28.57 \times 0.02 + \frac{843.54}{2} \times 002^2\right]$$

$$= 0.4026$$

This answer is clearly much closer to the theoretically correct value of 0.420 than the approximation based on duration alone, viz. 0.3636.

15.7   NON-GOVERNMENT BONDS

In much of our discussion of bonds we have implicitly assumed that the issuer of the bond will indeed pay the coupons and redemption proceeds in full and on time. This assumption is reasonable for issuers such as governments of politically stable and relatively wealthy economies such as the UK and the US.

However, bonds are also issued by numerous other providers such as supranational organisations (e.g. the World Bank, or the OECD), local authorities and municipalities, government agencies (e.g. Government National Mortgage Association) and corporations. The structure of the bonds (e.g. their coupons and coupon frequency, optionality, conventions about accrued interest, collateralisation, etc.) will differ markedly from issuer to issuer and indeed from issue to issue. In addition, some of the issuers may default on their obligations since they may not have access to funds when they fall due, unlike a government which has tax-raising powers.

There are at least two elements to the risks inherent in a default: the probability of the default occurring and the "recoverability". Depending on the structure of a bond, a default (e.g. the bankruptcy of the company that issued a corporate bond) will not necessarily result in complete loss of the invested capital.

In some cases, particularly if the bonds are collateralised (i.e. they are backed by a specific set of assets), the investors will recover part of their investment.

The assessment of credit risk (both default probability and recoverability) is a crucial part of analysing bonds. Several rating agencies (e.g. Moody's Investors Services, Standard & Poor's Corporation, and Fitch Investors Services) provide a rating service for bonds. The rating awarded to a bond depends on the ability to service the bond and thus will depend on the creditworthiness of the issuer, as well as the details of the issue itself, particularly its seniority and collateralisation.

Fitch and Standard & Poor's have ratings from AAA for the highest rating possible down to D, which are issues that are in default. The Moody's ratings look slightly different with Aaa corresponding to a Standard & Poor's AAA, for example. Issues that are AAA rated tend to be supranational issues. The next major rating band is AA and these are typically associated with financial institutions of high quality (international banks, for example). Bonds rated A may possibly default if economic changes are sufficiently adverse, but none the less currently have strong covenants. Bonds rated BBB have adequate protection and are still said to be of investment grade.

Bonds rated BB or B are considered "speculative". Bonds rated CCC or below are either in danger of default or already in default. The rating agencies subdivide the rating categories to provide more detail about the quality of the rated bonds. The non-government bond market is large (at least as big as the government bond market) and by far the majority of issues are rated. By value, the largest proportion of the market is rated AAA, but lower quality issues are also available in significant numbers. Investment banks generally offer derivatives such as swaps on credit risks, which make the market liquid and accessible to investors. Figure 15.2 shows the credit spread (the difference between the yields on corporate bonds and government bonds of roughly the same duration) for the UK.

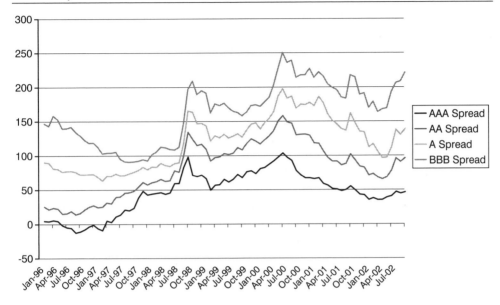

Figure 15.2

Source: UBS Warburg. Reproduced with permission.

The lower the quality of the bond, the higher the expected yield has to be to compensate the investor for taking the risk. Bonds occasionally change rating over time as the creditworthiness of the issuer, or economic conditions change. In some cases, the re-rating of a bond can have significant implications on the issuer as the structure of the bond may require that a down-rating be accompanied by specified steps (such as altering the assets held) to try to protect the interests of debt holders.

15.8 SOME APPLICATIONS OF THE CONCEPTS OF VOLATILITY AND DURATION

A manager of a portfolio of fixed-interest bonds will often not wish to hold them to redemption. Therefore it is the likely holding period return (see Section 2.9) which is of interest. The holding period return will depend mainly on the yield on which the bonds were first purchased and the change in the yield basis between the time at which they were bought and the time at which they were sold (as well as on other factors such as taxation, etc.). The volatility of a bond will give the manager an indication of the likely change in the price if the yield basis changes; from this, the possible change in the holding period return can be calculated.

A fund manager will also wish to consider volatility when selecting bonds for a portfolio at a time when interest rates are expected to change. If a reduction in yields is expected by a fund manager, a movement into longer-dated, more volatile, bonds may be regarded as desirable, because their price will increase more if the reduction in yields takes place; profits would therefore be maximised. However, if the manager's judgement is incorrect and yields rise rather than fall, losses would also be maximised by moving into longer-dated bonds.

If the manager expects yields to increase, a movement out of longer-dated bonds into shorter-dated bonds would minimise the reduction in the value of the portfolio. The manager could then move back into longer-dated bonds, at cheaper prices, after the increase in yield basis had occurred. Again, there is a risk of the manager making the wrong judgement; if yields fall rather than rise, the manager would have to repurchase the longer-dated bonds on a lower yield basis than that on which they were sold.

The above applications of the concept of volatility are examples of *policy switching*. The manager "takes a view" on the likely course of yields and the switch will lead to a profit if the view turns out to be correct.

So far, the discussion has focused on the way in which the values of fixed-interest bonds respond to a level change in yields. However, changes in interest rates are rarely, if ever, uniform along the yield curve. Often, for example, a tightening of monetary policy will lead to a rise in interest rates at the short end of the bond market and a fall in rates at the long end (because investors believe that the tightening of monetary policy will lead to a subsequent fall in inflation and interest rates). Therefore it may be useful to calculate measures of volatility so that, for example, the reaction to a change in short-term interest rates and long-term interest rates can be determined separately. This involves using separate discounting factors for payments received at different times and calculating partial differentials of the present value of the bond with respect to one or more of the discounting factors.

The concept of volatility can also be applied to other types of investment. It is possible, for example, to calculate volatilities of equity prices with respect to a change in the expected growth rate of dividends, or to the investor's expected rate of return. In the case of index-linked bonds, where payments are linked to a price index with a lag, the present value of the payments will be affected by the rate of inflation; again the volatility of the price with respect to a change in the inflation assumption can be calculated.

Institutional investors such as a life insurance company will compare the present value of liabilities with the value of assets, in order to ensure that the assets are sufficient to meet the liabilities as they arise. If interest rates change, the value of the assets will be affected. However, the present value of the liabilities will also change. It is one of the duties of the actuary and other senior managers of an insurance company to ensure that the office is not adversely affected by changes in financial factors, in particular by changes in the rates of interest.

One of the aims of an insurance company is to achieve the maximum return from investments, given the constraint of fulfilling the liabilities of the fund as they fall due. The problems caused by ignoring the liabilities when determining investment policy can be seen by considering an extreme example: if an insurance company has only a single liability which matures in one year's time, it would not be prudent, unless there were substantial free reserves, to invest in a bond maturing in 20 years' time. If interest rates were to rise, the price of the bond would fall and the office might be unable to meet its liability. Conversely, if the office has only a single liability which is to mature in 20 years' time, with a guaranteed maturity value, it would not be prudent to invest in short-term deposits; if interest rates were to fall, the office might not have sufficient money to meet its liabilities.

The *theory of immunisation* gives some guidance to an insurance company on the way in which it may invest its assets in order to ensure that certain fixed money liabilities can be met. The theory uses the concepts of volatility and duration discussed above. The alternative but less flexible theory of *absolute matching* will be discussed first.

Fixed-interest bonds will give rise to known *asset proceeds*, i.e. payments of interest or capital, at known times. Let the asset proceeds at time t be denoted by A_t. The office will also have a series of liabilities; some of these may be contingent liabilities, such as sums assured payable on the death of a policyholder, but, given a large number of policyholders, a judgement can be made about the expected payments to be made at various times. When considering the liabilities, the office can deduct, from the total liability, the premiums due from existing policies at each future time. The liability after deducting the premiums due is known as the net liability. The net liability at time t will be denoted by L_t.

In theory, it may be possible to match every liability outflow with a corresponding asset proceed, by purchasing fixed-interest bonds with appropriate coupon payments and maturity dates. If this is done, then $A_t = L_t$ for all values of t; in this case the office is said to be absolutely matched. Because every outgoing payment is matched by a corresponding incoming payment, no change in the rate of interest can affect the financial position of the office. If interest rates change, the present value of the liabilities of the office will rise and fall exactly in line with the market value of the assets of the office.

Absolute matching is difficult to achieve in practice without the use of over-the-counter swap arrangements. Usually, the portfolio of liabilities that the office has to meet is much more complicated than that described above. In many cases, premiums will exceed expected outgoings for insurance policies in the early years. Thus the net liability could be negative and it is not possible to purchase conventional fixed-interest bonds to match negative liabilities. Furthermore, policies may have options, etc., which make matching more difficult.

In the case of a portfolio of liabilities, in respect of which the initial outgoings are very high and no premiums are due after the inception date of the policy, the office may be able to purchase fixed-interest bonds so that it is broadly matched. However, even in this case, it would probably not go through the procedure of trying to match liabilities with assets in the absolute sense described above.

If the office has significant free reserves (or solvency margin), it could deliberately mismatch. A view would be taken on the likely future path of interest rates and an asset portfolio held such that, if interest rates moved in the expected direction a profit would be made.

15.9 THE THEORY OF IMMUNISATION

A less stringent, but more conceptually useful theory an office may consider when determining the allocation of assets to meet fixed liabilities is the theory of *immunisation*, as described by Redington (1952). Firstly, it will be useful to introduce some notation:

$V_a(\delta)$ = present value of the assets
$V_1(\delta)$ = present value of the liabilities

$V_a'(\delta)$ = first differential of the present value of the assets (with respect to the force of interest)

$V_l'(\delta)$ = first differential of the present value of the liabilities (with respect to the force of interest)

$V_a''(\delta)$ = second differential of the present value of the assets (with respect to the force of interest)

$V_l''(\delta)$ = second differential of the present value of the liabilities (with respect to the force of interest)

The analysis is made slightly easier if it is carried out using the force of interest, rather than the annual or half-yearly effective rate of interest. It will be assumed that the present value of the assets is initially exactly equal to the present value of the liabilities, so that any additional assets are invested separately. Therefore $V_a(\delta) = V_l(\delta)$.

If there is a small change in the force of interest, say to $\delta + h$, then, by Taylor's theorem, the present value of the assets will change to

$$V_a(\delta + h) = V_a(\delta) + hV_a'(\delta) + \frac{h^2}{2} \times V_a''(\delta) + \cdots$$

The present value of the liabilities will change to

$$V_l(\delta + h) = V_l(\delta) + hV_l'(\delta) + \frac{h^2}{2} \times V_l''(\delta) + \cdots$$

Higher-order terms may be ignored, if it is assumed that any change in the force of interest will be small. It has already been assumed that $V_a(\delta) = V_l(\delta)$; if it is also assumed that $V_a'(\delta) = V_l'(\delta)$, then $V_a(\delta + h) > V_l(\delta + h)$, after a change in the force of interest, if $V_a''(\delta) > V_l''(\delta)$, as h^2 will always be positive.

Thus the resulting present value of the assets will always be greater than the resulting present value of the liabilities, after an infinitesimal change in the valuation rate of interest (i.e. a small profit will be made from the change), if the following conditions are met at outset:

(1) The present value of the assets is equal to the present value of liabilities at the initial force of interest.
(2) The first differential of the asset values is equal to that of the liability values.
(3) The second differential of the asset values is greater than that of the liability values.

It should be noted that, if these three conditions hold, the function defined by the difference between the present value of the assets and that of the liabilities will be equal to zero at the outset. Furthermore, the function will have a first differential equal to zero and will have a positive second differential. If this function is plotted graphically against the rate of interest, the value of the function will be zero at the current rate of interest and be at a local minimum, so that a small change in the rate of interest will lead to the difference between the present value of the assets and liabilities taking a positive value (see Figure 15.3).

If these conditions are fulfilled, the investor is said to be immunised against small, uniform changes in the rate of interest. It has been assumed here that the valuation of liabilities is carried out at the same rate of interest underlying that which is used to value the assets. If the assets are valued at their market value, the rate of interest used to value the liabilities should be that underlying the market value of assets.

If $V_a(\delta) = V_l(\delta)$ and $V'_a(\delta) = V'_l(\delta)$, as is required by conditions (1) and (2) described above, then we can say that

$$\frac{V'_a(\delta)}{V_a(\delta)} = \frac{V'_l(\delta)}{V_l(\delta)} \tag{15.12}$$

Returning to the definition of volatility, discussed in Section 15.2, the condition described by equation (15.12) can be interpreted as the requirement that the volatility of the assets is equal to the volatility of the liabilities. As the problem has been analysed using volatilities taken with respect to a change in the *force* of interest, we can say that a requirement for immunisation is that the duration of the assets is equal to the duration of the liabilities.

If the problem had been analysed with respect to a change in the rate of interest (say the rate of interest convertible half-yearly), similar results would have been obtained, but the requirement would be that the volatilities with respect to a change in the *rate* of interest are equal. Thus, the modified durations of the assets and liabilities would have to be equal; this would, in fact, imply that their unmodified durations or discounted mean terms are also equal.

$V_a(\delta)$ can be written as $\sum A_t e^{-\delta t}$, where the summation is over all values of t. If this is differentiated twice with respect to the force of interest, to give $V''_a(\delta)$, we obtain

$$V''_a(\delta) = \sum t^2 A_t e^{-\delta t} + \sum t^2 A_t v^t$$

Similarly, $V''_l(\delta) = \sum t^2 L_t v^t$, again with the summation being over all values of t. Thus the condition $V''_a(\delta) > V''_l(\delta)$ can be written as

$$\sum t^2 A_t v^t > \sum t^2 L_t v^t$$

Consider the expression $\sum (t - \mu_a)^2 A_t v^t > \sum (t - \mu_l)^2 L_t v^t$, where μ_a is the discounted mean term of the assets and μ_l is the discounted mean term of the liabilities. When this is expanded, all the terms cancel, apart from $\sum t^2 A_t v^t$ and $\sum t^2 L_t v^t$, as long

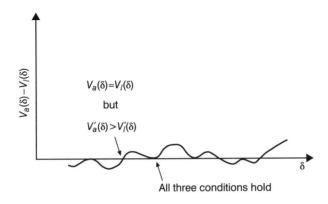

Figure 15.3

as μ_a is equal to μ_l. Thus $\sum t^2 A_t v^t > \sum t^2 L_t v^t$ can be written as $\sum (t - \mu_a)^2 A_t v^t > \sum (t - \mu_l)^2 L_t v^t$ and this third condition for immunisation can be interpreted as a requirement for the spread of the asset terms around the discounted mean term of the assets to be greater than the spread of the liability terms around the discounted mean term of the liabilities.

Finally, therefore, it can be said that if the following three conditions are fulfilled the office is said to be immunised against *small uniform* changes in the rate of interest:

(1) The present value of the assets is equal to the present value of the liabilities.
(2) The discounted mean term of the assets is equal to the discounted mean term of the liabilities.
(3) The spread of the asset terms around the discounted mean term is greater than the spread of the liability terms around the discounted mean term.

15.10 SOME PRACTICAL ISSUES WITH IMMUNISATION AND MATCHING

There are many problems with the practical implementation of the ideas discussed above, not least of which is that it is almost impossible to manage a bond portfolio so that the immunisation conditions are fulfilled all the time. The required asset distribution changes continuously over time (unless absolute matching is possible) therefore dealing costs would be incurred constantly. In addition to these practical, implementation problems, markets are highly unlikely to permit such simple strategies to have such a high probability of producing a profit. Indeed one of the fundamental premises in modern finance is that there is no such thing as a free lunch, i.e. arbitrage opportunities do not persist in the market. The shape of the yield curve and its evolution over time will actively prevent these opportunities.

However, the investment managers of an insurance company, working in conjunction with the actuary, will not wish to leave themselves too exposed and the concept of immunisation provides a useful framework for managing the "first order" risks. If the free reserves are small, they will wish to hold a bond portfolio such that, broadly speaking, the volatility or duration of the portfolio is of the same order of magnitude as the duration of the liabilities. Working within this constraint, the managers will invest in order to obtain the highest net yield. This will ensure that, if interest rates do move sharply, the likelihood of a substantial loss is relatively slim.

Both absolute matching and immunisation protect against profit as well as against loss (ignoring the small, second-order, terms in the case of immunisation). Therefore, there are various circumstances in which fund managers will seek to move away from what they believe to be the matched position. In practice, the fund manager will have some investment freedom because there will be free reserves or because only part of the liability may be guaranteed, etc. If the manager believes that interest rates are likely to move upwards (that is long-term as well as short-term interest rates), investments may be moved into relatively short-term bonds. If it is felt that interest rates are going to fall, the manager may move the portfolio into longer-term bonds. Dealing costs must always be covered in any such move. This situation is really a further example of policy switching, as described earlier.

Various hybrid forms of matching and immunisation also exist in practice. The cash flows over some specified near-term horizon, e.g. five years, will be matched, but the longer-dated liabilities will be immunised. The rationale behind this is that the short end of the yield curve exhibits a much wider variety of shapes than the long end, making immunisation practicably impossible. The long end experiences shifts that are approximately parallel, as required for immunisation theory.

More sophisticated stochastic models of interest rate behaviour can be used to manage bond portfolios. These allow for the possibility of interest rates over different terms changing by different amounts and can allow for different sizes of interest rate changes. An introduction to the idea of probability applied to financial mathematics is provided in the final chapter of this book; however, a detailed discussion of stochastic models is beyond the scope of this text and the reader is left to pursue further references listed at the end of Chapter 17.

REFERENCES

McCutcheon, J.J. and Scott, W.F. (1986), *An Introduction to the Mathematics of Finance*, Heinemann.
Phillips, P. (1987), *Inside the New Gilt Edged Market*, Woodhead-Faulkner.
Ranson, R.H. (1987), *Financial Aspects and the Valuation of Long Term Business Funds*, Institute of Actuaries.
Redington, F.M. (1952), "Review of the principles of life office valuations", *Journal of the Institute of Actuaries*, 78, 286–315.

16
Option Pricing Models

16.1 INTRODUCTION

In this chapter, consideration is given to theoretical models for pricing options and some basic investment strategies using options. Attention is focused primarily on traded stock options. It is assumed that the reader is familiar with what is meant by an option and is also familiar with the associated terminology. For a short introduction to traded options, the reader is referred to Chapter 7.

The two most popular option pricing models are the Black–Scholes model and the Binomial model. It is those models which are discussed in this chapter. Apart from introducing the models, it is shown how they may be implemented using worked examples. A link between the Black–Scholes and the Binomial model is established and a relationship between call option and put option prices is given. Furthermore, it is shown how to adjust both the Black–Scholes and Binomial models to accommodate dividends due to be paid on the underlying stock over the life of the option. The discussion is centred around European style options; that is, options which can only be exercised at expiry.

16.2 STOCK OPTIONS

As defined in Chapter 7, an option is the right to buy (or sell) a specified quantity of a given stock at a specified price on (or before) a given date in the future. The right to buy is called a *call* option; the right to sell, a *put* option.

The holder of an option will exercise his or her right at the expiry date, T, only if the option has value. A call option will be exercised only *if* the stock price at expiry, S_T, is greater than the exercise price, X, in which case the option is worth $S_T - X$. Thus at expiry,

$$C_T = S_T - X \quad \text{if } S_T > X$$
$$= 0 \quad \text{if } S_T \leqslant X$$

where C_T is the value of the call at the expiry date T.

This may be summarised mathematically as

$$C_T = \max\{0, S_T - X\}$$

Similarly, for a put option,

$$P_T = X - S_T \quad \text{if } S_T < X$$
$$= 0 \quad \text{if } S_T \geqslant X$$

where P_T is the value of the put at expiry, i.e.

$$P_T = \max\{0, X - S_T\}$$

The word "*if*" above provides a vital clue as to how the theoretical value of an option might be calculated. We need to assess the likelihood, or probability, that the stock price at expiry will be greater than the exercise price (or vice versa). We know that the exercise price is fixed, the only source of uncertainty being the stock price. If a probability distribution of the stock price at expiry is known, the so-called "real world" expected value of the option at expiry can be evaluated using standard results on statistical expectations introduced in Chapter 9. That is,

$$E[C_T] = E[\max(0, S_T - X)]$$

and

$$E[P_T] = E[\max(0, X - S_T)]$$

The final step in evaluating a theoretical option price is calculating the option price at time t, where t is any time prior to expiry, T. Invoking the so-called *risk neutrality* arguments (discussed in Section 16.4), the value of the option at time t is equal to the expected value of the option at maturity T discounted at the *risk-free* rate of interest, r. The *risk-free* interest rate is defined to be the yield, payable continuously, on a notional default-free bond (e.g. a government bond) of similar duration to the life of the option. Therefore,

$$C_t = e^{-r(T-t)} E_Q[C_T]$$

giving

$$C_t = e^{-r\tau} E_Q[\max(0, S_T - X)] \qquad (16.1)$$

where $\tau = T - t$. Similarly,

$$P_t = e^{-r\tau} E_Q[\max(0, X - S_T)] \qquad (16.2)$$

Notice that the discount factor, $e^{-r\tau}$, is in a form which assumes a continuously payable rate of interest and that expectation is now slightly different from the "real-world" expectation discussed earlier.

To evaluate equations (16.1) and (16.2), a suitable model for the evolution of stock prices over time is needed. This enables the probability distribution for the stock price at expiry to be found. Different models lead to different option pricing formulae. Particular examples are the lognormal process leading to the Black–Scholes model and the binomial process leading to the Binomial option pricing model. Adventurous readers may wish to develop their own models using, for example, empirical distributions.

16.3   THE RISKLESS HEDGE

Hedging strategies that remove certain risks from a portfolio have become not only practically very important but also contain some important theoretical insights into how assets and particularly derivative instruments may be priced.

We will consider the following very simple numerical example to show one of the important applications of riskless hedging. The model we will use may appear highly artificial, but it is useful for illustrative purposes and it also forms the basis for some of the models actually used in practice for pricing derivatives.

Suppose we have a simple market with only three types of asset: a share, a cash investment/borrowing facility and a European call option on the share. The share's price is currently 100p and it can move over the period of one month to either 133p (with probability 60%) or down to 75p (with probability 40%). The strike price for the option is 100p and it has a one month period to expiry. The risk-free rate of return on the cash investment is 5% per month.

The value of the call option in one month's time will be either 0, if the share price drops to 75p or will be worth 33p, if the share price rises to 133p. In order to price the option, the idea is to find some combination of purchases or sales in the share and the cash investment now so that we can exactly replicate the option's payoff in one month. If the combination of shares and cash have the same payoff as the option, then the cost of creating the combination must be the value of the option otherwise the market would permit an arbitrage opportunity. The number of shares bought is denoted by X, and Y denotes the amount invested in cash.

We refer to the case when the share's price rises to 133p as the Up state and the case when the share's price drops to 75p as the Down state. In the Up state, the value of the call option is 33p so the value of the combination, $X \times 133 + Y \times 1.05$, must be equal to 33 for it to replicate the payoff in the Up state. In the Down state, we would require $X \times 75 + Y \times 1.05$ to be equal to 0. We have two equations and two unknowns, X and Y, and so can find a single solution: $X = 33/58 = 0.5690$ and $Y = -33/58 \times 75/1.05 = -40.64$.

Because the portfolio of 0.5690 shares and a borrowing of 40.64p at a rate of 5% per unit of time has exactly the same payoff as the derivative in both the Up and Down states, the portfolio and the derivative must have exactly the same price to start off with, that is 56.90p − 40.64p = 16.26p.

What is very interesting with this pricing methodology is that it does not depend at all on the probabilities of the Up state or Down state occurring. This is slightly unnerving since most people would initially think that the value of an option to buy a share would depend on the share's expected return. In the simple case considered here, the expected return would be determined by the probabilities of the Up and Down states. For example, with the given probabilities, the expected return on the share is $0.6 \times 133 + 0.4 \times 75 = 109.18$. If the probabilities had been different, say, a probability of 50% that the Up state would occur and a 50% probability that the Down state would occur, the expected return would have been 104p. However, the price of the call option would be exactly the same, 16.26p.

To understand this apparently strange behaviour, we have to realise that the current price of the share already reflects the expected return. The fact that in our example the price of the share was 100p and not 95p or 105p means that the market had already discounted the share price to the appropriate level, given the risk of the investment. There is therefore no need to try to discount it all again when pricing a derivative that relies on the market price of the share. The market does all the hard work and we can use this to derive a more general way of pricing derivatives. This brings us on to the topic of risk neutrality.

16.4   RISK NEUTRALITY

Risk neutrality is probably best understood as being a mathematical trick to make pricing derivatives easier. The trick depends on what we discovered in the simple example in Section 16.3, namely, that the market price of securities already takes into account the expected returns and so any financial instrument that depends only on the price of securities already priced in the market will not itself depend directly on the expected returns.

Returning to the example of the previous section, we can illustrate the more general result that leads to the concept of risk-neutral pricing. In particular, we are going to demonstrate that the price of the derivative can be obtained as a (discounted) expected value calculation. In order to establish an expected value, we will need some probabilities to attach to the events of each of the two states occurring. Because the riskless hedge does not depend on the probabilities of the Up state or Down state, it is convenient to use probabilities that make the calculation simple. It turns out that the most mathematically convenient probabilities are those under which the expected return on the share is the same as the risk-free rate. We calculate the probabilities of Up and Down moves by solving the following equation for q, which we use to denote the "risk neutral" probability of the Up state:

$$133q + 75(1 - q) = 105.$$

The solution to the above yields $q = 30/58 = 51.7\%$.

Now it can be proved that the risk-neutral probability can be used to find the price of the call option directly by taking the option's expected return and then discounting it at the risk-free rate. The option's expected return is given by the probability of the Up state multiplied by its value in the Up state plus the probability of the Down state multiplied by its value in the Down state, i.e.

$$\text{expected value of option} = 33p \times 0.517 + 0p \times (1 - 0.517) = 17.069p$$

If we discount the option back one period, we get the current price of the option, i.e. price $= 17.069/1.05 = 16.26p$, which is exactly the same as the price obtained in the previous section by valuing the replicating portfolio.

This is a much easier way of pricing the option than going through the process of constructing the replicating portfolio and constructing the riskless hedge; we just calculate the risk-neutral probability, find the expected value of the derivative using the risk-neutral probability and then discount it at the risk-free rate. Under the assumption that the market is complete, i.e. that the value of the derivatives are entirely based on the value of existing assets in the market, the risk-neutrality trick will work for all derivatives. For example, if we buy a put option on the stock with a strike price of 90p, say, then we know that the value of the put option in the Up state is 0p and in the Down state is worth 15p (90p − 75p). The expected value of the put option is

$$0.517 \times 0 + (1 - 0.517) \times 15 = 7.245$$

which, when discounted at 5%, gives a value of $7.245/1.05 = 6.9p$.

The example above is a simple particular case and may appear artificial. However, the risk-neutrality concept can be extended to more complicated cases, although the proof that this is the case involves sophisticated mathematics. The steps in valuing a derivative are to find a model of all the different values that the derivative and the underlying asset can take and discount the expected value (calculated using risk-neutral probabilities) at the risk-free rate of return. The artificial Up state/Down state model (the so-called binomial model) is the basic building block for many models used in the real-world pricing of options and other derivatives.

The reason why the risk-neutrality trick works is that we have assumed that the market is complete, i.e. the derivative can be exactly replicated by existing assets in the market. This means that all the risk in the derivative can be hedged away and so investors will not demand a risk premium when pricing the derivative relative to other assets. In the apparently artificial case where the probability distribution of the "future states of the world" was such that all the underlying assets had exactly the same expected rate of return (the risk-free rate of return), then the derivative would also have the same expected rate of return. The value of the derivative could then be obtained by calculating its expected value based on the probability distribution and discounting it at the risk-free rate back from the time of payoff to the current date. We then demonstrated that the real world probabilities associated with the underlying asset values did not affect the price of the option obtained by replicating it. Consequently, it is "valid" to use the artificial risk-neutral case to value derivatives.

Example 16.1

Consider the case where there are two time periods before the call option expires. As in the earlier example, the share price currently has a price of 100p which can go up to 133p or down to 75p after one period. At the end of the second period, if the share price is 133p at the start, the price can be up to 177p or back down to 100p. If the share price is 75p at the start of the second period, then by the end of the second period, the price can go up to 100p or down to 58.5p.

The call option has a strike price of 90p and expires at the end of the second period. The risk-free rate of borrowing and lending is 5% per period.

Answer

We will answer this in two ways, first, by finding the replicating portfolio and, second, by using risk neutrality.

Figure 16.1 shows the possible values of share, the value of 100p invested in the risk-free asset and the value of the option at each point.

We have used S to denote the share price, R to denote the value of 100p deposited in a risk-free account and C to denote the value of the call option. The approach is to start with the known values at the far right and then work back to the current time on the left of the "binomial tree".

C1 is going to be calculated as the value of a portfolio that provides a payoff of 87p if the Up state occurs and 10p if the Down state occurs in time period 2, starting from the fact that an Up state has already occurred in time period 1.

We let X1 be the number of shares held in the replicating portfolio and Y1 be the amount deposited in the risk-free security at the end of time period 1, assuming that an Up move has occurred during time period 1. In order that the replicating portfolio provide identical payoffs to the option, we require

$$X1 \times 177 + Y1 \times (1.05) = 87$$

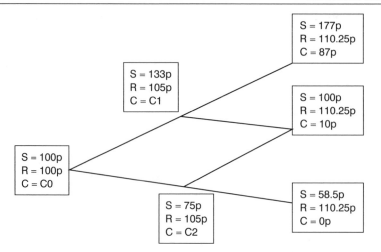

Figure 16.1   Values of shares, risk-free asset and option

and

$$X1 \times 100 + Y1 \times (1.05) = 10, \quad \text{i.e.}$$

$$X1 = 77/77 = 1 \qquad \text{and} \qquad Y1 = -85.71$$

The value of the replicating portfolio, and hence of the call option (C1), at the end of period 1, assuming an Up state at the end of period 1, is $1 \times 133 - 85.71 = 47.29$p.

C2 is going to be calculated as the value of a portfolio that provides a payoff of 10p if the Up state occurs and 0p if the Down state occurs in time period 2, starting from the fact that a Down state has already occurred in time period 1.

We let X2 be the number of shares held in the replicating portfolio and Y2 be the amount deposited in the risk-free security at the end of time period 1, assuming that a Down move has occurred during time period 1. In order that the replicating portfolio provide identical payoffs to the option, we require

$$X2 \times 100 + Y2 \times (1.05) = 10$$

and

$$X2 \times 58.5 + Y2 \times (1.05) = 0, \quad \text{i.e.}$$

$$X1 = 10/41.5 = 0.24 \qquad \text{and} \qquad Y2 = -13.43\text{p}$$

The value of the replicating portfolio, and hence of the call option (C2), at the end of period 1, assuming a Down state at the end of period 1, is $0.24 \times 75 - 13.43 = 4.57$p.

We now know the value of the call option at the end of period 1 in both the Up and Down states and we can interpret these as "payoffs". We can therefore find the replicating portfolio that will mimic the "payoffs" of the option over the course of period 1

$$X0 \times 133 + Y0 \times 1.05 = 47.29$$

and

$$X0 \times 75 + Y0 \times 1.05 = 4.57, \quad \text{i.e.}$$

$$X0 = 0.74 \quad \text{and} \quad Y0 = -48.25.$$

The replicating portfolio, and hence the value of the call option at the start of period 1 (C0), is $0.74 \times 100 - 48.25 = 25.6p$.

The risk-neutral solution requires that we find the probabilities such that the expected return on the share is the risk-free rate. This is exactly the same as in the example discussed in Section 16.4, viz., the probability of an Up move is 0.517. We can use this to derive the fact that the probability that the call option provides a payoff of 87p is $0.517 \times 0.517 = 0.267$; the probability that it provides a payoff of 0 is $(1 - 0.517) \times (1 - 0.517) = 0.233$; the probability that the payoff is 10p is $1 - 0.267 - 0.233 = 0.499$.

The value of the option is then calculated as the (discounted) expected payoff using risk-neutral probabilities is $(0.267 \times 87 + 0.499 \times 10 + 0.233 \times 0)/1.1025 = 25.6p$, as obtained from the replication portfolio approach.

However, the fact remains that in proceeding to more realistic examples, the mathematics required quickly goes beyond the scope of this book and requires, in particular, the language of stochastic calculus.

16.5   A MORE GENERAL BINOMIAL MODEL

The Black–Scholes model (see Section 16.8) is undoubtedly the most popular option pricing model in current use. However, many find the underlying mathematics too demanding and prefer to use the simpler Binomial option pricing model, which has gained considerable popularity. The methodology for the Binomial model was developed by Cox, Ross and Rubinstein and published in 1979.

The essential difference between this model and the Black–Scholes model is in the underlying model for the evolution of stock prices over time. Recall that, it is necessary to solve equations (16.1) and (16.2), i.e. solve

$$C_t = e^{-r\tau} E[\max(0, S_T - X)]$$

$$P_t = e^{-r\tau} E[\max(0, X - S_T)]$$

According to the methodology of the Binomial model, divide the time to maturity, τ, into n discrete time intervals of equal length τ/n. Thus, each interval of time may be indexed from 1 up to n. Assume that during each time interval, the stock price may rise by a multiple of e^u (greater than 1) with probability p, or fall by a multiple of e^v (less than 1) with probability $1 - p$.

Then over one time interval:

$$S_{t+1} = S_t e^u \qquad \text{with probability } p$$

$$= S_t e^v \qquad \text{with probability } 1 - p$$

u, v and p are constants satisfying $0 < p < 1$ and $v < r\tau/n < u$.

Over two intervals

$$S_{t+2} = S_t e^{2u} \qquad \text{with probability } p^2$$

$$= S_t e^{u+v} \qquad \text{with probability } 2p(1-p)$$

$$= S_t e^{2v} \qquad \text{with probability } (1-p)^2$$

Over two intervals there are three possible outcomes. The stock price increases in both intervals, the price increases then decreases (or decreases then increases), or the price decreases in both intervals.

Continuing the process, it can be seen that after k discrete time intervals the stock price, S_{t+k}, takes the value

$$S_{t+k} = S_t e^{ju + (k-j)v} \quad \text{with probability} \quad {}^k C_j p^j (1-p)^{k-j} \qquad j = 0, 1, ..., k \quad (16.3)$$

where j is the number of upward jumps (thus $k - j$ is the number of downward jumps). The parameter j has a *binomial* distribution (see Chapter 9 for a discussion of the binomial distribution).

Time at maturity is reached after n time intervals, therefore $S_T = S_{t+n}$. From equation (16.3) we know that

$$S_T = S_t e^{ju + (n-j)v} \quad \text{with probability} \quad {}^n C_j p^j (1-p)^{n-j} \qquad j = 0, 1, ..., n \quad (16.4)$$

Equation (16.4) gives the distribution of stock prices at maturity. Taking expectations

$$E[S_T] = \sum_{j=0}^{n} {}^n C_j p^j (1-p)^{n-j} S_t e^{ju + (n-j)v}$$

and equation (16.4) together with equations (16.1) and (16.2) leads to

$$C_t = e^{-r\tau} \sum_{j=0}^{n} {}^n C_j p^j (1-p)^{n-j} \max\{0, S_t e^{ju + (n-j)v} - X\} \qquad (16.5)$$

and

$$P_t = e^{-r\tau} \sum_{j=0}^{n} {}^n C_j p^j (1-p)^{n-j} \max\{0, X - S_t e^{ju + (n-j)v}\} \qquad (16.6)$$

Equations (16.5) and (16.6) are the call and put formulae given by the Binomial option pricing model, assuming there are no dividends payable on the underlying stock prior to maturity. To complete the model, we need to know the value of p and need to estimate the parameters u, v and n.

16.6 THE VALUE OF p

From the *risk neutrality* hypothesis (see Section 16.4) we know that, in a risk-neutral economy, the expected yield from all assets equals the risk-free rate of interest. Therefore,

$$E[S_{t+1}] = S_t e^{r\tau/n} \qquad (16.7)$$

where r is the risk-free rate of interest. Also, from the stock price model, we know that

$$E[S_{t+1}] = p S_t e^u + (1-p) S_t e^v \qquad (16.8)$$

Equating equations (16.7) and (16.8) and rearranging in terms of p gives

$$p = \frac{e^{r\tau/n} - e^{v}}{e^{u} - e^{v}}$$

Thus p is automatically specified by the choice of u and v.

16.7 ESTIMATING THE PARAMETERS u, v AND n

Choosing values for the parameters u, v and n is a decision which the analyst needs to make, based on empirical evidence. It is not unambiguous how these parameters should be estimated from data. However, u and v can be chosen so that, for large values of n, the binomial stock price process (equation (16.4)) approximates the lognormal stock price process used in the Black–Scholes model (see equation (16.11)). Furthermore, in the limit as n tends to infinity, the binomial option price equals the Black–Scholes price. Jarrow and Rudd (1983) show that to obtain the approximation, choose

$$u = (r - \tfrac{1}{2}\sigma^2)\frac{\tau}{n} + \sigma\sqrt{\frac{\tau}{n}} \qquad (16.9)$$

$$v = (r - \tfrac{1}{2}\sigma^2)\frac{\tau}{n} - \sigma\sqrt{\frac{\tau}{n}} \qquad (16.10)$$

where σ is the volatility of the underlying stock.

These results imply $p = \tfrac{1}{2}$ (as n tends to infinity).

Thus, u and v can be estimated using the risk-free interest rate, volatility of the underlying stock, time to maturity and number of discrete time intervals.

The final consideration is how many discrete time intervals, n, should be used. This is an arbitrary decision. Jarrow and Rudd (1983) consider that a value of $n = 300$ is more than sufficient and state that current practice at the time was to use a value of n in the order of 150 to 200. Obviously the larger the value of n, the more computer time needed to perform the calculations.

Example 16.2

Midwest stock is currently trading at 148p. Calculate the call and put option prices given by the Binomial option pricing model if the options are due to expire in 180 days, there are no dividends payable from now until expiry and:

(a) the exercise price is 150p;
(b) the risk-free rate is 10% per annum payable continuously;
(c) volatility is estimated to be 30%.

Divide the time to maturity into 25 intervals.

Answer

$$S_t = 148p, \qquad X = 150p, \qquad \tau = \frac{180}{365} \text{ years}, \qquad r = 0.10, \qquad \sigma = 30$$

also $n = 25$.

It follows that

$$e^{-r\tau} = 0.95188117$$

$$u = 0.04321974 \qquad \text{using equation (16.9)}$$

$$v = -0.04104988 \qquad \text{using equation (16.10)}$$

giving

$$p = 0.5$$

The intermediate calculations are shown in the body of Table 16.1. Values are shown to three decimal places only. The values in columns (1) to (6) refer to various parts of

Table 16.1

j	(1)	(2)	(3)	(4)	(5)	(6)
0	0.000	53.036	0.000	96.964	0.000	0.000
1	0.000	57.699	0.000	92.301	0.000	0.000
2	0.000	62.772	0.000	87.228	0.000	0.000
3	0.000	68.291	0.000	81.709	0.000	0.006
4	0.000	74.295	0.000	75.705	0.000	0.029
5	0.002	80.827	0.000	69.173	0.000	0.110
6	0.005	87.934	0.000	62.066	0.000	0.328
7	0.014	95.665	0.000	54.335	0.000	0.778
8	0.032	104.076	0.000	45.924	0.000	1.480
9	0.061	113.227	0.000	36.773	0.000	2.239
10	0.097	123.182	0.000	26.818	0.000	2.613
11	0.133	134.012	0.000	15.988	0.000	2.124
12	0.155	145.795	0.000	4.205	0.000	0.652
13	0.155	158.613	8.613	0.000	1.335	0.000
14	0.133	172.559	22.559	0.000	2.997	0.000
15	0.097	187.731	37.731	0.000	3.676	0.000
16	0.061	204.237	54.237	0.000	3.302	0.000
17	0.032	222.194	72.194	0.000	2.327	0.000
18	0.014	241.729	91.729	0.000	1.314	0.000
19	0.005	262.983	112.983	0.000	0.596	0.000
20	0.002	286.105	136.105	0.000	0.216	0.000
21	0.000	311.260	161.260	0.000	0.061	0.000
22	0.000	338.626	188.626	0.000	0.013	0.000
23	0.000	368.399	218.399	0.000	0.002	0.000
24	0.000	400.789	250.789	0.000	0.000	0.000
25	0.000	436.028	286.028	0.000	0.000	0.000
				Total	15.838	10.358

the intermediate calculations, specified as follows:

Column	Calculation
(1)	$^nC_j p^j (1-p)^{n-j}$
(2)	$S_t e^{ju+(n-j)v}$
(3)	$\max\{0, S_t e^{ju+(n-j)v} - X\}$
(4)	$\max\{0, X - S_t e^{ju+(n-j)v}\}$
(5)	Columns (1) × (3)
(6)	Columns (1) × (4)

The values of the summations in equations (16.5) and (16.6) are shown at the bottom of columns (5) and (6) respectively. All that remains is to multiply these values by the discounting factor, $e^{-r\tau}$. Therefore,

$$C_t = 0.95188117 \times 15.838$$

$$= 15.08 \text{ pence (to 2 decimal places)}$$

and

$$P_t = 0.95188117 \times 10.358$$

$$= 9.86 \text{ pence (to 2 decimal places)}$$

16.8 THE BLACK–SCHOLES MODEL

Although the concept of an option has been around for a very long time (at least as far back as Aristotle), two major innovations took place in 1973 which set the scene for a dramatic rise in the importance of options. The first of these was the opening of the Chicago Board Options Exchange in April 1973. The second was the publication, in May 1973, of a paper entitled "The Pricing of Options and Corporate Liabilities" by Fischer Black and Myron Scholes in the *Journal of Political Economy*. In that paper, Black and Scholes present their epoch-making model.

Alternative option valuation models had been developed previously by others: the key difference between these models and the Black–Scholes model is that Black and Scholes focus on the neutral option hedge to determine option value. Use of the model is computationally simple and it rapidly became the industry standard. The complete derivation of the model, however, is mathematically complex and goes beyond the scope of this book. Here, attention is focused on the probabilistic (or *heuristic*) derivation and on other more practical considerations of interest to practitioners.

Before introducing the Black–Scholes model itself, a worthwhile exercise is to take a look at the underlying model for the evolution of stock prices, which in this case is based on the lognormal distribution.

The lognormal distribution for stock prices assumes that logarithmic stock returns are normally distributed. That is,

$$\log\left(\frac{S_{t+\Delta t}}{S_t}\right) = \mu\Delta t + \sigma\sqrt{\Delta t}Z \tag{16.11}$$

where Z is the standard normal random variable with mean 0 and standard deviation 1
$S_{t+\Delta t}/S_t$ is the stock return over the interval t to $t + \Delta t$
μ is the mean logarithmic stock return per unit time
σ is the standard deviation of logarithmic stock returns per unit time

Greater insight into equation (16.11) can be obtained by rearranging it. Consider rearranging in terms of Z.

$$Z = \frac{\log\left(\dfrac{S_{t+\Delta t}}{S_t}\right) - \mu\Delta t}{\sigma\sqrt{\Delta t}} \qquad Z \sim N(0,1) \qquad (16.12)$$

Equation (16.12) is in the form of a standardised normal variable (see Chapter 9). In this case, the random variable is the logarithmic stock return, the mean is $\mu\Delta t$ and the standard deviation is $\sigma\sqrt{\Delta t}$.

Exponentiating both sides of equation (16.11) and multiplying by S_t gives

$$S_{t+\Delta t} = S_t \exp(\mu\Delta t + \sigma\sqrt{\Delta t}Z)$$
$$= S_t \exp(\mu\Delta t)\exp(\sigma\sqrt{\Delta t}Z) \qquad (16.13)$$

which shows that over the interval Δt, the stock price evolves at a constant rate, $\mu\Delta t$, and a random rate, $\sigma\sqrt{\Delta t}Z$.

From equation (16.13), we know that

$$S_T = S_t \exp(\mu\tau + \sigma\sqrt{\tau}Z) \qquad (16.14)$$

Equation (16.14) can be used in conjunction with equations (16.1) and (16.2) to complete the heuristic derivation of the Black–Scholes model. The algebraic manipulations are a little complicated and are likely to be offputting to some readers; for this reason, the derivation is left to Annex 16.1 and we shall instead move on to the Black–Scholes pricing formula itself, starting with call options.

16.9   CALL OPTIONS

Assuming that no dividends are payable on the stock prior to maturity of the option, the Black–Scholes call option price, C_t, is given by

$$C_t = S_t\Phi(h) - Xe^{-r\tau}\Phi(h - \sigma\sqrt{\tau}) \qquad (16.15)$$

where $h = \dfrac{\log(S_t/Xe^{-r\tau})}{\sigma\sqrt{\tau}} + \dfrac{1}{2}\sigma\sqrt{\tau}$

S_t = current stock price
r = risk-free interest rate
X = exercise price
τ = time to expiry (in years)
σ = volatility = standard deviation of logarithmic stock returns per unit time

$$\Phi(\omega) = \int_{-\infty}^{\omega} \frac{1}{\sqrt{2\pi}} e^{-y^2/2} dy \qquad \text{i.e. } P(Y<\omega) \text{ given } Y \sim N(0,1)$$

In some texts, the parameter h is written in an alternative form, as follows:

$$h = \frac{\log(S/X) + (r + \frac{1}{2}\sigma^2)\tau}{\sigma\sqrt{\tau}}$$

The reader should not be concerned about this since the two expressions for h are equivalent. It should be noted that *natural* logarithms are always used.

It will be noticed that the call price is a function of only five parameters; S_t, X, τ, r and σ. $\Phi(h)$ and $\Phi(h - \sigma\sqrt{\tau})$ are simply values from the cumulative standard normal distribution. They are probabilities and therefore lie in the range 0 to 1. For a discussion of the normal distribution, the reader is referred to Chapter 9.

It is revealing to take a closer look at the formula. Firstly, it does not depend on the mean return on the stock, but on its current market price and volatility only. As h tends to infinity, $\Phi(h)$ and $\Phi(h - \sigma\sqrt{\tau})$ both tend to 1, giving

$$C_t \simeq S_t - Xe^{-r\tau}$$

that is, as h tends to infinity, the value of the call tends to the stock price less the discounted value of the exercise price. This can happen if:

(i) The underlying stock price becomes very high relative to the exercise price (i.e. the option is deep in-the-money and time value becomes negligible compared with intrinsic value).

(ii) $S_t > Xe^{-r\tau}$ and the option is very close to expiry (i.e. $\tau \rightarrow 0$). In this case $C_t \simeq S_t - X$, since $e^{-r\tau} \rightarrow 1$ as $r \rightarrow 0$ and the option price is almost entirely intrinsic value.

(iii) $S_t > Xe^{-r\tau}$ and the volatility tends to 0. In this case, the stock price at expiry is known with certainty and the call is simply worth the stock price less the exercise payment at expiry, discounted to the present time.

Allowing h to tend to infinity may seem unrealistic. However, if h takes a value higher than 3, $\Phi(h)$ is very close to 1 ($\Phi(3) = 0.99865$). This implies that if the stock price is high (rather than very high) relative to the exercise price or if time to expiry or volatility become low (rather than tending to 0), then $C_t \simeq S_t - Xe^{-r\tau}$.

Additional insight can be obtained by examining how the call price reacts to changes in the underlying model parameters. This can be achieved intuitively, by thinking about what we would expect to happen when a model parameter changes, or mathematically, by looking at the *sensitivities* of the model. A sensitivity is simply the rate of change of the call price with respect to a change in one of the model parameters, keeping the rest of the parameters fixed. Mathematically speaking, this is the first partial derivative with respect to one of the parameters of interest.

Consider first the intuitive approach. As the stock price rises, the value of the net proceeds on exercise also rises, hence the value of the call rises. Similarly, as the exercise price falls, the value of net proceeds on exercise rises, hence the value of the call rises. As the time to maturity increases, there are two effects. The first is that there is more time for the option to expire in-the-money or out-of-the-money. Since the downside risk is limited (to the value of the call) it is reasonable to expect the value of the call to rise as time to maturity increases. The second effect is that the present value of exercise payments falls as time to maturity rises, again resulting in an increase in the value of the call. Both of these effects are in the same direction. As interest rates rise, the present value of exercise payments falls, resulting in an increase in the value of the call. As volatility rises, the stock price at expiry becomes more uncertain, and because the downside risk is limited this has a beneficial effect on the value of the call. Hence as volatility rises, the value of the call rises.

Does the Black–Scholes model confirm these observations? To answer this question, it is necessary to look at the sensitivities of the model. The sensitivities can be very useful to option traders and most are given names in option trading parlance. Calculating the sensitivities is an exercise in differential calculus. Table 16.2 shows the names, formulae and signs of the various sensitivities.

The positive signs show that as the stock price, time to maturity, interest rate or volatility increases, the value of the call increases (i.e. there is a positive relationship). The negative sign shows that as the exercise price rises, the value of the call falls (a negative relationship). This is in agreement with the earlier discussion. Thus, analysis of the sensitivities of the Black–Scholes call formula reveals that the theoretical call price reacts to changes in the model parameters in directions which would be expected.

By evaluating the formulae for the sensitivities, it is possible to assess their magnitude. Take, for example, the *delta*. It is the rate of change of the option price with respect to a change in the price of the underlying stock, and is given by the formula *delta* $= \Phi(h)$. $\Phi(h)$ is a probability and must therefore lie between 0 and 1. This means that the call price will never rise by more than a rise in the underlying stock, may sometimes rise by the same amount, but will generally not rise by as much.

Table 16.2 Sensitivities of the Black–Scholes call formula

Name	Formula[a]	Sign
Delta, Hedge ratio	$\dfrac{\partial C}{\partial S} = \Phi(h)$	+
	$\dfrac{\partial C}{\partial X} = -e^{-r\tau}\Phi(h - \sigma\sqrt{\tau})$	−
Theta	$\dfrac{\partial C}{\partial \tau} = \dfrac{S\sigma}{2\sqrt{\tau}}\Phi'(h) + Xre^{-r\tau}\Phi(h - \sigma\sqrt{\tau})$	+
Rho	$\dfrac{\partial C}{\partial r} = \tau Xe^{-r\tau}\Phi(h - \sigma\sqrt{\tau})$	+
Kappa, Epsilon, Vega	$\dfrac{\partial C}{\partial \sigma} = S\sqrt{\tau}\Phi'(h)$	+
Gamma	$\dfrac{\partial^2 C}{\partial S^2} = \dfrac{1}{S\sigma\sqrt{\tau}}\Phi'(h)$	+

[a] $\Phi'(y) = \dfrac{1}{\sqrt{2\pi}}e^{-y^2/2}$.

As h becomes large, $\Phi(h)$ tends to 1. Therefore, a deep-in-the-money call will have a *delta* near 1 and the call price will move (nearly) penny for penny with the underlying stock.

The *delta* is probably the most useful of the sensitivities and is used extensively when using options to *hedge* a portfolio. Sometimes the term *hedge ratio* is used. The terms *hedge ratio* and *delta* are synonymous. The hedge ratio shows how many stocks need to be held long (i.e. bought) for each call option held short (i.e. written) for the net position to be perfectly hedged over a short interval of time. The net position is perfectly hedged if losses made on the stock are offset by gains made on the option, or gains made on the stock are offset by losses made on the option.

The *delta* does not remain constant and changes as the underlying stock price changes. If the *delta* changes rapidly, the ratio of the number of stocks held to options written in a hedged portfolio will need to be changed often to keep the portfolio perfectly hedged. This is costly in time and commissions and is therefore undesirable. When considering options as a means of hedging a portfolio, it is helpful to have some idea of how much the *delta* changes as the underlying stock price changes. This can be calculated mathematically by working out the rate of change of *delta* with respect to the underlying stock price, and is called the option *gamma*. The *gamma* is the second partial derivative of the call price with respect to the underlying stock price and can be evaluated by differentiating the Black–Scholes formula twice.

$$gamma = \frac{\partial^2 C}{\partial S^2} = \frac{1}{S\sigma\sqrt{\tau}}\, \Phi'(h) > 0 \qquad (16.16)$$

An option with a high *gamma* is of little use for hedging, since it would involve having to readjust the hedge constantly.

So far, the discussion has centred around some equations which do not look particularly friendly. It is helpful at this stage to evaluate the Black–Scholes call formula and associated sensitivities using a particular example.

Example 16.3

Recall from Example 16.2 that Midwest stock is currently trading at 148p. Calculate the theoretical call option price using the Black–Scholes model for an option due to expire in 180 days if there are no dividends payable from now until expiry and

(a) the exercise price is 150p;
(b) the risk-free interest rate is 10% per annum payable continuously;
(c) volatility is estimated to be 30%.

(These are the same option specifications as for Example 16.2, to enable a comparison to be made between the Black–Scholes and Binomial models.)

Also, calculate the associated sensitivities, including *gamma*.

Answer

The five parameter values needed are

$$S_t = 148\text{p}, \qquad X = 150\text{p}, \qquad \tau = \frac{180}{365}\ \text{years}, \qquad r = 0.10, \qquad \sigma = 0.30$$

It follows that

$$\sigma\sqrt{\tau} = 0.21067407$$

$$e^{-r\tau} = 0.95188117$$

giving

$$h = 0.27570470$$

$$h - \sigma\sqrt{\tau} = 0.06503063$$

From a table of the cumulative standard normal distribution (or see Section 16.10),

$$\Phi(h) = 0.60861260$$

$$\Phi(h - \sigma\sqrt{\tau}) = 0.52593452$$

Hence the Black–Scholes call price is

$$C = 148(0.60861260) - 150(0.95188117)(0.52593452)$$

$$= 14.98 \text{ pence (2 decimal places)}$$

The call price given by the Binomial model with $n = 25$ was 15.08 pence. It would be even closer to the Black–Scholes call price if n were increased.

Furthermore,

$$delta = \partial C/\partial S \quad = 0.60861260$$

$$\partial C/\partial X \quad = -0.50062717$$

$$theta = \partial C/\partial \tau \quad = 19.650763$$

$$rho = \partial C/\partial r \quad = 37.032694$$

$$kappa = \partial C/\partial \sigma \quad = 39.916786$$

$$gamma = \partial^2 C/\partial S^2 = 0.01231775$$

16.10 COMPUTATIONAL CONSIDERATIONS

In evaluating the Black–Scholes call (or put) formula, perhaps the most difficult part is finding the appropriate values from the cumulative standard normal distribution, $\Phi(\omega)$, where

$$\Phi(\omega) = \int_{-\infty}^{\omega} \frac{1}{\sqrt{2\pi}} e^{-y^2/2} dy$$

Unfortunately, this integral cannot be evaluated analytically. Although values of $\Phi(\omega)$ can be read from statistical tables, this is not satisfactory from a computer programming point of view. However, $\Phi(\omega)$ can be approximated with reasonable accuracy using a polynomial approximation technique. One such technique, for $\omega \geqslant 0$ is given by

$$\Phi(\omega) \simeq 1 - \Phi'(\omega)(ax^3 + bx^2 + cx)$$

where $\quad x = \dfrac{1}{1 + p\omega}$

$p = 0.33267$
$a = 0.9372980$
$b = -0.1201676$
$c = 0.4361836$

$$\Phi'(\omega) = \frac{1}{\sqrt{2\pi}} e^{-\omega^2/2}$$

(This technique is accurate to about four decimal places.)

For values of ω less than zero, the fact that the normal distribution is symmetric can be used. Thus,

$$\Phi(-\omega) = 1 - \Phi(\omega)$$

where $\Phi(\omega)$ is calculated as above (see Abramowitz and Stegun, 1972).

Example 16.4

Use the numerical approximation technique above to evaluate $\Phi(h)$ from Example 16.3.

Answer

From Example 16.3, $h = 0.27570470$. In the equations above, we need to replace ω by h, giving

$$\Phi'(h) = 0.384064383 \quad \text{and} \quad x = 0.915986889$$

Therefore,

$$\Phi(h) = 1 - 0.384064383(0.9372980 \times 0.768542294 - 0.1201676$$

$$\times 0.839031981 + 0.4361836 \times 0.915986889)$$

$$= 0.60861260$$

which is the value of $\Phi(h)$ used in Example 16.3.

16.11   PUT OPTIONS

Assuming there are no dividends payable on the stock prior to maturity, the Black–Scholes put option price, P_t, is given by

$$P_t = Xe^{-r\tau}\Phi(\sigma\sqrt{\tau} - h) - S_t\Phi(-h)$$

where all symbols have been previously defined.

The Black–Scholes put formula is very similar to the call formula, except it appears to be written in reverse and the items in the brackets have been multiplied by -1. Like the call formula, the put formula is a function of only five parameters, S_t, X, τ, r and σ.

As h tends to minus infinity, $\Phi(-h)$ and $\Phi(\sigma\sqrt{\tau} - h)$ both tend to 1, giving

$$P_t \simeq Xe^{-r\tau} - S_t$$

That is, the value of the put is approximately equal to the discounted value of exercise payments less the stock price. In fact, if h is less than about -3, then $P_t \simeq Xe^{-r\tau} - S_t$. This can happen if:

(i) the underlying stock price becomes very low relative to the exercise price (i.e. the put is deep-in-the-money). In this case, $Xe^{-r\tau}$ is greater than S_t and $\log(S_t/Xe^{-r\tau})$ is negative.
(ii) $Xe^{-r\tau} > S_t$ and time to expiry is short.
(iii) $Xe^{-r\tau} > S_t$ and volatility is low.

Before calculating the sensitivities of the Black–Scholes put formula, consider how the put price would be expected to react to changes in the model parameters. As the exercise price rises or the underlying stock price falls, we would expect the put price to rise. As interest rates rise, the present value of exercise payments falls, resulting in a fall in the value of the put. As volatility rises, the probability of a favourable outcome rises (since the downside risk is limited by the value of the put) and we would expect the value of the put to rise. As time to maturity changes, the effect on the value of the put is not clear since there are two effects working in opposite directions. As time to maturity falls, the present value of exercise payments rises, resulting in an increase in the value of the put. However, at the same time, there is a lower chance of a favourable outcome. The dominant effect is not immediately obvious and depends on a number of factors.

The sensitivities of the Black–Scholes put formula, derived mathematically, are shown in Table 16.3. The signs of the sensitivities are in agreement with the earlier

Table 16.3   Sensitivities of the Black–Scholes put formula

Name	Formula[a]	Sign
Delta, Hedge ratio	$\dfrac{\partial P}{\partial S} = -\Phi(-h)$	$-$
	$\dfrac{\partial P}{\partial X} = -e^{-r\tau}\Phi(\sigma\sqrt{\tau} - h)$	$+$
Theta	$\dfrac{\partial P}{\partial \tau} = \dfrac{S\sigma}{2\sqrt{\tau}}\Phi'(h) - Xre^{-r\tau}\Phi(\sigma\sqrt{\tau} - h)$	$+$ or $-$
Rho	$\dfrac{\partial P}{\partial r} = -\tau Xe^{-r\tau}\Phi(\sigma\sqrt{\tau} - h)$	$-$
Kappa, Epsilon, Vega	$\dfrac{\partial P}{\partial \sigma} = S\sqrt{\tau}\Phi'(h)$	$+$
Gamma	$\dfrac{\partial^2 P}{\partial S^2} = \dfrac{1}{S\sigma\sqrt{\tau}}\Phi'(h)$	$+$

discussion. The most frequently quoted of the sensitivities are the *delta* and *gamma*. The put *delta* is usually quoted as a positive number (i.e. without the minus sign). Comparing call and put sensitivities given by the Black–Scholes formula for a given option specification, two interesting observations can be made:

(1) $\dfrac{\partial C}{\partial S} - \dfrac{\partial P}{\partial S} = 1$, i.e. $delta_{call} - delta_{put} = 1$

(2) $\dfrac{\partial^2 C}{\partial S^2} = \dfrac{\partial^2 P}{\partial S^2} = \dfrac{1}{S\sigma\sqrt{\tau}}\Phi'(h)$, i.e. $gamma_{call} = gamma_{put}$

These two relationships can be useful in practice and are a result of the put/call parity relationship which is discussed in section 16.16.

Example 16.5

Recalling the scenario given in Example 16.3, evaluate a put option on Midwest stock using the same option specification and the Black–Scholes put option formula. Also, evaluate the sensitivities given in Table 16.3.

Answer

From Example 16.3:

$$S_t = 148\text{p}, \qquad X = 150\text{p}, \qquad \tau = \frac{180}{365}\ \text{years}, \qquad r = 0.10, \qquad \sigma = 0.30$$

giving

$$\Phi(-h) = 0.39138740$$

$$\Phi(\sigma\sqrt{\tau} - h) = 0.47406548$$

and

$$P = 150(0.95188117)(0.47406548) - 148(0.39138740)$$

$$= \underline{9.76\ \text{pence}}\ \text{(to 2 decimal places)}$$

Further,

$$delta = \frac{\partial P}{\partial S} = -0.39138740$$

$$\frac{\partial P}{\partial X} = 0.45125400$$

$$theta = \frac{\partial P}{\partial \tau} = 5.3725457$$

$$rho = \frac{\partial P}{\partial r} = -33.380433$$

$$kappa = \frac{\partial P}{\partial \sigma} = 39.916786$$

$$gamma = \frac{\partial^2 P}{\partial S^2} = 0.01231775$$

From Example 16.3, we know that $delta_{call} = 0.60861260$ and $gamma_{call} = 0.01231775$, giving

$$delta_{call} - delta_{put} = 1 \quad \text{and} \quad gamma_{call} = gamma_{put}$$

16.12 VOLATILITY

The Black–Scholes model depends on five parameters. Of these, the exercise price and time to expiry are specified by the option contract. The current underlying stock price can easily be obtained from the market.

The *risk-free* rate of interest is the yield on a notional default-free bond of similar duration to the life of the option. There is some degree of choice involved here, although the formula is not particularly sensitive to the rate of interest and a reasonable value for this parameter can easily be chosen. The parameter which presents the most difficulty in its estimation is the volatility of the underlying stock.

Volatility is defined to be the standard deviation of logarithmic stock returns per unit time, where time is measured in years. In the derivation of the Black–Scholes model, volatility is assumed to remain constant over the life of the option. The validity of this assumption is dubious since, in practice, volatility may not remain constant over time. However, what is needed for the Black–Scholes model is an estimate of the volatility over the future life of the option. Typically, the volatility over the life of the option for a particular stock is estimated by measuring the volatility for that stock over the recent past, called the *historic volatility*. The use of historic volatility assumes that past volatility is indicative of future volatility, which may not be the case. However, its use is common and the method of calculation is described in the following section.

16.13 ESTIMATION OF VOLATILITY FROM HISTORICAL DATA

To estimate the historical volatility of a stock price, perform the following six steps:

(1) Record the closing prices of the stock on $N+1$ consecutive days. Label these closing prices $S_1, S_2, ..., S_{N+1}$
(2) Calculate the logarithmic daily return R_i, where

$$R_i = \log\left(\frac{S_{i+1}}{S_i}\right) \qquad i = 1, 2, ..., N$$

(Note: natural logarithms must be used.)

(3) Calculate the average (mean) daily stock return, $\bar{R}$, where

$$\bar{R} = \frac{1}{N} \sum_{i=1}^{N} R_i$$

(4) Calculate the sample variance of logarithmic *daily* stock returns where

$$\text{Sample variance} = \frac{1}{N-1} \sum_{i=1}^{N} (R_i - \bar{R})^2$$

(Note: See Chapter 8 for a discussion of the mean and sample variance.)

(5) Approximate the variance of the logarithmic *annual* stock returns. The variance in step (4) was calculated using daily data. This needs to be annualised by multiplying by the number of days in the year. An important consideration here is whether to use 365, the actual number of days, or 252 (or thereabouts), the number of trading days. Empirical research (see French, 1980) seems to indicate that trading days should be used, and indeed, the number of trading days is normally used in practice. This gives

$$\text{Annualised sample variance} = \frac{252}{N-1} \sum_{i=1}^{N} (R_i - \bar{R})^2$$

(6) Approximate volatility, the standard deviation of logarithmic returns per unit time, by calculating the square root of the annualised sample variance, giving

$$\hat{\sigma} = \sqrt{\frac{252}{N-1} \sum_{i=1}^{N} (R_i - \bar{R})^2}$$

where $\hat{\sigma}$ denotes an estimate of the volatility, σ.

An important consideration is the choice of the size of N used in the calculation. If N is too large, changes in volatility will not be detected quickly; if N is too small, volatility will appear to be erratic and will change too rapidly. A popular choice is $N = 30$, but a more stable estimate can be obtained by increasing the size of N up to 90 or 180.

16.14 IMPLIED VOLATILITY

So far, attention has been focused on calculating a theoretical option price given estimates of a few key parameters. In practice, the market price of an option will often differ from this theoretical price. How can this happen? One reason is that there are factors at work, other than those considered in the derivation of the model, which the model does not allow for. Another reason is that estimates of the key parameters may be unreliable. To rectify the first problem, a better model is needed, but when modelling it is necessary to balance a realistic portrayal with simplicity. The search for a better model could go on *ad infinitum*. The obvious solution to the second problem is to obtain more reliable estimates of the parameters. In the case of volatility, this is far from simple, which has led to the idea of looking at the problem in reverse. That is, find the value of volatility which, when used as an input to the Black–Scholes model, gives a theoretical price which is identical to the market price. The value of volatility implied by the market price is called the *implied* or *implicit* volatility.

Example 16.6

In Example 16.3, a theoretical call price of 14.98 pence was calculated for Midwest stock, with volatility estimated to be 30%. Suppose the market price for the equivalent call is 17 pence. What is the volatility implied by this market price?

Answer

By trial and error, the theoretical call price is 17 pence when a value of volatility equal to 35.05% is used in Example 16.3. Therefore, the market implied volatility for Midwest stock is 35.05%.

Many practitioners find it informative to calculate implied volatilities, and some make trading decisions based on implied volatility computer programs. For each stock, a range of implied volatilities can be computed based on the call and put prices for different exercise prices and durations to maturity. These can be combined using various techniques to arrive at an overall measure of market implied volatility for the particular stock under consideration. The results of a study comparing various alternative weighting schemes for calculating market implied volatilities have been published by Beckers (1981).

16.15 PUT/CALL PARITY

It is possible to derive relationships between prices of call and put options on the same underlying security with the same exercise price and maturity date. The relationships are known as put/call parity relationships. The exact form depends on whether dividends are payable on the underlying security over the life of the option.

Excel Application 16.1

Most of the parameters (namely, the risk-free rate of return, the strike price of the option, the current price of the underlying asset and the term to expiry) associated with the Black–Scholes formula can be observed directly in the market. However, the volatility is not directly observable.

In some cases it may be estimated by taking the standard deviation of the asset price over an historical time period, say, 30 days, and using that estimate. However, because options are traded, their prices are observable and it is possible to infer what the volatility must have been, assuming that the Black–Scholes model is correct. One can then use the volatility estimated from other options already traded in the market to price a new option.

Because the Black–Scholes pricing formula is rather a complicated function of the volatility, it is not possible in general to find an exact analytical solution and we have to use numerical methods.

Excel provides a useful function ("Goal Seek") that does just that. As an illustration, consider a European call option with strike price 105, term to expiry of six months, a risk-free rate of return of 5% per annum (continuously compounded) and assume that the current price of the underlying asset is 100. We shall assume that the option is priced in the market at 2.5.

The process involves setting up the Black–Scholes formula in a cell on a spreadsheet and then letting Excel search for the value of the volatility that makes the Black–Scholes price equal to the observed market price of 2.5. Then, assuming that the Black–Scholes model is correct, we will have an estimate of the volatility. Enter a "guess" for the volatility, say 10%, although any value will do, in cell B2. Enter the risk-free rate of 5% in cell B3; the time to expiry of 0.5 in cell B4; the current price of 100 in cell B5 and the strike price of 105 in cell B6.

In cell D3, enter the formula for "h", i.e.

=(LN(B5/B6) + (B3 + B2^2/2)*B4)/(B2*SQRT(B4)) and in cell E3, the formula for "$h - \sigma\sqrt{\tau}$", i.e. = D3 − B2*SQRT(B4).

The Black–Scholes formula, =B5*NORMSDIST(D3) − B6*EXP(−B3*B4)* NORMSDIST(E3) is entered in cell F3. Note that we have used the Excel function "NORMSDIST" to calculate the distribution function for the standard normal distribution.

The value displayed in cell F3 (if you have used a volatility guess of 10%) should be 1.8105. This value is lower than the market price of 2.5 and indicates that our guess of 10% for the volatility is too low. However, rather than use trial and error to find the correct value, we use the \Tools\Goal Seek drop down menu. This should bring up a dialogue box where you enter three elements: (1) the "Set Cell" should be entered as F3, (2) the "to value" should be entered as 2.5 and (3) the "by changing cell" should be entered as B2. Click on OK. In a very short period of time, the dialogue box should change to show that it has found a value and the number in cell B2 (the volatility) should have changed to 12.53%. This is the market-implied volatility.

According to the Black–Scholes assumptions, all options priced on the same underlying asset should be associated with the same market-implied volatility. However, in practice, the implied volatilities differ significantly for options of different strikes and terms to expiry. Extending the Black–Scholes model to allow for these variations in implied volatility is the subject of much current research.

For European-style options, with no dividends payable on the underlying security over the life of the option, the put/call parity relationship is given by

$$C_t = P_t + S_t - Xe^{-r\tau} \tag{16.17}$$

Equation (16.17) is important because it shows how to duplicate a call by buying one put option and one security, and financing this by borrowing $Xe^{-r\tau}$ at the risk-free rate. The cash flows of the call are created synthetically using the other securities. Equation (16.17) also shows how to find the price of the put given the price of the call (and vice versa). It is a theoretical relationship which is independent of the underlying price model used and is therefore valid for the Black–Scholes and Binomial models. However, the put/call parity relationship, as stated in equation (16.17), does not take into account transaction costs or the bid/offer spread and will not be strictly valid using market prices of calls and puts.

Example 16.7

Verify numerically that the put/call parity relationship as stated in equation (16.17) is valid for the Black–Scholes model, using the results of Examples 16.3 and 16.5.

Answer

From Example 16.3:

$$S_t = 148, \qquad C_t = 14.98, \qquad Xe^{-r\tau} = 142.78$$

Rearranging equation (16.17) gives

$$P_t = C_t - S_t + Xe^{-r\tau}$$
$$= 14.98 - 148 + 142.78$$
$$= 9.76$$

which is the same as the value of the put given by Example 16.5. Hence, the put/call parity relationship (equation (16.17)) is valid for the Black–Scholes model.

Example 16.8

Verify that the put/call parity relationship as stated in equation (16.17) is valid for the Binomial model, using the results of Example 16.2.

Answer

From Example 16.2:

$$S_t = 148, \qquad C_t = 15.08, \qquad Xe^{r\tau} = 142.78$$

Rearranging equation (16.17) gives

$$P_t = C_t - S_t + Xe^{-r\tau}$$
$$= 15.08 - 148 + 142.78$$
$$= 9.86$$

which is the same as the value of the put given by Example 16.2. Hence, the put/call parity relationship (equation (16.17)) is valid for the Binomial model.

16.16   ADJUSTMENTS FOR KNOWN DIVIDENDS

So far, we have assumed that there are no dividends payable on the underlying security over the life of the option. In practice, this assumption is unrealistic. However, it is possible to adapt the Black–Scholes and Binomial models to accommodate dividends.

The simplest approach is to assume that there are a finite number of known dividends due to be paid on the underlying security over the life of the option. As traded options typically have a maximum duration of nine months, this assumption is not unrealistic. Furthermore, it is unlikely that there will be more than two dividends paid over the life of the option. Assume there are two dividends d_1 and d_2 payable over the life of the option with ex-dividend dates t_1 and t_2 respectively. Dividends are allowed for in the Black–Scholes and Binomial models by replacing the current stock price, S_t, by S_t^* where S_t^* is the current stock price less the discounted value of known future dividends payable over the life of the option. That is,

$$S_t^* = S_t - d_1 e^{-r\tau_1} - d_2 e^{-r\tau_2} \qquad (16.18)$$

where $\tau_1 = t_1 - t$
$\tau_2 = t_2 - t$
$r = $ risk-free interest rate

This approach is justifiable since the holder of a European-style option will not receive dividends payable on the underlying security over the life of the option. According to equation (16.18), the stock price falls by the exact amount of the dividend as the stock goes ex-dividend. In practice, however, the stock price usually falls by less than the full amount of the dividend; typically the stock price falls by around 80% of the dividend. This effect is usually attributed to taxation. Some practitioners, therefore, reduce the stock price by the present value of the expected fall in the stock price on the ex-dividend date (e.g. $0.8d_i$).

The extension to more than two dividends payable over the life of the option is obvious. It is important to remember that a dividend is included in calculations only if its ex-dividend date occurs during the life of the option.

Example 16.9

KGB stock is currently trading at 250 pence. Calculate the theoretical call and put prices using the Black–Scholes model for an option due to expire in 250 days if there are two dividends payable, the first being 6 pence per share after 30 days and the second being $6\frac{1}{2}$ pence per share after 210 days. The exercise price is 245 pence and assume also that the risk-free interest rate is 10% per annum payable continuously and that volatility is 30%.

Answer

The parameter values are

$$S_t = 250, \qquad X = 245, \qquad \tau = 250 \text{ days} = \frac{250}{365} \text{ years}, \qquad r = 0.1, \qquad \sigma = 0.30$$

$$d_1 = 6, \qquad \tau_1 = 30 \text{ days} = \frac{30}{365} \text{ years}, \qquad d_2 = 6.5, \qquad \tau_2 = 210 \text{ days} = \frac{210}{365} \text{ years}$$

It follows that

$$e^{-r\tau_1} = 0.991814507$$

$$e^{-r\tau_2} = 0.944089558$$

$$S_t^* = 250 - 6(0.991814507) - 6.5(0.944089558) = 237.9125308$$

$$h = 0.281776416, \qquad \Phi(h) = 0.610942063, \qquad \Phi(-h) = 0.389057937$$

$$h - \sigma\sqrt{\tau} = 0.033494650, \qquad \Phi(h - \sigma\sqrt{\tau}) = 0.513366121,$$

$$\Phi(\sigma\sqrt{\tau} - h) = 0.486633879, \qquad e^{-r\tau} = 0.933799856$$

giving

$$C_t = 237.9125308(0.610942063) - 245(0.933799856)(0.51366121)$$

$$= 27.90 \text{ (to 2 decimal places)}$$

and

$$P_t = 245(0.933799856)(0.48663879) - 237.9125308(0.389057937)$$

$$= 18.77 \text{ (to 2 decimal places)}$$

Therefore, the call and put prices given by the Black–Scholes model are 27.90 pence and 18.77 pence respectively.

Example 16.10

Using the scenario set out in Example 16.9, calculate the equivalent call and put prices given by the Binomial model, with $n = 25$.

Answer

$$S_t^* = 237.9125308, \qquad X = 245, \qquad e^{-r\tau} = 0.933799856$$

$$r = 0.1, \qquad \sigma = 0.3, \qquad \tau = \frac{250}{365}, \qquad n = 25$$

giving

$$u = 0.051163 \qquad v = -0.04814 \qquad p = 0.5$$

The intermediate calculations are shown in the body of Table 16.4. Values are shown to three decimal places. The values in columns (1) to (6) refer to various parts of the intermediate calculations, specified as follows:

Column	Calculation
(1)	${}^nC_j p^j (1-p)^{n-j}$
(2)	$S_t^* e^{ju + (n-j)v}$
(3)	$\max\{0, S_t^* e^{ju + (n-j)v} - X\}$
(4)	$\max\{0, X - S_t^* e^{ju + (n-j)v}\}$
(5)	Columns (1) × (3)
(6)	Columns (1) × (4)

Table 16.4

(1)	(2)	(3)	(4)	(5)	(6)
0.000	71.391	0.000	173.609	0.000	0.000
0.000	78.845	0.000	166.155	0.000	0.000
0.000	87.077	0.000	157.923	0.000	0.001
0.000	96.169	0.000	148.831	0.000	0.010
0.000	106.210	0.000	138.790	0.000	0.052
0.002	117.299	0.000	127.701	0.000	0.202
0.005	129.547	0.000	115.453	0.000	0.609
0.014	143.073	0.000	101.927	0.000	1.460
0.032	158.011	0.000	86.989	0.000	2.804
0.061	174.510	0.000	70.490	0.000	4.292
0.097	192.730	0.000	52.270	0.000	5.092
0.133	212.854	0.000	32.146	0.000	4.270
0.155	235.078	0.000	9.922	0.000	1.538
0.155	259.623	14.623	0.000	2.266	0.000
0.133	286.731	41.731	0.000	5.544	0.000
0.097	316.669	71.669	0.000	6.982	0.000
0.061	349.733	104.733	0.000	6.377	0.000
0.032	386.249	141.249	0.000	4.553	0.000
0.014	426.578	181.578	0.000	2.601	0.000
0.005	471.117	226.117	0.000	1.193	0.000
0.002	520.307	275.307	0.000	0.436	0.000
0.000	574.633	329.633	0.000	0.124	0.000
0.000	634.632	389.632	0.000	0.027	0.000
0.000	700.895	455.895	0.000	0.004	0.000
0.000	774.076	529.076	0.000	0.000	0.000
0.000	854.899	609.899	0.000	0.000	0.000
			Total	30.107	20.332

It follows that

$$C_t = 0.933799856(30.107)$$

$$= 28.11 \text{ (to 2 decimal places)}$$

and

$$P_t = 0.933799856(20.332)$$

$$= 18.99 \text{ (to 2 decimal places)}$$

Therefore, the call and put prices given by the Binomial model are 28.11 pence and 18.99 pence respectively. These results are very close to the results given by the Black–Scholes model.

16.17 PUT/CALL PARITY WITH KNOWN DIVIDENDS

The put/call parity relationship can be restated to accommodate dividends payable on the stock over the life of the option. For European-style options, this relationship is given by

$$C_t = P_t + (S_t - d_1 e^{-rT_1} - d_2 e^{-rT_2}) - X e^{-rT} \qquad (16.19)$$

S_t in equation (16.17) has been replaced by S_t^* to arrive at the relationship above. That is, the stock price is reduced by the present value of dividends payable over the life of the option. Equation (16.19) is a general form of the put/call parity relationship for European style options. If there are no dividends payable on the stock over the life of the option (i.e. $d_1 = d_2 = 0$) then equation (16.19) reduces to equation (16.17).

Example 16.11

Verify numerically that the put/call parity relationship, as stated in equation (16.19), is valid for the Black–Scholes model using the results from Example 16.9.

Answer

Rearranging equation (16.19),

$$P_t = C_t - (S_t - d_1 e^{-rT_1} - d_2 e^{-rT_2}) + X e^{-rT}$$
$$= 27.90 - 237.9125308 + 245(0.933799856)$$
$$= 18.77 \text{ (2 decimal places)}$$

which is the same as the value of the put given by Example 16.9. Thus the put/call parity relationship in equation (16.19) is valid for the Black–Scholes model.

Example 16.12

Verify numerically that the put/call parity relationship, as stated in equation (16.19), is valid for the Binomial model using the results from Example 16.10.

Answer

Rearranging equation (16.19),

$$P_t = C_t - (S_t - d_1 e^{-rT_1} - d_2 e^{-rT_2}) + X e^{-rT}$$
$$= 28.11 - 237.9125308 + 245(0.933799856)$$
$$= 18.98 \text{ (2 decimal places)}$$

which is the same as the value of the put given by Example 16.10 (the discrepancy of 0.01p is simply due to rounding). Thus the put/call parity relationship in equation (16.19) is valid for the Binomial model.

16.18   AMERICAN-STYLE OPTIONS

With American-style options, the holder of the option has the right to exercise the option at any time prior to expiry. This additional flexibility can create difficulties in valuing the option correctly.

With call options, in the absence of dividends payable on the underlying stock over the life of the option, it can be shown that it is never optimal to exercise the option prior to expiry. Therefore, the option can be valued as if it is a European-style option. When dividends are payable on the underlying stock over the life of the option, it can be shown that it is only ever optimal to exercise the option immediately before the stock goes ex-dividend. This led Black to suggest an approximate procedure for taking account of the early exercise provision of American-style options. The method involves calculating the prices of European options that mature at each of the ex-dividend dates and the expiry date, and then setting the price of the American option equal to the maximum of these values. The procedure is explained in Black (1975).

A more complicated but more exact procedure for evaluating American-style call options has been suggested by Roll and discussed by Geske and Whaley. The model is more difficult to implement and considerably more difficult to interpret than the Black–Scholes model. The interested reader is referred to Roll (1977), Geske (1979, 1981), and Whaley (1981).

Empirical research (Whaley, 1982) has shown that these two alternative approaches for the valuation of American-style options rarely give prices which are very different from the value of the equivalent European-style option. Many practitioners, therefore, are happy to omit the additional computations involved in calculating the value of the American call, and simply use the value of the equivalent European call as an approximation.

It is possible that early exercise of American-style put options may well be optimal on a dividend-paying or non-dividend-paying stock. Unfortunately, there is no known analytic model for the correct valuation of American-style put options. The value of the equivalent European-style put is often used as an approximation, although this will tend to undervalue American-style puts since the additional flexibility of the early exercise provision will generally attract a higher price.

16.19   OPTION TRADING STRATEGIES

Options are used in a variety of ways. Sometimes they are used as stand-alone speculative investments by the investor to try to take advantage of some supposed insight into how the underlying asset might change in value. Another common use of options is in hedging out particular types of risk. The most common example in this area is the purchase of a put option on the underlying asset in conjunction with holding the asset. If the asset increases in value, the investor sacrifices the cost of the put, but enjoys the increased value of the asset. If the asset drops in value, the put option gives the investor the right to recover his or her capital. This strategy is sometimes referred to as portfolio insurance.

In this section we shall look very briefly at yet another possibility, namely option trading strategies where various "basic" options are used in combination. These combinations attempt either to take advantage of a less direct insight that the investor thinks that they have, or to hedge a particular type of risk that the investor does not want to bear. For example, during a particularly uncertain time in the markets, an investor may want to trade on the belief that the market will be volatile and will move sharply either up or down. If the investor simply holds assets in the market then clearly they will make money only if the market moves up. Conversely, if the investor sells assets to another investor now and agrees to buy them back at the ruling market price at some future date, then they will make money only if the market falls. However, with options an investor can construct a trading strategy that will make them money provided that the market moves sharply one way or the other.

Some option trading strategies are sufficiently common to have names. The particular strategy needed to take advantage of the belief that markets will move sharply either up or down is a *long straddle*. In a long straddle, the investor buys two options, one put and one call, both at the same exercise price. Each of the two options will cost the investor money to buy. If the share price moves above the exercise price, then the investor will exercise the call option (and forfeit the put option) and buy the share at the exercise price. They can then sell the share at the ruling market price and lock in a profit. If the share price falls, then the investor has the right to sell the share at the exercise price. They could buy the share in the market at the lower price and sell it on immediately at the exercise price and so lock in a profit.

Clearly, though, the "profit" has to be larger than the cost of the two options in order for it to be a genuine gain.

Example 16.13

An investor buys a put and a call on an asset currently trading at £100, both with exercise prices of £100, for a total cost of £5. Analyse the payoff to the investor at the date of exercise.

Answer

The price of the share will need to move by at least the cost of the options above or below the exercise price in order for the investor to make a profit. If the strike price is £100 and the share moves over £105, say £107, then the call option will be worth £7 (and the put option will be worth nothing) and the total strategy will net a profit of £7 − £5 = £2. If the share price drops below £95 to, say, £90, then the put option will be worth £10 (and the call option will be worth nothing) and the net profit from the strategy will be £10 − £5 = £5. If the share price is between £95 and £100, say £97, the investor will make the £3 from the put option (and nothing from the call options) less the cost of the options, i.e. a net loss of £2.

Holding a long straddle is a bet that the market will move significantly, either up or down, but will not stay close to current levels. In the jargon of option strategies, it is a volatility play.

An investor who believes the converse, that is, that the market will drift sideways and will not move sharply up or down, could enter a *short straddle*. This investor would sell the call option and the put option. The premium income from selling the options would usually be larger than the profit or loss associated with paying the owners of the call or put option if the market moves only a small way from its exercise price. On the other hand, if the market does move a long way then the investor can stand to lose (virtually) unlimited amounts of money, particularly if the share price shoots up and the investor does not own the share.

These strategies are illustrated in Figure 16.2, where the profit or loss is shown at the expiry date of the options.

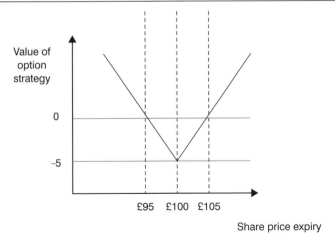

Figure 16.2   Payoff diagram

A fairly common variation on the long straddle is the *long strap*. In addition to that put and the call, the investor also buys a second call. The initial cost of this strategy will be higher than the straddle. However, if the share price increases, then the investor will stand to make a profit at a fast rate.

Example 16.14

Suppose that an investor buys three options on a share trading at £100 for a cost of £7.50, two calls and one put with a strike of £100. Analyse the payoff structure of the strap compared with the straddle.

Answer

If the share price increases to £105, then the investor will make £5 from each of the two call options (and the put option will expire worthless) thereby making a gain of £10 − £7.50 = £2.50. The conventional straddle would have just broken even (£5 gain from the call option, nothing from the put option and less the initial cost of £5 for the two options). Of course, if the market falls, then it will have to fall by at least £7.50, before the put option will generate a net profit. The long strap is therefore a "tilted" straddle. The investor is still betting on the market being volatile, but believes that it is more likely to be volatile "upwards" than "downwards".

The bearish parallel to the strap is the *strip*; this involves purchasing two puts and one call.
   A *strangle* can be thought of as a stretched version of the straddle. The idea is the same, the investor is wanting to make a volatility play, but finds that the straddle is too expensive. In order to reduce cost, the investor might purchase an out of the money call and an out of the money put.

Example 16.15

An investor buys a call option on a share currently trading at £100 at a strike price of £103 and a put option at a strike price of £97 for a total cost of £3. Explain when the investor will make a profit and compare with the straddle.

Answer

If the price of the asset remained at its initial level of £100, then both options would expire worthless and the investor would be out of pocket by the cost of the two options. The share price now has to move above £106, or below £94 in order for the strangle to generate a profit. The worst off that the investor can be is £3 down, compared with £5 down in the case of the straddle. See Figure 16.3.

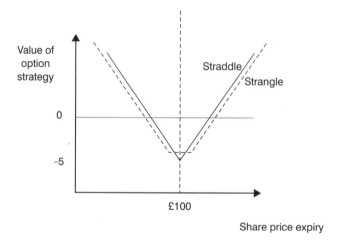

Figure 16.3 Payoff diagram with straddle and strangle

Spreads are also popular option strategies. These involve a directional call on the market (jargon for believing that the market will move in a particular direction, up or down) rather than a volatility play. The idea in a spread is that the investor will buy some protection (in case they have called the market incorrectly), but will help offset the cost of the protection by giving away the upper end of their potential profits.

For example, an investor believes that the market will go up. One way of acting on this is to buy a call option. If the market goes up, then the investor can exercise the call option and secure a profit. If the market goes down, then the investor will simply not exercise the option and will just lose the cost of the option. However, the cost of the option can be quite high and some investors will reckon it to be worthwhile to give up any profits that might arise if the market goes up extremely high in order to offset the cost of the call option. The strategy is therefore to buy one call that takes advantage of any modest upward moves in the market, but sell a call at a high strike price. This particular option is sometimes referred to as a bull spread.

Example 16.16

The current price of an asset is £100 and an investor buys one call option at a strike price of £100 for £5 and sells a call option at a strike price of £120 for a premium of £1.50. Analyse the payoff of the strategy for the investor.

Answer

If the market moves anywhere between £100 and £120, the investor will exercise the first option and secure a profit of the upward move less the net cost of the options. If the price of the asset were £110 at expiry, then the net profit to the investor would be £110 − £100 − £5 + £1.50 = £6.50. If the asset price fell anywhere below £100, both call options would be worthless and the investor's loss would be £5 − £1.50 = £3.50. If the price of the asset rose above £120, then the investor would of course exercise their option. However, the call option that the investor had sold would also be exercised and the investor would effectively have to pay out any profit above £120. So, for example, if the asset price rose to £126, then the investor would make £26 − £3.50 = £22.50 but would then owe £126 − £120 = £6 to the other investor. In this way, the total profit to the first investor would be £22.50 − £6 = £16.50. Figure 16.4 illustrates this and compares it with the payoff from a simple long call strategy.

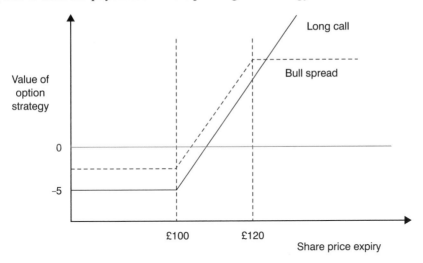

Figure 16.4 Payoff diagram with long call and bull spread

The converse of a bull spread is a bear spread. In this case the investor sells a call at a low exercise price and buys a call at a high exercise price. The idea here is that investors will gain a higher premium from the call they sell than the cost of the call they buy. The sold call is at a lower exercise price and hence is more likely to be exercised and so is more valuable to the purchaser. If the market moves down, both calls expire worthless and the investor pockets the premium difference. If the market moves up above the lower of the two exercise prices, then of course the investor will start to lose money. However, that loss is capped in the sense that if the price goes above the higher of the two exercise prices then they can exercise the second option.

The payoff diagram for a bear spread is given in Figure 16.5.

Figure 16.5   Payoff diagram for a bear spread

If we combine a bull spread with a bear spread, then we get a butterfly spread. A butterfly spread produces a small profit if the share price does not move much, much the same way as a short straddle. The difference between the short straddle and the butterfly spread is that significant moves in the market will result in significant losses for the holder of short straddle, but only a small capped loss for the holder of a butterfly.

The payoff diagram for a butterfly spread compared with a short straddle is given in Figure 16.6.

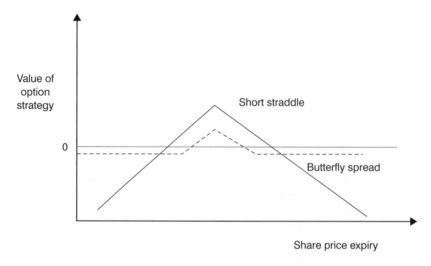

Figure 16.6   Payoff diagram with butterfly spread

16.20   STOCK INDEX OPTIONS

Traded options are available on several stock indices, for example the FT-SE 100, S&P 100, S&P 500 and NYSE indices. Options on a particular index may be European or American-style, occasionally both. All index options are cash settled. Assuming that returns on the index follow the lognormal process described in Section 16.8, the index options formulae using the Black–Scholes model are

$$C_t = I_t^* \Phi(h) - Xe^{-r\tau}(h - \sigma\sqrt{\tau}) \qquad (16.20)$$

$$P_t = Xe^{-r\tau}\Phi(\sigma\sqrt{\tau} - h) - I_t^* \Phi(-h) \qquad (16.21)$$

where $h = \dfrac{\log(I_t^*/Xe^{-r\tau})}{\sigma\sqrt{\tau}} + \dfrac{1}{2}\sigma\sqrt{\tau}$

$I_t^* = I_t e^{-y\tau}$
I_t = current index level
y = annual dividend yield (payable continuously)
X = exercise price
τ = time to expiry
r = risk-free rate of interest
σ = volatility = standard deviation of logarithmic index returns per unit time
$\Phi(\omega)$ = cumulative standard normal distribution

It will be noticed that equations (16.20) and (16.21) are very similar to the Black–Scholes formulae for stock options after allowing for dividends paid over the life of the option. It is assumed that the ex-dividend dates of stocks underlying the index are uniformly distributed over the calendar year. Strictly, equations (16.20) and (16.21) are only valid for European-style options and will tend to undervalue American-style options.

16.21   BOND OPTIONS

Options are available on a variety of specific government bonds. Like index options, it is a simple matter to apply the Black–Scholes model and derive theoretical pricing models for bond options. If there are no coupon payments due to be received over the life of the option, then the bond option call and put prices are given by

$$C_t = B_t \Phi(h) - Xe^{-r\tau}\Phi(h - \sigma\sqrt{\tau}) \qquad (16.22)$$

$$P_t = Xe^{-r\tau}\Phi(\sigma\sqrt{\tau} - h) - B_t \Phi(-h) \qquad (16.23)$$

where $h = \dfrac{\log(B_t/Xe^{-r\tau})}{\sigma\sqrt{\tau}} + \dfrac{1}{2}\sigma\sqrt{\tau}$

B_t = current bond price
X = exercise price
τ = time to expiry
r = risk-free rate of interest
σ = volatility of bond price
$\Phi(\omega)$ = cumulative standard normal distribution

If coupon payments are due to be received over the life of the option, then reduce B_t by the present value of coupon payments before applying equations (16.22) and (16.23). Therefore, coupon payments are treated in the same way as dividend payments for stock options.

The Black–Scholes model assumes that volatility is constant over the life of the option. Since the price of a bond equals its face value at the maturity date of the bond, bond price volatility falls with the passage of time. The bond price volatility tends to zero as the maturity date of the bond is approached. Therefore, the Black–Scholes model for bond options should only be used when the remaining life of the bond is much greater than the life of the option.

16.22 FUTURES OPTIONS

Futures options, as their name implies, are options on futures contracts. Options are available on an array of commodity and financial futures. In Chapter 7, it was shown that a general formula for the futures price of an asset is $F = S(1 + i)^\tau$. Using a continuously compounded rate of interest, $(1 + i) = e^r$, therefore,

$$F = Se^{r\tau}$$

where F is the futures price and S is the price of the underlying asset. Rearranging gives $S = Fe^{-r\tau}$.

Putting this expression for S into the Black–Scholes model gives

$$C_t = e^{-r\tau}[F_t \Phi(h) - X \Phi(h - \sigma\sqrt{\tau})] \qquad (16.24)$$

$$P_t = e^{-r\tau}[X \Phi(\sigma\sqrt{\tau} - h) - F_t \Phi(-h)] \qquad (16.25)$$

where
$$h = \frac{\log(F_t/X)}{\sigma\sqrt{\tau}} + \frac{1}{2}\sigma\sqrt{\tau}$$

F_t = spot futures price
X = exercise price
τ = time to expiry
r = risk-free rate of interest
σ = volatility of the asset underlying the futures contract
$\Phi(\omega)$ = cumulative standard normal distribution

Equations (16.24) and (16.25) form what is known as the Black model, since they were formally derived by Black in 1976.

16.23 CURRENCY OPTIONS

An investment in a foreign currency is equivalent to a security providing a known dividend yield, where the dividend yield is the risk-free rate of interest in the foreign currency. This is because interest earned on a foreign currency is denominated in the foreign currency. Currency options are evaluated using the Black–Scholes model adjusted for dividends. With stock options, the underlying asset was reduced by the discounted value of dividends. In this case, it is assumed that the underlying asset pays a known dividend yield, rather than discrete dividends. The underlying asset is the currency rate and the dividend yield is the risk-free rate of interest in the foreign currency. Then

$$S_t^* = S_t e^{-r_f \tau} \qquad (16.26)$$

where S_t = spot exchange rate
r_f = risk-free rate of interest in the foreign currency

Using equation (16.26) in conjunction with the Black–Scholes model gives

$$C_t = S_t^* \Phi(h) - X e^{-r\tau} \Phi(h - \sigma\sqrt{\tau}) \qquad (16.27)$$

$$P_t = X e^{-r\tau} \Phi(\sigma\sqrt{\tau} - h) - S_t^* \Phi(-h) \qquad (16.28)$$

where $h = \dfrac{\log(S_t^*/X e^{-r\tau})}{\sigma\sqrt{\tau}} + \dfrac{1}{2}\sigma\sqrt{\tau}$

$S_t^* = S_t e^{-r_f \tau}$
X = exercise price
τ = time to expiry
r = risk-free rate of interest in the domestic currency
σ = volatility of the exchange rate
$\Phi(\omega)$ = cumulative standard normal distribution

16.24   EXOTIC OPTIONS

The options that we have considered in this chapter are referred to as "vanilla" options. Investment banks and other providers now sell a range of very complex derivative products that enable a wide variety of risks to be hedged, or speculative investment positions taken. The payoff of some options will not depend on the price of the asset at the time at which the option is exercised, but rather at the highest price (or lowest price, or average price) at which the asset traded during the term of the contract. Some options depend on the price movements of more than one asset class. For example, a call option may only become exercisable on asset A if the price of asset B has fallen below a certain level. These options are sometimes referred to as exotics. From a technical perspective, pricing these options is very demanding and they are not normally traded on exchanges, but rather traded over the counter through investment banks.

The pricing and management of the risks associated with offering exotics currently demand a vast amount of resources, typically mathematically skilled individuals with the ability to implement their analyses on fast computers.

Annex 16.1   The heuristic derivation of the Black–Scholes model

The first step is to derive a useful result which is needed later. From the discussion of the stock price model in Section 16.8:

$$S_{t+\Delta t} = S_t \exp(\mu\Delta t + \sigma\sqrt{\Delta t}Z)$$

Taking expectations,

$$E[S_{t+\Delta t}] = S_t E[\exp(\mu \Delta t + \sigma \sqrt{\Delta t} Z)]$$

$$= S_t \exp(\mu \Delta t) E[\exp(\sigma \sqrt{\Delta t} Z)]$$

$$= S_t \exp[(\mu + \tfrac{1}{2}\sigma^2)\Delta t]$$

This last step is justified by using a standard statistical result based on *moment-generating functions* where the moment-generating function for a random variable X is defined to be $E[e^{tX}]$. For a normal random variable with mean $= 0$ and variance $= 1$, $E[e^{tX}] = \exp(t^2/2)$. It follows that $E[\exp(\sigma \sqrt{\Delta t} Z)] = \exp(\tfrac{1}{2}\sigma^2 \Delta t)$ after substituting $t = \sigma \sqrt{\Delta t}$ and recognising that Z represents a normal random variable with mean zero and standard deviation 1. Then,

$$E\left[\frac{S_{t+\Delta t}}{S_t}\right] = \exp[(\mu + \tfrac{1}{2}\sigma^2)\Delta t] \tag{A16.1}$$

However, we also know that

$$E\left[\frac{S_{t+\Delta t}}{S_t}\right] = \exp(r\Delta t) \tag{A16.2}$$

since, in a risk-neutral economy, all assets yield the risk-free rate of interest. Equating (A16.1) and (A16.2) gives

$$r = \mu + \tfrac{1}{2}\sigma^2 \tag{A16.3}$$

In the risk-neutral economy all assets return the risk-free rate, therefore

$$C_t = e^{-r\tau} E[C_T] \tag{A16.4}$$

and

$$S_t = e^{-r\tau} E[S_T]$$

That is, the value of the call at time t is equal to the value of the call at expiry, T, discounted at the risk-free rate and the value of the stock at time t is equal to the value of the stock at expiry discounted at the risk-free rate.

At expiry there are two possible outcomes, either the stock price is greater than the exercise price (the option is in-the-money) or the stock price is less than or equal to the exercise price (the option is out-of-the-money or at-the-money).

$$C_T = S_T - X \qquad S_T > X$$

$$= 0 \qquad S_T \leqslant X$$

i.e.

$$C_T = \max\{0, S_T - X\}$$

Substituting this expression into equation (A16.4) gives

$$C_t = e^{-r\tau} E[\max\{0, S_T - X\}] \tag{A16.5}$$

If equation (A16.5) can be evaluated, the value of the call at time t has been found.

The next step is to evaluate equation (A16.5) in conjunction with the stock price model as expressed in equation (16.14). From equation (A16.5):

$$C_t = E[\max\{0, S_T - X\}]e^{-r\tau}$$

This can be written

$$C_t = e^{-r\tau} \cdot 0 \cdot P(S_T \leqslant X) + e^{-r\tau} \cdot E[S_T - X \mid S_T > X] \cdot P(S_T > X)$$

where the expression $E[S_T - X \mid S_T > X]$ is the statistical notation for the statement "the expected value of $S_T - X$ conditional on S_T being greater than X". Therefore,

$$C_t = e^{-r\tau} \cdot E[S_T \mid S_T > X] \cdot P(S_T > X) - Xe^{-r\tau} \cdot P(S_T > X) \tag{A16.6}$$

Already this is beginning to resemble the Black–Scholes call formula. The final step is to evaluate $P(S_T > X)$ and $E[S_T \mid S_T > X]P(S_T > X)$. Using equation (16.14),

$$P(S_T > X) = P(S_t \exp[\mu\tau + \sigma\sqrt{\tau}Z] > X)$$

$$= P\left(Z < \frac{\log(S_t/X) + \mu\tau}{\sigma\sqrt{\tau}}\right)$$

$$= \Phi\left\{\frac{\log(S_t/X) + \mu\tau}{\sigma\sqrt{\tau}}\right\}$$

since $Z \sim N(0, 1)$.

From equation (A16.3), $\mu = r - \frac{1}{2}\sigma^2$, therefore

$$P(S_T > X) = \Phi(h - \sigma\sqrt{\tau}) \tag{A16.7}$$

where

$$h = \frac{\log(S_t/Xe^{-r\tau})}{\sigma\sqrt{\tau}} + \frac{1}{2}\sigma\sqrt{\tau}$$

Turn now to the remaining expression, $E[S_T \mid S_T > X]P(S_T > X)$. Written in integral form, this expression becomes.

$$I = P(S_T > X) \int_{y=X}^{y=\infty} S_T \cdot P(S_T = y \mid S_T > X)\, dy$$

where

$$I = E[S_T \mid S_T > X]P(S_T > X)$$

Using Bayes' theorem (discussed in Chapter 8),

$$I = P(S_T > X) \int_{y=X}^{y=\infty} S_T \cdot \frac{P(S_T = y)}{P(S_T > X)} \, dy$$

$$= \int_{y=X}^{y=\infty} S_T \cdot P(S_T = y) \, dy$$

after cancellation. Invoking equation (16.14),

$$I = \int_{y=X}^{y=\infty} S_t \exp(\mu\tau + \mu\sqrt{\tau}z) \cdot P(S_t \exp(\mu\tau + \sigma\sqrt{\tau}z) = y) \, dy$$

It will be noticed that integration is over the range of y, which represents the stock price at expiry. However, for each value of y from X to infinity, there is an equivalent value of z for which

$$S_t \exp(\mu\tau + \sigma\sqrt{\tau}z) = y \qquad (A16.8)$$

It is more convenient to think of evaluating the integral over the range of z, since the probability distribution of z has a simple form. If we are to do this, we need to make adjustments to the range of integration. From equation (A16.8),

$$z = \frac{-[\log(S_t/y) + \mu\sqrt{\tau}]}{\sigma\sqrt{\tau}}$$

When $y = X$, $z = -(h - \sigma\sqrt{\tau})$; when $y = \infty$, $z = \infty$. Therefore,

$$I = \int_{z=-(h-\sigma\sqrt{\tau})}^{z=\infty} S_t \exp(\mu\tau + \sigma\sqrt{\tau}z) \cdot \frac{1}{\sqrt{2\pi}} e^{-z^2/2} \, dz$$

$$= S_t \exp(\mu + \tfrac{1}{2}\sigma^2)\tau \int_{-(h-\sigma\sqrt{\tau})}^{\infty} \exp\left(\sigma\sqrt{\tau}z - \frac{\sigma^2\tau}{2}\right) \cdot \exp\left(-\frac{z^2}{2}\right) \frac{dz}{\sqrt{2\pi}}$$

Using equation (A16.3) and combining the exponentiated terms in the integrand gives

$$I = S_t \exp(r\tau) \int_{-(h-\sigma\sqrt{\tau})}^{\infty} \exp(-\tfrac{1}{2}(\sigma\sqrt{\tau} - z)^2) \frac{dz}{\sqrt{2\pi}}$$

To simplify this expression, make the change of variable $\omega = \sigma\sqrt{\tau} - z$ which implies $dz = -d\omega$. Again, we need to adjust the range of integration. When $z = -h + \sigma\sqrt{\tau}$, $\omega = h$ and when $z = \infty$, $\omega = -\infty$, giving

$$I = S_t \exp(r\tau) \int_{-\infty}^{h} \frac{1}{\sqrt{2\pi}} \exp(-\tfrac{1}{2}\omega^2) \, d\omega$$

$$= S_t e^{r\tau} \Phi(h) \qquad (A16.9)$$

Putting equations (A16.7) and (A16.9) into equation (A16.6) gives

$$C_t = S_t \Phi(h) - Xe^{-r\tau} \Phi(h - \sigma\sqrt{\tau}) \qquad (A16.10)$$

where

$$h = \frac{\log(S_t/Xe^{-r\tau})}{\sigma\sqrt{\tau}} + \frac{1}{2}\sigma\sqrt{\tau}$$

Equation (A16.10) is the Black–Scholes call formula. The equivalent put formula can be derived in a similar manner.

REFERENCES

Abramowitz, M. and Stegun, I. (1972), *Handbook of Mathematical Functions*, New York: Dover Publications.

Adams, A.T. (1989), *Investment*, Graham and Trotman.

Beckers, S. (Sep. 1981), "Standard deviations implied in option prices as predictors of future stock price variability", *Journal of Banking and Finance*, 5, 363–82.

Black, F. (July/Aug. 1975), "Fact and fantasy in the use of options", *Financial Analysis Journal*, 31, 36–72.

Black, F. (Mar. 1976), "The Pricing of Commodity Contracts", *Journal of Financial Economics*, 3, 167–79.

Black, F. and Scholes, M. (May 1973) "The pricing of options and corporate liabilities", *Journal of Political Economy*, 81, 637–59.

Cavalla, N.M. (1989), *GNI Handbook of Traded Options*, Macmillan.

Cox, J., Ross, S. and Rubinstein, M. (Sep. 1979), "Option pricing: a simplified approach", *Journal of Financial Economics*, 7, 229–63.

Coy, J. and Ross, S. (Jan. 1976), "The valuation of options for alternative stochastic processes", *Journal of Financial Economics*, 3, 145–66.

French, K.R. (1980), "Stock returns and the weekend effect", *Journal of Financial Economics*, 8, 55–69.

Gastineau, G. (1979), *The Stock Options Manual*, McGraw-Hill.

Geske, R. (1979), "A note on an analytic valuation formula for unprotected American call options on stocks with known dividends", *Journal of Financial Economics*, 7, 375–80.

Geske, R. (1981), "Comments on Whaley's note", *Journal of Financial Economics*, 9, 213–15.

Gladstein, M., Merton, R. and Scholes, M. (1982), "The returns and risks of alternate put option portfolio investment strategies", *Journal of Business*, Jan., 1–55.

Hull, J. (1989), *Options, Futures, and Other Derivative Securities*, Prentice-Hall International.

Jarrow, R.A. and Rudd, A. (1983), *Option Pricing*, Irwin.

Klemkosky, R. and Resnick, B. (Dec. 1979), "Put-call parity and market efficiency", *Journal of Finance*, 34, 1141–55.

Latane, H. and Rendleman, R. (May 1976), "Standard deviations of stock price ratios implied in option prices", *Journal of Finance*, 31, 369–82.

Roll, R. (1977), "An analytic formula for unprotected American call options on stocks with known dividends", *Journal of Financial Economics*, 5, 251–8.

Rubinstein, M. and Cox, J. (1985), *Options Markets*, Prentice-Hall.

Whaley, R.E. (1981), "On the valuation of American call options on stocks with known dividends", *Journal of Financial Economics*, 9, 207–11.

Whaley, R.E. (1982), "Valuation of American call options on dividend paying stocks: empirical tests", *Journal of Financial Economics*, 10, 29–58.

17
Stochastic Investment Models

17.1 INTRODUCTION

In most practical circumstances, the investment decision is not limited to a single time horizon. Rather, the investment strategy is one that has to endure for several time periods. Moreover, investors can usually alter strategy at any time in response to the investment environment that they have just experienced or that they may expect to experience. As a simple example, investors may have a rule that they always rebalance their portfolio so that the asset mix is the same at the start of each period.

Neat mathematically tractable solutions to such multi-period, dynamic problems are available only with very restrictive and unrealistic assumptions. Furthermore, decisions about strategy often involve discussions among several parties and it is useful to have a tool that enables one party to illustrate to another what the consequences of a particular planned course of action might be.

A stochastic investment model makes use of a large number of "random" projections to illustrate the risks and returns associated with different asset allocations and strategies.

In each projection (sometimes referred to as an iteration or simulation) the rates of return in all future periods for all the asset classes and other economic variables (such as inflation and yields) are generated according to a model that involves random elements. For example, a single six-period projection might look like:

	Period					
	1	*2*	*3*	*4*	*5*	*6*
Equity returns	10%	−20%	−13%	5%	0%	30%
Bond returns	3%	−1%	−3%	8%	15%	10%
Inflation	1.5%	2%	2.5%	2.8%	3.0%	3.5%

In this projection inflation happens to be rising. We could assess how various combinations of equity and bond portfolios might perform.

Of course one projection is of limited use, in the same way that using an "average" return for each period is of limited use. What can be done is to repeat the projection process a large number of times, say 5000, with different random elements. We can then get a picture of how the various portfolios performed under all conditions. In particular, we might want to focus on the "average" outcome across the projections and on the worst outcome in all the projections. We then not only have an indication of how the portfolios might perform on average, but we also have a measure of risk, i.e. how badly they might do. Alternative measures of risk and reward are also available.

What is of importance in an analysis, such as that described above, is the way in which the returns and economic conditions are "randomly generated". A strategy that appears excellent using one stochastic investment model may be disastrous under another. For example, consider again the strategy that encompasses the rule that the portfolio is rebalanced back to its initial asset mix at the end of each period. If the stochastic investment model generates its random returns in such a way that a period of high returns is followed by a period of low returns, then rebalancing will prove to be a good rule. If, on the other hand, the stochastic investment model generates its random returns in such a way that a period of high returns is likely to be followed by another period of high returns, the rebalancing rule may prove to be costly. The comparison of two strategies, one of which involves rebalancing and one of which does not, will depend crucially on the stochastic investment model. One would not want to recommend an investment strategy based on a model that is not realistic or that creates false expectations.

The good news is that statistics provide us with a rich set of tools for generating random returns in a multitude of ways that might be realistic. The bad news is that there is only tentative agreement, both in theory and based on empirical evidence, on exactly what are the "realistic" features of asset returns.

In this chapter, a variety of methodologies for generating returns with many of the features that some analysts consider realistic are outlined. Although some comments about how these features fit in with empirical and theoretical considerations, these are by no means exhaustive. The whole science of stochastic investment modelling is still at a relatively early stage of development and there is little to be gained from too much dogmatism.

Section 17.9 gives a brief description of part of a stochastic investment model developed by A.D. Wilkie that is well known among actuaries particularly those working in the UK and that has been used in practice. This model has been chosen mainly because it is well documented in publicly accessible journals and was one of the first models published. We are not endorsing its use for commercial purposes or indicating that this would be regarded as state-of-the-art modelling.

One of the major issues that has to be considered in developing a stochastic asset model is its scope and complexity. A model must be able to project the returns on the assets (and liabilities) that form part of the set of possible assets for the investor. The returns on all the asset classes must be projected consistently. For example, it should be unlikely (but not impossible) in the asset model that a projection involving consistent high nominal equity returns will be found in the same scenario as persistent deflation. Clearly, the correlation between asset classes will have to be taken into account in a way that makes sense theoretically. However, one would normally wish to avoid building a full model of the economy in order to make projections.

Some economists and econometricians have built very comprehensive models of the economy, generally intended for short-term projections. These models are typically of little use for the analysis of long-term investment strategies. In practice, such models would take too long to run a great many times, as required for producing a large number of projections into the long-term future. Furthermore, the inputs for such models are huge and would require the investor and/or analyst to have views not only on a great many economic variables, but also on the political management of the variables.

Conversely, a model that is too limited may produce implausible features in the projections. For example, a model of inflation that does not include interest rates or any economic factors and possible feedback mechanisms of interest rates on inflation, might arguably make the volatility of the inflation series look rather high.

Another investigation needed before constructing an asset model is the purpose to which it will be put. Some asset models are used for measuring short-term risk, e.g. the probability that a portfolio of holdings will lose more than 25% of its value in the next six months. For the short-term risk assessment projection, it is reasonable to aim for a model that captures as much as possible of the likely volatility of the elements of the portfolio. Hence its statistical qualities are likely to be of most importance.

For a model that is to be used for assessing investment strategies over the long term, it is necessary to avoid introducing features into the model that make some strategies implausibly attractive. For example, one would want to avoid a model that provided systematic over- or under-valuations in the projected series. If the model were used to compare strategies, these mispricings would make a strategy that exploited them appear optimal. If the mispricings failed to materialise in the real world (and we rarely observe unambiguous arbitrage opportunities in the market), the strategy that relied on the mispricings will fail the investor. It is more prudent to base a strategy on an arbitrage free market and allow the investor to take advantage of any transient opportunities if and when they occur. We would note, however, that it can be technically quite difficult to build a model that includes a lot of assets that does not introduce "mispricings".

17.2 PERSISTENCE IN ECONOMIC SERIES

Apart from randomness, one of the main features of economic series, whether they be returns on asset classes, interest rates or rates of inflation, is persistence, that is patterns that repeat themselves. Trend is perhaps the most obvious type of persistence. Seasonality (patterns that repeat themselves on a calendar-year basis) is also typical of many economic time series. Cyclical patterns that extend over periods (these periods range in length from days to many years) that are not linked to the calendar year can also be identified. The discussion in this chapter focuses mainly on the trend and non-calendar cycles. Seasonality is typically quite easy to remove from a time series because it is so regular and predictable. Indeed, many sources of official statistics deseasonalise figures before publication.

For the purposes of this chapter consider the following notional breakdown of the observed value from a time series

Observed value = long-term trend component + cyclical component

+ random component

Consider the value of a portfolio of equities over the course of a year. The long-term trend component will equal the current value of the portfolio escalated by the assumed long-term return on equities. The cyclical component may depend on the extent to which the current value of the portfolio was different from its long-term trend component. The random component will typically be modelled using a random variable drawn from a specified distribution.

The random component may also include correlation effects with the random components of other time series being modelled. For example, it would probably be necessary to ensure that there was a strong likelihood that a random shock to one stock market in the model was related to the other stock markets in the model. Figure 17.1 shows the value of selected stock market indices around the world in the late 1980s. It is

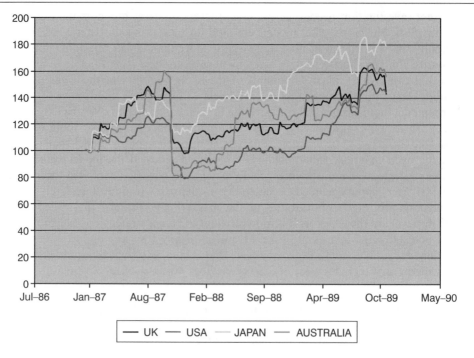

Figure 17.1

clear that in October 1987 and indeed on other dates, there was a "random" shock to all the markets. This feature is referred to as "cross-correlation" and it will include features that include time lags.

The long-term component in asset models intended for use over long periods into the future is the most critical. The long-term "average" returns on equities, bonds, cash, property, etc. will be absolutely crucial in determining which strategy is deemed to be optimal. It should be noted that these long-term components need not be static. It is sometimes assumed that the "paradigm" in which the model is operating shifts and so the long-term parameters also shift. We discuss "shifting paradigm" features further towards the end of the chapter. The long-term component will not, or course, be important for shorter-term models (e.g. assessing risk over the next day or week or month), for which the structure of the random component is typically most important. In many such cases the long-term component is actually omitted from the model entirely.

The cyclical component is in many ways the distinguishing feature of many models and is the component upon which much attention is focused, both in theory and in the search for empirical evidence. Figure 17.2 shows the short-term interest rates that have applied in the UK from 1946. One of the features of this graph is that short-term interest rates have varied significantly over the period (ranging from under 1% to over 18%). In addition, from one year to the next, "high" interest rates have tended to be followed by interest rates that are also "high".

Figure 17.3 shows the annual rates of inflation in the UK (as measured by rates of change in the Retail Prices Index) over the same period. It too shows a tendency for high rates of inflation to be clustered together.

Contrast this graph with the one depicted in Figure 17.4. This is a chart of the annual total returns earned on UK equities since 1946. The returns in this figure do not follow any clear pattern.

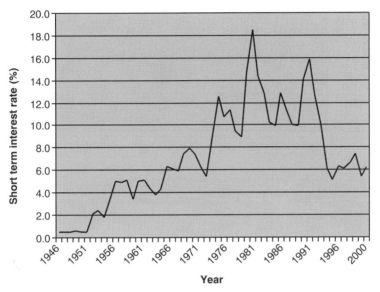

Figure 17.2   Short-term interest rates in the UK, 1946–2000

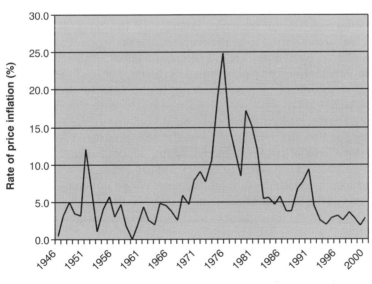

Figure 17.3   Annual rates of inflation

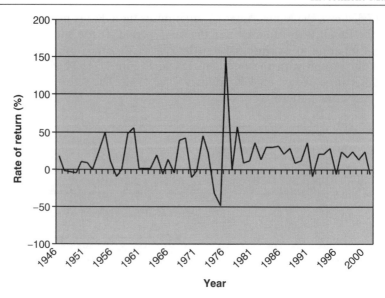

Figure 17.4   UK equity returns: annual since 1946

Building a stochastic investment model will necessarily demand that some stance be taken as regards the persistence of returns. Some researchers have argued using theoretical and empirical evidence that "momentum" effects caused by investor sentiment will lead to share prices systematically over- and under-shooting some underlying and unobserved economic value. Other researchers argue that the "momentum" effects are a statistical illusion and in fact there is no over- or under-valuation relative to the risks inherent in the markets. The latter set of researchers are often referred to as the efficient market proponents as they argue that the pricing offered by the market is efficient in that it instantly and fully reflects all available information. Any persistence in the market is argued to be an efficient and rational reflection of systematic trends in the risks (or other elements of the information set).

As discussed earlier, the requirement to build in momentum effects will depend very much on why and how the model is to be used. Other persistence effects that sometimes have to be considered in economic modelling are seasonal effects. For example, retail prices tend to show a marked (calendar) annual effect as a result of systematic variations in spending patterns through the year. We do not consider the modelling of seasonal effects in this chapter as our focus is more on financial instruments, which will typically discount known seasonalities and therefore do not exhibit very strong seasonal patterns.

Some studies into equity prices have suggested that there are seasonalities (turn of the year, turn of week, ...) in the returns earned. Although reasonable explanations have been offered as to why they may exhibit these features (in other words they are not necessarily statistical artefacts), it can equally well be argued that they will disappear after being pointed out.

17.3 AUTOCORRELATION

Before discussing how to build models, we first touch on a simple way of measuring whether or not a time series exhibits persistence. This measure is useful not only in deciding whether or not you may want to include persistence effects in your projections, but also in describing the features of your model.

Consider an economic time series, $I(t)$, which reflects the rate of change in some variable over the period $(t-1)$ to t. The autocorrelation (also referred to as serial correlation) of the series is given by the correlation of $I(t)$ with $I(t-1)$. So if $I(t)$ tends to be high when $I(t-1)$ has been high (and vice versa), then the series is said to be positively autocorrelated. If $I(t)$ is usually low after $I(t-1)$ has been high, then the series is said to be negatively autocorrelated. If there is no statistical relationship between successive values of $I(t)$, the series is said to be a random walk, or to have zero autocorrelation, or to be uncorrelated.

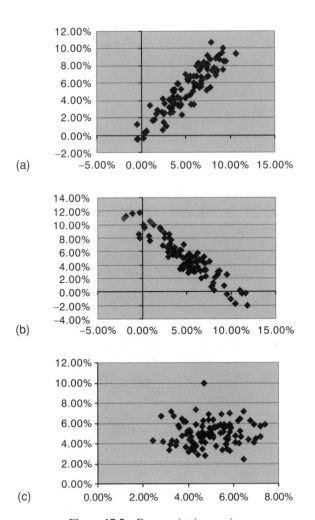

Figure 17.5 Economic time series

The three graphs in Figure 17.5 show scatterplots of $I(t)$ against $I(t-1)$ for (a) a positively autocorrelated series; (b) a negatively autocorrelated series; and (c) an uncorrelated series.

The corresponding plot for the annual rates of inflation in the UK over the period 1945 to 2000 is given in Figure 17.6.

High rates of inflation tend to follow high rates of inflation and low rates follow low rates, which suggests that inflation might be positively autocorrelated.

Although the above description of autocorrelation focused on the relationship between the value of the series in the one period and the value of the series in the next period, autocorrelation is a concept that can be applied to any statistical relationship between values in a series. For example, it might be that $I(t)$ is expected to be high after a high value of $I(t-1)$, but if $I(t-2)$ were high, then $I(t)$ might be expected to be low. In this example, $I(t)$ has a positive first-order autocorrelation (or lag 1 correlation) but negative second-order autocorrelation (or lag 2 correlation). For example, suppose that $\{I(t)\}_t$ represented inflation. If during period $(t-2)$ inflation were high, it would cause the monetary and fiscal authorities to implement policies during period $(t-1)$ that were intended to bring inflation down. If it took until period t for those policies to take effect, then the series would exhibit lag 2 negative autocorrelation.

The autocorrelation of an observed time series is typically estimated at each of a number of lags. The autocorrelation at lag k (where k is much smaller than n, the number of observations) can be estimated using

$$r_k = \frac{\sum_{t=k+1}^{n} (I(t) - \overline{I(t)})(I(t-k) - \overline{I(t-k)})}{\sum_{t=1}^{n} (I(t) - \overline{I(t)})^2}$$

where $\overline{I(t)}$ is the estimated expected value of the series at time t. The estimated expected value may come from a variety of methods. If $I(t)$ represents inflation and it can be assumed that the overall average rate of inflation is constant over time, $\overline{I(t)}$ would be constant and could be estimated using the arithmetic average of all the observations.

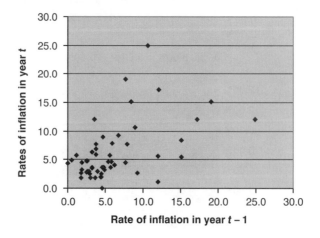

Figure 17.6 Annual rates of inflation

Partial autocorrelation

If $I(t)$ is positively correlated with $I(t-1)$ and $I(t-1)$ is positively correlated with $I(t-2)$, then, other things being equal, $I(t)$ will be correlated positively with $I(t-2)$. Therefore, even though it might appear as if an economic series has autocorrelation extending several lags, it is often the case that a model with only one level of autocorrelation will suffice. To check this, we can calculate the partial autocorrelation, which measures, for example, the correlation between $I(t)$ and $I(t-2)$ after taking into account the autocorrelation between the two that would be induced by a simple first-order autocorrelation.

The sample partial autocorrelation is typically calculated in a recursive manner as follows:

$$p_k = \frac{r_k - \sum_{j=1}^{k-1} r_{k-j}\phi_{k-1,j}}{1 - \sum_{j=1}^{k-1} r_j\phi_{k-1,j}}$$

where $\phi_{a,b} = \phi_{a-1,b} - p_a\phi_{a-1,a-b}$ and putting $\phi_{a,a} = p_a$.

So, for example, if we first note that $p_1 = r_1$, then

$$p_2 = \frac{r_2 - p_1 r_1}{1 - p_1 r_1} = \frac{r_2 - r_1^2}{1 - r_1^2}$$

Then, $\phi_{2,1} = p_1 - p_2 p_1$

so

$$p_3 = \frac{r_3 - \phi_{2,1} r_2 - p_2 r_1}{1 - \phi_{2,1} r_1 - p_2 r_2}, \quad \text{etc.}$$

Example 17.1

Suppose that the first-order autocorrelation for a time series were 0.8 and the second-order autocorrelation were 0.6. Calculate the second-order partial autocorrelation and comment on it.

Answer

$$p_2 = \frac{0.6 - 0.64}{1 - 0.64} = -0.11$$

The second-order autocorrelation of 0.6 is lower than would be expected if the series were a straightforward first-order autoregressive (AR(1)) process with first-order autocorrelation of 0.8. This suggests that there is a genuine, but small inverse relationship between the observations two time periods apart.

In empirical work it is of course important to recognise statistical significance in the magnitude of estimated partial autocorrelation coefficients. Quenouille (1949) has shown that under certain conditions, an approximate test for whether a partial autocorrelation at lag k is significantly different from zero is to compare it with the critical value of $\pm 2/\sqrt{n}$, where n is the number of observations. So, the estimated partial autocorrelation of -0.11 in the example above would be reliable evidence to reject a simple AR(1) model only if the number of observations had been greater than about 330.

17.4   THE RANDOM WALK MODEL

The random walk model is in many ways the simplest of all possible asset models. The movement of asset values under the random walk model is, as its name suggests, a series of random increments added to the current value of the asset. The size and direction of the random increment do not depend on the value of the asset or on any feature of the increments that have occurred in the past.

The model can be written as

$$X(t) = X(t-1) + Z(t)$$

where $X(t)$ is the asset value at time t and $Z(t)$ is the random increment.

When it comes to modelling, say, equity share prices, the random walk in this very simple form is often not plausible. For example, if the share price at time $t-1$, $X(t-1)$ were 100, then we would expect the size of the increments to be quite different from that if $X(t-1)$ were 10,000. A value of $Z(t) = 10$ would be quite significant if $X(t-1)$ were 100, but barely noticeable if $X(t-1)$ were 10,000.

Figure 17.7 shows a simple random walk. If we compare this with the total return index on UK equities given in Figure 17.8, it is clear that they are qualitatively very different.

However, we can quite easily modify the model to make something that could look more akin to real data.

Let $S(t) = \exp(X(t))$, or $\log(S(t)) = X(t)$, then $\log(S(t)) = \log(S(t-1)) + Z(t)$.

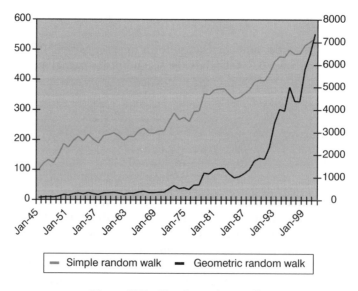

Figure 17.7   Simple random walk

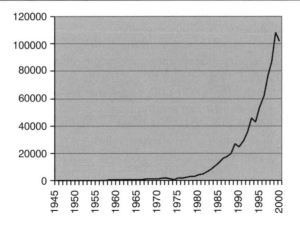

Figure 17.8   Total return index on UK equities

This is a random walk model. However, when we transform the equation back so that $S(t)$ is on the LHS, we obtain:

$$\text{or } S(t) = S(t-1)\exp(Z(t))$$

Now, the price at time t is the price at time $t-1$ multiplied by a random variable. This random variable can be interpreted as the return on the share and we now have a more realistic model, for example if $Z(t)$ were 10%, then we have the price of the share increasing by roughly 10% of its initial price. Actually, the increase will be $\exp(0.1) - 1 = 10.52\%$. The $Z(t)$ in this model should be interpreted as the rate of return expressed in continuously compounded form.

This model is properly known as the geometric random walk (and is also illustrated in Figure 17.7) and is very commonly used to model economic time series. This is usually what is meant when analysts talk of a random walk model in a stochastic modelling context. The geometric random walk is also referred to as geometric brownian motion if the random increments are drawn from a standard normal distribution. The transformation $\exp(Z(t))$ can be interpreted as a random variable with a log-normal distribution.

The geometric brownian motion and variations thereon are very popular for modelling equity share prices. There are a number of reasons for this. If the continuously compounded rates of return are the aggregate response of investors to many bits of information, this aggregate will approximately have a normal distribution according to the central limit theorem (see Section 10.3).

The log-normal distribution is also very convenient because if single period returns have a log-normal distribution, then compounded multi-period returns will also have a log-normal distribution. This is not true for many other distributions, e.g. the normal distribution. An additional benefit is that the underlying mathematics of the geometric brownian motion are well known and many important results have been derived based on it; this makes it a convenient assumption when it comes to, say, pricing derivatives of equities. The log-normal distribution, unlike the normal distribution for example, is also bounded below by zero, i.e. the worst possible return is -100%. This accords with the notion of limited liability for equity investors.

Empirical evidence suggests that, although the geometric brownian motion is a fairly reasonable model for equity prices, there are some important discrepancies. For example, equity prices tend to experience more extreme moves than would be expected under a log-normal distribution. One of the underlying reasons for these more extreme moves is that the geometric brownian motion supposes that the price of a share moves in a "smooth" fashion from one value to the next. In reality, share prices "jump" from one value to another if investors receive a particularly important piece of information or re-evaluate existing information suddenly.

Some investors believe that the evolution of a share's price depends not only on new information entering the market, but also on how the share's current price has been arrived at. For example, they might believe that there are momentum effects, perhaps underpinned by swings in market sentiment. Such momentum effects suggest that there is value to be gained by investing so as continue to back the "winners" from a previous period. Other theories suggest that momentum continues only so far before it becomes valuable to sell the winners as they "peak" and start backing those shares that had performed poorly over the past periods.

The types of investment strategy above require that there are systematic inefficiencies in the market and that they can be exploited to the benefit of those who are able to detect them. That is, they produce risk-adjusted returns to the investor in excess of that obtainable by the market as a whole. The empirical evidence for these strategies is largely anecdotal. And there is good reason to suspect that if anyone actually knew about a good strategy they would keep it to themselves. Proponents of the efficient markets hypothesis (EMH) can also explain superficial empirical contradictions of the hypothesis in terms of trends in the underlying riskiness of the market and hence changing expected returns.

Therefore, for the purposes of modelling, it is arguably prudent to assume that the equity market is efficient and that there is no way to predict whether the market will continue to rise, or start to fall without a change in the underlying state of the world.

Note that there is an important difference between models based on no-arbitrage and models that are based on efficiency. Strictly speaking, an arbitrage is an investment opportunity that yields a chance of a positive return to the investor with zero risk. Arbitrage opportunities might exist if it were possible to buy a share on a stock exchange for one price and sell it at the same time on a different exchange for a price that was more different than the frictional costs of enacting the trade. An efficient market is one step on; it states that expected returns (or the average of the simulated returns from the stochastic model) must be in line with the riskiness of the asset class. In other words, you cannot expect to get a high positive returns unless you take the requisite risk in the market.

17.5 AUTOREGRESSIVE MODELS

There are some economic variables that clearly do not follow a random walk. The Bank of England, for example, currently aims to keep inflation at a level of 2.5% per annum. It will start to cut or raise interest rates to encourage inflation back to its target level should it start to fluctuate.

Similarly, interest rates in the UK have not shown a tendency to drift off uncontrollably in a way that might occur if modelled using a random walk. The tendency to revert back to some average level is often referred to as mean-reversion.

Although autoregressive models do conceptually include models that exhibit mean aversion, in practice, there are very few economic series that do this. It is possible however, that these types of models may be useful for modelling extreme events. The case of hyperinflation is a possible example. If fiscal and monetary activity is not able to control inflation, then, high levels of inflation may presage a complete breakdown of confidence in the economy. Inflation may then become progressively worse, with the rate of increase in prices becoming faster. But for the remainder of this section, we consider only mean-reverting models.

The basic structure of a first-order autoregressive model is:

$$X(t) = \mu + \alpha(X(t-1) - \mu) + \varepsilon(t),$$

where $\varepsilon(t)$ is the random component, μ is the long-term component and $\alpha(X(t-1) - \mu)$ is the autoregressive (cyclical) component. For the model to be stationary (or mean-reverting in the sense that $X(t)$ never drifts off to plus or minus infinity) α must be between -1 and 1. In most practical applications in financial markets, α is non-negative.

The value of $X(t)$ can therefore be seen to comprise a long-term component plus some fraction of how far away $X(t-1)$ was from μ plus a random component. If $X(t-1)$ were much greater than μ, we would expect $X(t)$ to be greater than μ as well, but by a lesser amount.

Figure 17.9 shows three first-order autoregressive models with values of α that are 0.9, 0.5 and 0.1 respectively.

A value of α close to unity makes the model very much like a random walk. A value of α close to zero means that there is no cyclical component present and the time series is effectively a long-term trend around which there is random variation. If the rate of return on an asset is a zero α process (and there are no other lagged relationships within the series), then the value of the asset will follow a random walk with an α of unity. A value of α that is greater than unity in absolute value implies that the process is not stationary, i.e. its autocorrelation and autocovariance structure change with time. A negative value of α introduces negative autocorrelation where the series tends to jump from being greater than the trend value to below it and back again.

The conditional variance of an observation one time period in advance is given by the variance of the ε term, say σ^2. The unconditional variance of an observation, i.e. the variance based on no knowledge of what the current level of the series is, is given by $\sigma^2/(1 - \alpha^2)$. Again, it can be seen that the closer α is to zero, the more similar in value the conditional and unconditional variances become, i.e. the less useful knowledge about the current state of the series is in predicting the next value. The closer α is to one (or negative one), the larger the unconditional variance becomes.

Example 17.2

Suppose we have a series where $\sigma^2 = 100$ and that $X(0) = 90$ and $\mu = 100$.

(a) If $\alpha = 0$, calculate the conditional and unconditional standard deviation. Discuss in broad terms what values $X(1)$ and $X(1000)$ are likely to take on.

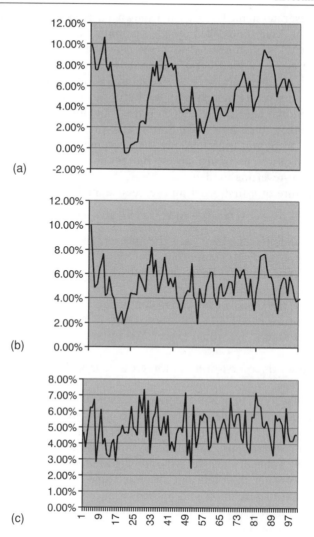

Figure 17.9 Autoregressive models

(b) If $\alpha = 0.71$, calculate the conditional and unconditional standard deviation. Discuss in broad terms what values $X(1)$ and $X(1000)$ are likely to take on.

Answer

(a) If $\alpha = 0$, i.e. there is no autocorrelation, then the unconditional and conditional standard deviations are both 10. The whole series of $X(t)$s will therefore tend to stay close to 100 (with a standard deviation of 10).

For example, $X(1) = 100$ plus a random number with a mean of zero and a standard deviation of 10. $X(1000)$ would also be 100 plus a random number with a mean of zero and a standard deviation of 10.

(b) If $\alpha = 0.71$, the conditional standard deviation is still 10. Thus, for example, $X(1) = 100 + 0.71 \times (90 - 100) = 92.9$ plus a random number with a mean of zero and standard deviation of 10. The unconditional variance will, however, now be $100/(1 - 0.5) = 200 = 14.1^2$.

Without any further information, $X(1000)$ would be equal to the mean of 100 plus a random number with a standard deviation of 14.1. The fact that the series tends to move in cycles because of the autocorrelation means that it can move away from its long-term average of 100 for several periods in a row. That means that we will be less certain about where the series is without current information about the series. A fairly crude way of thinking about this, is that if the process happens to be low (for example, suppose it is equal to 90), then even though the conditional mean for the process at the next time step is 92.9, the conditional standard deviation of 10 means that it is not unlikely that the process will move to, say, $92.9 - 10 = 82.9$. On the other hand, if the process had no autocorrelation, the likelihood of the process taking a value of 82.9 or lower is much smaller because the mean of the process reverts back to 100 immediately.

The covariance between $X(t)$ and $X(t - k)$, $Cov[X(t), X(t - k)]$ is simple to derive as:

$$Cov(X(t), X(t - k)) = \alpha^k \frac{\sigma^2}{1 - \alpha^2}$$

and the autocorrelation, $Corr(X(t), X(t - k))$, is given by α^k. If α is positive (but less than one), the autocorrelation will "die out" exponentially. The interpretation here is that any shock to the process will have impacts on subsequent values of the process, but the magnitude of the impact will decrease with time. For example, a shock to the rate of inflation process in one period will affect not only the inflation rate in that period and the next, but also the subsequent periods.

If the parameter α is negative, the autocorrelation alternately changes sign as the lags increase. Thus the autocorrelation between the observation and its immediate predecessor is negative (i.e. a high value of the predecessor is more likely to be followed by a low value). The autocorrelation between the observation and the two lags prior is positive, i.e. a high value is likely to be followed by a high value in two periods' time.

A simple kth order autoregressive model can be written as:

$$X(t) - \mu = \sum_{j=1}^{k} \alpha_j (X(t - j) - \mu) + \varepsilon(t)$$

Although stochastic asset models have been developed that use asset models incorporating very high order autoregressive features, the vast majority of asset models use at most second-order models. Apart from statistical issues (such as the difficulty in estimating higher order parameters from the time series typically available), lower order models are easier to interpret and understand.

Again, because stochastic asset models are usually used in a prospective, "predictive" sense, it is rare that only historical statistical input is used to parameterise in the model. Users will typically want to adjust the parameters based on their own (or their clients') guesses about the future (perhaps to undertake stress testing or what-if scenario analysis) and it becomes extremely hard to do that sensibly unless the parameters have a fairly simple economic interpretation.

17.6 ARIMA MODELS

Although autoregressive models (AR models) are by far the most commonly encountered type of model in stochastic asset models, a family of models called the ARIMA family exists that can be used to model different types of time-dependencies. The AR in ARIMA stands for autoregressive, the I for integrated and the MA for moving average. Box and Jenkins (1976) popularised these models and provided a methodology for identifying, fitting and checking their fit.

A time series such as an inflation index or share price has a somewhat obvious time-dependency: the level of the index or the magnitude of the share price is roughly the same from one time period to the next. Even share prices, although volatile, have the same order of magnitude over quite long periods. What is less obvious is how the *changes* in the level of the index (rate of inflation) or share price (the return on the share ignoring dividends) are related from one period to the next. The focus is therefore on the differenced series, i.e. the series of differences or changes from one period to the next. The integrated series (the original observations) has properties that are derived from those of the differenced series.

The MA model enables quite different types of time dependency to be modelled. A first-order MA model is given by:

$$X(t) = \mu(t) + u(t)$$

where

$$u(t) = \phi\varepsilon(t-1) + \varepsilon(t),$$

and ϕ is the MA parameter.

The unconditional variance of the process can be derived as $\sigma^2(1 + \phi^2)$. The first-order autocorrelation, $Corr(X(t), X(t-1)) = \phi/(1 + \phi^2)$, but the correlations at further lags are zero.

The practical importance of an MA process is that it can be used to model series where a shock to one observation will impact on that observation and the next, but not on those observations that follow. The "lifetime" of a shock in an MA process is given by its order — so a first-order MA process has a lifetime of one — unlike an AR process where the lifetime is theoretically infinite (although decaying in importance at exponential rates).

Specific members of the ARIMA family of models are usually specified as ARIMA(p, d, q), where p indicates the order of the AR model, d indicates the frequency of differencing and q indicates the order of the MA model. So, for example, an inflation index model might be specified as ARIMA $(1, 1, 0)$, indicating that a first-order AR model has been used, that the series has been differenced once and that no MA terms have been included. We can therefore note that the model is given by:

$$I(t) = \mu + \alpha(I(t-1) - \mu) + \varepsilon(t),$$

where $I(t) = Q(t) - Q(t-1)$ and $Q(t)$ is the inflation index. In order to model "geometric" price growth, $I(t)$ is usually defined to be the difference in the logarithm of the inflation index. In this case $I(t)$ is not interpreted as the change in the level of the price index, but rather as the continuously compounded rate of change in the index, i.e. the force of inflation in continuously compounded form. Mathematically,

$$I(t) = \log(Q(t)) - \log(Q(t-1)) = \log(Q(t)/Q(t-1))$$

or

$$Q(t) = Q(t-1)\exp(I(t)).$$

Projecting the series is conceptually quite easy with ARIMA models. For example, consider the inflation model above. Provided we have estimates of α, μ and σ and can observe $Q(t)$ and $Q(t-1)$ and hence calculate $I(t)$, $Q(t+1)$ can be projected to be $Q(t) \times \exp(I(t+1))$, where

$$I(t+1) = \mu + \alpha(I(t) - \mu) + \sigma Z$$

and where Z is a randomly generated number from the normal distribution (or whichever distribution is chosen for the random shocks).

17.7 ARCH MODELS

In some cases, time series do not exhibit any unambiguous autocorrelation, but nevertheless do exhibit time-dependent statistical properties. In particular, some series, although serially independent, have time-dependent, "autocorrelated" volatility structures. In other words, not only does σ depend on time, i.e. should be written as $\sigma(t)$, but $\sigma(t)$ depends on either previous levels of volatility, or on previous shocks to the series itself.

As an example, equity returns measured over short periods, such as a day or week, display "bursts" of volatility (see Figure 17.10) even though there is little evidence that there is any autocorrelation in the returns themselves.

Other examples where there is clear-cut evidence of some autocorrelation in the series itself and where models with autoregressive volatility structures have been used are inflation, exchange rates and interest rates (Engle, 1982; Domowitz and Hakkio, 1985; Pagan and Ullah, 1986; Engle et al., 1987).

A broad family of models has sprung up to capture the time-varying, autoregressive volatility, namely ARCH models. As with the other sections in this chapter, we have not covered the models in any great depth, but have rather focused on providing an understanding of the simplest members of the family, some of which are encountered in practice.

ARCH stands for autoregressive, conditionally heteroscedastic. The term "heteroscedastic" indicates that the variance of the process changes through time. The qualifier "conditional" indicates that the level of volatility depends on some other random variable. The "autoregressive" indicates that the conditioning variable is the process itself.

At its simplest, an ARCH (Engle, 1982) model can be represented as:

$$X(t) = \mu + \sigma(t)Z(t)$$

where $Z(t)$ is an independent, standard normal variable and

$$\sigma^2(t) = \gamma_0 + \gamma_1[\sigma(t-1)Z(t-1)]^2$$

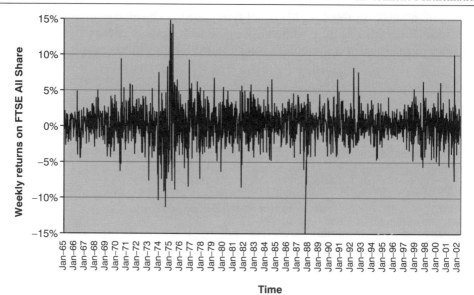

Figure 17.10 Weekly equity returns

A shock (a large positive or negative Z) to the model will affect not only the current observation of $X(t)$, but will also increase (assuming that γ_1 is positive) the variance of the next observation (and hence increase the likelihood that the next observation will be "extreme").

A generalised ARCH model (GARCH, see Bollerslev, 1986) is very similar but includes an explicit link between the variances in successive periods, i.e.

$$\sigma^2(t) = \gamma_0 + \gamma_1[\sigma(t-1)Z(t-1)]^2 + \gamma_2\sigma^2(t-1)$$

The effect of this additional term is to make the error structure less sensitive to shocks that occur when the process is in a low volatility state and to make the volatility exhibit longer cycles. For example, it might be considered desirable in an inflation model that a price shock that occurred when the inflation rate had been stable for some time (i.e. the inflation process had low volatility) would be less likely to "destabilise" inflation rates than if the process had been more volatile previously. A simple ARCH model would imply that the shock had virtually the same impact on future volatility whatever the previous level of volatilty.

The ARCH effect can also feed back on the mean of the process itself (this variation is referred to as ARCH-M), viz:

$$X(t) = \mu + \beta\sigma^2(t) + \sigma(t)Z(t)$$

with $\sigma(t)$ as in the ARCH process,

$$\sigma^2(t) = \gamma_0 + \gamma_1[\sigma(t-1)Z(t-1)]^2.$$

Engle *et al.* (1987) have used such a process in modelling long bond yields: the higher the underlying volatility, the higher the excess redemption yield over shorter-term instruments.

Excel Application 17.1

The use of Excel spreadsheets alone is not a very efficient way of implementing a large-scale asset-liability model and is not to be recommended under current technology. However, there are some Add-In products (such as @Risk from Palisade Corporation) that can be used to construct models. In addition, implementing models using Excel VBA (Visual Basic for Applications, the "macro" language associated with Excel) is often fast enough for many practical purposes.

Nevertheless, an Excel spreadsheet can be used to generate sample projections that will enable you to get a feel for the differences between the types of models considered in this chapter. As an example, we show how to create a sample path for an inflation index $(Q(t))$ that has the following structure:

$$Q(t) = Q(t-1)\exp(I(t))$$
$$I(t) = 4.5\% + 0.6 \times [I(t-1) - 4.5\%] + \sigma(t)Z(t)$$
$$\sigma^2(t) = 2\%^2 + 1 \times [\sigma(t-1)Z(t-1)]^2$$

$Z(t)$ is a standard normal random variable and $Q(0) = 100$, $I(0) = 4.5\%$ and $\sigma(1) = 2\%$.

Enter 100 in cell A1 and 4.5% in cell B1. Column A will contain the simulated Q series and column B will contain the simulated rates of inflation.

In cell C2 enter 2%. Column C will contain the variances.

In cell D2 enter the formula =NORMSINV(RAND()). This formula will generate a random normal variable in cell D2, which will change every time the spreadsheet is recalculated. This can be done manually by pressing the function key F9. The function RAND() generates a pseudo-random number from the uniform distribution between zero and unity. NORMSINV is a function that returns the inverse of the normal distribution function, i.e. the quantile from the standard normal distribution associated with a given (cumulative) probability.

You can turn off the automatic recalculation feature in the \Tools\Options menu in order to avoid the spreadsheet changing frequently. You then just have to remember to press F9 (manual recalculation) when you want to see the effect of any changes you then make.

In cell B2 enter $= 4.5\% + 0.6*(\text{B1} - 4.5\%) + \text{C2}*\text{D2}$. This should update the value of the rate of inflation in the first period, i.e. I(1).

In cell A2 enter $= \exp(\text{B2})*\text{A1}$. This should update the inflation index at time 1.

Copy the function in D2 to D3. This should just provide you with another random standard normal variable. In cell C3, enter $= \text{SQRT}(2\%\,\hat{}\,2 + 1*(\text{C2}*1)2)\hat{}\,2)$. This should produce a result that will be the volatility of the residual process for time period 2.

Copy the functions from A2 and B2 down into A3 and B3.

The functions in the range {A3:D3} can be copied down the rows in the spreadsheet in order to create a sample path of whichever length you choose. When graphed, a length of 100 or more should be sufficient to give you some feel for the features of the model. It is probably most instructive to graph column B, i.e. the series of rates of inflation. You should be able to see the "bursts" of volatility as well as the fact that the series usually cycles around 4.5%.

Do not be too disconcerted if you discover #NUM "errors" in your simulated series. This just indicates that the model has ended up generating rates of inflation that are too extreme for the numerical precision in Excel. Press F9 a couple of times and you will get a more useful simulation. The errors indicate that the model we have chosen is probably not very useful (unless of course we want our model to produce such extremes). You can get a more stable model by reducing the ARCH effect, i.e. try $\gamma_1 = 0.5$, instead of 1. Or try a GARCH model.

17.8 ASSET-LIABILITY MODELLING

Asset-liability modelling, in its broadest sense, is the joint modelling of the assets and the liabilities. In many cases, for example pension liabilities, the liabilities depend on many of the same factors as do the assets, e.g. interest rates, credit spreads, inflation rates, etc.

By projecting forward the assets and liabilities together, you are able to assess how the fund (assets less liabilities) will evolve over time. In the example of a pension fund, asset-liability modelling should enable you to assess how different asset strategies affect the funding position and solvency of the scheme over time.

Different types of funds have differing concerns. A trust fund that has no regulatory solvency requirements and for which outflows from the fund are under the complete control of the trustees may want a very different investment strategy from a bank writing derivatives, where liabilities are marked to market daily.

Asset-liability models are used for a variety of purposes. Sometimes the investment strategy is largely fixed and the model is used to check what impact a change to taxation rates, or a change to demographic variables, will have on the projected fund levels. Sometimes asset-liability models are implemented within an optimiser so that an optimal investment strategy can be developed. For example, it may be considered desirable to maximise the expected surplus in the fund after a period of, say, 30 years, subject to a less than 5%, say, chance that the surplus will be negative.

Unless all the asset and liability returns can be assumed to have a multi-variate normal (or one of a limited number of alternative) distributions, mean-variance approaches are not necessarily appropriate. For example, if the strategy permits options to be bought or sold, or if the asset strategy is dynamic and can change depending on the projected state of the world, it is difficult to avoid using an asset-liability model in order to assess how it will work.

Asset-liability models can also be used to value liabilities (or assets for which there are no ready markets). If it is possible to find a combination of assets that will, with certainty, match the liability cash flows, then the value of the liability must be the same as the value of those assets. Given that it is usually possible to find the value of the assets by looking up their price in the market, the liability can then be assigned a value.

More generally, the combinations will not be a static set of assets, but rather a "time series" of portfolios that vary through time depending on the state of the world and how that in turn affects the liability cash flows. These "dynamic hedges" are a very powerful way of using asset-liability models, but unfortunately usually require considerable sophistication. This second type of asset-liability modelling is usually found in banks and other "sell-side" institutions.

Asset-liability modelling for institutional funds, such as pension funds, involves some significant, if subtle, issues. These have been highlighted by Tepper (1981), Black (1980) and more recently by Exley *et al.* (1997) in the UK. The conventional argument runs that because equities have a higher expected return than bonds, it is appropriate for a defined benefit pension fund to invest in equities so that the higher expected return will lead to a lower contribution rate from the company to the fund. This lower contribution rate is in turn supposed to benefit the company's shareholders and make them more amenable to providing the employees with generous benefits.

However, the equity investment in pension funds creates additional risk, not only for the members of the scheme, but also for the shareholders. After all, if the pension scheme is underfunded, it will be the shareholders that have to make up that deficit. This will mean that shareholders are "forced" to hold some lower risk assets (such as cash and bonds) in their personal accounts in order to dampen the risk associated with their investment in shares. If the pension scheme were to change its investment strategy to hold bonds instead of equities, for example, the contribution rates into the pension scheme are likely to increase, but the risk associated with the sponsoring company will have decreased. This will enable the shareholders to change their personal holdings from bonds to shares so that they are exposed to the same level of risk (and return) as before.

The point is, no matter what the investment strategy of the pension fund, the individual shareholders will be able to rearrange their personal holdings so that their personal risk-return preferences are satisfied. Excluding so-called "second-order" effects (such as taxation anomalies, implicit options available to sponsors and some scheme members and market imperfections), the asset allocation strategy of the pension fund is irrelevant and there is little to be gained from trying to find an optimal investment strategy based on conventional methods. The optimal investment strategy should be derived by analysing how the second-order effects associated with different investment strategies impact on the different stakeholders of the pension scheme, e.g. the members of the scheme, the shareholders of the sponsoring company, the advisors to the scheme, the Inland Revenue, etc.

17.9   THE WILKIE MODEL

The Wilkie model is the name for a family of models, developed and subsequently refined by A.D. Wilkie, starting in 1980. The models were initially developed to determine the reserves needed for particular types of life insurance product, but have subsequently become widely used in the UK and beyond in areas such as pensions consultancy and general investment strategy.

The Wilkie model has achieved prominence mainly because it has been published in full (and therefore discussed widely) and was the first published formalisation of a stochastic investment model. Many other actuarial consultancies and investment banks have developed their own models. In some cases aspects of these models have been disseminated in journals and conferences, but key elements remain proprietary. The Wilkie model focuses on modelling the "long term". It therefore encompasses some features that detractors have claimed are unrealistic and we shall discuss one of these in due course.

The Wilkie model is also a discrete model in the sense that it models prices and yields at annual intervals. It does not say anything about how a price has changed from one value at the start of the year to another at the end of the year. This has limitations in that it ignores any risk or opportunity within the year and instruments such as options are difficult to incorporate. Some researchers have attempted to expand the model to allow for continuous aspects, e.g. Kemp (1999) and Chan (1998).

The advantage of the discretisation is that it is mathematically simpler to specify and, arguably, accords with the way in which assets held by institutions such as pension funds are monitored in practice.

The Wilkie model is predominantly a statistical model in that much of its structure is determined from data analysis and the fitting of standard time series models to the data. The estimated model parameters have, though, typically been "adjusted". In some cases, e.g. exchange rates, the relationships motivated by economic theory have been retained even when data analysis might have suggested otherwise. In other cases, the statistical features have been retained even if they contradicted conventional economic wisdom.

We use the following notation to describe some elements of the Wilkie model (although we will leave out many of the variables contained in the model and hence also the relationships between the ones illustrated here and those other variables):

$I(t)$ is the force of inflation during year t;
$Y(t)$ is the equity dividend yield at the end of year t;
$G(t)$ is the force of dividend growth during year t and
$R(t)$ is the real yield on irredeemable index linked bonds at the end of year t.

The force of inflation is assumed to follow an AR(1) model:

$$I(t) = QMU + QA[I(t-1) - QMU] + QSD \times QZ(t)$$

where QMU represents the long-term average force of inflation, QA is the autoregressive parameter, QSD is the conditional standard deviation and $QZ(t)$ represents a standard normal innovation. Although Wilkie recommends that practitioners use judgement to calibrate the model, he also provides the following "base case" recommendations for the parameters: $QMU = 0.047$; $QA = 0.58$; $QSD = 0.0425$.

Once the forces of inflation are modelled, a price index can easily be generated:

$$Q(t) = Q(t-1) \times \exp\{I(t)\}.$$

The equity dividend yield is built up from several component relationships:

$$Y(t) = \exp\{YW \times I(t) + \log(YMU) + YN(t)\}.$$

The first term in the exponent represents an impact from the force of inflation on the yield; the second term is a "mean" term and the last term contains the additional random element and is itself an AR(1) term of the form

$$YN(t) = YA \times YN(t-1) + YSD \times YZ(t),$$

where YA is the autoregressive parameter, YSD is a conditional standard deviation and YZ is a standard normal random variable.

The dividend yield can therefore be thought of as being a function of a multiple of the force of inflation plus a constant plus an autoregressive process.

Wilkie's recommended values for the parameters are: $YMU = 0.0375$; $YA = 0.55$; $YSD = 0.155$ and $YW = 1.8$.

The force of growth in dividends is given by:

$$G(t) = DW \times DM(t) + DX \times I(t) + DMU + DDZ(t),$$

where

$$DDZ(t) = DY \times YSD \times YZ(t-1) + DB \times DSD \times DZ(t-1) + DSD \times DZ(t)$$

and

$$DM(t) = DD \times I(t) + (1 - DD) \times DM(t-1).$$

Loosely, the force of growth in year t is a function of $DM(t)$, which represents some weighted average of past forces of inflation, plus a proportion of current inflation plus a constant (DMU) plus a fairly complicated "random innovation" (DDZ).

The "random innovation" is actually the sum of a proportion of the random innovation in the yield process, YZ, from a year ago plus a proportion of last year's random innovation in the growth process itself plus a genuine, new, random innovation for this year.

The values recommended by Wilkie are: $DW = 0.58$; $DX = 0.42$; $DMU = 0.016$; $DY = -0.175$; $DB = 0.57$; $DSD = 0.07$; $DD = 0.13$.

The force of growth can then be used to generate a dividend index: $D(t) = D(t-1) \times \exp(G(t))$ and this in turn can be used along with the yields to generate an equity price index:

$$P(t) = D(t)/Y(t).$$

The model for real interest rates also contains at its heart an AR(1) process:

$$\log(R(t)) = \log(RMU) + RA[\log(R(t-1)) - \log(RMU)] + RRZ(t)$$

where

$$RRZ(t) = RBC \times CSD \times CZ(t) + RSD \times RZ(t).$$

The logarithm of the real interest rate is therefore an AR(1) process, with a complicated innovation term, RRZ. The innovation term is the sum of a proportion of the innovation term for the model for long-term nominal interest rates (which we do not discuss here) and an independent innovation term.

The suggested parameter values are: $RMU = 0.04$; $RA = 0.055$; $RSD = 0.05$; $RBC = 0.22$; $CSD = 0.185$.

At first sight, even this cut-down version of the Wilkie model can seem quite complicated as it has many parameters and there are many relationships across the elements of the model. One of the best ways of understanding the model is to try to implement it, for example using a spreadsheet.

We can make a few general comments about the properties of the model. The inflation rate model is a fairly straightforward mean-reverting model; high inflation will tend to persist, but gradually moves back towards some average level. Similarly, dividend yields will mean revert around a level that is related to the current level of inflation. The dividend growth equation is superficially the most complicated, but broadly, dividend growth will be related to long-term inflation levels. The real interest rate model is also a mean-reverting model so although interest rates can drift up, for example, and will then stay high for some years, they will tend to revert back to a mean level over time.

17.10   A NOTE ON CALIBRATION

Although there are many well-documented statistical procedures for estimating the parameters of models from a given dataset, in the context of stochastic investment models these are only of moderate importance. This is for several reasons: (a) data may not be available because the asset has not existed before (or has not been measured); (b) the historical time period may contain very unusual circumstances, or may be considered irrelevant for projections into the future; (c) there is often considerable sampling error involved in estimating parameters (i.e. the confidence intervals are wide) and the analyst will have to decide which actual value to use. The calibration of models in practice is therefore usually a blend of theory, data-based analysis and subjectivity. For example, interest rates may be modelled by starting with a theoretical model that precludes arbitrage. The parameters of the model might be adjusted so that (a) the year-on-year volatility of the interest rates matches historical experience and (b) the average long-term interest rate matches the analyst's own opinion, which may well differ from the historical average.

Several statistical procedures such as Bayesian estimation (Black and Litterman, 1992) or resampling (see Michaud, 2001) exist that can formally combine data analytic and other sources of information. These are used in practice, although in by far the majority of cases, calibration remains a dark art.

17.11   INTEREST RATE MODELLING

Although many of the statistical models outlined in the earlier sections can be used to model interest rates in a stochastic investment model, interest rate modelling does require a special mention. As discussed in Chapter 2, interest rates at various maturities are very closely related. Unless done very carefully, modelled interest rates at various durations will lead to arbitrage opportunities within the model. This is undesirable as discussed in Section 17.1.

Various researchers have created yield-curve models that are sufficiently flexible to mimic historical statistics but avoid arbitrage opportunities. A full understanding of the models requires some knowledge of stochastic calculus, which is not covered in any detail in this book, but can be found in Hull (2000), for example.

However, we do present two related, simple models of yield curves in order to give a flavour of how such models work and look in practice.

The first model shown is known as the Vasicek model and is an example of the type of model known as a one-factor "equilibrium" model, described in Vasicek (1977). In this model, an equation is specified for how the "short rate", denoted r, moves from one time period to the next and, using the relationships described in Chapter 2, how the rest of the yield curve must then move to preclude arbitrage. The "short rate" in this context should be thought of as the continuously compounded rate of interest over a very short time period, Δt. Using rather loose notation, the equation for the short rate can be written

$$r(t + \Delta t) - r(t) = \alpha \Delta t (\mu - r(t)) + \sigma \Delta t \cdot Z(t) \qquad (17.1)$$

where

α is a mean-reversion rate
μ is a mean short rate
σ is a volatility parameter
$Z(t)$ is an independent standard normal random variable

Equation (17.1) can be re-arranged to make it look more like the autoregressive, mean-reverting processes we have looked at earlier in the chapter:

$$[r(t + \Delta t) - \mu] = (1 - \alpha \Delta t)[r(t) - \mu] + (\sigma \Delta t)Z(t)$$

Therefore, the larger α is, the quicker the short rate regresses to its mean, μ. There is one technical issue to be aware of: the process for the short rate is actually in the risk-neutral world and so it is theoretically incorrect to think about the model for the short rate as if it were in the "real" world. However, in practice, it often does not make much difference where such a simple model is concerned.

Equation 17.1 can be used to project short rates and Vasicek shows that the price at time t of a zero-coupon bond paying 1 at maturity at time T is given by

$$P(t, T) = A(t, T)e^{-B(t, T)r(t)}$$

where

$$B(t, T) = \frac{1 - e^{-\alpha(T - t)}}{\alpha}$$

and

$$\log A(t, T) = \frac{[B(t, T) - (T - t)][\alpha^2 \mu - \frac{1}{2}\sigma^2]}{\alpha^2} - \frac{\sigma^2 B^2(t, T)}{4\alpha}$$

when $\alpha = 0$, $B(t, T) = (T - t)$ and $\log A(t, T) = \dfrac{\sigma^2 (T - t)^3}{6}$.

Example 17.3

An analyst has set up a stochastic investment model and is using a Vasicek model for the interest rate component with parameters:

$$\alpha = 0.10$$
$$\mu = 0.05$$
$$\sigma = 0.02$$

In one of the simulations, the projected short rate moves from 0.08 in projection year 1 to 0.07 in projection year 2. Calculate the simulated total return on a two-year coupon-bearing bond "issued" and "bought", in projection year 1 and "sold" in projection year 2. The coupon is 0.1 per unit nominal and is paid annually in arrears.

Answer

Projection year	1	2
Short rate	0.08	0.07
Price of bond	$P^*(1, 3)$	$P^*(2, 3)$

We denote the price per unit nominal of the coupon-bearing bond at time t by $P^*(t, 3)$. The total return over the year is given by:

$$R = \frac{P^*(2, 3)}{P^*(1, 3)} + 0.1$$

If we denote the price per unit nominal at time t of a zero-coupon bond maturing in projection year T by $P(t, T)$ then

$$P^*(2, 3) = 1.1P(2, 3)$$

and
$$P^*(1, 3) = 0.1P(1, 2) + 1.1P(1, 3)$$

and
$$P(1, 3) = A(1, 3)e^{-B(1, 3)0.08}$$

$$P(1, 2) = A(1, 2)e^{-B(1, 2)0.08}$$

$$P(2, 3) = A(2, 3)e^{-B(2, 3)0.07}$$

So
$$P(1, 2) = 0.9245$$

$$P(1, 3) = 0.8573$$

$$P(2, 3) = 0.9334$$

$$\Rightarrow \quad P^*(2, 3) = 1.0267$$

$$P^*(1, 3) = 1.0355$$

$$\Rightarrow \quad R = 1.0916,$$

i.e. an effective rate of return of 9.16% p.a.

The second example of an interest rate model is the Hull–White model. It is an example of a "no-arbitrage" model. Although the Vasicek model does not permit arbitrage, its simplicity means that it will usually not "fit" the current term structure. In other words, although the Vasicek model can be used to project theoretically consistent yield curves in the future, it cannot exactly match the starting position. The Hull–White model can be interpreted as a generalisation of the Vasicek model that allows for exact initial fitting. Heath, Jarrow and Morton (1992) provide the more comprehensive framework for models of this sort.

Using the same notation as before, the short-rate process in the Hull–White model is given by:

$$r(t + \Delta t) - r(t) = [\theta(t) - \alpha r(t)]\Delta t + \sigma \Delta t Z(t)$$

and

$$P(t, T) = A(t, T)e^{-B(t, T)r(t)}$$

$$B(t, T) = \frac{1 - e^{-\alpha(T - t)}}{\alpha}$$

$$\log A(t, T) = \log\frac{P(0, T)}{P(0, t)} - B(t, T)\frac{\partial \log P(0, t)}{\partial t}$$

$$-\frac{1}{4\alpha^3}\sigma^2\{e^{-\alpha T} - e^{-\alpha t}\}^2\{e^{2\alpha t} - 1\}$$

where $P(0, t)$ denotes the current (time 0) price per unit nominal of a zero-coupon bond of maturity t. These prices can generally be found in the financial press or can be derived from published bond prices. The partial derivative $\partial \log P(0, t)/\partial t$ is simply the negative of the continuously compounded yield associated with the zero-coupon bond.

17.12 VALUE AT RISK

Value at risk (and variations thereon) have become popular measures of risk, especially among the banking community. However, investors have also started to use these measures as regular "marking to market" has become more prevalent. Roughly speaking, the A%-value at risk is the (smallest) amount of capital that you could lose in a given time period with probability $(1 - A)\%$. Another (approximate) way of thinking about the value at risk is that you could be $A\%$ confident that your loss would not be worse than the A%-value at risk.

For example, consider a portfolio of investments whose value follows a random walk with steps that are normally distributed with mean 1% per month and standard deviation 5% per month and that the current value is £100m. The 95% value at risk for one month would then be £100m $\times$ (1% $-$ 1.645 $\times$ 5%) = £7.2m. The investor could be 95% sure that the loss over the month would not be worse than £7.2m. Another way of thinking about this is that if the investor could relive the month many, say 1000, times and record the loss each month, the 50th-worst loss would be about £7.2m.

In the case above (i.e. a random walk with normally distributed increments), there is a clear relationship between the value at risk and the mean and standard deviation of the return process. If we fix the mean, the value at risk and standard deviation will both increase and decrease together. If we fix the standard deviation, the value at risk will move up as the mean is decreased and move down as the mean is increased.

While standard deviation remains the pre-eminent measure of risk within the fund management (buy-side) environment, value at risk dominates the banking and derivative (sell-side) industries. The popularity of value at risk is partly due to the fact that it is reasonably easy for people to envisage and partly because standard deviation is not an appropriate measure of risk for investments that have discrete or distribution mixes of discrete and continuous distributions.

For example, a call option (as might be sold by a bank) can take on a range of values at exercise if the underlying instrument is above the strike price. However, if the price of the underlying instrument is anywhere less than the strike price, then the derivative will have the same value, i.e. 0, since it will not be exercised. The distribution of the value of the call option is therefore partly continuous (since it can take on any value in a range) and partly discrete (since it has non-zero probability mass at a particular value). Unless the call option is a long way in the money, the standard deviation of its value is not a good indicator of its risk.

Value at risk makes much more sense for portfolios that contain derivatives and other securities that have a non-normally distributed return process. But it is difficult to obtain exact analytical expressions for value at risk except in special circumstances and we therefore typically have to revert to other techniques. The most common alternatives are bootstrapping and simulation.

In bootstrapping, historical data are used repeatedly to see what might have happened to a portfolio. Suppose that we have ten years of monthly returns for a particular asset class. We might be fairly confident that the data set provides us with reasonable information about the distribution of monthly returns, but, because there are only ten non-overlapping years of data, we are unable to say anything with great confidence about the annual return distribution. In particular, we are unable to calculate a 95% VaR with any conviction.

The bootstrap methodology involves repeatedly (say, 1000 times) drawing, at random, 12 months of information from the original data set of 120 months. In some of the random draws of 12 months, we might draw the same month of original information more than once. At the end of this process we will have 1000 "bootstrapped" years of information and we will then be able to calculate the 50th worst year and that would represent our 95% VaR. Implemented in this way, we are assuming that the returns in consecutive months are independent and identically distributed. Variations on the bootstrap have been developed that enable more complicated sampling plans to be instigated (see Efron, 1982).

An alternative to bootstrapping is to use the monthly information to estimate the parameters of a distribution, for example the μ and σ for a normal distribution. Once we know the distribution, we can then draw random numbers from the distribution as many times as we need. For example, we might generate 12,000 random numbers from that distribution to represent 1000 simulated years of monthly data. We can then look up the 50th worst annual return and use that as our estimate of a 95% VaR.

The advantage of a bootstrap approach is that it uses actual data from the past to form the basis of the sample. No assumptions have to be made as to what distribution the returns come from (other than that they all come from the same distribution and are independent). On the other hand, because the bootstrap uses actual data, it might miss out on some extreme cases, which in a risk-assessment exercise are possibly the important ones. For example, the worst monthly (continuously compounded) return on an asset in the past 120 months might be -5%. This would mean that the worst possible annual return (continuously compounded) that we could find in our bootstrap sample is $12 \times (-5\%) = -60\%$. We might know from economic reasons that even worse returns are possible and would want them to feature when it came to measuring levels of risk. If instead we interpreted the observed monthly returns as a random sample from a statistical distribution such as the normal distribution, or t-distribution or some other distribution that provided the appropriate features such as skewness and kurtosis and then used random drawings from the distribution to make up the simulation, we might well find simulated annual returns that were worse than -60%.

Excel Application 17.2

Bootstrap

Suppose that you have available the following 24 monthly returns on an index and that you further wish to calculate the 70% VaR for the quarterly return on a derivative product that provides a return each month equal to the larger of the monthly index return and −10%.

Enter the information (including headings) below into range A1:B25 of a spreadsheet.

In cell C2, enter the formula = max(b2, −10%). The value in C2 should be 4.0%, or 0.04 (depending on the formatting that you have chosen for the cell). Copy the formula into the range C3:C25. So, for example, the value in C3 should be −10% (or −0.1). Column C now contains the returns on the derivative product and you might want to enter in a label in cell C1 such as "Derivative returns".

We now need to set up some random numbers so that we can construct random quarterly returns for the derivative product. To do so, we can use Excel's random number generator. You will find this in the \Tools\Data Analysis drop down menu (if this option is not available, you will have to use \Tools\Add Ins to load the Data

Table 17.1

Date	Index returns (%)
Jan-99	4.0
Feb-99	−15.6
Mar-99	14.9
Apr-99	35.5
May-99	34.0
Jun-99	44.7
Jul-99	−33.7
Aug-99	5.3
Sep-99	31.9
Oct-99	−11.7
Nov-99	−3.8
Dec-99	−23.8
Jan-00	−26.9
Feb-00	−9.6
Mar-00	−5.5
Apr-00	−32.4
May-00	−1.4
Jun-00	1.9
Jul-00	12.7
Aug-00	2.7
Sep-00	3.5
Oct-00	2.6
Nov-00	36.9
Dec-00	8.3

Analysis Add In). Under \Tools\Data Analysis, click on Random Number Generation in the option list. This will then provide you with an input form. In the box for number of variables, enter 3 (we will need 3 months to generate each quarter). In the box "Number of random numbers" enter 1000 (this is the number of bootstrap samples that we will be using in this — fairly small scale! — bootstrapping exercise). Under "Distribution" select the Uniform distribution since we want each month to have an equal chance of being selected. In the parameters section, enter 1 and 25 for the range of values. Click the radio button next to Output range and enter D2 in the space provided. Then click OK. What we have asked Excel to do is to generate 1000 sets of uniformly distributed random numbers between 1 and 25 in the block of cells with upper left cell D2. This may take several seconds depending on the need of your machine.

We now have to convert these numbers into the months that we are selecting. In cell G2, enter the formula $= INT(D2)$. This asks Excel to give us the integer part of cell D2. Copy the formula into the whole range G2:I1001. We now have to look up the derivative returns associated with the randomly selected month. In cell J2, we enter the formula $= OFFSET(\$C\$1, G2, 0)$. This asks Excel to find the contents of the cell that is G2 rows below cell \$C\$1 and 0 rows to the right of it (i.e. in column C itself). For example, if cell G2 contained a 2, then the formula in cell J2 should find the entry in cell C3, i.e. -10%.

Again, we copy this formula into the range J2:L1001. We now just have to compound up the monthly returns to get the quarterly return on the derivative. In cell M2 we can then enter $= (1 + J2)^*(1 + K2)^*(1 + L2) - 1$. This formula should be copied across into the range M2:M1001. The one thousand cells in M2 to M1001 give us the 1000 bootstrapped quarterly derivative returns. The 70% VaR can be calculated by entering the following formula in cell N2: $=$ percentile(M2:M1001, 0.3). This asks Excel to provide us with the 30th percentile (30th smallest number) of the 1000 random quarterly returns.

The disadvantages of a measure such as value at risk are that (a) one needs to specify A%, and the ordering of projects according to riskiness can vary significantly depending on A%; (b) it is mathematically difficult to work with (for example, you would have to recompute the value at risk each time a new investment is added to the portfolio in order to get an accurate estimate); and (c) it is not sub-additive.

This last disadvantage may sound technical, but it is quite a simple concept and an important limitation of VaR. If you were an investor with several portfolios and you knew that the values at risk in each of the portfolios were acceptable to you, then you would want to be sure that the value at risk of your total investment (the aggregate of all the portfolios) was also acceptable. For example, if you had ten portfolios of equal size and the value at risk in each portfolio was £1000, then you would expect that the total value at risk to be less than £10,000. Unfortunately, this is not true for value at risk and certain other measures of risk, and is therefore not a coherent measure of risk in general.

An example of a measure of risk that is coherent and is related to value at risk, is referred to as expected shortfall. Expected shortfall is loosely defined as the expected value of the "worst" $(1 - A\%)$ of the outcomes.

Example 17.4 (adapted from Artzner, 1999)

A bank has lent a customer £9500 for a period of one year at a rate of interest of 5.26%. Suppose that the customer will default on the loan (i.e. will pay nothing back to the bank) with a probability of 3%.

(a) What is the 95% VaR for the bank in respect of the single customer?
(b) Suppose, however, that the bank provides 100 loans of £95 each to 100 independent customers, each at a rate of interest of 5.26%. What is the VaR in this case?
(c) By comparing the answers to (a) and (b), discuss one of the flaws in using VaR as a measure of risk.
(d) Calculate the expected shortfall measure of risk in each case and show that this provides a more coherent picture of the risks.

Answer

(a) In respect of the one customer, the bank's risk as measured by a one-year 95% VaR is zero, because the probability of default is lower than the VaR level. You can think of performing a simulation 10,000 times; in 300 of the 10,000 simulations the bank will receive 0 and in the remaining 9700, it will receive 10,000. That makes the expected return to the bank equal to 9700. However, the 95% VaR is the $5\% \times 10{,}000 = 500$th worst case, which will be 10,000. Compared with the mean of 9700, this strictly speaking makes the risk "negative" but risk is usually limited to be zero or positive.
(b) In both this case and the previous case, the bank has paid out £9500 and expects to get £9700 in return after allowing for defaults. In this second case, the total return to the bank can be approximated by a normal distribution (see Section 9.19) with a mean of $0.97 \times 100 \times 100 = 9700$ and standard deviation of $(100^2 \times 100 \times 0.97 \times 0.03)^{0.5} = 170.6$. The 5th percentile of this distribution is therefore $9700 - 1.645 \times 170.6 = 9419$. In the context of a simulation that is repeated 10,000 times, the 500th worst case would be approximately 9419. This represents a risk of just under 300 relative to the mean.
(c) Based on the 95% VaR, the portfolio of 100 contracts of £95 each is riskier than a single contract of £9500. In reality, virtually no-one would agree with this analysis. The more diversified book of business is clearly preferable (when examined on its own). It is the measure of risk that is inappropriate. The anomaly can be seen also in that the 95% VaR for each individual loan of £95 is zero, which if added up over the 100 contracts is still zero. This is different from the amount derived by looking at the contracts in aggregate; in particular, looking at the contracts individually and then adding them up indicates a misleadingly low risk figure.
(d) If we look now at the sizes of the risks, then we get a different picture. In the case where we sell only one loan with a repayment value of 10,000, 3% out of the worst 5% of cases will involve a loss (relative to the expected return of 9700) of 9700 and 2% out of the 5% will involve a small "profit" of 300. That works out as an average loss in the worst 5% of cases of 5700.

In the case of the portfolio of 100 loans, the calculation of the average of the worst 5% of outcomes can be approximated using conditional expectations using the normal distribution. As an exercise, you can check that when X has a normal distribution with mean μ and standard deviation σ

$$E[X \mid X < c] = \mu - \sigma^2 \frac{\phi\left(\dfrac{c - \mu}{\sigma}\right)}{\Phi\left(\dfrac{c - \mu}{\sigma}\right)}.$$

Where $\phi(.)$ denotes the standard normal density function and $\Phi(.)$ denotes the standard normal distribution function:

Using the calculations from earlier, the expected return in the worst 5% of cases can then be calculated as about 9348, i.e. an average loss (relative to the average of 9700) of 352. This is clearly much lower than in the single loan case, as we would "intuitively" expect.

Alternatively, we can estimate the expected shortfall using a quick simulation analysis.

Excel Application 17.3

Using \Tools\Data Analysis select the random number generator. Fill in 1 as the number of random variables; 10,000 as the number of random numbers; Binomial as the appropriate distribution; 0.03 as the p-Value and 100 as the number of trials.

If you enter the A1 as the output range, you should then get 10,000 numbers in the range A1 : A10,000. Using \Data\Sort from the dropdown menu, sort these numbers from largest to smallest. In cell B1, enter $= 1000 - 100*A1$ and then copy this formula into the range B1 : B10,000. In cell C1 enter the formula $=$ average(b1 : b500). This calculates the average loss, relative to the maximum possible return, in the worst $500/10,000 = 5\%$ of cases. You should get a figure of around 9300. This represents an average loss of about 400 relative to 9700, as we calculated using the normal approximation. You can also check that the value in B500 is about 9400, as we earlier estimated the VaR.

Repeat the above exercise, but change the binomial distribution to have a number of trials of one and multiply the numbers by 10,000 instead of 100. Remember to sort the figures in column A and you should see in cell C1 an estimate of the average expected loss in the worst 5% of cases (relative to the maximum possible return) in the single loan case. This should be a number within a few hundred of 4000, i.e. a loss of about 5700 relative to the average of 9700.

REFERENCES

Artzner, P. (1999), "Application of coherent risk measures to capital requirements in insurance", *North American Actuarial Journal*, 3, 2.

Artzner, P., Delbaen, F., Eber, J.M. and Heath, D. (1998), "Coherent risk measures", *Mathematical Finance*.

Black, F. (1980), "The tax consequences of long-run pension policy", *Financial Analysts Journal*, 36.

Black, F. and Litterman, R. (1992), "Global portfolio optimization", *Financial Analysts Journal*, Sept./Oct.

Bollerslev, T. (1986), "Generalised autoregressive conditional heteroscedasticity", *Journal of Econometrics*, 31.

Box, G.E.P. and Jenkins, G.M. (1976), *Time Series Analysis: Forecasting and Control*, San Francisco: Holden-Day.

Chan, T. (1998), "Some applications of levy processes to stochastic investment models for actuarial use", *ASTIN Bulletin*, 28.

Domowitz, I. and Hakkio, C.S. (1985), "Conditional variance and the risk premium in the foreign exchange market", *Journal of International Economics*, 19, 47–66.

Efron, B. (1982), *The Jackknife, the Bootstrap and Other Resampling Plans*, SIAM, Philadelphia.

Engle, R.F. (1982), "Autoregressive conditional heteroscedasticity with estimates of the variance of UK inflation", *Econometrica*, 50, 987–1007.

Engle, R.F., Lilien, D.M. and Robins, R.P. (1987), "Estimating time varying risk premia in the term structure: the ARCH-M model", *Econometrica*, 55.

Exley, C.J., Mehta, S.J.B. and Smith, A.D. (1997), "The financial theory of defined benefit pension schemes", *British Actuarial Journal*, 3, 835–966.

Heath, D., Jarrow, R. and Morton, A. (1992), "Bond pricing and the term structure of interest rates: a new methodology", *Econometrica*, 60, 77–105.

Hull, J.C. (2000), *Options, Futures and Other Derivative Securities*, Prentice-Hall.

Kemp, M.H.D. (1999), "Pricing derivatives under the Wilkie model", *British Actuarial Journal*, 6, 28, 621–35.

Michaud, R. (2001), *Efficient Asset Management: A Practical Guide to Stock Portfolio Optimization and Asset Allocation*. Oxford University Press.

Pagan, A. and Ullah, A. (1986), *The Econometric Analysis of Models with Risk Terms*, discussion paper, Centre for Economic Policy Research.

Quenouille, M.H. (1949), "A method of trend elimination", *Biometrika*, 36.

Tepper, I. (1981), "Taxation and corporate pension policy", *Journal of Finance*, 36.

Vasicek, O.A. (1977), "An equilibrium characterization of the term structure of interest rates", *Journal of Financial Economics*, 5, 177–88.

Wilkie, A.D. (1986), "A stochastic investment model for actuarial use", *Transactions of Faculty of Actuaries*, 39, 341–73.

Wilkie, A.D. (1995), "More on a stochastic asset model for actuarial use (with discussion)", *British Actuarial Journal*, 1 5, 777–964.

Compound Interest Tables

1%

n	i 0.01 d 0.009901 $(1+i)^n$	$i^{(2)}$ 0.009975 $d^{(2)}$ 0.009926 v^n	$i^{(4)}$ 0.009963 $d^{(4)}$ 0.009938 $a_{\overline{n}\rceil}$	$i^{(12)}$ 0.009954 $d^{(12)}$ 0.009946 $s_{\overline{n}\rceil}$	δ 0.009950 $(Ia)_{\overline{n}\rceil}$	n
1	1.010000	0.990099	0.9901	1.0000	0.9901	1
2	1.020100	0.980296	1.9704	2.0100	2.9507	2
3	1.030301	0.970590	2.9410	3.0301	5.8625	3
4	1.040604	0.960980	3.9020	4.0604	9.7064	4
5	1.051010	0.951466	4.8534	5.1010	14.4637	5
6	1.061520	0.942045	5.7955	6.1520	20.1160	6
7	1.072135	0.932718	6.7282	7.2135	26.6450	7
8	1.082857	0.923483	7.6517	8.2857	34.0329	8
9	1.093685	0.914340	8.5660	9.3685	42.2619	9
10	1.104622	0.905287	9.4713	10.4622	51.3148	10
11	1.115668	0.896324	10.3676	11.5668	61.1744	11
12	1.126825	0.887449	11.2551	12.6825	71.8238	12
13	1.138093	0.878663	12.1337	13.8093	83.2464	13
14	1.149474	0.869963	13.0037	14.9474	95.4258	14
15	1.160969	0.861349	13.8651	16.0969	108.3461	15
16	1.172579	0.852821	14.7179	17.2579	121.9912	16
17	1.184304	0.844377	15.5623	18.4304	136.3456	17
18	1.196147	0.836017	16.3983	19.6147	151.3940	18
19	1.208109	0.827740	17.2260	20.8109	167.1210	19
20	1.220190	0.819544	18.0456	22.0190	183.5119	20
21	1.232392	0.811430	18.8570	23.2392	200.5519	21
22	1.244716	0.803396	19.6604	24.4716	218.2267	22
23	1.257163	0.795442	20.4558	25.7163	236.5218	23
24	1.269735	0.787566	21.2434	26.9735	255.4234	24
25	1.282432	0.779768	22.0232	28.2432	274.9176	25
26	1.295256	0.772048	22.7952	29.5256	294.9909	26
27	1.308209	0.764404	23.5596	30.8209	315.6298	27
28	1.321291	0.756836	24.3164	32.1291	336.8212	28
29	1.334504	0.749342	25.0658	33.4504	358.5521	29
30	1.347849	0.741923	25.8077	34.7849	380.8098	30
35	1.416603	0.705914	29.4086	41.6603	499.5669	35
40	1.488864	0.671653	32.8347	48.8864	629.6907	40
45	1.564811	0.639055	36.0945	56.4811	769.7982	45
50	1.644632	0.608039	39.1961	64.4632	918.6137	50
55	1.728525	0.578528	42.1472	72.8525	1074.9620	55
60	1.816697	0.550450	44.9550	81.6697	1237.7612	60
65	1.909366	0.523734	47.6266	90.9366	1406.0169	65
70	2.006763	0.498315	50.1685	100.6763	1578.8160	70
75	2.109128	0.474129	52.5871	110.9128	1755.3210	75
80	2.216715	0.451118	54.8882	121.6715	1934.7653	80
85	2.329790	0.429223	57.0777	132.9790	2116.4477	85
90	2.448633	0.408391	59.1609	144.8633	2299.7284	90
95	2.573538	0.388570	61.1430	157.3538	2484.0241	95
100	2.704814	0.369711	63.0289	170.4814	2668.8046	100

2%

n	i 0.02 d 0.019608 $(1+i)^n$	$i^{(2)}$ 0.019901 $d^{(2)}$ 0.019705 v^n	$i^{(4)}$ 0.019852 $d^{(4)}$ 0.019754 $a_{\overline{n}\|}$	$i^{(12)}$ 0.019819 $d^{(12)}$ 0.019786 $s_{\overline{n}\|}$	δ 0.019803 $(Ia)_{\overline{n}\|}$	n
1	1.020000	0.980392	0.9804	1.0000	0.9804	1
2	1.040400	0.961169	1.9416	2.0200	2.9027	2
3	1.061208	0.942322	2.8839	3.0604	5.7297	3
4	1.082432	0.923845	3.8077	4.1216	9.4251	4
5	1.104081	0.905731	4.7135	5.2040	13.9537	5
6	1.126162	0.887971	5.6014	6.3081	19.2816	6
7	1.148686	0.870560	6.4720	7.4343	25.3755	7
8	1.171659	0.853490	7.3255	8.5830	32.2034	8
9	1.195093	0.836755	8.1622	9.7546	39.7342	9
10	1.218994	0.820348	8.9826	10.9497	47.9377	10
11	1.243374	0.804263	9.7868	12.1687	56.7846	11
12	1.268242	0.788493	10.5753	13.4121	66.2465	12
13	1.293607	0.773033	11.3484	14.6803	76.2959	13
14	1.319479	0.757875	12.1062	15.9739	86.9062	14
15	1.345868	0.743015	12.8493	17.2934	98.0514	15
16	1.372786	0.728446	13.5777	18.6393	109.7065	16
17	1.400241	0.714163	14.2919	20.0121	121.8473	17
18	1.428246	0.700159	14.9920	21.4123	134.4502	18
19	1.456811	0.686431	15.6785	22.8406	147.4923	19
20	1.485947	0.672971	16.3514	24.2974	160.9518	20
21	1.515666	0.659776	17.0112	25.7833	174.8071	21
22	1.545980	0.646839	17.6580	27.2990	189.0375	22
23	1.576899	0.634156	18.2922	28.8450	203.6231	23
24	1.608437	0.621721	18.9139	30.4219	218.5444	24
25	1.640606	0.609531	19.5235	32.0303	233.7827	25
26	1.673418	0.597579	20.1210	33.6709	249.3198	26
27	1.706886	0.585862	20.7069	35.3443	265.1380	27
28	1.741024	0.574375	21.2813	37.0512	281.2205	28
29	1.775845	0.563112	21.8444	38.7922	297.5508	29
30	1.811362	0.552071	22.3965	40.5681	314.1129	30
35	1.999890	0.500028	24.9986	49.9945	399.8813	35
40	2.208040	0.452890	27.3555	60.4020	489.3486	40
45	2.437854	0.410197	29.4902	71.8927	581.0553	45
50	2.691588	0.371528	31.4236	84.5794	673.7842	50
55	2.971731	0.336504	33.1748	98.5865	766.5275	55
60	3.281031	0.304782	34.7609	114.0515	858.4584	60
65	3.622523	0.276051	36.1975	131.1262	948.9060	65
70	3.999558	0.250028	37.4986	149.9779	1037.3329	70
75	4.415835	0.226458	38.6771	170.7918	1123.3164	75
80	4.875439	0.205110	39.7445	193.7720	1206.5313	80
85	5.382879	0.185774	40.7113	219.1439	1286.7354	85
90	5.943133	0.168261	41.5869	247.1567	1363.7570	90
95	6.561699	0.152400	42.3800	278.0850	1437.4833	95
100	7.244646	0.138033	43.0984	312.2323	1507.8511	100

3%

n	i 0.03 d 0.029126 $(1+i)^n$	$i^{(2)}$ 0.029778 $d^{(2)}$ 0.029341 v^n	$i^{(4)}$ 0.029668 $d^{(4)}$ 0.029450 $a_{\overline{n}\rceil}$	$i^{(12)}$ 0.029595 $d^{(12)}$ 0.029522 $s_{\overline{n}\rceil}$	δ 0.029559 $(Ia)_{\overline{n}\rceil}$	n
1	1.030000	0.970874	0.9709	1.0000	0.9709	1
2	1.060900	0.942596	1.9135	2.0300	2.8561	2
3	1.092727	0.915142	2.8286	3.0909	5.6015	3
4	1.125509	0.888487	3.7171	4.1836	9.1554	4
5	1.159274	0.862609	4.5797	5.3091	13.4685	5
6	1.194052	0.837484	5.4172	6.4684	18.4934	6
7	1.229874	0.813092	6.2303	7.6625	24.1850	7
8	1.266770	0.789409	7.0197	8.8923	30.5003	8
9	1.304773	0.766417	7.7861	10.1591	37.3981	9
10	1.343916	0.744094	8.5302	11.4639	44.8390	10
11	1.384234	0.722421	9.2526	12.8078	52.7856	11
12	1.425761	0.701380	9.9540	14.1920	61.2022	12
13	1.468534	0.680951	10.6350	15.6178	70.0546	13
14	1.512590	0.661118	11.2961	17.0863	79.3102	14
15	1.557967	0.641862	11.9379	18.5989	88.9381	15
16	1.604706	0.623167	12.5611	20.1569	98.9088	16
17	1.652848	0.605016	13.1661	21.7616	109.1941	17
18	1.702433	0.587395	13.7535	23.4144	119.7672	18
19	1.753506	0.570286	14.3238	25.1169	130.6026	19
20	1.806111	0.553676	14.8775	26.8704	141.6761	20
21	1.860295	0.537549	15.4150	28.6765	152.9647	21
22	1.916103	0.521893	15.9369	30.5368	164.4463	22
23	1.973587	0.506692	16.4436	32.4529	176.1002	23
24	2.032794	0.491934	16.9355	34.4265	187.9066	24
25	2.093778	0.477606	17.4131	36.4593	199.8468	25
26	2.156591	0.463695	17.8768	38.5530	211.9028	26
27	2.221289	0.450189	18.3270	40.7096	224.0579	27
28	2.287928	0.437077	18.7641	42.9309	236.2961	28
29	2.356566	0.424346	19.1885	45.2189	248.6021	29
30	2.427262	0.411987	19.6004	47.5754	260.9617	30
35	2.813862	0.355383	21.4872	60.4621	323.1139	35
40	3.262038	0.306557	23.1148	75.4013	384.8647	40
45	3.781596	0.264439	24.5187	92.7199	445.1512	45
50	4.383906	0.228107	25.7298	112.7969	503.2101	50
55	5.082149	0.196767	26.7744	136.0716	558.5155	55
60	5.891603	0.169733	27.6756	163.0534	610.7282	60
65	6.829983	0.146413	28.4529	194.3328	659.6539	65
70	7.917822	0.126297	29.1234	230.5941	705.2103	70
75	9.178926	0.108945	29.7018	272.6309	747.3997	75
80	10.640891	0.093977	30.2008	321.3630	786.2873	80
85	12.335709	0.081065	30.6312	377.8570	821.9840	85
90	14.300467	0.069928	31.0024	443.3489	854.6326	90
95	16.578161	0.060320	31.3227	519.2720	884.3968	95
100	19.218632	0.052033	31.5989	607.2877	911.4530	100

4%

n	i 0.04 d 0.038462 $(1+i)^n$	$i^{(2)}$ 0.039608 $d^{(2)}$ 0.038839 v^n	$i^{(4)}$ 0.039414 $d^{(4)}$ 0.039029 $a_{\overline{n}\rceil}$	$i^{(12)}$ 0.039285 $d^{(12)}$ 0.039157 $s_{\overline{n}\rceil}$	δ 0.039221 $(Ia)_{\overline{n}\rceil}$	n
1	1.040000	0.961538	0.9615	1.0000	0.9615	1
2	1.081600	0.924556	1.8861	2.0400	2.8107	2
3	1.124864	0.888996	2.7751	3.1216	5.4776	3
4	1.169859	0.854804	3.6299	4.2465	8.8969	4
5	1.216653	0.821927	4.4518	5.4163	13.0065	5
6	1.265319	0.790315	5.2421	6.6330	17.7484	6
7	1.315932	0.759918	6.0021	7.8983	23.0678	7
8	1.368569	0.730690	6.7327	9.2142	28.9133	8
9	1.423312	0.702587	7.4353	10.5828	35.2366	9
10	1.480244	0.675564	8.1109	12.0061	41.9922	10
11	1.539454	0.649581	8.7605	13.4864	49.1376	11
12	1.601032	0.624597	9.3851	15.0258	56.6328	12
13	1.665074	0.600574	9.9856	16.6268	64.4403	13
14	1.731676	0.577475	10.5631	18.2919	72.5249	14
15	1.800944	0.555265	11.1184	20.0236	80.8539	15
16	1.872981	0.533908	11.6523	21.8245	89.3964	16
17	1.947900	0.513373	12.1657	23.6975	98.1238	17
18	2.025817	0.493628	12.6593	25.6454	107.0091	18
19	2.106849	0.474642	13.1339	27.6712	116.0273	19
20	2.191123	0.456387	13.5903	29.7781	125.1550	20
21	2.278768	0.438834	14.0292	31.9692	134.3705	21
22	2.369919	0.421955	14.4511	34.2480	143.6535	22
23	2.464716	0.405726	14.8568	36.6179	152.9852	23
24	2.563304	0.390121	15.2470	39.0826	162.3482	24
25	2.665836	0.375117	15.6221	41.6459	171.7261	25
26	2.772470	0.360689	15.9828	44.3117	181.1040	26
27	2.883369	0.346817	16.3296	47.0842	190.4680	27
28	2.998703	0.333477	16.6631	49.9676	199.8054	28
29	3.118651	0.320651	16.9837	52.9663	209.1043	29
30	3.243398	0.308319	17.2920	56.0849	218.3539	30
35	3.946089	0.253415	18.6646	73.6522	263.5414	35
40	4.801021	0.208289	19.7928	95.0255	306.3231	40
45	5.841176	0.171198	20.7200	121.0294	346.1228	45
50	7.106683	0.140713	21.4822	152.6671	382.6460	50
55	8.646367	0.115656	22.1086	191.1592	415.7976	55
60	10.519627	0.095060	22.6235	237.9907	445.6201	60
65	12.798735	0.078133	23.0467	294.9684	472.2481	65
70	15.571618	0.064219	23.3945	364.2905	495.8734	70
75	18.945255	0.052784	23.6804	448.6314	516.7212	75
80	23.049799	0.043384	23.9154	551.2450	535.0315	80
85	28.043605	0.035659	24.1085	676.0901	551.0470	85
90	34.119333	0.029309	24.2673	827.9833	565.0042	90
95	41.511386	0.024090	24.3978	1012.7846	577.1284	95
100	50.504948	0.019800	24.5050	1237.6237	587.6299	100

5%

n	i 0.05 d 0.047619 $(1+i)^n$	$i^{(2)}$ 0.049390 $d^{(2)}$ 0.048200 v^n	$i^{(4)}$ 0.049089 $d^{(4)}$ 0.048494 $a_{\overline{n}\rceil}$	$i^{(12)}$ 0.048889 $d^{(12)}$ 0.048691 $s_{\overline{n}\rceil}$	δ 0.049790 $(Ia)_{\overline{n}\rceil}$	n
1	1.050000	0.952381	0.9524	1.0000	0.9524	1
2	1.102500	0.907029	1.8594	2.0500	2.7664	2
3	1.157625	0.863838	2.7232	3.1525	5.3580	3
4	1.215506	0.822702	3.5460	4.3101	8.6488	4
5	1.276282	0.783526	4.3295	5.5256	12.5664	5
6	1.340096	0.746215	5.0757	6.8019	17.0437	6
7	1.407100	0.710681	5.7864	8.1420	22.0185	7
8	1.477455	0.676839	6.4632	9.5491	27.4332	8
9	1.551328	0.644609	7.1078	11.0266	33.2347	9
10	1.628895	0.613913	7.7217	12.5779	39.3738	10
11	1.710339	0.584679	8.3064	14.2068	45.8053	11
12	1.795856	0.556837	8.8633	15.9171	52.4873	12
13	1.885649	0.530321	9.3936	17.7130	59.3815	13
14	1.979932	0.505068	9.8986	19.5986	66.4524	14
15	2.078928	0.481017	10.3797	21.5786	73.6677	15
16	2.182875	0.458112	10.8378	23.6575	80.9975	16
17	2.292018	0.436297	11.2741	25.8404	88.4145	17
18	2.406619	0.415521	11.6896	28.1324	95.8939	18
19	2.526950	0.395734	12.0853	30.5390	103.4128	19
20	2.653298	0.376889	12.4622	33.0660	110.9506	20
21	2.785963	0.358942	12.8212	35.7193	118.4884	21
22	2.925261	0.341850	13.1630	38.5052	126.0091	22
23	3.071524	0.325571	13.4886	41.4305	133.4973	23
24	3.225100	0.310068	13.7986	44.5020	140.9389	24
25	3.386355	0.295303	14.0939	47.7271	148.3215	25
26	3.555673	0.281241	14.3752	51.1135	155.6337	26
27	3.733456	0.267848	14.6430	54.6691	162.8656	27
28	3.920129	0.255094	14.8981	58.4026	170.0082	28
29	4.116136	0.242946	15.1411	62.3227	177.0537	29
30	4.321942	0.231377	15.3725	66.4388	183.9950	30
35	5.516015	0.181290	16.3742	90.3203	216.9549	35
40	7.039989	0.142046	17.1591	120.7998	246.7043	40
45	8.985008	0.111297	17.7741	159.7002	273.0886	45
50	11.467400	0.087204	18.2559	209.3480	296.1707	50
55	14.635631	0.068326	18.6335	272.7126	316.1439	55
60	18.679186	0.053536	18.9293	353.5837	333.2725	60
65	23.839901	0.041946	19.1611	456.7980	347.8520	65
70	30.426426	0.032866	19.3427	588.5285	360.1836	70
75	38.832686	0.025752	19.4850	756.6537	370.5571	75
80	49.561441	0.020177	19.5965	971.2288	379.2425	80
85	63.254353	0.015809	19.6838	1245.0871	386.4845	85
90	80.730365	0.0123807	19.7523	1594.6073	392.5011	90
95	103.034676	0.009705	19.8059	2040.6935	397.4833	95
100	131.501258	0.007604	19.8479	2610.0252	401.5971	100

Investment Mathematics

	6%				
	i	$i^{(2)}$	$i^{(4)}$	$i^{(12)}$	δ
	0.06	0.059126	0.058695	0.058411	0.058269
	d	$d^{(2)}$	$d^{(4)}$	$d^{(12)}$	
	0.056604	0.057428	0.057847	0.058128	
n	$(1+i)^n$	v^n	$a_{\overline{n}|}$	$s_{\overline{n}|}$	$(Ia)_{\overline{n}|}$	n
1	1.060000	0.943396	0.9434	1.0000	0.9434	1
2	1.123600	0.889996	1.8334	2.0600	2.7234	2
3	1.191016	0.839619	2.6730	3.1836	5.2422	3
4	1.262477	0.792094	3.4651	4.3746	8.4106	4
5	1.338226	0.747258	4.2124	5.6371	12.1469	5
6	1.418519	0.704961	4.9173	6.9753	16.3767	6
7	1.503630	0.665057	5.5824	8.3938	21.0321	7
8	1.593848	0.627412	6.2098	9.8975	26.0514	8
9	1.689479	0.591898	6.8017	11.4913	31.3785	9
10	1.790848	0.558395	7.3601	13.1808	36.9624	10
11	1.898299	0.526788	7.8869	14.9716	42.7571	11
12	2.012196	0.496969	8.3838	16.8699	48.7207	12
13	2.132928	0.468839	8.8527	18.8821	54.8156	13
14	2.260904	0.442301	9.2950	21.0151	61.0078	14
15	2.396558	0.417265	9.7122	23.2760	67.2668	15
16	2.540352	0.393646	10.1059	25.6725	73.5651	16
17	2.692773	0.371364	10.4773	28.2129	79.8783	17
18	2.854339	0.350344	10.8276	30.9057	86.1845	18
19	3.025600	0.330513	11.1581	33.7600	92.4643	19
20	3.207135	0.311805	11.4699	36.7856	98.7004	20
21	3.399564	0.294155	11.7641	39.9927	104.8776	21
22	3.603537	0.277505	12.0416	43.3923	110.9827	22
23	3.819750	0.261797	12.3034	46.9958	117.0041	23
24	4.048935	0.246979	12.5504	50.8156	122.9316	24
25	4.291871	0.232999	12.7834	54.8645	128.7565	25
26	4.549383	0.219810	13.0032	59.1564	134.4716	26
27	4.822346	0.207368	13.2105	63.7058	140.0705	27
28	5.111687	0.195630	13.4062	68.5281	145.5482	28
29	5.418388	0.184557	13.5907	73.6398	150.9003	29
30	5.743491	0.174110	13.7648	79.0582	156.1236	30
35	7.686087	0.130105	14.4982	111.4348	180.2410	35
40	10.285718	0.097222	15.0463	154.7620	201.0031	40
45	13.764611	0.072650	15.4558	212.7435	218.5655	45
50	18.420154	0.054288	15.7619	290.3359	233.2192	50
55	24.650322	0.040567	15.9905	394.1720	245.3128	55
60	32.987691	0.030314	16.1614	533.1282	255.2042	60
65	44.144972	0.022653	16.2891	719.0829	263.2341	65
70	59.075930	0.016927	16.3845	967.9322	269.7117	70
75	79.056921	0.012649	16.4558	1300.9487	274.9086	75
80	105.795993	0.009452	16.5091	1746.5999	279.0584	80
85	141.578904	0.007063	16.5489	2342.9817	282.3585	85
90	189.464511	0.005278	16.5787	3141.0752	284.9733	90
95	253.546255	0.003944	16.6009	4209.1042	287.0384	95
100	339.302084	0.002947	16.6175	5638.3681	288.6646	100

8%

n	i 0.08 d 0.074074 $(1+i)^n$	$i^{(2)}$ 0.078461 $d^{(2)}$ 0.075499 v^n	$i^{(4)}$ 0.077706 $d^{(4)}$ 0.076225 $a_{\overline{n}\rceil}$	$i^{(12)}$ 0.077208 $d^{(12)}$ 0.076715 $s_{\overline{n}\rceil}$	δ 0.076961 $(Ia)_{\overline{n}\rceil}$	n
1	1.080000	0.925926	0.9259	1.0000	0.9259	1
2	1.166400	0.857339	1.7833	2.0800	2.6406	2
3	1.259712	0.793832	2.5771	3.2464	5.0221	3
4	1.360489	0.735030	3.3121	4.5061	7.9622	4
5	1.469328	0.680583	3.9927	5.8666	11.3651	5
6	1.586874	0.630170	4.6229	7.3359	15.1462	6
7	1.713824	0.583490	5.2064	8.9228	19.2306	7
8	1.850930	0.540269	5.7466	10.6366	23.5527	8
9	1.999005	0.500249	6.2469	12.4876	28.0550	9
10	2.158925	0.463193	6.7101	14.4866	32.6869	10
11	2.331639	0.428883	7.1390	16.6455	37.4046	11
12	2.518170	0.397114	7.5361	18.9771	42.1700	12
13	2.719624	0.367698	7.9038	21.4953	46.9501	13
14	2.937194	0.340461	8.2442	24.2149	51.7165	14
15	3.172169	0.315242	8.5595	27.1521	56.4451	15
16	3.425943	0.291890	8.8514	30.3243	61.1154	16
17	3.700018	0.270269	9.1216	33.7502	65.7100	17
18	3.996019	0.250249	9.3719	37.4502	70.2144	18
19	4.315701	0.231712	9.6036	41.4463	74.6170	19
20	4.660957	0.214548	9.8181	45.7620	78.9079	20
21	5.033834	0.198656	10.0168	50.4229	83.0797	21
22	5.436540	0.183941	10.2007	55.4568	87.1264	22
23	5.871464	0.170315	10.3711	60.8933	91.0437	23
24	6.341181	0.157699	10.5288	66.7648	94.8284	24
25	6.848475	0.146018	10.6748	73.1059	98.4789	25
26	7.396353	0.135202	10.8100	79.9544	101.9941	25
27	7.988061	0.125187	10.9352	87.3508	105.3742	27
28	8.627106	0.115914	11.0511	95.3388	108.6198	28
29	9.317275	0.107328	11.1584	103.9659	111.7323	29
30	10.062657	0.099377	11.2578	113.2832	114.7136	30
35	14.785344	0.067635	11.6546	172.3168	127.7466	35
40	21.724521	0.046031	11.9246	259.0565	137.9668	40
45	31.920449	0.031328	12.1084	386.5056	145.8415	45
50	46.901613	0.021321	12.2335	573.7702	151.8263	50
55	68.913856	0.014511	12.3186	848.9232	156.3251	55
60	101.257064	0.009876	12.3766	1253.2133	159.6766	60
65	148.779847	0.006721	12.4160	1847.2481	162.1547	65
70	218.606406	0.004574	12.4428	2720.0801	163.9754	70
75	321.284530	0.003113	12.4611	4002.5566	165.3059	75
80	471.954834	0.002119	12.4735	5886.9354	166.2736	80

10%

n	i 0.1 d 0.090909 $(1 + i)^n$	$i^{(2)}$ 0.097618 $d^{(2)}$ 0.093075 v^n	$i^{(4)}$ 0.096455 $d^{(4)}$ 0.094184 $a_{\overline{n}|}$	$i^{(12)}$ 0.095690 $d^{(12)}$ 0.094933 $s_{\overline{n}|}$	δ 0.095310 $(Ia)_{\overline{n}|}$	n
1	1.100000	0.909091	0.9091	1.0000	0.9091	1
2	1.210000	0.826446	1.7355	2.1000	2.5620	2
3	1.331000	0.751315	2.4869	3.3100	4.8159	3
4	1.464100	0.683013	3.1699	4.6410	7.5480	4
5	1.610510	0.620921	3.7908	6.1051	10.6526	5
6	1.771561	0.564474	4.3553	7.7156	14.0394	6
7	1.948717	0.513158	4.8684	9.4872	17.6315	7
8	2.143589	0.466507	5.3349	11.4359	21.3636	8
9	2.357948	0.424098	5.7590	13.5795	25.1805	9
10	2.593742	0.385543	6.1446	15.9374	29.0359	10
11	2.853117	0.350494	6.4951	18.5312	32.8913	11
12	3.138428	0.318631	6.8137	21.3843	36.7149	12
13	3.452271	0.289664	7.1034	24.5227	40.4805	13
14	3.797498	0.263331	7.3667	27.9750	44.1672	14
15	4.177248	0.239392	7.6061	31.7725	47.7581	15
16	4.594973	0.217629	7.8237	35.9497	51.2401	16
17	5.054470	0.197845	8.0216	40.5447	54.6035	17
18	5.559917	0.179859	8.2014	45.5992	57.8410	18
19	6.115909	0.163508	8.3649	51.1591	60.9476	19
20	6.727500	0.148644	8.5136	57.2750	63.9205	20
21	7.400250	0.135131	8.6487	64.0025	66.7582	21
22	8.140275	0.122846	8.7715	71.4027	69.4608	22
23	8.954302	0.111678	8.8832	79.5430	72.0294	23
24	9.849733	0.101526	8.9847	88.4973	74.4660	24
25	10.834706	0.092296	9.0770	98.3471	76.7734	25
26	11.918177	0.083905	9.1609	109.1818	78.9550	26
27	13.109994	0.076278	9.2372	121.0999	81.0145	27
28	14.420994	0.069343	9.3066	134.2099	82.9561	28
29	15.863093	0.063039	9.3696	148.6309	84.7842	29
30	17.449402	0.057309	9.4269	164.4940	86.5035	30
35	28.102437	0.035584	9.6442	271.0244	93.6313	35
40	45.259256	0.022095	9.7791	442.5926	98.7316	40
45	72.890484	0.013719	9.8628	718.9048	102.3172	45
50	117.390853	0.008519	9.9148	1163.9085	104.8037	50
55	189.059142	0.005289	9.9471	1880.5914	106.5090	55
60	304.481640	0.003284	9.9672	3034.8164	107.6682	60
65	490.370725	0.002039	9.9796	4893.7073	108.4502	65
70	789.746957	0.001266	9.9873	7887.4696	108.9744	70

12%

n	i 0.12 d 0.107143 $(1+i)^n$	$i^{(2)}$ 0.116601 $d^{(2)}$ 0.110178 v^n	$i^{(4)}$ 0.114949 $d^{(4)}$ 0.111738 $a_{\overline{n}\rceil}$	$i^{(12)}$ 0.113866 $d^{(12)}$ 0.112795 $s_{\overline{n}\rceil}$	δ 0.113329 $(Ia)_{\overline{n}\rceil}$	n
1	1.120000	0.892857	0.8929	1.0000	0.8929	1
2	1.254400	0.797194	1.6901	2.1200	2.4872	2
3	1.404928	0.711780	2.4018	3.3744	4.6226	3
4	1.573519	0.635518	3.0373	4.7793	7.1647	4
5	1.762342	0.567427	3.6048	6.3528	10.0018	5
6	1.973823	0.506631	4.1114	8.1152	13.0416	6
7	2.210681	0.452349	4.5638	10.0890	16.2080	7
8	2.475963	0.403883	4.9676	12.2997	19.4391	8
9	2.773079	0.360610	5.3282	14.7757	22.6846	9
10	3.105848	0.321973	5.6502	17.5487	25.9043	10
11	3.478550	0.287476	5.9377	20.6546	29.0665	11
12	3.895976	0.256675	6.1944	24.1331	32.1467	12
13	4.363493	0.229174	6.4235	28.0291	35.1259	13
14	4.887112	0.204620	6.6282	32.3926	37.9906	14
15	5.473566	0.182696	6.8109	37.2797	40.7310	15
16	6.130394	0.163122	6.9740	42.7533	43.3410	16
17	6.866041	0.145644	7.1196	48.8837	45.8169	17
18	7.689966	0.130040	7.2497	55.7497	48.1576	18
19	8.612762	0.116107	7.3658	63.4397	50.3637	19
20	9.646293	0.103667	7.4694	72.0524	52.4370	20
21	10.803848	0.092560	7.5620	81.6987	54.3808	21
22	12.100310	0.082643	7.6446	92.5026	56.1989	22
23	13.552347	0.073788	7.7184	104.6029	57.8960	23
24	15.178629	0.065882	7.7843	118.1552	59.4772	24
25	17.000064	0.058823	7.8431	133.3339	60.9478	25
26	19.040072	0.052521	7.8957	150.3339	62.3133	26
27	21.324881	0.046894	7.9426	169.3740	63.5794	27
28	23.883866	0.041869	7.9844	190.6989	64.7518	28
29	26.749930	0.037383	8.0218	214.5828	65.8359	29
30	29.959922	0.033378	8.0552	241.3327	66.8372	30
35	52.799620	0.018940	8.1755	431.6635	70.7807	35
40	93.050970	0.010747	8.2438	767.0914	73.3596	40
45	163.987604	0.006098	8.2825	1358.2300	75.0167	45
50	289.002190	0.003460	8.3045	2400.0182	76.0669	50
55	509.320606	0.001963	8.3170	4236.0050	76.7252	55

Student's *t* Distribution: Critical Points

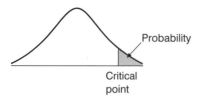

Probability

Critical point

Probability	0.10	0.05	0.025	0.01	0.005
$\nu = $ 1	3.078	6.314	12.706	31.821	63.657
2	1.886	2.920	4.303	6.965	9.925
3	1.638	2.353	3.182	4.541	5.841
4	1.533	2.132	2.776	3.747	4.604
5	1.476	2.015	2.571	3.365	4.032
6	1.440	1.943	2.447	3.143	3.707
7	1.415	1.895	2.365	2.998	3.499
8	1.397	1.860	2.306	2.896	3.355
9	1.383	1.833	2.262	2.821	3.250
10	1.372	1.812	2.228	2.764	3.169
11	1.363	1.796	2.201	2.718	3.106
12	1.356	1.782	2.179	2.681	3.055
13	1.350	1.771	2.160	2.650	3.012
14	1.345	1.761	2.145	2.624	2.977
15	1.341	1.753	2.131	2.602	2.947
16	1.337	1.746	2.120	2.583	2.921
17	1.333	1.740	2.110	2.567	2.898
18	1.330	1.734	2.101	2.552	2.878
19	1.328	1.729	2.093	2.539	2.861
20	1.325	1.725	2.086	2.528	2.845
21	1.323	1.721	2.080	2.518	2.831
22	1.321	1.717	2.074	2.508	2.819
23	1.319	1.714	2.069	2.500	2.807
24	1.318	1.711	2.064	2.492	2.797
25	1.316	1.708	2.060	2.485	2.787
26	1.315	1.706	2.056	2.479	2.779
27	1.314	1.703	2.052	2.473	2.771
28	1.313	1.701	2.048	2.467	2.763
29	1.311	1.699	2.045	2.462	2.756
30	1.310	1.697	2.042	2.457	2.750
40	1.303	1.684	2.021	2.423	2.704
60	1.296	1.671	2.000	2.390	2.660
120	1.289	1.658	1.980	2.358	2.617
∞	1.282	1.645	1.960	2.326	2.576

where ν the number of degrees of freedom.

Areas in the Right-hand Tail
of the Normal Distribution

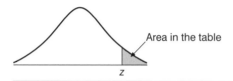

Area in the table

z

z	0.00	0.01	0.02	0.03	0.04	0.05	0.06	0.07	0.08	0.09
0.0	0.5000	0.4960	0.4920	0.4880	0.4840	0.4801	0.4761	0.4721	0.4681	0.4641
0.1	0.4602	0.4562	0.4522	0.4483	0.4443	0.4404	0.4364	0.4325	0.4286	0.4247
0.2	0.4207	0.4168	0.4129	0.4090	0.4052	0.4013	0.3974	0.3936	0.3897	0.3859
0.3	0.3821	0.3873	0.3745	0.3707	0.3669	0.3632	0.3594	0.3557	0.3520	0.3483
0.4	0.3446	0.3409	0.3372	0.3336	0.3300	0.3264	0.3228	0.3192	0.3156	0.3121
0.5	0.3085	0.3050	0.3015	0.2981	0.2946	0.2912	0.2877	0.2843	0.2810	0.2776
0.6	0.2743	0.2709	0.2676	0.2643	0.2611	0.2578	0.2546	0.2514	0.2483	0.2451
0.7	0.2420	0.2389	0.2358	0.2327	0.2296	0.2266	0.2236	0.2206	0.2177	0.2148
0.8	0.2119	0.2090	0.2061	0.2033	0.2005	0.1977	0.1949	0.1922	0.1894	0.1867
0.9	0.1841	0.1814	0.1788	0.1762	0.1736	0.1711	0.1685	0.1660	0.1635	0.1611
1.0	0.1587	0.1562	0.1539	0.1515	0.1492	0.1469	0.1446	0.1423	0.1401	0.1379
1.1	0.1357	0.1335	0.1314	0.1292	0.1271	0.1251	0.1230	0.1210	0.1190	0.1170
1.2	0.1151	0.1131	0.1112	0.1093	0.1075	0.1056	0.1038	0.1020	0.1003	0.0985
1.3	0.0968	0.0951	0.0934	0.0918	0.0901	0.0885	0.0869	0.0853	0.0838	0.0823
1.4	0.0808	0.0793	0.0778	0.0764	0.0749	0.0735	0.0721	0.0708	0.0694	0.0681
1.5	0.0668	0.0655	0.0643	0.0630	0.0618	0.0606	0.0594	0.0582	0.0571	0.0559
1.6	0.0548	0.0537	0.0526	0.0516	0.0505	0.0495	0.0485	0.0475	0.0465	0.0455
1.7	0.0446	0.0436	0.0427	0.0418	0.0409	0.0401	0.0392	0.0384	0.0375	0.0367
1.8	0.0359	0.0351	0.0344	0.0336	0.0329	0.0322	0.0314	0.0307	0.0301	0.0294
1.9	0.0287	0.0281	0.0274	0.0268	0.0262	0.0256	0.0250	0.0244	0.0239	0.0233
2.0	0.02275	0.02222	0.02169	0.02118	0.02068	0.02018	0.01970	0.01923	0.01876	0.01831
2.1	0.01786	0.01743	0.01700	0.01659	0.01618	0.01578	0.01539	0.01500	0.01463	0.01426
2.2	0.01390	0.01355	0.01321	0.01287	0.01255	0.01222	0.01191	0.01160	0.01130	0.01101
2.3	0.01072	0.01044	0.01017	0.00990	0.00964	0.00939	0.00914	0.00889	0.00866	0.00842
2.4	0.00820	0.00798	0.00776	0.00755	0.00734	0.00714	0.00695	0.00676	0.00657	0.06639
2.5	0.00621	0.00604	0.00587	0.00570	0.00554	0.00539	0.00523	0.00508	0.00494	0.00480
2.6	0.00466	0.00453	0.00440	0.00427	0.00415	0.00402	0.00391	0.00379	0.00368	0.00357
2.7	0.00347	0.00336	0.00326	0.00317	0.00307	0.00298	0.00289	0.00280	0.00272	0.00264
2.8	0.00256	0.00248	0.00240	0.00233	0.00226	0.00219	0.00212	0.00205	0.00199	0.00193
2.9	0.00187	0.00181	0.00175	0.00169	0.00164	0.00159	0.00154	0.00149	0.00144	0.00139

z	0.00	0.01	0.02	0.03	0.04	0.05	0.06	0.07	0.08	0.09
3.0	0.00135									
3.1	0.00097									
3.2	0.00069									
3.3	0.00048									
3.4	0.00034									
3.5	0.00023									
3.6	0.00016									
3.7	0.00011									
3.8	0.00007									
3.9	0.00005									
4.0	0.00003									

Index

Note: Page references in *italics* refer to Figures and Tables